to mother
from stetson -
Mother's Day - 1956
with love

AMERICAN IN ITALY

by

Herbert Kubly

SIMON AND SCHUSTER
New York

FOURTH PRINTING
LIBRARY OF CONGRESS CATALOG CARD NUMBER: 54-8641
DEWEY DECIMAL CLASSIFICATION NUMBER: 945.092
MANUFACTURED IN THE UNITED STATES OF AMERICA
BY AMERICAN BOOK-STRATFORD PRESS, INC., NEW YORK

FOR

Lila and Robert Dibble and Leonard Schach

Table of Contents

"The Creator made Italy from designs by Michelangelo."

MARK TWAIN

"If Western civilization is to save its body, it must save its soul too."

ADLAI STEVENSON

Foreword

Italy is the land of human nature. Italians are an undistorted people rich in soul and wise in the mysteries of the human heart. They have produced an unusually large proportion of the world's great saints and more than their share of great sinners.

In America we are extremely communication-minded. Books are written about communication; universities offer courses in it. American industry spends upward of a hundred million dollars a year to communicate the virtues of free enterprise, and Congress appropriates almost two hundred million dollars a year to spread American good will abroad. In Italy, through the Economic Co-operation Administration and other agencies, the United States has invested three and one half billion dollars in Italian friendship.

What are the returns on our investment?

In the Italian general election of 1948, an important test between Communism and friendship for the United States, the Communists were defeated by the pro-American Christian Democrats. Since then the influence of the Christian Democrats has declined steadily. The Communist block has gained more than one and a half million supporters, most of them youths from twenty-one to twenty-five years old voting for the first time. Neo-Fascists have gained two million votes. In Rome the Fascists gather on each anniversary of Mussolini's death in the Piazza del Popolo to give their salute and shout, "Long live the Duce!"

In other words, the biggest and most expensive public-relations campaign in American history is failing. The rise in Italian Communism and Fascism is in direct proportion to the decline in American prestige. We are not convincing the people of Europe that we are a leader worth following.

W. H. Whyte, Jr., in his alarming book, Is Anybody Listening? *speaks of the myth abroad "that for all our bathtubs and our cars and our sky-scrapers we are without moral purpose; that we are the New Carthage—all money and no spirit; that we are, in short, a country without a soul." According to Mr. Whyte, this myth already "has sapped the will of our allies, made those who benefited from the ECA cynical of its purpose; and each month it grows more in virulence, ready to attack at each crisis."*

Why are we unable to discredit this myth? Says Mr. Whyte: "Our congenital dislike of abstract thought has at last come home to roost. We have failed to determine what it is we wish to communicate."

For fourteen months I was in Italy under a Fulbright research grant of the United States State Department. One of the first things I learned on arriving there is that the Italian dearly loves to talk. From Piedmont and the northern Alps to the African coast of Sicily I talked with people. Sometimes I talked before classes of university students or on radio broadcasts, but mostly I talked with individuals. I was warmly welcomed and hospitably entertained. Everywhere I made friends.

I found that anti-Americanism is an abstract, impersonal sentiment hardly ever directed toward an individual. The Italian feels betrayed, abused, and rejected, not by Americans, but by America. This is because we have not paid him the courtesy of listening to him. In carrying out our vast and expensive communications program we have forgotten that communication is not a stream flowing in one direction, but a reciprocal exchange of experience and ideas.

The Italian deserves to be heard, for he has much to tell. He would like to tell us how, in his overcrowded country, next to Germany the most war-destroyed in Europe, he and his family live on bread and macaroni in one or two rooms without sanitation facilities. He would like us to know there are more than two million unemployed, and that if he is lucky enough to work, it is probably for less than a dollar a day. If he is a southern peasant, he would like us to understand why he and his neighbors are idle while thousands of acres of hereditary lands owned by Milanese and Roman nobility lie fallow and unproductive. He would like to explain to us why, at the war's end, he thinks we fell into a Communist trap and joined with the wrong side, the landlords and the rich minority who preserved themselves through Fascism by supporting Mussolini and are doing the same now by courting Americans. He would like us to know that when young Italians become Communists or Fascists they are less the victims of Left or Right propaganda than they are of the shameful conditions in which too many of them must live. Until we realize all these things and find in ourselves some of the Italian's love and humility, we will not understand him or learn to communicate with him.

Because the Italians taught me communication, this is a book of communication. It is also about the beauties, the virtues, and vices of a country and a people. Where identity might embarrass friends I have changed names. When Italians speak English I have tried to record their speech faithfully and convey its full flavor and charm. The result is, I think, a book of the heart. I hope there is understanding in it. I offer it not in a spirit of cool appraisal, but with love.

I owe much to many. For the privilege of a lifetime I am indebted to the Fulbright Commission; for encouragement, to Prof. Helen C. White, Dr. Annette C. Washburne, and to Rosemary B. Blackmon; for asylum, while working, to Mrs. Ralph Linton; for checking Italian language references, to Fritz Flükiger, and for editing, to Charlotte Seillin. My greatest gratitude goes to my Italian friends, who, loving to talk, made this book possible.

HERBERT KUBLY

New Haven, Connecticut, November 1954

CHAPTER 1

ONWARD CHRISTIAN SOLDIERS

THE SAILING was an off-season one. Passengers gathered somberly out of the gray October mists. A black-shawled Italian grandmother sobbed good-by in the arms of her American relatives. Black-robed nuns and priests thumped up the gangplank on their way to Rome for the dogma of the assumption of the Virgin. There was none of the gaiety that is traditional to a sailing. It was all as dark and damp as an embarkation on the Styx.

To simulate some joy, I gathered the dozen people who had come to see me off for a drink in the bar. Above the din of loading we heard singing. The song was "Onward Christian Soldiers." Some American priests at the bar heard it too; they quickly gulped their whisky and ordered another. On a little platform in the ballroom a score of black-clothed men and women were crowded around a slight tense young man at a piano. After four vigorous unmusical stanzas of "Onward Christian Soldiers," the somber choir launched into "Nearer My God to Thee."

"It's Friday the thirteenth," my sister said glumly, as indeed it was. The whistle blew, and the priests went quietly below deck. The hymn singers departed, but the young man at the piano continued to pound. I said my own good-bys. As the ship pulled away from the pier, stewards dutifully hurled rolls of confetti which became soggy with rain and fell into the river slime. Harbor fog covered the Statue of Liberty, but no one noticed. Despite the gloomy parting, I was happy to be off. The three weeks before sailing I had spent painfully in a hospital repairing a slipped disc in my back; I was still unable to walk without canes and I was looking forward to the therapeutic rest of a voyage. More than that, the routine of a midwestern university had begun to pall on me, and I needed the stimulation of new people and new places.

I

A large nun, a medium-sized nun, and a small nun paced back and forth across the deck like the three bears, mumbling prayers. Nuns and priests were not the only pilgrims on board; judging from the purposeful air worn by everyone, especially the intense piano player, we were a cargo of pilgrims traveling with a mission.

My mission was to turn swords into plowshares. I was a Fulbright professor on my way to Italy; to understand my role one had to go back to the end of the war in 1945 when the United States had billions of dollars worth of military equipment in storage depots throughout the world. In 1946 Congress passed the Fulbright Act, authorizing the sale of these supplies to foreign powers for credit rather than cash, the credit to be used for the educational exchange of persons between the United States and the debtor country. The first Fulbright professors went abroad in 1948; since then more than sixteen thousand teachers and scholars had been sent into twenty-six countries as diverse as England, France, Germany, Burma, Japan, and Iran. Two thousand nationals of these countries were brought to the United States for study. My directive from Washington said "Your ultimate purpose is to further good will and understanding between the United States and other countries . . . in the direction of ultimate world peace."

I was not alone. There were sixteen of us professors on board, all hand-picked out of American universities. I had not met any of my colleagues. From the list I learned that we included an Indiana professor of Greek going to study ancient geometry, a Chicago political scientist to study Italian politics, a West Virginia lady to lecture in Rome on American history, a Harvard archaeologist to photograph Norman mosaics in Sicily, a Cornell linguist to teach Italians the science of languages, and an Oregon seminarian to study the history of religion. The most formidable was a lady authority on Petrarch. My own project was to study the use of the theater in international communication. How it all was going to work into *objective: peace* was not yet clear.

We were innocents going abroad; innocents to whom Washington had given few hints other than that we were to present our Italian allies with a strong case for American democracy. Our first lesson in democracy came quickly, even before we left New York. When we embarked we discovered that the committee in Washington had booked professors from Harvard and Yale into first-class cabins and those of us not in the ivy league into second-class cabins.

The dining steward gathered five of us second-class professors for our first meal. One was a frail, anxious little classics professor. He had been assigned a cabin with two strangers. "When I told the steward I found privacy absolutely essential, he was very rude," the classicist wailed. It was not the only indignity he had suffered. He was not sure whether his trunk, sent on ahead from his midwest university, was on board. It contained a year's supply of American toilet articles, including two dozen rolls of Scott tissue. "If the purser doesn't find the trunk, I don't know what I'll do," he moaned. "You simply can't get those things in Italy." Even without these disasters, the professor had been nervous about leaving America. "I was undecided right up to last week whether I should come," he said. "If Uncle Joe [Stalin was still very alive] starts anything, I'm going straight home." I introduced the subject of our work in Italy. "I'm going to do *my* research in the Vatican library," one scholar said. "I expect to live at the American Academy. They speak English there."

In the doorway, I saw the young piano player speaking to the steward. He waved his hands excitedly, but the two kept their voices lowered, and I could not hear what the argument was about. Whatever it was, the piano player failed to make his point and disappeared. Sitting alone at a table was a commanding young woman whose long black hair covered her face like a sort of screen. She was smoking through a long cigarette holder and spoke to the waiter in a voice that was deeply accented. I wasn't alone in my interest. Near by a tall fair youth, also alone at a table, watched her over his wineglass. Though she gave no sign, I was certain she was aware of both of us. Later, when coffee was served in the lounge, she was still alone. I went to ask if I might join her, arriving at her table almost at the precise moment as the fair young man.

She tossed aside enough of her hair to see us. "I am very fortunate," she said huskily. "Already I am to meet the second and third most interesting men in the dining room. You are third," she said pointedly to me, "because you walk with a cane. I cannot resist men with canes."

I asked who the *most* interesting man was. She pointed to a circle of priests. A tall athletic-looking young man wearing a sweater was identifiable only by his clerical collar. "The prettiest man on board," she said, "and Jesus gets him instead of me. It is very tragic."

"I think it will be an interesting crossing," I said.

"An Italian ship is always more interesting," she said. "On English and American ships the crew doesn't make advances to ladies."

The young man was Max Johann, a Swiss who was by vocation a chemist and by avocation a skiing champion. "I am Renata Fiori," the girl said. Fiori is Italian for "flowers." Because the name was so unusual I seemed to remember having heard or seen it before. Then I recalled the list of Fulbright professors.

"*Doctor* Renata Fiori?" I asked. I had never seen anyone look less like a Professor of Literature. She appeared to be in her late twenties.

"I guess you are surprised?" she said.

"Well, yes. Sort of."

"I could tell," Dr. Flowers said. "Men are very self-centered about such things." She turned to me. "You know," she said, "you are crazy to leave an American university to go to Italy. Italy is extremely dirty and the people are quite impossible. I am Italian. Naturally I know."

I remarked that one with such feelings was a peculiar choice for a mission of good will. "It is a terrible mistake," she said. "I expect to regret it very much. But it is necessary that I go to visit relatives." Though her parents were Americans of long standing, she had spent part of her childhood with an aristocratic Tuscan great-aunt who had tried to change her from an American into an Italian. If not a genius, Dr. Flowers seemed at least a prodigy. At the age of twenty-four she had finished her doctor's thesis on Petrarch. Its subsequent publication established her as an authority on Italian literature.

"What will you contribute to world peace?" I asked.

"I will see when I arrive," she replied. "I do not expect very much. Italians are too stupid to learn anything."

At their table the priests hailed a waiter for a brandy benediction to their meal. As it was being poured, the young piano player stepped like a dark conscience into the lounge. He crossed the room to the piano and angrily began to beat out "The Old Rugged Cross." The priests quietly emptied their snifters and started out on deck. One by one, passengers disappeared. The piano continued to thunder in the empty lounge.

In the evening Dr. Flowers, Max Johann, and I arranged with the steward to take our meals together. "I decided to wear something *saaxy* for dinner," Dr. Flowers said. "I hope you like it." The Swiss and I did. It was a shoulderless black affair which did well by her full figure. It could not be said she was a striking beauty. But her style, manner of dress, her husky voice, hazel eyes and the original things she said made her an engaging companion. She told us how reprehensible she found the Italians' moral code.

"They think an unmarried girl should preserve herself," she said. "What a cockeyed idea. It is okay for a married woman to have a lover but not an unmarried one. I think it should be the other way. If I were married, why should I take a lover?"

I really couldn't say. The priests were entering the dining room. The tall blond one was among them. "It is very sad," Dr. Flowers said. "When he gets to Rome they will trim his hair to a little golden halo on his pink scalp. They will make him wear a robe which will flap in the wind like an old woman's, and his lovely blue eyes will be shaded by a soup-bowl hat. God made him so beautiful and now he must be sacrificed back to God." She considered it all for a moment and then said, "If either of you have a chance, ask him for me if he has any temptation of the flesh."

The waiter said something I did not understand. "Don't you know Italian?" Dr. Flowers asked. I replied that I'd studied grammar, but had had no experience with conversation. "Then I will give you conversation lessons," she said. We agreed on an hour a day, and the next afternoon she came to my cabin. I had been resting and wore a flannel robe over my clothes. "You are very many types," Dr. Flowers said. "Very fascinating. On deck you are the nature-boy type, and in cabin you are the bedroom type." She was in a temper. After lunch she had climbed into a lifeboat to take a sunbath and was spied upon by deck hands, dark agile little Neapolitans wearing berets who scrambled about the riggings with brushes and buckets of paint. When she scolded them for peeping, they ordered her to abandon her perch lest a sudden lilt of the ship should pitch her into the sea. "Immoral little monkeys," she called them. I sat at the desk and she handed me an Italian *Pinocchio* from the ship's library.

"*Legga!*" she ordered. "Read!" She threw herself on the bed to listen

She was wearing black satin shorts and a plunging blouse. I read somewhat falteringly a paragraph or two.

"Bravo," she applauded. She looked around the large cabin, which was equipped for four, and said, "I am crowded in a small cabin with two pious housemaids making a holy year pilgrimage. Naturally we are not very *simpatiche*. You have so much space I think I will move in with you."

I said that I had arranged for a stateroom to myself because I was convalescing. "It's okay," Dr. Flowers said. "I'm used to it. During the war I was in a ward with twenty men. They were *all* disabled." I explained that my spine was in a brace, that it was necessary for me to rest long hours, and that I had been warned against any bodily exertion for at least two months.

"My Gawd!" Dr. Flowers said. "What a boat!"

After that our lessons went off in businesslike fashion. Occasionally there was competition from the cabin across the corridor where the three different-sized nuns spent long hours in prayer. Dr. Flowers said they were members of a praying order and she was certainly right. At mealtime they prayed loudly in the dining room. Each morning they bounced to the prow of the ship where they lined up like a trio of gargoyles, the wind whipping their black robes like shrouds as they read their morning breviaries in unison. During the day they covered the ship gathering subject matter for the prayers which they droned late into the night. Nothing escaped their attention. Dr. Flowers' scant costumes, my crippled back, the whisky drinking of the priests, the love-making under the lifeboats at night, all were grist for their mill. One afternoon a cabin maid was accused by a passenger of stealing a lipstick. Despite the maid's swearing by the Virgin Mary that she had not stolen the lipstick, the three nuns prayed loudly the night through for the wretched girl.

The gayest religious on board was Father Rocco, a Neapolitan priest returning home from a visit with American relatives. Father Rocco had a passion for American sports clothes. He appeared on deck in an assortment of Palm Beach shirts, brown suède sandals, maroon gabardine slacks, and, for a Neapolitan touch, a red sash around his belly. Evenings he danced tarantellas, sang risqué dialect songs, and chased girls over the decks like Harpo Marx. One night at a dance Dr. Flowers made an appointment for him to hear her confession in the ship's chapel. When it was over, she reported, "I made up a wonderful confession and when I finished it I began to cry. He said, 'Never mind, girlie, never mind. We are all

God's sinners!' " Father Rocco's disguise was so complete that the praying nuns did not know he was a priest until the fifth day at sea. When they found out, they overlooked the ship's venial sins and spent hours praying for Father Rocco's immortal soul.

The congenial American priests gave both the nuns and Father Rocco a wide berth. They passed their time reading and smoking cigars on deck, where I visited with them. The tall fair one whom Dr. Flowers had conceded to Jesus was Father Mulholland, a philosophy instructor in a New England college. He was twenty-five years old and six feet, four inches tall; as a youth he had trained for professional baseball. It had not been easy for him to give up athletics; in the monastery where he lived he had organized brothers into baseball and basketball teams. Now he was going to Rome to study for two years. On the ship he was never without his breviary, which, he said, "is a handy little gadget. For some reason bores always start talking to priests, and whenever a bore starts on me, I open my breviary and begin to read. It works every time." I relayed to Father Mulholland Dr. Flowers' question about his fleshly temptations and her concern for his golden hair.

"Tell the doctor I am sorry," he said, "but my studies and the reading of the mass protect me from temptation and build up my strength. Tell her she should not worry about my hair. Vanity and pride are sins worse than lust. I have liked too much the flattery of women and I am frequently guilty of the sin of pride. For four years I have prayed to become bald so to free myself from the attentions of women. Now at last my prayers are being answered; my hairline is receding and my hair is becoming thin. I thank God daily for this blessing." While we were talking the young pianist appeared in the lounge. "Here comes Gallstones," a fat young Jesuit said. "Five to one it's 'Rock of Ages.' " The strange musician glanced darkly in our direction and then went to the piano and beat out "Rock of Ages."

"We will now all rise and sing," said the Jesuit. The priests did not know who the elusive young pianist was. "It's a vicious circle," the Jesuit said, "he seems to play because we drink, and his playing drives us to drink."

"I think he is a troubled young man," Father Mulholland said.

The priests went to their cabins, and I crossed the lounge and introduced myself to the pianist. He gripped my hand like a vise. I could feel the moisture of his palms.

"Carl Raymond is the name," he said. "The *Reverend* Carl Raymond."

His lean face was flushed with color and his dark eyes flashed. His black hair was immaculately groomed; his clothes were cheap but neat. There was something quite delicate about him, all except his hands, which were long and stronger than the rest of him. I offered him a cigarette, which he refused. "I don't smoke," he said sternly. "Are you a Christian?"

The question startled me, but I stood my ground. "Yes, I am," I said.

"A Protestant?"

I was.

"I thought you might be a Jew," he said. "I'm so happy to know a Christian. There are so many sinners on board."

"There are!" I exclaimed.

"Oh, yes," he said. "Those priests who pretend to be men of God drink whisky and smoke cigars. Down in third class there are jugs of wine on the table. I explained to the steward that I could not eat with men who drank wine, but he would not let me take my meals up here. It is like a prison down there, six men to a cabin, all smelling of wine." He glanced at my cigarette. "Do you live according to the precepts of the Bible?" he asked.

"I try to," I said.

"What does the Bible mean to you?" he asked.

"A moral teaching," I said.

"Do you believe what it says?" he asked.

"I believe it as poetry rather than history," I replied.

He reacted as if I'd said the Bible were a hoax. "I knew it," he wailed. "You have no rock, no foundations. Men who have no rock are sinners." I asked about himself, and he babbled in the manner of lonely people when they have found a listener. He told me he was thirty-one years old, that his family was Pennsylvania Dutch, and he was one of twelve children reared in the Reformed Church. By raising chickens he had earned enough money to attend a southern evangelistic college where he interested himself in dramatics and played the leads in plays. He also discovered sin; the fighting of it was now the major passion of his life. "The world must be cleansed of sin," he said, "to prepare for the coming of Jesus."

This tortured, distorted young man was going to the land of the gentle St. Francis to make brimstone Methodists. It was a sobering thought.

After that the Reverend Raymond seemed to consider me a friend. Whenever he saw me with the priests he sulked unhappily in a corner, as if my fellowship with them were a sort of betrayal. One afternoon I invited him to join Father Mulholland and me for afternoon tea. It did not go well. The Reverend Raymond said he had been praying for strength to fight sin when he reached Italy because he had heard the Italians were very promiscuous.

"It would be better to pray for understanding and tolerance," Father Mulholland replied. I said I thought a Latin's frank enjoyment of sex was healthier than an Anglo-Saxon's dark preoccupation with the sin of it.

"Don't you Freud boys read the Bible?" the Reverend Raymond said hotly.

This was rough on Father Mulholland, who nevertheless heard it coolly without a change of expression. "Yes," he said, "I read it."

"You intellectuals have no foundation, no rock," the evangelist said to the priest. "Only simple unintellectual people have faith."

"Was the Bible written by ignorant men?" the priest asked.

"The Bible is divine revelation. It is the Word of God."

"So it is," Father Mulholland said. "But it was written by men of learning to be read by men of learning. You will remember from Thomas Aquinas . . ."

"Who is he?"

"One of our boys," Father Mulholland said.

"An intellectual, I suppose."

"I'm afraid so," the priest said. "What is the Protestant creed?"

"A faith in the teachings of the Bible," the minister said.

"I believe it is faith in man's redemption from sin through Christ's blood," the priest said. "Even Italian sins are redeemable."

The Reverend Raymond stood up and looked down at us with the wrath of a Luther. "Don't you know that the Bible says, 'He that increaseth knowledge, increaseth sorrow?' " he asked. Then he crossed to the piano and thundered out "Onward Christian Soldiers."

"He is a very religious man," Father Mulholland said gently. "He will have an unhappy time in Italy, for he shall have to live with human beings. He may even be stoned. That, I think, is what he wants. I think it would please him to be stoned."

The second last day of the voyage our ship docked for a day in Palermo, the capital of Sicily. It was my first view of Italian soil. I stood on the deck remembering Goethe's words when he looked on the city from the harbor in 1787. "A most glorious view . . . the most beautiful headland in the whole world."

Though the view was the same, now it was more shocking than glorious. In 1943 Palermo was brutally bombed. Its harbor was repaired, but the surrounding quarters were still in ruins, and the people were not yet aroused from weariness and despair. A crowd of students wearing paper carnival hats were gathered on the dock to greet us. They sang Sicilian songs, words I did not understand and melodies that were at the same time gay and tragic. Behind them the city, brooded over by blue-gray mountains, shone brilliantly in the morning sun with the luminosity of decay. When Dr. Flowers, Max Johann, and I stepped from the ship, it was into a land of beggars. They clutched at us like hungry beasts; terrible cripples, children covered with dirt and sores, black-hooded old ladies and squalling babies carried by women who wailed, *"Il bambino è affamato* [the baby starves]." I was filled with horror; very soon I had given away all my Italian currency despite Dr. Flowers' urgings to ignore the beggars. Her scorn for them seemed to me shameful. "They are all professionals," she said. "The babies are not hungry. They cry because the women pinch their bottoms to make them cry. Most of the women are not even the mothers. They borrow the babies for begging."

She may have been right. Still the despair was more real to me than any I had seen, and I could not accustom myself to it. Wherever we went, the mantle of death lay over the city. The population was in mourning. Women were robed in black, men wore the inevitable black arm band, and the doors of houses wore black swatches of cloth as if the dark angel had passed over the city.

"They love death," Dr. Flowers said. "Death is their hobby. For each death in the family a Sicilian must wear mourning for a year. Since families are large and infant mortality high, no one ever lays aside his black. There is always someone a Sicilian can mourn for."

It was true; the signs of dying were everywhere. We walked up the street of the coffin makers where the shops were open to let in daylight. Inside, industrious gnomes beat together coffins, some plain narrow boxes and others ornately carved with cupids and skulls. On our way out we met a funeral, a procession festive with flowers, the coffin riding in high splendor on a horse-drawn wagon, the first mourners following in an old motorcar and the others in horse-drawn carriages. We followed it away from the sea. Where the bombs had been less devastating the city had a garish oriental beauty. It was the middle of the autumnal growing season, and a profusion of bougainvillaea, clematis, and roses grew over the houses as over tombs.

In the heart of the town, at the Piazza Quattro Canti, a wasted old witch selling newspapers shouted shrilly, "Extra! Newborn babe kills obstetrician! Extra! Priest marries prostitute!" Only tourists like us paid any attention to her. Donkeys, dainty-hooved, silver-gray creatures wore regal trappings of silver and feathered headdresses as fantastic as an Eastern potentate's. The two-wheeled carts to which the docile little beasts were hitched were wondrous works of art. A Sicilian peasant will live in squalor and starve his children for a cart decorated with the Virgin in glory, Venus on her shell, or the heroes of the crusades. The cart is his object of pride, his lifetime extravagance; on weekdays he hauls cabbages and fodder in it, on Sundays his wife and children.

People filled the streets, shy languid women and girls, moving with Eastern softness, men defiant and fiercely noble, and children with straight brown legs, heads matted with curls, dark eyes flashing supercilious wisdom. The children were the most bewitching of all, like angels in a corrupted paradise.

In the afternoon two English-speaking guides on a sight-seeing bus whipped us in indecent haste through a montage of tourist shrines. We saw sybaritic palaces, mosaiced chapels, and cloistered gardens of hibiscus and lemon trees. Through each we were followed by beggars, wailing their monosyllabic sorrows, tugging at our sleeves like nagging furies. The climax of the excursion was a pilgrimage to the summit of Monte Pellegrino, the shrine of Palermo's patroness, St. Rosalie. The legend of Rosalie re-established in the twelfth century the cult of the Virgin which Latin Catholics had borrowed from pagan antiquity. The maid Rosalie was from a noble family named Sinibaldi which arranged her betrothal to a Palermo courtier. To avoid losing her chastity, Rosalie crawled to the top of the barren limestone mountain to live like a beast in a cave until her death. Since its discovery in the sixteenth century, the cave has been one of the great shrines of religious pilgrims.

Our bus snaked back and forth on the flank of the bleak mountain. Bands of boys harvested prickly pears, and men with donkeys collected dried cactus for fuel. The driver skillfully navigated the bus through hairpin curves, climbing beyond the cactus where there was only rock and a bleak wind to chill the bones. We stopped at a little plaza, from which steps led to a church built over Rosalie's cave. Inside the grotto, it was dismal and dank; moisture dripped from the walls. In the dark heart of it shone the recumbent figure of the saint, a life-sized statue of white marble clothed in gleaming gold.

Goethe had been entranced. "A lovely female form," he wrote. "It was executed so naturally and so pleasingly that one almost fancied it must breathe and move." Presumably styles have changed, both in saints and female figures. As I looked at the woman lying in voluptuous elegance like a Titian Venus, I had a more irreverent association. She bore a remarkable likeness to Mae West. Surrounding the statue was a macabre treasure of ex-voto gifts brought by pious Sicilians whose physical ailments the saint had miraculously cured. For the most part these gifts, which overflowed into several rooms of an orphanage next door, were silver and gold images of healed organs and limbs, literally thousands of glistening hearts, heads, stomachs, intestines, livers, kidneys, and genitals, and shelves of hands, feet, arms, and legs. There was even a silver donkey's leg presented to the saint by a grateful master.

A bell tinkled in the orphanage and a band of little boys led by a young pinch-faced monk clomped double-file down a stairway and out of doors. They were solemn-faced orphans of war, some of unknown American fathers. Wearing wooden shoes and ragged little shirts and shorts, they stood shivering in the harsh wind, their flesh pimpled by the cold. The monk clapped his hands together and ordered the little boys to run and play in order to keep warm. I thought of the saint's gold dress and the obscene silver hanging in the cave.

When we returned to the city it was dark.

The bus twisted through the empty narrow streets. Gusts of rain blew in from the sea and spattered the windows, and ahead of us two men crossed, carrying a shining new coffin on their shoulders.

It was our last night at sea and the ship was as gay as a carnival. There was champagne at dinner, and later confetti and dancing in the ballroom. The grandmother who had sobbed in New York was shrieking hilariously as she sprayed everyone with a jet of water from an artificial tulip pinned to her black dress. The American priests drank an extra brandy and the Neapolitan Father Rocco's green shirt was lacquered to his back with sweat as he danced the tarantella with two girls at one time. In his corner the Reverend Raymond sulked like John Wesley in Babylon. Max Johann and I missed Dr. Flowers. As we approached the end of our voyage her mood had changed from flippant gaiety to moroseness. Often she interrupted my conversation lessons to speak of her hatred for Italy and her regret for ever having left New York. Max confided to me that one evening on deck she had wept hysterically and threatened to plunge into the sea. Together we searched, first her cabin, then on the deck. We found her at the railing, moodily contemplating the dark sea.

"If only the voyage did not end and the boat sailed on and on forever," she said.

"I can hardly wait for it to end," said Max, who was going on to Genoa.

"I am not going ashore in the morning," Dr. Flowers said. "I will stay on the ship and return to America."

"Of course you'll go ashore," I said.

She began to weep. "I can't," she wailed. "She'll tell me I'm ugly, my clothes are bad, my hair is a mess. . . ."

"Who?" I asked.

She did not answer. "She hates me. Ever since she first knew me she hated me," she sobbed. "I want to go back to America, I want to go back. . . ."

We took her inside and gave her a drink. Soon she was calm, and when I went to my cabin she and Max were dancing. I could not sleep; instead I lay awake for a long time thinking of the strange torment of Dr. Flowers. When I awoke in the morning the ship was at rest in the Neapolitan bay. Framed in my porthole was a view I had seen on hundreds of pictures. The blue morning mists were rising from the city and a white cloud spiraled gently over Vesuvius' cone. It was eight o'clock. I dressed and joined the bustle of debarkation. In the lounge an elderly and fiercely commanding woman waved a long-stemmed black lace umbrella at me. She was a formidable figure. A black plume rose from her hat and furs dangled from her sharp shoulders. Her manner was as imperious, her gestures as dramatic as an operatic soprano's. The woman waved aside several ship's attendants.

"Do you know where my niece is?" she asked me.

"Who is your niece?" I knew the answer.

"Dr. Renata Fiori. Have you seen her?"

In a moment Dr. Flowers appeared. I hardly knew her. She was a pale, trembling little girl, her eyes were red from weeping. The two women fell into each other's arms and kissed. "Where have you been?" the voice shrilled. "I have waited for a half hour. The car is waiting. My dear, you look terrible. Have you been sick? When was your hair done? That dress is very unbecoming. You might be a little more considerate. I've been up since six o'clock. . . ." They went off, Dr. Flowers running alongside her mother, her hand grasped firmly as a naughty child's.

On deck I found the Fulbright professors. Our baggage was already expedited by an efficient man from the American Embassy. There was nothing left to do. I promised to see Max Johann in Zurich and Father Mulholland in Rome. In the lounge the Reverend Raymond, who was going on to Genoa, beat out a defiant "Onward Christian Soldiers."

CHAPTER 2

CITTÀ SANTA, ANNO SANTO

"Faith is made here, and believed elsewhere."
—A ROMAN SAYING

THE HOLY CITY in a holy year, the mother city to which all roads lead. We came to it by bus from the south over the new Appian Way. Ancient castles brooded on the mountaintops like silent gray fortresses. A biblical languor lay over the soft valleys. In the olive groves and vineyards men and women were gathering in the summer. Youths herded sheep on the slopes and maids came from the wells balancing water bottles on their heads. Oxen pulled plows between rows of lemon and orange.

The new city outside the wall was like a lower-class American suburb with its acres of garish boxlike tenements without trees or grass. Passing into the anicent city through the gate of San Giovanni we were at once in the midst of Rome's religious world's fair. We stopped before the Lateran Church, the cathedral of the world, and one of the five basilicas of the holy-year pilgrimage.

The piazza was alive with bands of the faithful zigzagging over the pavements with a divine compulsion, racing zealously across Rome from one basilica to another. Nuns and priests seemed to float on the wind which billowed their robes like sails. And what a variety of sails. The bright scarlet of a German order, purple ones from Spain, and green from France stood out against the somber browns and blacks from Ireland and America. Opposite the church is the *Scala Santa*, twenty-eight holy stairs which, according to legend, are those from the palace of Pontius Pilate which Christ ascended on the day of his crucifixion. The stairs must not be defiled by human feet. Pilgrims were climbing them on their knees, painstakingly lifting themselves up, women, sweating from the effort, sobbing and kissing each steep step; crippled old men shaking with the ague; children, their knees too short, raising themselves by their elbows. The twenty-eight steps, according to multi-lingual placards, are stained with the blood of Jesus and the tears of popes, and the reward for climbing them is an indulgence of nine years, which, if the penitent desires, can be applied to a soul in purgatory. As they do about all their multitudinous relics, Romans keep a discreet silence about the holy stairs. But the pilgrims believed.

Rome, which had beatified the little rape victim Maria Goretti earlier in the year, was now preparing for its second holy year climax, the announcement of the dogma of the Virgin's assumption. The crowds were so great that the American Embassy had been hard pressed to find rooms for our busload of Fulbrights arriving in the midst of them. The bus, unloading its cargo one and two to a hotel, left the classics professor and myself at the Bellavista Milton, a hotel with an English-speaking staff. It was filled at the moment with pilgrims from Switzerland. The manager, an Austrian woman who had married an Italian, told us we would have to share a room until after the assumption dogma. "*Ach*, this pilgrims," she said. "*C'est impossible*, a room *privata*! Pilgrims is good for hotels. But now is too much. When is over this holy year is good."

The beautiful view for which the hotel is named was on the Pincio Gardens. I heard the barking of dogs and cries of "Yoicks!" and looked out on red-jacketed horsemen in a steeplechase.

The hotel was two blocks from the Via Veneto, the fashionable boulevard which is the heart of Rome's English-speaking island. Kiosks were papered with American newspapers and magazines; posters advertised American movies, a troupe of American Negro dancers, and Dixieland music by the "Roman New Orleans Jazz Band." This short, wide street was the American Rome; a rich, free-spending community of expensive hotels, American cocktail bars, sidewalk restaurants, gasoline stations, and, at its foot, the American Embassy. It was the gay new Rome of the spendthrift G.I.'s of the middle forties, of UNRRA and the Marshall Plan, and of motion-picture companies; a city of tourists, actresses and diplomats, and now pilgrims. Viewed from a café table of the Veneto, Rome was rich and Italy an Eden.

The weather was cold and rainy; in our hotel there was no heat. Our room was damp and raw as a tomb. The classicist was miserable, his trunk had appeared briefly in Naples and had disappeared again. The bottle of wine he had ordered for supper had cost him one hundred of the 317,111 lire we were being paid each month, and he was sure the waiter had cheated him.

He stayed in bed nursing his wretchedness, and I joined the pilgrims,

taking a trolley to the Vatican. On the way I read a newspaper, the Eng-
lish-language tabloid called *The Rome Daily American*. It contained pes-
simistic articles about the imminence of war, society columns filled with
the social doings of the Embassy set, and a page of personal notices. "Nice
elegant lady, 35, owns furnished apartment, would marry American gentleman with high culture," one of them announced. A man advertised:
"Stanfordites in Italy interested in alumni get-together, contact me."

Long lines of pilgrims filed through Vatican turnstiles to see the Papal
art treasures. Admission cost one hundred and fifty lire for pilgrims and
twice that for others. While I waited, a youth came to ask if I were
American; he had, he said, two pilgrim's passes and by using one I could
cut my fee in half. I accepted, more grateful for his companionship than
for the saving of twenty-four cents. His name was Ernesto Pirola and he
was a twenty-two-year-old medical student from Turin on a university
holiday. He was strongly built, and he had black curly hair and black eyes.
He wore contrasting tweed trousers and jacket such as any American student might wear. I would have taken him for Spanish rather than Italian,
and he told me he had a Spanish grandmother. Communication was not
easy. He spoke hardly any English; my conversational Italian was still
laborious. But he knew the galleries and enjoyed the role of guide. It was
a staggering undertaking. Droves of ardent pilgrims bounced through the
rooms as if the paintings were stations of the cross; multilingual gallery
guides outshouted each other in French, German, English, and Italian.
Skillfully Ernesto maneuvered me through the labyrinth of corridors and
rooms, weaving in and out of crowds to find his own high spots in the
gallery. We made stops at a series of Venuses, including Praxiteles' Knido
Venus, which Ernesto described with a sigh as "the perfect woman," at
the youthful Belvedere Apollo, and at Laocoön and his sons bound together by serpents, a bewildering piece of frozen motion which Ernesto
said was the finest statue in the world. In the Vatican library he showed me
entrancing miniatures on illuminated manuscripts, and in a room of Etruscan pottery he slyly pointed out the vases with pornographic decorations.

Ernesto's strategy was to move against the tide of pilgrims, so the pic-
ture galleries were at the end of our tour. The crowds were thickest in the
Raphael room; instead of moving along, bands of pilgrims remained there
to cluck excitedly over the *Coronation*, the *Foligno Madonna*, and the
Transfiguration. "It is considered the finest painting in the world,"
Ernesto said of the *Transfiguration*. "Raphael was working on it when he

died, and it was carried behind his coffin at his funeral." The corpulent
figures of Christ and two apostles were heavily suspended in mid-air like
angels hoisted by pulleys in a baroque theater. *"Troppo dolce,"* Ernesto
said. "For me, too sweet." We moved on to the room which was his
favorite. It contained a collection of saints' martyrdoms, dark and murky
in color and painted in the luridly naturalistic style of the seventeenth
century. In one murderous canvas a dog licked the dripping human body;
in another—Guido Reni's *Crucifixion of St. Peter*—a youth wearing a red-
feathered cap gaily drove a spike through flesh. The most shocking of all
was Poussin's disemboweling of St. Erasmus. The sight of the saint's intestines wound around a windlass transfixed a band of monks that were
crowded about it with masochistic pleasure, as if they were trying to re-
create the incident with themselves as victims.

"È bello," Ernesto said, awed as the monks. I moved away. "You do
not like it?" Ernesto asked.

"It is interesting," I said.

"It is also beautiful," Ernesto replied.

We passed through the long tunnel corridor, which leads to the Sistine
Chapel. Here was the greatest crush of all. Pilgrims, with their eyes glued
upward, stumbled over each other like sheep. A blanket of stale air lay
heavy over the box-shaped room; instead of light there was twilight. The
paintings were dark with the fog of centuries. Yet the crowd, feeling the
overpowering presence of Michelangelo, was subdued and silent before his
terrible moral lesson. The cycle of man, from the creation to the final
deluge, was complete in every detail; in its dim visibility the last judgment raged furiously. The muscular young Adam, the heroic prophets and
sibyls, the Christ a raging Hercules standing on stone, and the laughing
satyrlike youths belong to a fleshly pagan eternity rather than to a spiritual Christian one. They are citizens not of a lute-plucking *paradiso* of
divine spirits, but of an Olympus where flesh is divine.

We saw what we could. Pilgrims streamed in. When we could no longer
move or breathe the fetid air, we left. At a neighborhood *trattoria*, we
stopped for some wine and spaghetti.

"You are the first American I have ever spoken to," Ernesto said. He
was full of curiosity. Had I ever been in Hollywood?—it was a question
I was to be asked over and over again—and did I know Linda Darnell?
"Is it true in America the universities provide medical students with
microscopes?" he asked. I said I believed they did. "In Italy it is other-

wise," he said. "I must pay fifty thousand lire for a microscope. Many students who would study medicine do not do so because they cannot buy the microscope. It is very difficult for a student to pay fifty thousand lire."

It was the last day of Ernesto's Rome visit; he was leaving by train for his school in Turin in two hours. Had he made his pilgrimages to the five basilicas? I asked.

"Only two," he replied. "I have gone to the museums and to the theaters. It is a convenient time to come to Rome. For a pilgrimage you have a school holiday. Railroads are cheaper, and one can eat and sleep in student houses. Rome is very beautiful," he said, "but I do not like it."

I asked him why.

"The people of Italy do not like Rome," he said, "because Rome is not Italy. When the war was over, the cities of Italy shot their Fascist leaders. But not the Romans. In Rome the Fascists are now in the government and in society, just as they were before the war. Many are nobility who have become very American in their tastes. They speak English and when they entertain in their palaces, the Americans are their favorite guests." Ernesto spoke rapidly, carried along by feeling. "In Rome there are few factories and no true laboring classes. Everyone works for the government and the embassies or as servants to diplomats. Rome is rich from living off its visitors, so its loyalty is not to Italy. To be governed by Rome is for Italians like being governed by a power outside, for Rome is not part of us. If you wish to know Italians, you must go to Bologna and Florence and Naples. You must come to Turin. It is a city very beautiful." Turin was Italy's Detroit, the center of her automotive industry. I supposed it was a crowded industrial town and suspected Ernesto's enthusiasm for its beauty as chauvinistic.

At another table two French priests were asking a waiter if it were true that the Pope had returned from his summer palace and would hold a public audience that afternoon? The waiter shrugged; he did not know, but if the priests wished, they might inquire of the sentry standing guard at a gate of the Vatican wall across the street. The guard was tall, with great coarse peasant's hands and a soft face. He had straw-blond hair and blue eyes, a perfect type to wear the bright blue doublet and tam-o'-shanter of a Swiss guard's uniform. I spoke to him in German-Swiss.

"Yes, it is true," he replied in the same dialect. "There will be an audience at four o'clock." He examined me closely. "From where in Switzerland do you come?" he asked.

I said I was American.

"Never heard of an American speaking Swiss like that," he said, implying that Swiss was a chosen language, the speaking of it a rare privilege. I explained that I was of Swiss ancestry, and the dialect had been my childhood language. *"Unglaublich,"* he muttered, "for an American, impossible." An American tourist couple asked him if they might go inside the Vatican city. He did not understand them, so I translated the question. He answered that only residents and official Vatican visitors could enter inside the walls. After the couple left, he asked me if I should like to go in. I said I would, very much. "Very well," he said, "it is permitted us to invite our relatives. I will take you as my cousin from Switzerland. My name is Hilarius Hessler. If you are to be my cousin, you must remember to call me Larry. Of course," he added, glancing sharply at Ernesto, "it will be necessary for you to be alone."

Ernesto, who did not understand Swiss, grasped the point nonetheless. "It is time for me to go to the railroad station," he said. We shook hands. "I beg you to come to Turin," he said. I promised to try and thanked him for the pilgrim's pass and for conducting me so efficiently through the galleries. "I am the richer," he said. "I now have an American friend. *Ciao,*" he said in parting. It was the intimate greeting of Italians for close friends.

With Ernesto out of the way, Hilarius Hessler warmed up considerably. He spoke an elemental mountain patois full of peasant vulgarisms and profanities practically impossible to translate into English. It was disconcerting to discover that, despite his name, he was completely without humor. He introduced me as his cousin to the guard who replaced him, and we passed inside the gate. He apologized for discriminating against my Italian friend. It was necessary, he said, to keep out the *"gottver-dammte cinque,"* a phrase most literally translated as "God-damned wops." What he said went roughly like this: "We can't have those uncivilized wops around; they steal everything that isn't nailed on. Of course, some wops are better than others, but even the best ones you have to watch. They're all damned skirt chasers; they got a skirt inside their skull and that's all." Larry's mouth drooped about an inch on one side so that his face wore a perpetual leer. I suspected it came from infancy thumb-sucking. He caught me looking at it. "If it disturbs you looking at me, we can say good-by," he said. He was a narcissist and hypersensitive about his mouth. To change the subject I asked him how one became a Swiss guard of the Pope.

"Mi mues Katholisch, witzig, jung und hübsch sy and ich bin alles
[One must be Catholic, clever, young and handsome, and I am all those
things]. The letters from your priest and bishop are easy to get." Elaborately he reviewed the historical heroics of the Swiss guards. "To guard
the life of the Pope is the most glorious responsibility in the world," he
said. He told me he was twenty-four years old, had been a furniture carpenter in a mountain village in Canton St. Gallen, and was "in service"
for two years. "After eighteen more years I will be pensioned," he said.
"By that time I shall have saved enough money to buy a hotel on Capri.
One of the guards bought a hotel on Capri last year and made a profit of
five million lire in eight months." Larry was frugal, banking every copper
of his money toward the day when he would realize his ambition. "Then
a man is free and life is beautiful," he said with feeling. "To be in one's
own hotel with the money coming in and the wops doing all the work."
To augment his savings, Larry had developed a lucrative week-end
hobby. He took trips to Capri, Ischia, Venice, Sorrento, and Tuscany to
make camera color slides which he showed to church groups in Switzerland for a price. "At a hundred francs an evening, it all helps," he said.

Inside the thick walls was a tiny medieval state, one hundred acres of
gardens, courtyards, heavy artillery ramps, and a post office. One court was
filled with some antiquated cannons and a score or so of old United States
Army trucks and jeeps. This Larry called a "graveyard of American
arms"; speaking to me as a fellow Swiss, he made no effort to conceal
his anti-Americanism. *"Das sind Saucheibe, d'Amerikaner"*—the vulgar-
ism is untranslatable— "They got their money for this junk and most of
it doesn't run. I would never go to America. Never! Nothing but labor
revolutions and Communist uprisings all the time." I said that in spite of
what he might have read in his newspapers, there had never been a Communist uprising in America, and I wasn't sure what he meant by "labor
revolutions." Without paying me attention, he continued his monologue
of the self-centered trivia with which his head seemed to be filled. "I have
taken two hundred and eighty-seven colored slides in the Roman forum.
My Arc of Constantine against the sunset is a *meisterwerk*! Of course the
sunsets in Italy are nothing compared to sunsets in Switzerland. Evening
on the Matterhorn! *There* is a sunset for you!"

I asked Larry if I might take a photograph of him. He posed with a
girl's foolish coquetry. A guard approached us wearing the blue, red, and
yellow spangled parade uniform. On his head was a burnished plumed

helmet, and he carried a spear. The sight of him sent Larry into a steely temper. "The guard captain is jealous of me because I appeared thirty-seven times in a motion picture of the Vatican made by an American film company," he said. "So he has not called on me for today's procession. But it amounts to nothing. It is a very small affair, and after all . . ." Larry spoke with apostolic revelation, *"Ich ha's Maria Goretti treit!* [I carried Maria Goretti!]"

In the guards' quarters, I had the feeling I was in a tiny twenty-third canton. Swiss was the only language spoken. Larry's room was a clean, pleasant cell decorated with Swiss scenery calendars. In the clubrooms downstairs the newspaper racks were filled with Swiss newspapers; the walls were decorated with beefy William Tells and Arnold von Winkel-rieds in a series of frescoes from Swiss legend and history. In the kitchen the cook, a stolid burgher from Basel, stood before six barrels of wine, each of which was taller than himself. A Swiss waiter served us *Schinken* and *Schweizer Käse,* which we washed down with Swiss beer. I asked Larry if guards married. "Certainly not," he said sternly. "To be a guard, one must remain a bachelor. Of course, some keep women in outside apartments where they go on their days off, and a few are *Wybersuecher,* skirt chasers, as bad as the wops. But of course all the women are wops and I—if I can't have a good clean Swiss girl—I don't have any!" He continued his Bae-deker. "We are in service two days and every third day is a free day. In-side where we lead normal Swiss lives, it is not bad. But the days of out-side are *veruckt. Uberall, italiener.* We have our own Swiss doctor and *coiffeur.* We don't want any greasy wop cutting our hair." When we had finished with our lunch, he took me to the guard's private chapel and a theater equipped with a movie projector. "Here we have jazz music and we put on shows. Now and then we even dance."

"Then you bring women in," I said.

"Of course we do not have women. They are not allowed inside the gates," he said. "We have it most *lustig* on *Schmutzige Zystig.*" I said my knowledge of Swiss life did not include "greasy Tuesday." "It is the Tues-day before Lent," Larry explained, "the day when wives cuckold their hus-bands, and husbands betray their wives. *Ach, das isch lustig!*" I tried with difficulty to imagine the gaieties of *Schmutzige Zystig* inside the austere and holy wall. "On Easter we do the passion here," Larry said, pointing to a stage. "I am Mary Magdalene!"

Larry returned to his post at the gate, and I walked around the wall to

St. Peter's Square. The weather was fitfully alternating between rain and sun; at the moment the portal of Christendom shimmered wetly in a flash of brightness. In spite of Larry's caviling, the audience later in the afternoon was to be a significant one. It was the last before the proclamation of the Assumption dogma; the Pope had just announced that the Virgin had twice appeared to him during the holy year, and thousands of pilgrims wanted to see for themselves how he had withstood the experience. The piazza, a great wheel about an obelisk hub, was as bustling with movement as a suddenly disturbed insect colony. Motor scooters and small autos whirred helter-skelter over the pavements, and horse cabs filled with American sailors clopped up to the St. Peter's stairway. Pilgrim buses with Swiss and French license plates jammed the avenues. Coveys of nuns hovered under umbrellas; tonsured monks and student priests with souptureen hats chattered alien tongues; bands of uniformed school children marched solemnly behind flapping sisters. The *carabinieri* did nothing to maintain order; preening their tricornered plumed hats, their red-striped trousers, and their curving swords, they were a conspicuous part of the circus.

The audience scheduled to be outside on the square was still an hour away, so I entered the basilica. It was as busy as a subway station and almost as noisy. Bands of chanting, torch-bearing pilgrims crisscrossed briskly from one chapel to another. They were as multilingual as babel; many wore the provincial dress of southern Italy, France, and Spain. Almost hidden in a corner behind the holy doors, which are opened to pilgrims on holy years, I came upon the most beautiful thing I had yet seen in Rome, Michelangelo's *Pietà*. The utter purity of this eloquent statue is out of context in the baroque temple; and it is set so high that one almost misses the luminous delicacy with which the face of the dead is fashioned. But the sorrow is overwhelming in the frail boy's body with its slender child's limbs translucently radiant, lying so dead on the lap of the mother. There is nothing quite like it. Except for the *Pietà* and the celebrated bronze of St. Peter, whose toes have been worn away by human lips in centuries of devout kisses, the art of St. Peter's is shocking. Bernini, whose colonnade outside is his masterpiece, is responsible for much of it. Neapolitan born, this artist covered Rome with his southerner's passion for the florid and pretentious. His most bizarre creations are in St. Peter's— especially the tortuously twisted baldachin directly under Michelangelo's dome and the series of grotesque sarcophagi for the bodies of popes.

Most of the paintings in St. Peter's are by Bernini contemporaries; they are large, fat, and empty, a final vulgarization of Michelangelo and the beginning of that sentimental school of religious art still seen on church calendars. Over the altar I encountered for the second time the bowels of Erasmus, this time in a mosaic reproduction of the Poussin painting. In the Sacristy I saw the holy treasures and jeweled relics of Christendom, passing in a slow line by glass cabinets filled with primitive crucifixes from Constantine and Justin, popes' brooches and rings, with chalices of Byzantine brilliance and elaborately rococo crowns and scepters mounted with diamonds, topazes, emeralds, and rubies. Arabian nights' splendors, symbols of monarchy and the omnipotent oligarchy of the Kingdom of Heaven. Here dazzled pilgrims were carefully watched by stalwart *carabinieri* who never took their hands from the hilts of their swords.

For a hundred lire I rode an elevator to the roof. A village thrived on top of the basilica. Photographers were taking pilgrims' pictures, booths sold postcards, and a post office sent them; a variety of bazaars offered cheap rosaries, guidebooks, bits of saints' bones, Benedictine liqueurs, and a confusion of the cheap *bibelots,* which the Germans so aptly call *kitsch.* Signs everywhere warned "Do not spit" and "Do not write on the walls." I saw no one spit, but the work of the amateur muralists was evident everywhere. An Italian with a pencil is seldom idle; the pencil is his form of protest. The slogans and drawings found in American railroad stations and public lavatories decorate some of Italy's most venerable public monuments. Inside St. Peter's the scrawling was prosaic enough—usually names and addresses and a few *"Morte al Papa,"* roughly meaning, "Pope, drop dead!" On the roof it was more pungently Rabelaisian. One amateur drawing suggested that the stalls of the roof-top public urinals drained by pipes into the sacred vessels of the sanctuary below.

Down on the piazza, a sea of people had gathered. It was raining again. In the elevator I found myself thinking of the Holy Father's frail health. In the basilica, fences of boards and rope had been set up, dividing the floor into sections like an animal fair. The great temple was illuminated by the flickering light of thousands of candles, making an awesome effect, more theatrical than religious. Over loud-speakers came an announcement that because of the weather the Pope's audience had been shifted indoors. Immediately a roaring tumultuous wave of humanity burst through the doors. Cowled nuns, barefoot monks, and lay citizens of a score of countries poured to the railing hoping to reach out to touch the Holy Father as he passed by. I found myself a place near a roped aisle through which I expected the Holy Father to make his entrance. In less than three minutes the basilica was so crowded there was not even space to move one's feet. Rampaging multitudes continued to press through the doors like sheep in a storm. Those in the back pushed those in front to get closer. The clamor of languages was deafening. Grandmothers caught in the claustrophobic nightmare clutched rosaries and shouted for mercy; nuns chanted prayers. In different parts of the basilica groups burst into song, mostly hymns to the Virgin. A young farmer raised his little boy to his shoulder. *"Giù!"* the cries went up. "Take him down. We too wish to see."

"A child," the father replied. "He has a right to see the Father." "Down! Down! Down!" the crowd shouted. The father tried to lower the child and found he couldn't; there was no space left for the child beneath his shoulder.

The Holy Father's appearance, scheduled for four o'clock, was delayed. Tension mounted. Children screamed, women became hysterical and wept. Each time the red curtains by the holy door rippled, the cry went up, *"Allora, Jetzt, Maintenant, Now!"* But he did not appear; the curtains were ruffled by functionaries hiding behind them. A hidden choir sang hymns, and prayers in various languages were read over the speakers. Then, when the suspense had become unbearable, a shower of holy moisture fell like rain on the fifty thousand souls in the temple. It came from under the ceiling, sprinkled by priests pacing a catwalk. The rich baroque church shimmering with light was as tense as a theater at curtain time. The people joined in a hymn; it was as if Latin had miraculously become the common tongue of men. The procession commenced: the guards, bishops wearing gold embroidery and ermine, scarlet-caped Knights of Malta, the entire aristocracy of the church robed according to its holy station, and finally Pius himself, riding his *sedia gestatoria* on the shoulders of twelve damasked stalwarts.

Skeletal thin and wan, he was, indeed, a man who must husband his physical strength. With raised arms he welcomed his guests, turning his body to the right and to the left with the impersonal mechanical gesture of a marionette. A film of a smile stretched across the thin lips, a smile fighting against the sadness and the compassion in the face.

To the people the man was divine: their emotion could be aroused by none less than a god. It began with a great surge of shouting and the flutter of thousands of white handkerchiefs. *"Evviva il Papa, prego Papa,"* and words I could not understand, rolled over the temple like slow thunder. Slowly he bobbed forward in his chair, his expression never changing. Women wailed and men sobbed as they thrust blindly toward the rope hoping to touch him. Thousands turned their backs to watch him in little mirrors which they held in the air. I wondered what this mass of humanity was worshiping. How much of the exaltation and the prostration was to the Godhead symbolized and how much was man's need to bow to man, to the disastrous dark fetish of Nuremberg and the Piazza Venezia? They had come from everywhere for this; which of them could tell me why they had come?

He spoke. In Italian, in German, in French, in Spanish, in English he welcomed them all and prayed with them for peace in the world, saying the same in each tongue slowly, sincerely, with precise and carefully meas-ured articulation. He seemed a humble man, whether naturally or deliberately, one could not tell. Everyone understood him, and that was the most impressive thing of all, that no man, unless he were deaf, could fail to understand. But men tire, and even before he had finished speaking, the crowd, having seen him, began to file from the doors. Down the steps they clattered pell-mell, chattering over how he looked rather than what he said, scurrying in different directions across the square. From out of the crowd a balloon rose over the obelisk and floated slowly in the direction of the temple; attached to it was the black flag of Fascism. Then we remembered a forgotten date; it was the twenty-eighth anniversary of Benito Mussolini's successful march on Rome.

I rode back in a trolley with a band of Canadian nuns who sat in a quiet sort of ecstasy. Suddenly one turned to me and spoke. She was small and delicate; her face was young, pale, and pretty. "I kissed his hand twice," she said, softly mumbling the words like a prayer. "I kissed his hand when he came in and then I moved front and kissed his hand again. I kissed it twice." She sank back into her silent reverie.

The Assumption dogma was proclaimed and the holy year subsided. A Canadian plane crashed on a frozen mountain in France, killing fifty-eight pilgrims, and back in Sydney a band of disillusioned Australian pilgrims announced that Roman thieves had robbed them of their wallets and purses.

In Rome one felt the difference. The streets were a little less crowded and people moved with Mediterranean languor. Since the departure of the Swiss pilgrims, I had taken note of some of the other residents of the hotel.

Most of them were Army and Navy attachés and civilian employees of the American Embassy. Some were bachelors; some were awaiting the arrival of their families from America; others had their wives and children with them. In the dining room one could always tell the tables of Americans by the Nescafé, Worcestershire sauce, Carnation milk, and tea brought from America.

They were not a happy lot. Those for whom Rome was the first foreign station moped about the hotel reading paperback novels and longing for Texas or Pennsylvania. Sight-seeing didn't interest them. Week-ends officers played golf on a course reserved for their use. Doggedly determined not to learn a foreign language, they frequented only English-speaking bars and restaurants. In the dining room they sent Italian foods back to the kitchen and demanded steaks.

"Americans are *pazzi* [crazy]," the waiter said to me one night in a fit of temper. His name was Pietro; he was twenty-five years old and a Veronese. He spent an hour each afternoon studying English with a priest, and he practiced his conversation on me. He told me he lived during the war with twenty other boys in a cave in the mountains. For two years they scrounged like animals, eating game, fruit, and nuts. After the war Pietro had a brief period of prosperity dealing in black-market goods, stolen cars, and American cigarettes, but that passed quickly, and now for four years he had been a waiter. In a month he earned thirty thousand lire—approximately forty-eight dollars—of which he had to pay eight thousand for his own room in a lodging house. He had three loves—fast cars, women, and horses. "Cars cost two million lire," he said. "No use thinking about a car. A horse costs a thousand lire an hour. A woman—ten *minuti*—five hundred lire! The horse is a better investment!"

For four days three American fliers from a German base were grounded in Rome because of bad weather. They fretted away the time playing rummy and pining for Germany. One night they ventured out to seek women. "Pigs, nothing but Dago pigs," they reported in the morning. "And the price they ask they must think they're Lana Turner. You ought to see the women in Frankfurt. Don't cost much and they know what to do." The American military's nostalgia for German was strongest in officers who once had served there and were now stationed in Rome. "Germans are human beings like us," they said. "They know how to live. Germans are clean. German food is good to eat, not like this garbage. Who can get along with Italians? You can't even talk with them; they're crazy all of them." An officer discussing soldiers: "You can make a soldier out of a German; he knows how to fight! Give him an airplane and he'll run it and take care of it. But you'll never make a soldier out of a lousy dago. No wonder they lost the war. They'll wreck a piece of machinery every time."

Nonmilitary Americans liked Italians better. Everywhere they were having a good time. Sunday afternoon at the Teatro Argentina was like a concert in Carnegie Hall. Leonard Bernstein was a guest in the royal box, and other boxes held composers Aaron Copland, Gian-Carlo Menotti, Lukas Foss, Gail Kubik, Harold Shapiro, and the pianist Leo Smit. An Italian screen writer named Enzo Corelli, full of opinions about the American invasion of Rome, said: "We are being conquered by Americans and their money. But then, Romans have always been conquered, ever since antiquity. Everywhere you look in Rome you see ruins, all monuments to our conquerors. Frankly we don't give a damn. We don't like war and we'd rather be conquered than fight. We were conquered twice in the last war— first by the Germans, then by the Americans. No one cared much. You Americans have faith. You believe in yourselves, your gadgets, and your mechanical superiority. You have no humility and a wonderful innocence about your faith in yourselves. We Romans believe in nothing, we don't even believe in the Catholic Church. Having no faith and no innocence, we are wise. When you Americans come to conquer us with your riches, we permit ourselves to be conquered. We know we need you, so we grant you your innocence and your faith, and we laugh at you ever so slyly."

Enzo invited me to visit Cinecitta, the collection of film studios from which came such films as *Open City* and *Bicycle Thief*. Film City was a handful of ramshackle, unheated sheds in which at the moment two projects were under way, both of them American—Orson Welles' *Othello*, and Gian-Carlo Menotti's *The Medium*. Menotti was in his second day of shooting the opera's torture scene. Men on ladders were directing home-made spotlights on the American dancer Leo Coleman, who as the deaf mute was lying on a small bed. Though the studio was icy cold, the actor was undressed to the waist, his body greased with vaseline. A stand-in for Marie Powers, the American star of *The Medium*, was dripping hot wax from a burning candle on Coleman's face. Menotti was delighted with the effect.

"Isn't it lovely?" he said. "Sooooooo sadistic!"

With each drop of wax Coleman winced. Menotti told him to clench his fists so that the veins on his arms would stand out and further the impression of agony. Miss Powers was sent for. She came from her dressing room wearing a gaudy dressing gown. Menotti handed her the candle. *"Silenzio!"* Menotti shouted. *"Comincia la musica!"*

The pre-recorded music began to play and the cameras began to roll. Miss Powers raised the candle. With clenched fists Coleman waited. The hand that held the candle trembled and the candle dropped to the floor.

"No! No!" Miss Powers cried, "I can't do it."

"But we've been doing it all day," Menotti said.

"I can't do it." Miss Powers burst into tears. "I can't do it to poor Leo."

Menotti was exasperated. *"Maria* darling," he said, "you think I want to hurt Leo? I've been doing it to him for three hours. Look, he's still alive!"

Miss Powers wept. "Oh, don't get upset," Menotti wailed. "You are being very silly, *Maria.*"

The shooting was halted and Miss Powers went to her dressing room to collect herself. In a quarter of an hour she reappeared and the scene was made. The fifth take satisfied Menotti and shooting ended for the day.

It was All Souls' Eve. To observe the holy day Enzo suggested a visit to the church of the Capuchins, the macabre sanctuary of Hawthorne's *The Marble Faun.* It was close to the American Embassy and next door to the Jickey Club, which was advertising American Negro dancers. Inside, the church was dark and musty. A cowled friar led us into the crypt, four chapels built of human bones, the bones of four thousand Capuchins carefully dismembered, assorted, and arranged into designs as an old lady might sort glass beads and string them into flowers. Walls are lined with pelvic shells, laid one on another like fish scales or tiles on a roof. Ribs are fashioned into lamp shades and ceiling moldings; the altars are built of grinning skulls, and the crucifixes above them of femurs. By far the most versatile bones in the designing of the chapels were the vertebrae. With their assortment of lumbars the monks achieved true baroque elegance; these they arranged like mosaics on the walls and ceilings, fitted into rosettes, scallopings and flutings, chains and ribbons, and complicated floral patterns. One master arrangement is a great wreath filled with intertwining hearts, formed from vertebrae and curved lower ribs. Our silent guide genuflected before each altar. He sensed my horror and in a voice hardly more than a whisper he explained, "It is our purpose never to forget for a minute that we must die. We wish to remind all men who come here of their own mortality and the futility of life on earth."

I thought of the gray, death-loving brothers, dressed in the color of moles, groveling in the dark earth, doodling with human bones for the glory of God. We went upstairs and out into the city dusk. It was going to be a dark, wet night. In America it was Halloween, time for a party. Enzo invited me to one. It was on the top floor of a bastillelike *palazzo*. Each time a guest arrived a gate key was rolled inside a newspaper and dropped from a window to the street. Our host was a bearded artist who had painted his walls black and decorated them with drawings of nudes, some vaguely pornographic. Half-finished abstract paintings stood on easels; on the floor a huge mattress was covered with a stained spread. I felt immediately at home; a decade ago I had been to dozens of parties just like it in Greenwich Village. From the hand-wound phonograph came the garish cacophony of an obscure atonal composer. The guests were young writers, painters, actors. About half of them spoke English, some well. Unshaven men drank cheap cognac; slinky long-haired women dressed in plain black and wearing no make-up smoked cigarettes in long holders. By far the most striking person there was a tall blonde girl, dressed in black like the others, but thinner and with more style. Her long body was finely structured, her face pretty and alive. With a lean, graceful hand she worried a choker of pearls knotted at her throat. She had a natural and graceful elegance; the pearls gave her a queenly air. She was talking English to a young American Negro, a novelist expatriated to Rome.

More guests arrived. One of them, a small, youthful looking, smartly dressed white-haired woman, Enzo knew well. She was a baroness, a woman of prewar affluence and position in Rome who now worked as a teacher in the Roman schools. Her husband was a professor; his brother, a Mussolini supporter, had been shot by partisans at the end of the war. The baroness had a son and a daughter; the son was a doctor, the daughter was a dancer with the Rome opera company. Enzo introduced us; she spoke English with Oxonian perfection. She believed America was preparing for still another war.

"It does seem tragic that the American people wish more war," she said. "You see, we Italians have never wanted war. We have no love for fighting. Yet we are always drawn into wars we do not want. We have always had to fight when we haven't wanted to. We are a tired people, too tired for war and too poor. If there is another war, you will find us completely uncooperative. We think that nothing worse than another war can happen to us, so we will offer no resistance and we will not fight."

"Italians cannot be so easily absolved from guilt of war," I said. "If another war were to come, the guilt would not be with Americans, who are concerning themselves with international affairs. The guilt would lie in the inertia and indifference of which you boast."

"We are not a cowardly people," the baroness said. Small though she was, she herself gave me a feeling of strength and courage. "Our inertia is despair, not fear. Perhaps it will help you to understand us if I tell you my story of the last war.

"Because of my husband's family our name was a very unpopular one when the Fascists fell," she began. "Of course it was dangerous for us to stay in Rome. I left our flat in charge of servants who pretended to be the owners and moved my family and my parents into Tuscany. A kind bishop took in my parents; my husband took an assumed name and disappeared as a laborer. My older son went into a monastery and masqueraded as a monk, and the younger boy hid out in a bombed theater in Florence. He enjoyed this very much; it stimulated his fantastic imagination. For nine months I did not hear from my husband or my sons. In order to get food for myself and my parents I taught English to the Italian brides of American and English soldiers. The girls' husbands paid me in food from their military commissaries. I felt very guilty teaching those poor girls English. They all thought they were Cinderellas; to their young husbands they were glamorous, mysterious creatures. Mercy! I would think, what a cruel thing to be doing, teaching them their husbands' languages. They had at least their passion and their love-making. When they were able to speak, their disenchanted husbands would discover what terribly boring little creatures they were. They didn't have one single thing in common with their soldiers but sex; there wasn't one subject they had to talk about. They devoutly believed learning their husbands' language would solve everything; they didn't dream that for two peoples so distinctly different in tradition and experience, the problems only begin once the language is spoken. You poor things, I used to think. If I didn't need the food so desperately, I'd never consent to do this to you.

"My husband's brother was named Dante; he was the elder by three years. I remember him starting out as a boy, a handsome, strong lad, full of idealism for the improvement of Italy and the life of Italian people. This was in the twenties when Mussolini was the hero of all the young idealists. Naturally Dante became his follower. Dante always believed passionately in what he did, that is until the last years, when disillusionment set in. But he was a strong and loyal man who could not desert his friends even when he knew what the end would be.

"My older son was named for his uncle. He also is handsome. He has the same idealistic urge to help the Italian people and Italy. I see little difference in his idealism for the Communists from the other Dante's idealism for the Fascists. My son is so much like his uncle. I watch with a sad heart, because I know so well the end of the road. Dante has a baby, two years old, also a boy. So you see what I fear? That it will go on, this blood sacrifice of the male while we women look on and survive, always survive. That is the fate of Italy."

She had spoken eloquently and I felt compassionately toward her even though I knew that there were women in Germany, France, and England who could tell much the same story. I thought of the losses of American families and told the baroness of the Sullivans of Iowa whose four sons had died at sea.

"We live in Homeric times," she said with finality. Having told her story, she wanted to talk no more about it.

The probability of war was the main subject of conversation in the room. The princess of the pearls was talking of it with the Negro novelist. I asked Enzo to present me to her.

"She is very fancy," he said, "a duchess on one side of her family and a marchesa on the other. She works for the American government."

She eyed me with a superior sort of interest. "You are obviously American?" she said.

"Obviously," I replied. "What is your name?" I had not understood Enzo.

"My *full* name?" she asked.

"I'll promise to remember it forever."

"My name is Michela Cecilia Maria Monica Gabriela . . ." She went on and on. "When they took me to be christened, my mother was prepared with sixteen names, but the padre refused to go beyond thirteen. Thirteen is for us a mystical number."

"What are you called?"

"Michela," she said. There was an empty chair beside her. I did not see the cat asleep on it and I sat on the animal. "Is it bad luck to sit on a cat in Italy?" I asked.

"Sometimes for the cat," Michela said. "Like all Americans, you are very nervous. I shall never go to America. I am sure no one ever relaxes there. I would rather stay in Europe and die with the others than live someplace where I couldn't relax."

"Is that the choice left mankind?" I asked. "Hypertension in America or death in Europe?"

"When the war comes, it will be that," she said, pulling at her pearls. She spoke with mocking gaiety. "Of course there is going to be a war. If not immediately, it will come in a year or two. We're on the brink." She waved her hand about the room taking in the languid party guests. "This is our last gasp. Russia will march. Italy, France, all of western Europe will be quickly occupied."

"I don't understand why, if you really believe that, you're not more disturbed," I said.

"Why get upset?" she said. "When it comes, it comes. We're much too seasoned with war to worry about man's last convulsion. Life is worth nothing." She looked about the room. "I am bored and I am hungry and I must go to work for you Americans in the morning. Would you like to go someplace to eat?" I asked her if she hadn't come with someone. "You mean with a man?" she said coldly. "At this time I am hostile to men. I have quarreled with my lover in Paris, and my boy friend in Rome has no soul. He says that to him I am only a piece of flesh!" She tugged so hard on the pearls I feared they would break. "Is not a man who would say a thing like that a beast?" I agreed of course. We got our coats and went creakingly down in the *ascensore.*

In the cortile of the *palazzo* Michela had her Vespa, the motor scooter named for a wasp which is Italy's most popular means of transportation. I sat on a tiny ledge behind her, my coat dangling over the back of the machine. Her slippered toe pressed a button. "Brrrrumph." The motor exploded like gunfire in the courtyard. We jerked out of the gate and up a hill at breakneck speed. The night was bitter. I bounced crazily on the ledge, one hand holding my cap and the other embracing her waist so I would not fly off. Her skirt flapped like a flag and my coat ballooned behind us like an umbrella as we careened at a sickening angle around corners of the ancient city. As we passed the Ministry of Foreign Affairs a bomb exploded. Leaflets proclaiming the reaffirmation of Fascism fluttered over the Roman pavements like autumn leaves. Like Circe, the sorceress, Michela on her chariot was flying me to the gods knew where. I remembered how life meant nothing to her and that she was hostile to men, as we circled the Colosseum like daredevils in a hippodrome.

CHAPTER 3

A HOUSE IN MILAN

IN THE WESTERN QUARTER of Milan is the Pensione Gemma. It was there that the American Consulate reserved me a room when I went to Milan in January.

After a train ride through the glittering sun and cold blue skies of the mountains, Milan was oppressive. The afternoon, gloomy and dark under a blanket of fog, recalled Pittsburgh before smoke control, when street lights were never turned off during the twenty-four hours. Milan is the commercial and industrial center of Italy; a nondescript modern city with an American personality. Its people are busy; they move as if they had a place to go and were anxious to get there. Romans call a man who can't relax a *Milanese*.

People were gathered around the station in agitated clusters. A few carried signs. "Go home, *Americano*," one said, and another, "*Italia per gli Italiani*." My cab driver explained that the American director of NATO, General Dwight Eisenhower, was in Rome on an official visit, and Milan, a Communist city with a Communist mayor, was showing its displeasure. "There are too many Americans in Italy," the driver said. "The time has come to send them home. If an American wished to hire my cab today I would not accept him."

I gave him the address of the Gemma and we started out. The streets were littered with anti-American posters; four-letter Anglo-Saxon words were scrawled on the walls. It was a monotonous ride over miles of houses and shops as dreary as Chicago's sprawling acres except that here there were blocks of ruins left by bombs.

"Swedish or English?" the driver asked, leaning back.

"American," I said, thinking he would stop the car. He thought better of it and continued driving without a word. It started to rain. Rows of

pink neon signs flickering wetly were so oppressive I wanted to return
to the train and continue to Florence. But I had to stay—at least long
enough to make a university lecture and hear some opera performances at
La Scala. In the fog the driver had his troubles with the address. Found
at last, the Gemma was anything but reassuring. It stood out in a street
of nondescript apartment houses, an old *palazzo* with Moorish minarets.
There was a tower in one corner like a silo. From its balcony hung a frayed
red rug. A shining brass plate with "Gemma" in elegant script was attached to the door. I rang the bell. After an uncomfortable wait it was
opened a few inches by a slatternly woman in a black dress and a dirty
apron. Her face was empty of expression and her hair was untidy. I gave
my name. She called something which sounded like "Fanny" and opened
the door for me.

Inside I heard footsteps on the parquet floors. A girl appeared, young
and slender, wearing the same nondescript costume as the woman, but
it could not hide her prettiness. Her large eyes and hair were dark; in the
shadows of the hall I could not see whether they were brown or black.
Her skin was soft and fresh. She hardly looked at me as she bent down
to pick up my bags. When she took hold, I was startled by her hands.
They were coarse and red and too large for her frail body. As the door
shut behind us a heavy iron bar clanked into place. The inside of the
Gemma was as startling as the outside. Its style, if it had any, was a
cluttered Moorish baroque with ornately curlicued woodwork and stained
mosaic floors. In the center of the hall was the *ascensore,* a narrow grilled
bird cage suspended by a strand of cable. The air was as musty as the
inside of an old chest.

The older woman left me in the front parlor to await the Signora
Gemma. The hysteria of an Italian-version soap opera filled the room
from a small portable radio standing on a grand piano. On the walls were
pictures of a romantic period, showing the Alhambra and Venice by
moonlight. Old books and some original folios of Dante were displayed
under glass. The furniture appeared stiff and uncomfortable. Aspidistras
grew from marble urns in the corners. The signora entered with a German
police dog which licked her hand. She was a tall woman with a deceptively
soft voice. One could see that she was used to commanding. She held her
head high so as to see me through her thick lenses. Over her dress she wore
a sweater, for the house was dank and chilly.

"The reservations are for a professor," she said, as if a mistake had been made.

"I am a professor," I said.

"Professor of what?" she asked. I had learned that to be a professor of either speech or theater was considered as American conceit. "Of literature," I replied.

"Then you will be interested in my original of Dante," she said.

I replied that the folios were impressive. The signora introduced me to the dog, whose name was Occhio, Italian for "Eye," and her daughter, whose name was Felicia. Tall and nearsighted like her mother, Felicia was an ill-at-ease spinster, gracelessly trying to imitate her mother's hauteur. The signora said she had another American guest, a student of voice from Chicago, named Signor Kegler. Without a doubt, I would find him a sympathetic companion. Her terms were reasonable—twenty-two hundred lire a day for full *pensione*—with no discount for meals missed. The domestic who had let me in now took me to my room. With some misgivings I followed her into the *ascensore*. The two of us filled the cage; in it we creaked and groaned to the top. We entered a tower room, the highest in the house. It was dark and cold and smelled like a tomb. There were marble columns in the corner and cornices under the ceiling. A faded velvet hung across the window. I drew it aside to let in light and discovered a door leading to the balcony I had seen from the outside. I looked down into a drab winter garden. The room was no cleaner than it smelled, and except on the most obvious surfaces the dust lay thick. For fear of soiling my clothes, I decided against unpacking my bags. The tiny sink was grimy and only the cold-water tap worked. Glumly I lay on the bed, wondering what to do. The cotton blankets were stained and stale-smelling; I sagged deep into the lumpy mattress. I felt like a prisoner, trapped not so much by the iron bolt on the door downstairs as by a compelling air of mystery. In relief on the ceiling above me was a design of fruit, the peaches and pears like opulent breasts.

I was awakened from sleep by a knock on the door. "Hi!" A tall and lanky youth greeted me. "The old lady told me you were here."

It was the American voice student named Kegler. "Call me Jim," he said. In the macabre atmosphere of the Gemma he seemed like an old friend. He told me he was in Milan to become an operatic baritone, a project financed with weekly checks sent to the American Express by his druggist father in Los Angeles. The checks paid for two or three lessons a week, for standing room tickets for every performance at La Scala, and for girls. He was twenty-one years old. Though he spoke no Italian, he had through two weeks of observation learned a lot about the Gemma.

"You're not going to like the joint at first, but just stick around until you're over the hump," he said. "It's on the sloppy side and the food takes a strong gut, but once you stop fighting it, right away it's home sweet home. Of course it's a little on the exotic side. But there's nothing to worry about. Nothing at all. Just remember I'm always right next door."

From the hall I could hear the voice of Edith Piaf singing *"De l'autre côté de la rue."*

"Jack, the French kid, plays records all the time and leaves his door open for everyone to hear. He don't like to miss anything that's going on. Next door to Jack is Sven. He's a Swede studying to be a tenor and he talks English. The one you really want to know about is the Swiss baroness."

It was the first time I'd heard of a Swiss baroness.

"Well, she says she's Swiss and she looks like a baroness. Talks English. She's got the room at the end of the hall but she lives in the bathroom. She's a hazard when you have to get in. She's in there now. Keep your door open . . ."

Kegler kicked open the door of my room. It faced the door of the bathroom, which was beside the *ascensore*.

". . . and you'll get an eyeful of her coming out. The sight will drive your blood pressure up."

I said I did not like my door open.

"You're going to have to get used to it open. You shut it here, you're antisocial." We sat with our eyes on the bathroom door. I asked about the servant girl known as Fanny.

"So you noticed her? Say, isn't the little slave a sweet dish? I think the old witch bought her. There's a spook of a chambermaid named Maria. The cook you won't want to see once you've eaten a meal. Then there's Fanny. The signora picks on all three of them, and Maria and the cook pick on Fanny. She's the catch-all. She works from seven in the morning until ten at night. Only time she ever gets out of the joint is a couple hours on Sunday afternoons. I seen her crying a couple times; wouldn't be surprised if they beat her. She's no dumbbell, Fanny ain't. Soon as the doctor puts me back in training, which will be in about two weeks, I'm gonna take her out one Sunday."

The door of the bathroom opened and released a cloud of steam. Through the vapors appeared a woman, supple, slender, and young. She wore a gown of soft stuff, a flimsy veil which clung about her like a mist. Her head was turbaned in a towel. "Hallo," she said. Her voice startled me.

Kegler waved. "I can't meet your friend now," she said. "I'm not in condition." The voice was raw and tired. Every word seemed to require an individual effort. She swept with long steps to her room, leaving the door not quite shut. A strong cloud of scent remained behind. "When *I'm* in condition . . ." Kegler mumbled, wiping imaginary sweat from his brow. He turned to me and said, "See what I mean?"

Below a gong sounded dinner. The dining room was on the first floor, next to the signora's den. Like every other part of the Gemma it was dimly lit and cold. Small tables were crowded against each other. Fanny, who served them all, had set my place at Kegler's table. At a corner table for three sat the signora, her daughter Felicia, and Occhio. The trio was served before the guests. The dog, sitting stiffly on a chair, ate his portions from a plate. Most of the tables were occupied by single persons. They chatted across the room in Italian, French, German, and English. "Jolly hell, this fog, isn't it?" a sparrowy little Englishman was saying to whoever could understand. "Never anything like it in London. Got myself lost the other night and it took two hours to find the old hole. Tried to buy myself a cup of tea. You wouldn't believe it, the slop that passes for tea in this country. Best they can do is a bloody cup of dreadful railroad tea."

"He's in Milan selling Scottish tweeds," Kegel said.

A plump, pinkish youth bowed formally as he passed our table on his way to his own.

"That's Jack. He lives in Toulon and is here spying on a tool factory his father owns." A broad-shouldered blond young man I guessed to be Sven, the Swedish tenor, entered. Fanny was moving quietly through the room, carrying bowls of soup. When she brushed by me, I felt the frailness of her body. In the soft light her limpidly luminous eyes seemed full of sadness. She laughed softly at a guest's sally, but her mirth had the catch of sorrow in it. Her hands laid a plate of soup before me, and I looked at the swollen peasant fingers, calloused from washing dishes and cleaning, the nails clipped short. She saw me looking and withdrew her hands. Across the room the Englishman railed on about tea. "They expected me to drink it without milk. Barbarians! Kept telling me they had no milk. I can well believe it. Who could find a cow to milk in this bloody fog."

Though she couldn't understand the Englishman, Fanny gave me a wickedly elfish glance that was pure mischief and left no doubt in my mind what she thought of him.

"Like her, don't you?" Kegler said.

"She's pretty," I said.

"And deep too," he said. "I'm telling you, she's a tender bitch."

In the hall the *ascensore* creaked to rest and the metal door clicked shut. I felt a stir in the air, a military coming-to-attention by the men in the room. Floating on a cloud of perfume and scarves and long blond hair like a nymph in Botticelli's *Spring*, the baroness entered the room. "Good evening," she rasped hoarsely to us. "*Buona sera*" to the signora and "*Bonsoir*" to the Frenchman.

A hush fell over the room. The baroness was talking to the Swede whose table was next to hers. She spoke English with a German accent.

"I'm staying only another week," she said. "You see, I'm here on business, looking after some Italian investments. . . ."

Kegler broke into guffaws of laughter. The signora glared at him from her own corner. On the chair beside her Occhio gulped a boiled bone.

"I stay at the Gemma to rest." The voice rattled on. "The bustle of a large hotel is unbearable to me. My days are taken up and when evening comes I simply want to get into a hot tub and steam."

Kegler could stand it no longer and got up and left. The tenor asked the baroness her business. "Import and export," she said. "We're an Argentine firm with offices in Europe." I thought of the woman in an Evelyn Waugh novel who ran a chain of bordellos in South America and wondered what the baroness' commodity might be.

"Cattle," she explained to the Swede. "Cattle from the Pampas. Does that surprise you? I'm not the cattle type, I know. But then I always surprise people. You see I'm a schizophrenic," she said as she might have said, "I'm a Methodist." "All Swiss are schizophrenic, and I'm half Swiss. Swiss are insane and have terrible tempers. I'm insane and my temper is unspeakable. That's why I control it with baths. Hot water soothes me."

We ate silently. The food was distinguished neither by quality nor quantity. Each time she passed my table on her back-and-forth errands, Fanny roguishly rolled her eyes. She carried out plates and returned with bowls of nuts. Signora Gemma opened pecans for Occhio. The crackling of nutshells competed with the gravel voice of the baroness. "Very soon I shall go to New York for two months," the baroness said. "When I am there I shall take out papers for American citizenship. In the next war America will naturally be the only safe place." Now she addressed me directly. "Sir, do you know, will I be able to apply for citizenship when I am in New York?" she asked.

I explained that for an immigration visa it was necessary to get on the waiting list of the country of which one was born, and find an American citizen as a sponsor.

"That will be no problem at all," she said. "I know some very nice gentlemen in America who would be happy to sponsor me."

I added that after sponsorship five years of uninterrupted American residence would be necessary for citizenship.

"That will make a problem," the baroness said. Then with an artificial laugh that cut through the room like a saw, she said, "Of course, I can always marry an American. Everything would be so simple. That's what I'll do, I'll marry an American and be safe from the bombs."

The turn of conversation awed even the Englishman and the Swede to silence. Perhaps they were, like myself, frightened by the baroness' desperation. Her hysteria was the hysteria of the fugitive. From what was she a fugitive? I wondered. For a moment the only sound in the room was the crackling of nuts. Then she said to me, "What brings you to Milan, sir?"

I said I had come to hear some performances at La Scala. She laughed, but without mirth. "We have much in common," she said. "I have worked in the theater. I was *Rosalind* in Paris, and in Germany I directed Bertold Brecht."

She babbled on. I was uneasy as one is in the presence of people who have lost their self-control. The signora got up from the table and, with her daughter and dog following, left the room. It was the signal that the meal was over. On the way out I met Fanny. She smiled a mischievous smile which conveyed a world of meaning.

Upstairs Kegler was eating some food which Fanny had brought him.

"She says she's an Argentine cattle baroness," I said. "Forget her. She's strictly trouble. She's looking for a passport and she'll do anything to get it."

"Okay, I'll promise her a passport," Kegler said.

Sven had found an Italian girl friend, a dancer in a *rivista*. Kegler and the Frenchman were going downtown with him to see the show and invited me to go along. Next to operas and motion pictures, *rivistas*—revues—are the most popular form of theater in Italy. According to American standards, they are inexpensively staged, but the material is usually fresh and provocative, and a good barometer of Italian public opinion on current events.

I walked through the fog with the Frenchman. Speaking Italian, he told me his name was Jacques d'Albert and that he was twenty-two years old. He was petulant and completely humorless. His plump little body fidgeted nervously. "Are you married?" he asked me. I said I wasn't. "Then you are divorced?" he said. I asked him why he raised the question.

His eyes flashed angrily. "Americans are always marrying and divorcing," he said. "Americans are immoral people who do not know the meaning of love and marriage. My parents have been married thirty years. They have nine children and are as happy as the day they were married."

I offered my congratulations and wished the same for him.

"It will be the same," he said. "My fiancée writes me every day. She will never love anyone else but me. I never look at other women. In America it is different. Every American has been divorced at least once."

I tried to convince Jack that American divorce was not as easy as he thought, that his impression, a common one in Europe, was derived from the widely publicized marital chaos of Hollywood.

"In any case, when an American marries, he does not believe it is forever," Jack said. "He knows when he tires of his wife he can easily divorce her. To get a divorce it is necessary only to sign some papers at the city hall. I know."

The title of the *rivista* was *Chi vuol esser lieto sia!* a line from the poetry of the Medici Lorenzo the Magnificent which means, "Let us be merry (for who knows what will happen tomorrow)." The audience was preponderantly male, the expensive front rows being filled by the Italian equivalent of tired businessmen. The aisles and promenade were filled with standees, many of them young men in uniform, who paid two hundred lire, or thirty-two cents, for their tickets. As in an American burlesque house, a wide, carpeted runway jutted into the theater. The show opened on this plank, where a dozen dancing girls established a quick rapport with the audience.

"*Mamma mia,*" Kegler exclaimed. "Did you ever see such pretty belly buttons?" The chorus was young, perhaps under eighteen, practically

naked, and extremely saucy and pretty. Their curved young bodies were
fresh and innocently voluptuous. No one cared that the girls were not
talented either in singing or dancing; the sight of their bodies was enough.
Sven greeted his friend, a pert vivacious brunette. Beside me Jack fidgeted
until he was shaking the entire row. "Jesus," said Kegler, "can't you hold
your ass still?" Jack drew himself up primly. "My ass, it is tranquil," he
replied loftily in English.

The skits most enjoyed by the audience were those satirizing American
influences in Italy. In one, Italian brothels were operated under the supervision of NATO. The hero, a sad-faced Chaplinesque little man, spent
days of frantic pursuit collecting the necessary government documents to
make a brothel visit. Finally, when he was able to present his accumula-
tion of multicolored stamped documents to a row of functionaries at the
brothel gate, they informed him that he still lacked one document, the
written permission of his wife, also to be stamped by NATO.

In another, an Italian explorer suffered months of travail over frozen
ice fields to post an Italian flag in a presumably undiscovered arctic territory. When he finally arrived, the territory was already staked by Coca-
Cola, Metro-Goldwyn-Mayer, Shell Oil, and other American firms doing
business in Italy.

The show went on until one o'clock, at which hour twelve girls rode onto
the stage on one old white horse. By this time the girls and the audience
were old friends; the entire house sang and shouted. The tired horse
brought the evening to a close by leisurely urinating on stage. This im-
promptu climax sent the theater into pandemonium but failed to ruffle
the girls.

Sven invited us backstage to meet his friend. Kegler and I welcomed
the invitation, but not Jack—or "Tranquillity," as Kegler had already
named him. "He is not a typical Frenchman," Sven observed.

When the girls had dressed we met them all. They were as fresh and
delightful at close range as in the theater. Many had cautious mothers
standing by.

Kegler and I said good night and started for home. We mounted a
crowded tram and paid our fare, stuffing into our pockets the colored slips
of paper given as tickets on Italian trolleys but seldom collected. We
pushed to the front of the car, where we hung from straps and rocked with
the crowd as the car jolted through the fog. A conductor, singling us out,

asked for our tickets. We fished the pink scraps from our pockets. The conductor refused to take them.

"Wrong color," he said. I replied we had just purchased them. "Red tickets for daytime," he said impatiently, "green tickets for night."

With his insolent manner he suggested we were riding without having paid. "I do not know about color," I said. "I have just bought these tickets from the conductor in the rear."

"The tickets are old!" His bark drew the attention of everyone in the car. I could hear men grumble nastily to one another. "Rich Americans and they want to ride for nothing," someone said.

"You can check the tickets with the man in the back," I said.

The conductor shrugged and directed me down the aisle. It was jammed with riders who had come on after us, and who watched us hostilely. It would have been useless to try to push to the rear.

"If you want to ride you must pay," the conductor said.

The fare was thirty lire, hardly more than five cents, but I was determined not to pay it twice.

"Pay," the man shouted.

"Let's get the hell out of here," Kegler said. He was frightened. So, as a matter of fact, was I.

"Pay or get off!" The conductor's cry was picked up now by passengers. "Pay or get off!" they shouted. "Go home, Americans! We don't want you in Italy!" "The war is over!" "Go home, Ike!"

Outside, the night was dense with fog. If we did not ride to our stop we would certainly be lost. I knew there was no solution but capitulation. We paid the second fare, an act accepted as an admission of guilt, and the passengers enjoyed their triumph. I asked a man if we were approaching our stop, the Piazza della Giovane Italia. He replied with obvious pleasure that we were already well past it. This cheered all the passengers greatly, and when we disembarked at the next stop, there was merriment in the tram.

The mist was so thick we could not read the street signs. We followed the tram tracks back until we bumped into an old man huddled on a wooden crate with a parcel of newspapers beside him. I asked directions, and without raising his face from his collar he jerked his hand to the left. I bought a morning paper from him and folded it in my pocket. We trudged on, not knowing where we were. Finally we found a policeman who gave us detailed directions which in another twenty minutes brought us to the door of the Gemma. Kegler turned his key in the lock; we could hear the rattle of the iron bar inside. There was no light; we had to feel our way to the staircase. The *ascensore* was shut off, so we climbed the narrow stairs with the light of burning matches. In my room I unfolded the newspaper and read of anti-American demonstrations throughout Italy. Four were dead, including a nineteen-year-old youth shot by *carabinieri* in Sicily. I braced a chair against the door of my room, undressed, and tossed on the battered mattress trying to find a comfortable hollow.

I was awakened in the morning by angry women's voices. In the hall, Maria the maid was calling the baroness a whore; from her door the baroness was calling Maria a dirty pig. When they saw me their morning amenities came to an end. Outside, the fog seemed to have lifted, for a bit of sunlight flickered through my dirty panes. When fog lay on the city, my tower room was dark even in midday. Maria brought a breakfast of bread and gray coffee on a soiled and sticky tray. The baroness was floating through the hall, her head wrapped in a towel, her face pink from steam. "Cheers!" She waved, and disappeared into her room.

Though on the seamy side, life at the Gemma, as Kegler had predicted, was never dull. From Fanny, Kegler and I learned that the signora was distressed because we occasionally appeared at meals in sweaters instead of jackets. Tranquillity's door was always open, and our floor rang with French jazz from his phonograph. It was preferable to the shrieking soap operas which echoed up the stairway from the signora's parlor. A few times at night I heard soft tappings on my door, but I did not bother to find out who it was.

In the midst of all this, Fanny maintained her strange and sweet gentility. She told me she was twenty years old, the eldest child of a large country family, and had come to the Gemma when she was eighteen. Except for two brief holidays with her family and the free Sunday hours, she never stopped working. She found her happiness in the fleeting friendships of occasionally kind guests about whom she could weave her romantic fantasies as she went about her household drudgeries. Americans were her favorites. She was happy when Kegler and I were around. If either of us missed a meal she was as disconsolate as if we had personally slighted her. When I was out she took my phone calls, announcing herself as "*La segretaria privata del professore.*" On opera evenings she waited in the hall to fix my tie and tell me how "chic" I looked.

On free days I visited art galleries, expeditions in which Kegler trotted along without enthusiasm. We spent a chilling day in the drafty chambers of the Castello Sforzesco, a mighty fortress built in the 1450's by the Sforza family and decorated by Leonardo. We went to the Pinacoteca de Brera, where pictures are as pleasantly hung as in Washington's National Gallery, and to the Pinacoteco Ambrosiana, an unheated bombed castle where an exceptional collection is probably the worst hung in Italy. Here a guide brought out a folio of Leonardo's drawings. They were unbelievable treasures; with our coats drawn tight, we huddled over them like misers. There were nudes glowing with physical beauty; grotesques showing the monstrousness of flesh and meanness of souls; animals in fierce combat and children with the innocence of heaven in their faces.

After these drawings I felt ready to visit Leonardo's *Last Supper*. For ten days I had lived in the shadow of the masterpiece of the world, for the convent of Santa Maria della Grazie where Leonardo painted his *cenacolo* on the refectory wall was but two blocks from the Gemma.

As I entered the convent, the sickening odor of wet lime burned in my nostrils. An attendant showed me photographs of the chapel after the August 1943 bombing of Milan. "A miracle!" he said. "Only the *cenacolo* remained." The photograph showed the wall of Leonardo's painting standing in a crumbling heap of rubble.

I passed through a turnstile into a new bare room. Scaffolding and ladders covered freshly concreted walls. Under the ceiling three workmen were leisurely plastering. The room was dark with its own dusty fog. I looked through the scaffolding at the pale ghost of a painting, a gentle shadow that was hardly more than the outline of a picture. Long before bombs threatened the *Last Supper*, it had endured the devastating corruptions of time. It had begun to flake almost immediately after Leonardo painted it in 1498. Mildew attacked it; century by century it rotted away. Finally, early in this century, a restorer by the name of Cavaliere Cavenaghi attempted to fill in the obliterations with Leonardo's own tempera; after the war, restoration was continued by another great restorer named Mauro Pelliccioli. It was obvious that he would succeed, the dying painting would survive. I saw the twelve disciples, clustered in violent and agitated groups of three, caught in a terrible moment. Their Leader has just broken the serenity of the gathering.

"One of you shall betray Me."

Each man's face is a mirror of the soul beneath. In the midst of the animation is Jesus, withdrawn and infinitely sad with His knowledge of the human frailty about Him. As I gazed up at the divine mystery of the Christ, little clouds of slake floated down from the scaffolding. A bell tinkled in the outer hall and the guide came to tell me it was time to leave. I walked the two blocks to the Gemma, where Fanny was waiting inside the door. "*Dove va?*" she asked as usual.

"*Al cenacolo*," I said. She did not seem to know of what I was speaking, so I added, "The painting by Leonardo."

"I have never seen it," she said. I must have shown my astonishment, for she hastened to explain. "On Sunday there is hardly time for a cinema, and, if the weather is fair, a walk in the public gardens. When, signore, could I find time to go?"

Kegler and I went to the opera my last night in Milan. While I was dressing someone knocked on my door. I opened it and found the baroness, resplendent in fox and jewels, ready to go out for the evening.

"You are going to the opera," she said. "I love opera. It is the greatest of all art forms." She opened a large alligator bag. "I've come to show you my passport," she said. "It says that I was born in Switzerland." I looked where she pointed and read "Lucerne, May 2, 1920." "You see I am Swiss! You didn't believe me, did you?" She returned the passport to her bag, opening it wide enough for me to see the vast quantities of currency it contained, and not only lire, but Swiss and French francs and even American dollars. "It's useful to have a little of *every* kind," she said, catching my glance. "Now I must go. I'm meeting a friend," she said haughtily and swept to the *ascensore*.

It was one o'clock when Kegler and I returned to the Gemma. A ceiling light was burning dimly in the hall of our floor. Sitting on the last step at the top was the baroness. The blond mist of her hair flowed loosely about her shoulders, her furs were on her lap. In the soft light she was beautiful.

"Oh, sir," she whimpered. "At last you have come. Mine is such a foolish misfortune."

She sobbed out a distraught story. "Sir, I have lost my key and I am locked out of my room. I have been sitting here in the cold by myself for an hour waiting for someone to help me. I don't know what to do or where to go."

I asked where she thought she had lost her key.

Kegler was shaking with excitement. "How we gonna find a key in the fog?" he asked.

"Oh, no, sirs, it can never be found," the baroness said. "You see, I went to visit a friend, and her son—he is a strong boy of eighteen—took the key from my bag. He did it in jest, sir, overpowering me to take it, and then dropping it in the toilet and flushing it away. He is a very playful boy. He said now that I didn't have the key I would have to stay and sleep with him. But of course I wouldn't do anything like that, his mother being my dear friend. She scolded him, but what is the good of that? I have no key."

Kegler cursed under his breath.

"What did you say?" the baroness asked him.

"Sorry as hell about the key," he said. He rang bells and knocked on doors. We might have been in a tomb for the response he got. The noise aroused only Occhio, who barked somewhere in the chambers below. Increasing the volume of her weeping, the baroness began to empty the contents of her alligator bag on the parquet floor, strewing out hairpins, the wads of Italian, French, Swiss, and American money, cosmetics, handkerchiefs, and, in case we'd missed the point, some contraceptives. She made a tearful inventory.

"You see, gentlemen, no keys. I'm a respectable girl," she said, picking up the contraceptives and returning them to her bag. Kegler began to shout, and the echoes of his cries and Occhio's barks ricocheted up and down the stairs. Finally someone appeared, a night-crawling old harridan in curlpapers and a ragged wrapper. I'd never seen her before so I supposed it was the cook. I explained the circumstances and she invited the baroness to spend the night in her room. The two women went down the stairs together.

"Tomorrow I'm going to Florence with you for four days. Too dangerous staying around here."

In the morning we waited in the gloomy hall of the Gemma for a taxi. The strange staff of the house was gathered around to say good-by and collect tips. The signora overcharged me two thousand lire, but I was not up to arguing with her and let it go. All morning Fanny had been quiet and evasive. I knew it was because of my leaving and it made me sad.

Fanny carried my bags to the curb, not permitting me to touch them. When she had lifted them into the cab I gave her a folded banknote.

"*Ritorna?*" she whispered. I nodded. Yes, I would return. She burst into tears and ran weeping back into the cavernous door.

"*Andiamo,*" I said to the driver, anxious to be away. Neither Kegler nor I spoke. I was thinking of the frail Cinderella locked in the formidable Gemma fortress, dreaming there of a gallant Prince Charming who would rescue her. An American prince, no doubt.

On the train we found a compartment occupied by two priests and an old man whose white hair curled richly from under a blue beret. We rolled by ruins, always so conspicuous near the railway tracks of bombed cities, out of the fog of Milan. A bright sun dazzled our eyes and bits of white cumulus sped like swans across the blue sky. Herders grazed their sheep on winter's brown rubble, and women, their skirts billowing in the wind, harvested January leeks. I looked at Kegler.

"Geeze!" he said huskily. "That Fanny! What a tender bitch!" His eyes were filled with tears.

CHAPTER 4

FOG

ONE DAY WHEN, during my stay in Milan, I went to the American Consulate to pick up my mail, I found a dozen armed soldiers guarding the entrance. A street speaker was ranting before a milling crowd about "American military imperialism." After I identified myself, I was allowed to enter. Inside I struck up a conversation with two young Italians who had come to inquire about their applications for fellowships to American universities. The woman at the desk had discouraging news for them.

"It is very confusing," one said, as the three of us left. "It is on our records that we were anti-Fascists during the war. In the eyes of your Senator McCarran we are dangerous radicals."

"That is the same as being a Communist," the other said. "It would have been easier if we had been Fascists."

I invited them to have coffee with me. We crossed the Piazza della Scala, where we met an American jeep loaded with armed Italian soldiers, to a café beside the opera house. My guests' names were Davido Carboni and Fausto Filippi. Both spoke English, and both had Americanized nicknames, Davido's being "Dave" and Fausto's "Phil." Both were painters, and both worked as free-lance writers for Milanese journals. Dave, twenty-five, was the son of a well-known artist. He was lean and dark and of a brooding disposition. Phil was twenty-seven, shorter and more solidly built, with fair hair and blue eyes. His disposition was merrier. He had been a student of Dave's father and was established, both as a writer and an artist. The summer before he had studied art at an American-operated school in Austria, and he felt *simpatico* to the Americans he had met there.

As we talked, a man passed before the statue of Leonardo carrying a sign. It read, "Go home, *Americano.*"

"You see how it is?" I said. "America doesn't want you and Italy doesn't want me."

"This is a harvest America must reap," Dave said. I asked him what he meant. "When America supported the conservatives she betrayed the Italian people," he said. "The Communists are clever enough to pretend to be the people's party. Naturally they are anti-American."

Phil took a more moderate view. "America is blamed for too much," he said. "The people of Italy expect everything to come easy and are unwilling to help themselves."

Both young men hoped to study theater design in America, and perhaps to stay to make successful careers. In Italy they felt hopelessly trapped. "Not being Communists makes great hardships," Phil said. "The theaters which offer opportunities for young men are controlled by Communists and unless you are a Communist you cannot work in them."

I asked them what they believed was Italy's solution.

"Socialism," Phil said. "In a country so crowded as Italy Socialism is the only way of government. But it will take a long time. Unfortunately we have no great leaders in Italy."

The conversation turned to love. An Italian is never so happy as when he is sad about a love affair. Phil was meeting a marchesa in five minutes.

"She is a beautiful selfish girl of noble blood, with very great money," he said. "Four years ago I love her very much and she is my mistress. She went for the summer to her family's villa on Lake Como and I stayed in the hot city to work for my newspaper. That summer she was unfaithful to me many times and when she returned she found pleasure in telling me about it. Though I loved her still, I ended our relationship. This year I have read in the newspapers of her engagement to a count; she had gone to England to study and was to return to marry in August. Last week she telephoned me. She said she was in trouble. In England she had an affair with a Swedish student and now is awaiting a *bambino*. Since, of course, she wishes to marry her count and not tell him, she asked me to arrange an abortion for her. I love little babies; I would like to marry and have many. But now I will help the girl I love to destroy her baby. Life is very tragic."

"Italian girls are impossible," Dave said. "Either they are stupid peasants who want only to make many babies, or they are rich and snobbish virgins who want to marry counts and dukes."

"Mine was not a virgin," Phil said. "She was rather more a nymphomaniac." He said good-by and departed.

"I like American girls," Dave said. "They are free-minded and democratic." We watched Phil cross the square and wait under the statue. In a moment the girl arrived with a handsome boxer dog. She was a modish slim-legged blonde in a mink coat. The dog tugged impatiently on his leather leash as Phil went off with her to arrange the abortion.

"Italy is sick," Dave said in a flash of violence. "We are a corrupt and degenerate people. We have no spirit and no faith."

Dave and I left the café and cut through a line of women carrying signs which said in Italian, "America! The aggressor of Korea," and "I do not wish my son to go to war again."

"Do not be disturbed," Dave said. "In Italy anything is an excuse for a demonstration. Demonstrations are our national pastime." We walked past the expensive shops of the Galleria where the prices were even higher than in Rome. The women going in and out of the shops were beautiful mannequins of ice wrapped in furs.

"I hate the rich," Dave said. "To be rich in Italy one has to be selfish and cruel. There is no other way."

Everywhere the tempo was speeded up in a way I had not felt since leaving New York. Unlike other Italian cities, there were few beggars on the streets. One old man slept quietly against a sunny wall while his buff-colored mongrel dog, walking on his hind legs in a top hat and cutaway coat, begged for him with a tin cup. We entered the cathedral. It was dark and quiet and overwhelmingly spacious. A soft rose light from the Gothic windows illuminated the melancholy interior. We stopped before a window showing the children of the Old Testament.

"My father made this window," Dave said. "He used his children for models. I am David; Jacob, Isaac, and Joseph are my brothers. It was before the war. Father was against Fascism, and when the war came we were enemies of the state. My mother's brother was a resistance leader with a price of five million lire on his head. My father and my oldest brother were arrested and taken to Germany. I and another brother were warned by the underground that we were next to be arrested, so we escaped to Switzerland and worked in the underground there. My mother remained in Milan. So she wouldn't starve, some friends organized a benefit sale of my father's paintings. Until we returned after the war my mother believed all of us dead.

"My father was a prisoner at Dachau where he saw thousands of Jews starved and cremated. When he was liberated he was feeble and sick. For two months before he returned to Italy the Americans took care of him and helped him build up his strength. My brothers are now a composer, a writer, and a student of philosophy. I am a painter like my father."

Dave asked me if I would like to meet his parents. I said I would and he invited me to tea. Late in the afternoon he came for me and we walked a mile or so to his home. Dave talked about his family. "The war changed my parents from young people to old people," he said. "Now my father is convalescing from an operation. We live in the same apartment as before the war, but these days we have become quite poor. It is necessary for all of us to help each other by living at home. Even my brother who is married has come home to live with his wife and two babies."

We took an elevator to the top floor of an apartment house and entered into a high-ceilinged living room. It was a room jammed with pictures, books, and handsome old furniture. In a well-ordered Italian household hosts do not appear until the guests are comfortably seated, so while we waited silently I looked at the father's paintings. They were strong and richly colored. I was struck by a portrait of a willowy, dashing young woman wearing a cape and red flowers in her hair. "My mother," Dave said. "She had an English grandmother." While I was looking at it, a gaunt elderly woman came into the room. She moved with a fiercely noble air. Only the eyes were those of the portrait. They were strong and defiant even though the face was tragic and infinitely sad.

The father followed heavily on a cane. He was a handsome man who wore a beret in the house to keep his bald head warm. We spoke Italian, with Dave acting as interpreter when necessary. The mother brewed tea and served rich little cakes while I explained my purpose in Italy and told them what I had seen. The mother interrupted in a voice that was full of sorrow and came deep from the throat. "Do you think there will be another war?" she asked.

"I don't know," I said, "I don't know any more than you know. But I believe it can be avoided and I hope it will."

"Then why do you rearm the Germans?" said the mother. "If the Germans are rearmed, there will be another war."

I tried to explain the political expediency of rearming the Germans, but the mother would not be convinced. I pointed out Italy's share of responsibility for the world's troubles.

"It was not the Italian people," she said. "Our corrupt leaders followed the example of the Germans. The Germans are responsible. The Germans!" Rocking back and forth, she chanted her hatred. "The Germans are wicked people. They love only to kill. America does not know the evil of the Germans." She turned suddenly to her son. "Show him!" she said. "Let him see for himself the evil."

Dave explained that his father had brought back to Italy some drawings which he had made in the concentration camp. "Perhaps he would rather not see them," the father protested. "They are not easy to look upon."

I said I would see them. After some more discussion, the mother brought out a bundle and placed it on the coffee table before us. It was wrapped in heavy old paper and tied with a worn knotted cord. While he untied the parcel, Dave explained that in Dachau his father made drawings on bits of paper which he hid from the Germans. After the liberation, while convalescing in an American hospital, he had made others from the raw scars of his memory. Slowly the drawings were unfolded, odd scraps of paper laid on the coffee table for me to see. They were, indeed, almost too horrible. An artist's imagination goes beyond the camera's scope; they were more shocking than any photographs or motion pictures of Dachau. I began to feel sick, and still they continued dropping to the table, one by one, while the mother stood behind me watching, trembling in hatred for the Germans. The father paid little attention. He drew calmly at his pipe, as if by putting the impressions on paper he had permanently sealed his memory. My revulsion was for the drawings rather than the sadism, the mass starvation and nakedness they recorded. As long as such pictures existed they would fire human hatred.

"I think the drawings would be better destroyed," I said. "Until men can erase such deeds from their memories, men and nations will never look with compassion upon each other."

The father heard me calmly.

"What would you destroy?" the mother said, her voice stark as a Medea's. "Paper, only paper. You can burn paper but you cannot destroy the memory of the heart. Ah, signore, memory is strong when you have sent a husband and five sons to war."

I remembered that Dave had mentioned only three brothers. I sensed a danger signal and did not inquire then about a fourth. Later while walking back to the Gemma Dave told me when his father and oldest brother were taken to Germany, and he and another brother escaped to Switzerland, there was still a younger brother who remained in Milan with the mother. The boy, Peter, aged sixteen, went one night to attend a partisan meeting in the home of a friend and was never seen again. "We have heard that he was tortured to death by sadistic Nazis," Dave said. "This, mother does not know. We try to forget Peter. His name is never mentioned."

The next day, Phil Filippi invited me to see his paintings. The apartment was full of fresh green landscapes warmed by a Van Gogh sort of light and brooding sensitive portraits, several of which were of a white-haired old lady. "My grandmother," Phil said. "She is beautiful for painting and she is a model who costs me nothing." He was, indeed, a mature and gifted artist. I asked if he sold his paintings. "It is the same in the galleries as in the theaters," he said. "Galleries are owned by Communists and unless you are a Communist it is difficult to show and sell pictures. Life is difficult for an Italian artist, so he thinks how happy one would be in America where pictures are sold because they are good and not because of how the artist thinks." He brought out still another painting of the grandmother and said, "Even if America should welcome me, it would be difficult for me to leave my grandmother. I fear every day that today perhaps she will die. She is so old, and still she lives, and so long as she lives I cannot leave her."

One evening Dave and Phil took me to the Piccolo Teatro. The Piccolo Teatro, or "little theater," is a successful example of government-subsidized theater. Both the municipal government of Milan and the national government in Rome contribute to the support of the resident repertoire company which plays in an old palace owned by the city. It produces classic and contemporary art plays in Milan for nine months of a year; the other three months it tours Italy, England, France, and Switzerland. The theater's permanent director, Giorgio Strehler, is believed by many to be the best young director in Italy. Dave's brother, Joseph, was the theater's music director.

The play we saw was George Buchner's long-winded rhetorical drama of the French Revolution, *Danton's Death*. By moving action down into the auditorium, Director Strehler brought the static script to life and achieved a feeling of expansiveness despite his shallow stage. It was a technique borrowed from the American social theater of the thirties, especially Clifford Odets' *Waiting for Lefty*.

When the play was over we went backstage to meet Signor Strehler. He was a small wiry man in his middle thirties, good looking, with graying hair. Austrian ancestors accounted for his German name; he was a native of Trieste. We spoke German. He had never been to America; nevertheless he was very aware of American theater. Of Broadway he took a dim view, speaking earnestly, instead, of the short-lived Group Theater and the early years of the Theater Guild. "They both succumbed to false ideals," he said. "So one is dead and the other has become the most commercial of all. If theater does not fulfill its function of communication, it does not deserve to survive."

Most contemporary plays Signor Strehler did not consider worth his attention. His season's repertoire included Goldoni, Molière, Ibsen, Musset, Bertold Brecht, and two American plays, Thornton Wilder's *Skin of Our Teeth* and Tennessee Williams' *Summer and Smoke*, but no modern Italian writers. "Today most writers have nothing to say," he said. "They are confused and without ideals. It is the sickness of our faithless times." Strehler defended the *rivista* as "the one type of contemporary theater that communicates." "The *rivista* brings back to our theater the important elements of the erotic and the bawdy," he said. "In our preoccupation with psychological drama we have lost these characteristics of our early and classic theater. They are important to the theater and it is good to have them back."

The next evening I took Dave to a performance at La Scala. I wore a dinner jacket; Dave, who ordinarily heard operas from student galleries, arrived in a respectable enough dark suit, but wore a pair of white socks that shone forth like beacons from under his trouser cuffs. When I picked up the guest tickets at the box office I discovered we had been assigned to the *palco reale*, or royal box. A battalion of footmen in pantaloons, wearing keys on golden chains like wine stewards, bowed us through golden halls and up marble staircases. A major-domo unlocked the door of the gold and crimson stall of the Vittorio Emanueles and Umbertos of Italian history. Since the box was in the direct center facing the stage, it was a wonderful post from which to survey the house. High in the lofts the heads of students and music lovers reminded me of Daumier's drawings of the Paris galleries. Several tiers of boxes were crowded with bourgeois. Society milled in the orchestra below. Dave, forgetting where he was sitting, looked down on the men, formal as penguins, and the women glistening with aigrettes and diamonds. "Ghosts!" he muttered. "Their day is spent. They're dead but they don't know it."

The opera, Giordano's *Andrea Chénier*, was, like *Danton's Death*, about the French Revolution. A mob of frenzied revolutionaries wearing red bandannas rioted on the stage and a span of Belgian draft horses pulled a load of political prisoners in what looked like an old-fashioned brewery wagon. Supers shouted, "To the guillotine!" and "Off with their heads." Dave pointed to the patrons in the boxes around us. "They don't know the opera is about them," he said. During intermissions, as we walked through the promenades and salons, I could feel the white socks drawing attention to us. Scornfully David identified for me Milan's nobility, the Sforzi, the Borghesi, and the Visconti. Many of the princes and counts were kissing ladies' hands. "It is why they all have such bad health," Dave said. "They are always eating microbes."

The soprano was the distinguished Maria Caniglia; the tenor was young Mario del Monaco. In the last-act death pact the soprano took a deep breath and with a loud fortissimo swung the tenor's backside to the audience. A moment later while embracing her in love's death, he whirled her around in order to face the audience himself. Like a struggle of pythons it continued to the final breath. They kept their grip on each other even during the curtain calls. When the tenor, as is the custom, kissed the soprano's hand, he appeared to be biting a piece out of it. "Gorgeous George and Mr. America," said Dave, who, like many young Italians, followed American wrestling.

Outside, a caravan of chauffeured limousines crawled slowly under the theater canopy. From the square, students and workers watched society pour into the night. Their signs were leaning against the statue of Leonardo. *"Evviva la pace,"* one of them read. "Long live peace." From a parked jeep the armed militia watched.

We went on to a bachelor party of young American businessmen. Since Milan is a commercial rather than a tourist center, many Americans in the city are representatives of American business firms. This is one reason why Milan is more virulently anti-American than most Italian cities. Our host represented a western Pennsylvania steel mill of which his father was a corporate owner. He had an Italian name; the father was a native Milanese who had prospered in America. Except for servants, the son lived alone in a luxurious apartment permanently maintained by the family. We were let in by a maid. The Americans at the party were crowded around a piano singing songs of Cornell University from which several had been graduated. Some young Italians sat quietly by. The guests represented the Radio Corporation of America, Eastman Kodak, American Express, and several oil companies. Conversation dealt with contracts and profits, Cornell, American and Italian football, and women. The host, a fat youth of twenty-five, was lamenting his poverty.

"I cannot afford to marry," he wailed. "But even if I could afford it, whom would I marry? Italian girls are cows with no initiative. American girls are too independent. The only thing to do is marry an American girl and bring her to Italy to housebreak her. An American girl trained to know her place like Italian women would make a good wife. But who can afford it?" Listening to him, the young Italians only partly masked their scorn. "Of course, there is no point to marrying even if you could afford it," the fellow continued. "There's going to be war. In less than a year we'll be at war. We're keyed to war; we can't escape it." *

His opinions were shared by a junior member of America's diplomatic corps who described his own charmed existence. "It's the life!" he said. "I've got an apartment. I've got servants. Plenty of opera seats. I go up to Austria to ski several times a winter. Women are willing and liquor is cheap. But the end's coming. I feel it. When it comes, any American who doesn't clear out within twenty-four hours after the Communists take over is a dead duck. I'm whipping down to Genoa in my Buick and getting on the first boat. I got a guy down there looking out for me."

I reminded him that the duties of consular officials in time of war included the evacuation of American nationals.

"Listen, when the time comes it's sink or swim, every man for himself," he said. "I'm saving *my* skin."

When we left the party two of the cynical young Italians rode down the elevator with us. Paying no attention to me, one said in Italian, "Another war to feed fat American *maiali!*" The word meant pigs.

"So they can marry and breed more pigs," the other said. At the front door they bowed and bid me a gracious *buona sera*.

I continued to hear opera at La Scala. One Sunday afternoon Herbert von Karajan, the great Austrian conductor, led a magnificent *Tannhäuser* with the splendid Austrian soprano Elisabeth Schwarzkopf singing Elisabeth. As if to demonstrate their Austrian endurance the pair appeared the following evening in *Don Giovanni*. It was a joyful, audacious lark, the outstanding Mozart production in my memory. Next day I toured the house and visited with the executive director, Antonio Ghiringhelli.

Like the Piccolo Teatro, La Scala is supported by government assistance from Rome. Money for subsidy is collected by a national amusement tax on all entertainment and sports. Dr. Ghiringhelli was displeased that much of the large entertainment revenue collected in Milan's prosperous

* This was in January, 1951.

film houses and sports arenas was being spent by the government to subsidize opera in the poor towns of southern Italy and Sicily. He would have preferred it all returned to his opera house. On this point he quarreled with the Ministero degli Spettacoli, the government bureau in Rome which administered theater subsidization. "In the old days kings supported opera," the director said. "Kings were men of culture; today we have *piccoli* functionaries who are ignorant of culture and awed by their own power."

I found myself completely out of sympathy with his notion that less prosperous communities should be denied opera so that he might have more money to spend at La Scala. Our interview came to a hasty end. The next time I went to the opera my seats were no longer in the royal box, but in a high side box from which only two-thirds of the stage was visible. Perhaps Dave Carboni's white socks had something to do with the switch.

The last visit to the opera house was for the Italian première of Gian-Carlo Menotti's *The Consul*. Menotti's Italian invasion was a stormy one. Expatriated to America for twenty-five years, but still an Italian citizen, Menotti had returned to barnstorm his homeland with the operas which had been so phenomenally successful in America. Two months before, *The Medium* had been dismally received in Genoa. How much of the unfavorable criticism of that opera could be credited to a resentment toward Menotti for casting his fortune with America, and how much to a genuine distaste for his music, was difficult to say. With *The Consul* at La Scala, Menotti was putting his reputation in his own country to a second and greater test. In the salons of Milan, however, *The Consul* was a success before it opened, and its composer the darling of society. At the dress rehearsal English-speaking countesses and duchesses gushed in Hollywood superlatives. But at the official première, it had rougher sledding. On the gargantuan La Scala stage the little opera was almost lost; played by the large orchestra, its music was too loud. "People are always saying my plays get in the way of my music," the composer said. "Now for once they can hear the music." The Italians heard it, but not with pleasure. A critic and his friends came with police whistles in their pockets. When the music started they began a battle of sound. Singers hoarsely tried to outshout the din. Each bravo brought a barrage of angry boos. Everyone knew that the opera had been a success in America and the opposition was determined to prevent it from happening in Italy. "This is a dirty mess!" a woman's voice screamed. "Down with America! Long live Italy!" another voice called out. The biased blasting by the critics in the morning made it clear that if Verdi had composed *Aïda* in America, it would have received the same treatment.

I met another young journalist who became my friend at Bocconi University. This newest of Milan's institutions for higher learning is a modern concrete and glass structure as functional as an American biscuit factory. It has no campus; most of its students would not have time to use one. Bocconi provides a first-class liberal education for middle- and lower-class young people who could not otherwise afford it. *Dottoressa* Giovanna Cantoni, professor of American literature, warned me I need make no concessions in my lecture on contemporary American literature and theater. I could, she said, speak to them just as I would to my own students at home. She was wrong. Very quickly I discovered that my lecture must be pitched somewhat differently, for Mrs. Cantoni's pupils were more familiar with the writings of Herman Melville, Nathaniel Hawthorne, Eugene O'Neill, Thornton Wilder, and William Faulkner than were my own graduate students at the University of Illinois. There were twice as many girls as boys in the class; the girls, especially, understood and spoke English perfectly. Mrs. Cantoni had lived during the war in London and several of her students had studied in England. Students from other classes wandered in, and a reporter, a slight, intense youth with a cast in one eye feverishly made notes.

At the end of the lecture I invited discussion. Among the questions students asked were:

"What is the philosophy behind the American theater?"

"Is Blanche DuBois in *A Streetcar Named Desire* a typical American woman?"

"Why did the center of the American creative writing shift from New England in the nineteenth century to the South in the twentieth?"

"Was *All the King's Men* based on fact?"

"Is it true that the film *Pinky* was banned in America for fear of race riots?"

"What is the highest salary in Hollywood?"

"Have you ever witnessed a lynching?"

"Why doesn't Aaron Copland write an opera?"

There was no anti-Americanism in the questions, only doubts and a great desire to understand. They were young people with an overwhelming curiosity and an eagerness to like America despite many misconceptions. The two hours enriched me more than they enriched Mrs. Cantoni's students.

The professor and I lunched in the student refectory, a vast room as crowded and noisy as one in an American university. Italians have never accepted the cafeteria idea, so students were waiting on table. While we ate, one of the girls from the class brought her father to the table. He was a humble elderly man who told me he played second violin in the orchestra of La Scala. I told him how much I had enjoyed the *Don Giovanni*.

"But you have heard Mozart at *Il Metropolitano*," he said.

"Never with so much pleasure," I said.

"Grazie, signore, grazie!" He bowed graciously, as proud as if he himself had sung the *Don*.

"My father does not know many Americans," the girl said in English. "It pleases him very much to speak to one."

I asked Mrs. Cantoni why her girls spoke English better than the boys.

"Most of the girls have been to England," she answered. "In order to learn the language they have gone there as domestics and children's nurses.

"You must have noticed that our young people have a great hunger for everything that is American," the professor said. "Of course, all of them want desperately to go to America. They are prevented from going first by the expense, and second, by your law which turns away anyone who has ever been a Fascist. In Italy that includes most of our young people, who had to belong to Fascist youth organizations in order to attend schools.

"It would be so much better if you welcomed our young people to visit you. Nothing would bring as much understanding and friendship to our country and yours as an exchange of students. Our young people are rootless. They are searching for something solid. They worship America for its freedom of opportunity. Whenever an Italian youth is exposed to America he returns completely enthusiastic for the American way of life. The ones with Communist tendencies are exactly those with whom most can be done. Communism is an idealism of youth that has nothing to do with Russian politics. Unfortunately, in Italy it is the only idealism left to youth. But give students Thomas Paine and Thomas Jefferson and see what will happen!"

Dr. Cantoni spoke of the crying need of Italian universities for books of American literature. "This is an emergency," she said. "We have almost none such books. The students are hungry to read about the American way of life. They want the classics of Hawthorne, Longfellow, Poe, and Melville, as well as the contemporaries. Our universities are poor and such books are expensive to buy. If only your government or some private organization could understand this terrible hunger. The books would be devoured."

I thought of the endless dusty rows of "classics" in the second-hand bookshops in downtown New York, and the miles of unread shelves in the parlors of America. I promised Professor Cantoni I would see what could be done.

The boyish-looking reporter who had been in the classroom appeared at the table. He was carrying a camera, and he asked if he might take a photograph of me to accompany an article in his journal. While he was taking it, Professor Cantoni lowered her voice to say that he was reporter for a Communist newspaper which might distort what I had said.

"I have also been a journalist, so I know the problems of reporting public speeches," I said to the reporter. "Since most of my remarks were extemporaneous, I wonder if I might read your article before you submit it."

"Are you afraid because I am a Communist?" he asked in Italian.

I was not prepared for such candor. "There is the problem of translation," I said. "Things said in English do not always appear the same in Italian."

"You can trust me," he said, looking at me with such sincerity that I felt I could. "But I would be very happy if you would come to my home tonight," he said. "It is a new home, for I have been married only three weeks. I should like my wife to know you."

I said I would come. I wrote down the address he gave me and directions to get there by tram.

"My name is Giusto Vittorini," he said.

"Like the author," I said, thinking of Elio Vittorini, whose fine novel, *In Sicily*, I admired.

"He is my father," the reporter said.

Dr. Cantoni told me Giusto's parents separated when he was a boy and he had lived a lonely life. Three years before he had traveled to Yugoslavia and returned an admirer of Tito's. A year ago he had been awarded a scholarship to the same American school in Austria which Phil Filippi attended, but Giusto was denied a visa to leave Italy because of his political beliefs.

"It was a shame," Professor Cantoni said. "He is very eager to learn and would doubtlessly have become enthusiastically pro-American at the school. He is a perfect example of the dilemma of our young people; a very sensitive boy who has no awareness of the true nature of Communism and sees in it a solution for the social ills of Italy. He *believes* he is a Communist because he cannot close his eyes to the unhappiness about him. 'Giusto' means 'The Just,' and it is a good name for him. Of course, if the Communists ever took Italy, Giusto would be in Siberia in two weeks."

That night was foggy, as usual. I rode a tram into the heart of the city and took another in an opposite direction. After a long ride I got off at the end of the line. A small dark-haired girl came up to me and introduced herself as Signorina Sirotti, a student friend of Giusto's who had come to guide me to his home. As we walked through the soft night she told me she had studied in England for a year and that she had filed application at the American Consulate for a scholarship in America. The apartment to which she took me was in a new building in an open and unsettled area. Giusto met us at the door and thanked me for coming to see him. He was twenty-one years old and so frail in appearance he seemed much younger. His candor and sincerity were as disarming as a child's. "Elena," he called.

In a moment Giusto's bride came from another room to greet me. She had been his childhood sweetheart. She was an extremely pretty girl with dark hair and eyes. In my presence she was quiet and shy; as she led us into the living room she moved modestly with a classic sort of languor. The apartment, new and pleasant, was sparsely furnished. On the shelves were books by Thornton Wilder and William Saroyan, authors whom Giusto's father had translated into Italian, as well as books of other American writers. On one wall among Modigliani and Van Gogh reproductions was a framed portrait of Premier Stalin.

Elena spoke no English and Giusto spoke it badly, so we talked Italian. Signorina Sirotti translated for us when necessary. Though he was a student, Giusto was supporting himself and his bride with his earnings as a journalist. His ambition was to be a motion-picture writer and director; he spoke rapidly and excitedly of Hollywood's John Huston, whose *Asphalt Jungle* he thought was the finest film he had seen. Now he was writing his university dissertation on American films and he pumped me with questions about Hollywood. Beyond the work of Huston and Charlie Chaplin, Giusto had few good things to say about American movies.

"Most Hollywood films are fairy stories for adults," Giusto said. "They are not about human beings because the people who make them are isolated from all human problems except their own abnormal ones."

"Still the Italian people prefer the Hollywood fantasies to their own realistic films," I said.

"People who live in poverty are not entertained by realism," Giusto said. "They welcome any kind of escape, but even while they are enjoying your films, they mistrust and resent you for being so remote from the human community."

About Hollywood I did not argue, for I was in agreement with Giusto. "You have said Hollywood is an abnormal phenomenon," I said. "Hollywood may seem remote to the human community, but that is no evidence that America is removed from it. It seems to me America has become very much a part of the human community. Whether it has wanted to or not, it has had to take its place as a leader."

"Because America fears for her security," Giusto was quick to reply. "Americans are too rich to understand the problems of the poor. They are anti-poor, and a majority of the people in the world are poor."

"America is anti-Communist," I said. "That is not the same thing as being anti-poor. In America we believe that there are better ways than Communism to help the poor peoples of the world and maintain the human community."

"America's anti-Communism is self-preservation and not compassion for the poor of the world," Giusto said. While he talked, Elena served coffee and cognac.

"Why are you a Communist?" I asked.

"It is not for myself," he said. "I have enough. I know I will not be better off under a Communist government. But there are too many people who have nothing. They are my brothers and as long as they have nothing I cannot be content because I have plenty."

"But you must understand what Communism is," I said. "When you do not have freedom you cannot have brotherhood."

"Some people in the world believe Communism is bad and some people believe it is good," he said. "You think it is bad and I think it is good. It is hard to say who is right."

Giusto spoke of the poor farmers of Calabria and Sicily about whom his father wrote. "Farmers are starving and land is idle," he said. "They cannot work it because it is owned by rich aristocrats in Milan and Rome."

"It is true, man is entitled to his portion of land," I said. "The small landowners are the most precious portion of the state." I was quoting from Thomas Jefferson.

Giusto looked at me in surprise. "That is what the Communists say," he said. "We think alike, you and I. You understand something which y ⁻r country does not understand."

"The idea is not mine," I said. "It is Thomas Jefferson's. Ownership of the land by the worker is one of the democratic principles upon which America was founded."

"Then your government has forgotten," Giusto said vehemently. "In Italy we have a government that must pledge itself to oppose land reform in order to receive the financial support of the landowners. This is the government your government supports. You see, we have only two strong parties, the reactionary one supporting the interests of a rich minority, and the liberal one supporting the poor majority. The second one is the people's party of Italy. It is called the Communist party. Because it has that name the Americans will not try to understand it."

"Americans are more realistic," I said. "The Communist state is not an ideal, but a deadly practicality. Those who follow it idealistically are sheep lured by promises into a police state as bad as or worse than any the world can remember. Do you think there is any freedom in Poland and Czechoslovakia? Would Italy, if it became Communistic, be any different? Isn't it better to keep the wolf out of the fold than to trust to drawing his teeth and claws after he shall have entered?"

"A figure of speech . . . ," Giusto said.

"Yes. But it's not my figure of speech. Thomas Jefferson said that too."

Giusto looked at me for a moment. He started to speak and couldn't. When words finally came, his voice was trembling. "I am confused," he said. "I am very confused. I am yet a boy. I think like a boy. I suppose I must grow older and think older, but I do not like it. Two years ago I thought like this. . . ."

He drew a straight line on a piece of paper.

". . . and now I am already thinking like this."

He drew a broken waving line.

"Already I am compromising, and I am unhappy. I compromise because I must live in the world, because now I have a wife and a home. I fear I will compromise more and more until I will hate myself. I am afraid, because I am not strong. I am very weak. . . ."

Tears came to his eyes and his words came to a stop. Elena, who had sat quietly in the shadows, rose from her chair and went to comfort him.

I read his report of the lecture. It was carefully written and we changed only a few phrases. When it was time for the last tram I said good night. Giusto put on a beret and walked with me to the station.

"We walk through fog," he said.

"It is always fog in Milan," I said.

"It is always fog in Italy," Giusto said. He thought of his bride waiting for him in their apartment. "It is the first time I have left her alone," he said, and then, asserting the sex superiority so deep seated in every Italian male, he added, "But she will have to get used to it."

We waited for the tram. "You have read my father's books?" he asked. I replied I had.

"I wish I might be more like my father," he said. "I should like you to know him. Would you like to meet him?"

I said I would.

"I will try to arrange an appointment. He does not see many people and he will not have a telephone. Even I must write for an appointment to see him." The tram rumbled toward us. "I do not have many friends," Giusto said. "I did not expect ever to have an American friend. Will you let me write you?"

"I would be honored," I said.

"If there is anything I can do for you, you must tell me," he said.

"There is," I said. "You can take the picture of Stalin from the wall." He looked troubled and did not reply. "I think one day when you look back on your first home with your beautiful wife you will be happier if you remember it was not there," I said. I mounted the tram. As it jerked away Giusto waved from the fog.

CHAPTER 5

RED LETTUCE IN PIEDMONT

DURING MY STAY in Milan, I took a two-day sabbatical from its tense, hostile atmosphere to visit my friend, Ernesto Pirola, the student I had met in the Vatican museum my first week in Rome.

Rain pelted drearily through the fog when I boarded the train for Turin. Like the smoker on a New York–Boston run, my second-class compartment was filled with salesmen and clerks carrying briefcases. A thin, tense youth read an auto-racing magazine. Italy's automotive industry is divided between Milan and Turin, and motor racing is the regional sport. As the train plunged toward the mountains of Piedmont, the rain turned to snow. Through the steamed glass I looked out on an American winter. The landscape of the flat Po valley, mostly rice swamps and almond orchards, was as monotonous as the Jersey flats. The youth took a raisin loaf from his pocket and munched on it while he read. The clerks told smoking-room stories about the effect of inflation on prostitutes, the problems of Italians trying to emigrate to the United States, and the vocalism of Mary Margaret Truman, who, they said, was going to sing *La Traviata* at La Scala as a term of the NATO plan for Italy.

The tourist books made little of Turin, except to say that it was the home of the Savoy rulers of Piedmont and the Kingdom of Sardinia and for four years, from 1861 to 1865, the first capital of the Kingdom of Italy. Because of its automobile factories it was known as the Detroit of Italy.

The trip was a short one, hardly two hours. From my window I saw a spacious and elegant city. At the head of the track Ernesto was scanning passengers, apparently as uncertain that he would recognize me as I was that I would recognize him. I had believed him to be a poor student and was surprised by his groomed splendor. He had dressed formally, as if for a state occasion, in a black overcoat, a silk muffler, and black leather gloves. The clothes gave him an austere dignity and he seemed older than I remembered him. His black hair was uncovered and his face beamed with cold. His curious Spanish eyes flashed warmly.

"Welcome to Torino," he said in halting English. I was surprised by the station wagon to which he led me, for in Italy any kind of car is a mark of affluence. The city lay around us in broad sweeping lines, its wide streets bordered with palaces of classic design. Beyond, the snow-covered mountains, dividing Italy from France, rose from the mists like a white wall.

"You did not know Torino was so beautiful," Ernesto said, speaking Italian now. The courtly atmosphere was more French than Italian. On cinema marquees I saw French films advertised. "We are Italy's French city," Ernesto said. "We are not very popular with other Italian cities."

We went to a restaurant for lunch. He told me he had acceded to his father's wishes and switched his studies from medicine to commerce. In return, his father was building a house for him behind the family villa in Pindove, a small industrial town some twenty kilometers from Turin. I asked if he were going to be married.

"Yes, I have become engaged," he said as if this were an incidental detail. I congratulated him and asked if he had a picture of his fiancée. He didn't; his wallet contained only photographs of himself and his brothers. When I asked if I would meet the girl, he seemed surprised. He shrugged, as if it were not important. "She is a good girl," he said. He never mentioned her again. It was quite typical, this indifference of the self-centered Italian male toward the girl he has selected to marry.

When we finished eating, Ernesto announced an itinerary for an afternoon's sight-seeing; if we were to accomplish it we must begin at once. We drove through wide streets and broad piazzas, past palaces, theaters, and the university. "In Torino we permit the sun to enter," Ernesto said. "There is a law that no man can make a building more than one and a half times the width of the street. An industrial firm built its house too high and had to take four stories off." We crossed the Po to the Parco del Valentino, a hilly park with a reproduction of a medieval village and castle. From the basement stables with straw boxes for soldiers' beds, up to the ducal chambers and dining halls in the towers, it was a fascinating place. Ernesto raced me through it like a professional guide, lingering at only two places. The first was before a fresco of a fountain of youth into which tottered senile old men who emerged as glowing youths. The second attraction that held Ernesto was the prison dungeon under the floor of the cortile. Here the cells were furnished with heavy chains and stocks and a variety of torture devices. Ernesto explained the purpose of the iron gates in the floors. "There are cells underneath where prisoners were starved to death," he said. "Through the gates the prisoners above could hear the dying groans of the prisoners below. When they cried for water those above made their toilet down through the grates." In another cell Ernesto pointed out deep oil vats with trap doors. "Through these the prisoners were dropped for frying," he said.

I shuddered. Ernesto's emphasis on the macabre made sight-seeing a grisly affair. His was an Italian soul. Sadism, cruelty, and brutality runs through the history of Italy; it is natural that these things should also flow in Italian blood. Yet through the same blood flows a Jordan of love and affection; an Italian is always expressing his love for someone. The mingled currents of the dark and the light are what set apart the Latin soul from those of the rest of the world. In my own Anglo-Saxon spirit northern inhibition had submerged both the night and the day. Ernesto's appetite for the grotesque and the violent was as normal to him as my repulsion was to me.

We continued from shrine to shrine, from one dark symbol of human violence to another. From the medieval castle we went to the Accademia delle Scienze, an austere palace containing archaeological and Egyptian museums and a picture gallery. The Egyptian rooms were cold as an igloo and so dark one had to strain one's eyes to see. Ernesto raced me through a gruesome assortment of burial urns containing the intestines of ancient nobility and a variety of mummies both human and animal, including sacred crocodiles, dogs, cats, and bulls. The only other visitors in the museum were a pair of hand-holding lovers who giggled over the mummies. The prize display was the 3,300-year-old tomb of a man of affluence named Hai and his wife Mrije. This astounding monument to necrophilia was furnished with an eternity's supply of bread, palm fruits, cheeses and pastes, jars of embalmed swallows, linens, beds, and builders' tools. The two lovers behind us found Hai's toilet cabinet side-splitting, and the dismal rooms rang with young life finding merriment in death. Ernesto found a primitive adding machine in the tomb. "For scoring the years of eternity," he said.

The picture galleries upstairs were as gloomy as the tombs. Ernesto passed up a long-tressed Botticelli Venus for a beheaded John the Baptist, an arrow-riddled Sebastian, a bare-breasted Barbara being flagellated.

Ernesto's favorite room was one devoted to Savoy portraits. Here was a dynasty, a roomful of kings on horses and queens on thrones, of dukes and duchesses and endless royal children. The children were the most intriguing. Serious, puffy-cheeked babies in bonnets and lace, wearing religious medals, clutching at flowers or squeezing a little captive bird; elegant little dukes in velvet doublets and long-curled little duchesses, all curiously unbending little adults looking wise beyond their years. Ernesto explained their relationships to each other and their places in history. A three-year-old bambino was wearing the red robes of a cardinal cut down to size. "Emanuele Filiberto!" Ernesto said admiringly. "A great general who defeated the French at Saint-Quentin. Then he came home and made himself into a despot."

"Success went to his head," I said.

Ernesto looked at me sharply. "Emanuele Filiberto built Savoy into a rich and powerful monarchy," he said.

From the Accademia we climbed to the Basilica of Superga, a great domed church modeled after Rome's Pantheon, which rises over the mists of the Po like an apocalypse. Superga is the church into which an airliner carrying an Italian football team crashed during a fog, killing all on board. At the wall where the plane crashed, wreaths of frozen flowers rattled in the wind. Inside the church, Ernesto led me below the floor into a shadowy white marble grotto. We walked along a dead white corridor lined with saccharine statues of bereavement and death. The Stygian passage opened into a network of white chambers. These were the burial chambers of the Savoys. Rows of white sarcophagi were arranged according to families. It was an awesome sight, this clustering together of dead kings like barnacles to a rotting hulk. At the head of each royal encasement was a white marble skull carrying a golden crown; each interred king and duke wore his diadem in death.

Among the tombs Ernesto was at ease, almost happy, for an Italian loves necrophilia and its symbols; they bring him courage to face the fear of death. "We meet the children in the gallery again," he said. He took pains to identify the individual tombs with the portraits in the gallery. "Remember the baby in white lace holding the linnet? Well, here he is!" I looked down on a white skull wearing a golden coronet. "This is the *infante* who rolled the hoop." Dead in battle or bed, the unbending serious children of the pictures were here at the end of their cycle.

It was a pleasure to come up from the cellar into the out-of-doors, even though it was snowing again and Turin was invisible in the fog. With terrifying indifference, Ernesto coasted down the hairpin curves. I sat with eyes closed until Ernesto shifted back in gear and we rolled over the Po into town. The weather was too thick to set out for Pindove. We parked the car and walked through the storm, passing a bookstall where books were sold like potatoes, two hundred lire a kilogram, to a little theater, where sensational posters advertised "Burmah with snakes, an incredible spectacle!" The admission was small. Judging from the steady line moving in and out, it was not a place to tarry long. We bought our tickets and fell in. The line moved slowly. Inside, a knot of excited men were gathered about the attraction: a thin man of middle years, naked except for a loin covering, lying in a glass cage with—according to the testimonials—a hundred and fifty serpents.

"He has not come out or eaten any food for forty days," Ernesto told me. "His goal is fifty-six days. If he reaches it, he will have set the world's record." My first impression was that of a medieval painting of the inferno with clusters of serpents consuming the bodies of the damned. The difference was that in the frightful box there was a minimum of activity. Both Burmah and the snakes seemed to be in a torpor, and not the least bit aware of the babbling *voyeurs* outside the glass.

"*E bello!*"

"*Bellissimo!*"

With sixteen more days to go the enterprise was prospering; people were coming every day to check on its progress, Ernesto said. Beside us two men were counting the snakes.

"It is not possible, one hundred and fifty," one argued loudly.

"I have counted one hundred and thirty-nine," the other said. "It is very possible there are one hundred and fifty." Together they started counting again, but it was a hopeless enterprise. My stomach would take no more of the spectacle.

"*Ne ho abbastanza.*" It was enough for me! I departed, Ernesto following at my heels. "It does not please you?" he asked, a hurt tone in his voice.

"I am not fond of snakes."

"But it is a very interesting scientific experiment," Ernesto insisted.

The wet cold snow felt good on my face. We walked across a vast piazza which was the heart of the town, acres of spacious pavements facing the Royal Palace of the Kings of Sardinia and Italy, and the Palazza Madama, residence of the royal ladies. "On this square at the end of the war soldiers killed Communists," Ernesto said. "The bodies of the Communists were hung from the windows and parapets and all the people came to see the spectacle. It was like a great *festa*!" He pointed to where the bodies had hung.

"Did you see them?" I asked.

"No, that was not my good fortune," he said. "There was also fighting in Pindove. Thirty were killed. My brothers and I manned a . . ."

He was talking too fast for me to understand.

"Bup, bup, bup, bup . . . ," he shouted, manning an imaginary machine gun. His voice echoed across the empty piazza like real gunfire. I did some mental arithmetic; in 1943 Ernesto was hardly fourteen years old.

"Did you kill men?" I asked.

He looked at me with scorn. "Does one shoot machine guns at the leaves in trees?" he asked.

As night fell the storm increased. Ernesto telephoned his father, who reported the country roads ice covered and suggested that we remain in Turin for the night and drive to Pindove in the morning. We arranged for a hotel room and bought tickets for a performance at Milan's Piccolo Teatro, which was presenting its repertoire in Turin that week. The bill was *Estate e fumo*, an Italian version of Tennessee Williams' *Summer and Smoke*, a play I remembered as a dismal failure in New York. Under Giorgio Strehler's sensitive touch the Italian company brought it to glowing life. By treating it as a small play, Director Strehler made a virtue of the script's wistful tenderness. It was the first play Ernesto had ever seen and it engrossed him deeply. "It is a story of America," he said, of the frustrated tragedy of the minister's daughter, Alma Winemiller, "but it happens often in Italy. The difference is that in Italy she would not be the daughter of a padre." After the play, our walk to the hotel took us through the Piazza Castello, where the bodies had hung from the windows. It had stopped snowing and the night was clear and cold. "Do you think there will be another war?" Ernesto asked. It was the subject everyone in Italy was talking about.

"I believe it is possible to avoid war," I said. "Every week we gain now will strengthen the cause of peace."

"I think there will be another war," Ernesto said. "I think it will be necessary to kill more Communists."

The morning dawned gray, with more snow. After breakfast we set out for Pindove, thirty kilometers northwest of Turin and twenty kilometers from the French border. The narrow winding road was busy with peasants on morning errands. Donkey carts hauled grain; oxen pulled loads of hay and women carried winter vegetables on their heads. The fog was thick enough so we could see neither man nor beast until we were almost on them. Still, Ernesto drove in true Italianate fashion, his foot hard on the accelerator and his hand never off the horn. Neither the donkeys nor the women with cabbage headdresses gave any indication that they heard us coming. We careened from side to side, missing beasts and pedestrians. Occasionally the little Fiat skidded wildly over a patch of ice, which for Ernesto made the ride merrier. His gaiety made me giddily fatalistic, as if destiny had preordained the outcome of the ride. I have no memories of the Piedmont landscape.

Shouting above the wail of the horn and leaning toward me to make himself heard, Ernesto told me about his home and family. The house was named Villa Annabella after the mother who died of cancer in 1939, three years after the birth of her youngest son. "Pindove is an industrial village so we have political trouble and many battles over labor matters," Ernesto said. "My father is manager of a railroad car factory and we are always having to protect ourselves against the Communists." Ernesto's oldest brother, Aristide, was a priest. His hobby was skiing, so he was well pleased with his assignment to a mountain parish on the French border. A second brother, Riccardo, and a sister, Cecilia, were married and living away from home. Ernesto was next; he and Arturo commuted from the Villa Annabella to the University of Turin. The youngest brother, thirteen-year-old Silvestro, was at a boarding school.

It was apparent that the Pirolas were as rightist as the friends I had left in Milan were leftist. Signor Pirola was an industrialist who worshiped America's manufacturing genius and vehemently hated Communists. Politically he was a Monarchist, hoping for the return to power of his friend, Savoy Umberto II, the last King of Italy. His five sons, whom he ruled like a king, called him Pasha.

The mountains of Pindove were hidden by the fog, but one could feel the pressure of their presence. We tooted through the village and up a hill, jerking to a stop beside the stone wall of a medieval-looking manor house. *"Guarda al cane,* beware the dog!" a sign warned. Ernesto pulled a rope and in a moment a grinning little woman of middle years came to open a heavy iron gate bolted with chains. This was Lidia, the house-keeper. The gate locked behind us with a heavy click. Chained to a dark conifer was a great barrel-chested dog. He lunged at me, clanking the chain, growling and spitting saliva. I would have bet on him against his weight in lions. Loose, he would have devoured me on the spot. "He is necessary because of the Communists," Ernesto said.

Pasha came to the door. He was an overweight Ezio Pinza, a handsome man with graying hair, hearty in body, voice, and manner. His name was Tommaso, but Pasha was an appropriate moniker. With him was his fourth son, Arturo, a lean, poetic-looking boy of eighteen. My coat was hardly hung away before Pasha poured me a glass of vermouth, and when I was finished, another. Before I could drink the second, Pasha ushered us into the dining room. The house was grand inside, with marble stairs, parquet floors, and windows stained like church windows. The walls were hung with oil paintings, and statues, mostly classic females, stood in the corners. I was seated at Pasha's left. At his right in the place of *la mamma* sat Lidia, indicating that her place in the household was considerably above that of an ordinary servant. Ernesto and Arturo sat at the table's end.

We began with a platter of *antipasto* which was a meal by itself. Pasha talked constantly; his sons only when he addressed them. Since he knew no English and talked with a swift exuberance, our conversation was not easy. Occasionally Ernesto would assist as translator.

"You find Italy beautiful?" Pasha asked.

"More beautiful than I imagined."

Pasha shrugged. "It is the most beautiful country in the world. But beauty is for the eyes. . . ." He pointed to his eyes. ". . . and not for the stomach. Italy is empty in the stomach." He rubbed his.

"In your household there seems to be plenty for the stomach." I said. Lidia was following an *antipasto* with soup and a new wine. "I am not accustomed to hospitality like this."

"Ah, you are in *Piemonte*," Pasha said. "The most cultured, refined, and hospitable province in Italy. The *Piemontesi* are the aristocrats of Italy. . . ."

As Pasha spoke of culture and refinement his mouth was filled with food. He and his handsome sons enjoyed food like no one I'd ever seen. Bending low over their plates, they ladled it in with a minimum of motion and a maximum of suction. They finished each course long before I did. I apologized for my habit to *mangiare lentamente*; I was no match for Pasha in combining conversation with eating.

"Have you been in the south?" Pasha asked. I had not, but said I was looking forward to Naples and Sicily.

"You will see only poverty," he said. "Do not think Naples and Sicily are representative of Italian culture. For that you must come north, where we know how to treat an American."

Obviously the fatted calf had been slaughtered. For two hours, Lidia hopped up and down changing the plates and bottles, all at the signal of Pasha, who directed the banquet as a conductor directs a concert. The fortissimo movement of the gastronomical symphony was clearly the spaghetti course. The quantity of spaghetti on each plate would have made a meal for a stonemason. The Pirola men used the fork only to guide the ends of the long strands to their mouth; after that it was like a vacuum cleaner taking up the fringe of a rug. I tried to focus on the paintings on the wall, but it was no use. Closing my eyes only made it worse, for then I imagined they were taking it in through their navels. With their mouths full of food, they had to suck the wine through their teeth. While this was going on, Pasha discoursed exuberantly on the sublime beauties of Dante and Petrarch, writers who, he was surprised to discover, were read in America. In his questions about America, Pasha indicated some knowledge of American geography. When I said I was a native of Wisconsin, he asked if I had been born in "Waukeemill." I corrected his pronunciation, but he went right on praising "Waukeemill," his favorite American city. His enthusiasm was based on the excellence of some machine tools his factory had imported from a Milwaukee foundry. "Waukeemill is a city most distinguished," he said. "It would bring me great happiness if one of my sons would go to Waukeemill and become a foreman in a big factory there." We drank a toast to Waukeemill.

The roaringly masculine banquet continued; the housekeeper brought forth steaks with potatoes and vegetables. "Lidia," Pasha roared, *"il Bardolino!"* She came running with still another bottle. *"Ah, il Bardolino,"* Pasha sang, "one of the great wines of Piedmont." I had already tasted *Barolo, Barbera* and *Barbaresco,* and several other wines of Piedmont. The bottles stood on the table before me like pins in a bowling alley. Pasha uncorked the newest and filled the glasses. "To the United States of America," he toasted. Ernesto and Arturo silently packed away food; I wondered how long it would be before they would lose their slender waists and become man-mountains like Pasha. A jet-colored Tom leaped like a leopard onto the buffet and ate anchovies from the discarded *antipasto* platter.

"Umberto," Pasha roared. The cat dropped silently back to the floor. "He is named for my friend the King," Pasha said. The cat was as massive in his way as the dog. I told Pasha both beasts resembled him. It was a fine joke; Pasha started slapping me around with the hilarity of it. I discovered to my amazement that I was talking Italian freely, despite a confusion of verb forms and genders. I told Pasha it was the first moment since I'd arrived in Italy that I felt uninhibited in the new language.

"*Bravo*," he bellowed. "*Bisogna celebrare! Lidia! Porta lo sciampagna!*" The housekeeper, ripping drunk, clattered laughing into the cellar. The champagne was delivered and popped. The first glass was to President Harry S. Truman, the second to Dean Acheson. "The most distinguished diplomat in the world," Pasha said. While this was going on, Lidia served a salad.

"I think I must be drunk," I said. "That lettuce appears red."

"The lettuce *is* red," Lidia shouted, jumping up and down with glee.

"Red lettuce is winter lettuce," Pasha said. "Lidia grows it in the hot-house."

"Is it red in the summer too?" I asked.

Lidia almost collapsed with merriment. "No, no," she screamed, "in summer it is green." She had only to look at me to be convulsed with shrieks. Look at him, an American! her eyes kept saying. He doesn't even know red lettuce!

"In America we have red cabbage and red onions, but I have never seen red lettuce."

"I will give you some seed to take back." Lidia said.

"It will do no good," Pasha said. "In America it will grow green. It is only in Piedmont that lettuce grows red." He sent Lidia for still another bottle, this time French cognac. She tumbled into the basement; I could hear her down there, guffawing among the bottles. Pasha pushed bowls of nuts and tangerines at me. "Eat! Eat much!" he said. "Tangerines are better for health than penicillin."

Lidia shouted from the basement; Pasha shouted back a shelf number, and Lidia returned with a bottle. We toasted an end to war, to everlasting peace and friendship between the United States and Italy. Pasha turned sentimental. The dead mother's picture was brought out. It had a little wreath of flowers garlanded over the frame and showed a sensitive woman drawn with illness (it was made the year before her death, Pasha explained). Obviously the sons, who had their good looks from Pasha, had taken their gentle mildness from her. Other snapshots were brought out, a hundred of them, over which we pored for an hour. They showed the children at all ages and Pasha with his friend, the abdicated Umberto II. When we finished, Pasha gave me an assortment of the photographs to take back to America, portraits of himself and the mother, of all the children, including the priest, Aristide, on skis, and one of Ernesto and Arturo as small boys wearing their Fascist youth uniforms. They were pictures of an extraordinarily handsome family.

I was suddenly aware that it was late. In order to catch the evening train for Milan I would have to hurry. Ernesto and Arturo took me on a quick tour of the house. There was a large library with books filed in sections labeled "Italian," "Latin," "English," "French," and "German." I was shown the bedrooms of Pasha and his sons. Over the head of each bed hung a crucifix and a military rifle. "It is necessary to protect one's self," Ernesto said. "In a Communist town one cannot go to bed without a gun." He opened the bedside cabinet beside his own bed. On the lower shelf was a machine gun and a cartridge of bullets. "In case a revolution breaks out at night we are ready," Ernesto said. Each with his own arsenal, Pasha and his sons were prepared. The room of Aristide, the priest, was the same as the others.

We went into the cavernous cellar where room after room was filled with racks of wine, champagne, and cognac. Slyly Ernesto reached behind a wine shelf to press a secret button. A wall of wine bottles creaked open, revealing a dark secret chamber. "For hiding in the revolution," Ernesto said. "No one can ever find it." As the wall slid back into place, a dead swallow dropped from a wine shelf to my feet. "Umberto also keeps his treasures here," Ernesto said, kicking it aside.

Outside, Rocco rattled his chains as he leaped at me. Pasha urged me to return for a long visit in June when the Piedmont weather was "the most beautiful in Italy." If I could by chance invite Dean Acheson for a visit, he would be happy to prepare a worthy *festa* for him. Pasha slapped me on the back with lusty guffaws and Lidia led Ernesto and me through the gate. As we drove away, her laughter rang behind us. It was snowing again. We slithered through the storm. Ernesto informed me that I was not yet finished with the hospitality of Piedmont. Wine and food were not enough for a dear friend from America. Together we would go to the finest night club in Turin. The girls were young and beautiful; as a dessert to the feast, he would introduce me to any one of my choice.

I explained I had to take the train and there would not be time. Ernesto was disturbed. "Has something displeased you?" he asked. I replied nothing had; the visit had been a memorable one, but it was necessary for me to return to Milan. "What have I done to offend you?" he asked. "You are my dear friend. I have no friend so dear as you. It displeases me to have you leave offended."

Nothing I could say convinced Ernesto I was not offended with him. We drove in silence to Turin. We picked up my bag at the hotel and then went to the station where I had to wait a few minutes for my train.

"I know what offended you," Ernesto said. "It was the guns. You did not like the guns."

His dark olive eyes looked worried in the dim light of the station.

"I must tell you that when I was a soldier I was a very bad soldier," Ernesto said. "I hate war and killing. It is against my nature to take human life. I could not be a soldier again."

The train was loading, and I took his hand to say good-by.

"I have never killed a man," he said. "You must believe me, I could not kill a man. I am too much of a coward. Now I have told you the truth."

CHAPTER 6

MY FRIEND TULLIO

MY MOST INTIMATE FRIEND in Italy was Tullio Vacini of Florence. Our friendship was not a smooth one. We were vastly different; to each other we seemed to be exaggerated embodiments of our respective countries. He did not understand my American love for efficiency and order, my flat-footed candor and lack of subtlety. I was exasperated by his inefficient lack of what he called *"i virtuosi Americani,"* by his subtle evasiveness, his vagueness and irresponsibility. At times it seemed that instead of two individuals trying to get along, we actually were Italy and America trying to understand each other. It required tolerance, sympathy, patience, and humor. It was in humor that Tullio and I were most compatible.

I came upon him on a January Sunday in the Botticelli room of the Uffizi Gallery. He was a slight blond young man standing before the vast canvas *Spring.* English, I thought, for he wore a buff camel's-hair coat and carried a copy of George Orwell's *1984.*

A pair of middle-aged American tourists entered the room. The husband loitered before *The Birth of Venus;* his wife, busting out of a mink coat, nagged him impatiently on. "The gallery closes in half an hour," she scolded. "How can we see all the paintings if you keep stopping all the time?" The reluctant husband followed his wife into the next room.

"She will have to take herself on a bicycle," the young man said in the crisp staccato English of continental Europeans. "There are a thousand more paintings to see."

"I'll bet she sees them all," I said.

"Americans are very foolish peoples," the young man said. "They do not look at paintings, they count them." Now I was thinking he was German or Swedish.

"I am Italian," he said. I confessed I had been quite certain he wasn't.

78

"I suppose you think I should look like a brother to Anna Magnani," he said. "It is what Americans think, that we are all black-haired peasants who have no dignity or self-control."

"Fruit peddlers, gangsters, bootleggers, stone cutters, and opera singers," I said. "And you all eat spaghetti."

He looked at me with a pained expression. "Is that what Americans think?" he asked. "That is terrible! That is *just* terrible!"

"What do Italians think of as a typical American?" I asked.

"A rich man who has no culture and no soul," he said.

"That is terrible," I said. "That is just terrible!"

We laughed and moved into a gallery of Del Sartos. I realized I was up against an unusual individual. "Do you like Del Sarto?" he asked.

"Not especially," I said. "I like earlier painters better—like Angelico and Giotto."

"For an American your tastes are somewhat superior," he said. "Americans like best the sentimental Raphaels and Del Sartos."

"What," I asked, "do you have against Americans?"

"Their lack of humility," he said. "Because they know so well how to run machines and make money they think there is nothing else to know."

"Is there anything you like about them?" I asked.

"Yes," he said. "They are so sure of themselves. They are so hearty and they live passionately."

I said that passionate living was a relative thing, that for me it was being in Florence at that moment.

"For rich Americans it is easy to live passionately," he said. "For us Italians it is not possible. Our passion is despair, the passion of the poor."

The noon bell clanged. On our way out we stopped a moment before a Gozzoli painting of a Medici hunting procession. "I should have liked to live in those times," my companion said wistfully. "Then I should have lived passionately."

We introduced ourselves. He told me his name was Tullio Vacini. I invited him to lunch with me. He accepted with the alacrity of the lonely and offered to take me to a *trattoria* for students and workers where tourists were unknown. We walked along the Arno on the side where the sun had warmed the street. The city was in the midst of *carnevale*. Masked Florentines showered us with confetti and beat us with rubber truncheons. Under the Ponte Vecchio a regatta of festooned gondolas filled with musicians and singers glided down the river. We followed dominoed Pierrots and masked children to Santa Croce, the magnificent old church that is the Westminister Abbey of Florence. From the piazza, filled with carnival celebrants, we turned into a winding little street. Carts drawn by adolescent boys harnessed like donkeys rattled over the stones. At the end of the street was the *trattoria* run by a family Rosetti. It had no other name. Inside, nothing divided the eating room from the kitchen, where the Signora Rosetti and her daughters labored over steaming kettles. The tables were covered with white paper, which inspired customers to graphic and mysterious doodles, which they left for the pleasure of subsequent diners. The room was in an uproar of argument and laughter, and the sounds of hungry men enjoying their food.

We sat with three young workers who welcomed us by offering wine and a long loaf of bread. "In America do you have *pane* [bread] like this?" one asked, adding a phallic pun. The adolescent Rosetti daughter who waited on us giggled brazenly at my faulty Italian and then went into the kitchen and convulsed the family with an imitation of me. Our meal was excellent, from the thick *minestrone*, through a *bistecca* and salad, a liter of Chianti, and a dessert of fresh strawberries in Marsala wine.

Tullio told me his story. He was twenty-seven; during his childhood he lived with his parents and an older sister on a Tuscan farm. From his father, a member of an old Tuscan family, Tullio learned to hate Fascists. When the war started he joined a band of adolescent partisans hiding out in the mountains. At seventeen he was a seasoned soldier, shooting up Fascist ammunition depots and living off the generosity of peasants in the hills. At home the Fascists took the father to jail as a hostage for the son. Eventually the father died of a heart condition. Tullio spoke of him with tears in his eyes.

"I was too young to be prepared for my father to die," he said. "It was a very sad disappointment. I had never had conversations with my father about the important things in life. When he died my sadness was tremendous. He didn't know I loved him. I do not think much about a heaven when I die, except that I hope for one thing—I would like to talk with my father only long enough to tell him that I did love him."

When the war was over, Tullio enrolled as a student in architecture at the University of Florence. After two years of inflation his mother's money gave out, and she went to live with her daughter, now the wife of a Milanese candy manufacturer. She begged Tullio to come with her, but Tullio chose to stay in Florence. "Once you have lived here, it is hard to leave this beautiful city," he said. "Even though you know one day you may die violently in the decaying beauty."

In Florence there were always Americans. To Tullio, wandering sometimes hungry through the art galleries and along the Arno, they were "privileged angels to whom God has given the world like a play toy, to do with as they wish." So he might be able to speak to them, he studied English. "I began to burn with an urge to go to America," Tullio said, speaking in Italian. "Not to stay, for I am Italian and even now that Italy is so sick, I love her. But I should like to know the Americans in their homes and in their own country, to learn the secrets that make a people so strong. If I learn these things, perhaps I can return with their knowledge and with it help my people."

He thought he would study architecture in America, so he sought out facts on Frank Lloyd Wright and the architecture schools at Cornell and the University of Illinois. "In Italy are many people without houses," he said. "So I have great interest in your mass housing projects." He went to the office of the United States Information Service to apply for an exchange-student scholarship. He received no encouragement. "It is necessary for an Italian to know someone who is a good friend to the American diplomats to be considered for a scholarship," Tullio said. "I found I did not know such people."

Failing with a scholarship, Tullio worked out another plan to get to America. He took a job in the American Express office. His English made him valuable to his employers, but the hours were long and he had to drop his university studies. It was his duty to handle the banking accounts of American tourists, to cash their traveler's checks and to receive their American bank drafts and money orders and transfer them into lire. "There are Americans that gets to spend a thousand dollars a month," he said, expecting it would shock me as much as it did him. For upwards of fifty hours of this work a week, Tullio was being paid thirty thousand lire a month, or approximately forty-eight dollars. During the tourist season there were long hours of overtime, often until midnight. "There is so much unemployment in Italy, especially in the white collars," Tullio said, "that it is easy for American firms to take advantage. But it is a very bad example of capitalism in Italy, and it helps to make Italians into Communists."

Tullio's job with American employers brought the unanticipated hardship of a lonely life. "Because in Florence many people are Communist, I have lost all my student friends. They think when I work for Americans I am betraying my own people. The Americans with whom I work in the office know I am too poor to be their friend and they have no wish to see me when the hours of work are finished. Some of the patrons are very nice, but you do not make a friend of someone who is in Florence for a week. For two years I have not had a friend. I am lonely because I have wished to be the friend of Americans.

"I work very hard to please the American company. As the years go by, I am still hoping that I will one day yet make of myself an architect. When I make myself think realistically, I know it is a foolish hope and that I am born not to have a future. I am not a Communist, but there are many times I cannot help to think that I must be foolish not to be one. I guess I still like very much America, or I wouldn't suffer so much for her."

I poured us both some wine and we drank. "I will tell you the truth," Tullio said. "With America, we Italians are very much like a castoff lover. We say Americans who can have everything they want care only for what they can possess. We say they have no spirit and no love, and we are contemptuous of Americans who have no soul, for we are Italians who live in the soul. We say we do not care about the things that Americans care about. But that is not true. We care for them too, only we know we can never have them. So it gives us courage and satisfaction to speak with contempt of Americans who have no souls. We would like more than anything in the world to have the things they have, but since we cannot have them, we pretend to ourselves that we do not want them. We pretend to hate the Americans. But we do not hate them. To us they are really gods whom we worship and love. It is very hard for us to be honest. You see, we are also very proud, and it is easier for us to be Communist than to be honest."

Our three companions were finished with their eating. One passed among his friends a small can of American pipe tobacco. They rubbed it with their fingers to feel its texture, smelled it, brushed it against their faces, and finally filled their pipes with it. They brushed up every truant flake from the table and pressed it into the bowls, and then earnestly ignited it and began drawing in the smoke with beatific pleasure.

"We Italians are all very much alike," Tullio said. "These men are Communists. They have many bitter thoughts about America, and at their meetings their leaders tell them America is an evil country. But the tobacco is dear to them because it has come from your land. You see now how they *really* feel about America."

The owner of the tobacco told his fellows, "In America a man smokes a whole can each day."

One of his companions said, "It is not possible to smoke a whole can in a day."

"For an American it is quite possible," the owner said.

"Even if they have lost their faith in America, they have not lost their love," Tullio said. "An Italian thinks an American can do anything, even smoke all of a can of tobacco. We are simple-minded people. If you tell an Italian you take him to America, he thinks everything is solved for him. In America he will be rich and have a wonderful life with a can of tobacco every day. Going to America is for him like going to heaven after you die, except it is more difficult to go to America."

In my pocket were tickets for a matinee performance of *Falstaff* at the opera house. I asked Tullio if he could go.

"You mean you invite me?" He was incredulous. I explained that the tickets had been given me by the manager and I had no one to occupy one of the seats.

"If I go to the opera," he said, "I must save for two weeks to sit in the gallery. Who but an American could be so casual and say a half hour before a performance, 'Would you like to come and sit in the box?' You see what I mean when I say Americans live passionately?"

To get to the opera house at the other end of the town, we had to follow the Arno. While we walked he told me in English of his experiences with American patrons of the American Express. At the moment he was involved in an across-counter flirtation with an American girl who used her tangled finances as a daily excuse to come to him for consultation. Since Tullio knew the financial condition of almost every American in Florence, he knew that she was rich. "I think she has for me some love," Tullio said, "but I can't love girls who are rich from their beginnings. They are stupid."

How, I asked, had she revealed her stupidity?

"She think she is flattering me when she say, 'You don't seem Italian to me at all. You are so American!'" Tullio also knew an American lady journalist. "At least people *says* she is a journalist," Tullio said. "She is just out from the hospital where she went because she was bit by an Italian man."

"Where did the man bite her?" I asked.

"In her room," Tullio replied. "I think it would be very dangerous to bite her. You would doubtlessly get hydrophobia."

As we crossed Via Tornabuoni by the Ponte Trinita, a middle-aged American lady asked us for directions to Camillo's, a restaurant favored by American tourists. It was obvious that she took Tullio for an American. When we had given her the direction, she bubbled: "Don't you just love Florence?"

I said I did.

"It's so much nicer than any of the other cities," she said. "There aren't nearly so many Dagos." Then she left.

"What does 'Dago' mean?" Tullio asked when we had parted from her. I told him the word probably came from "Diego," the Spanish "James," and that it was used in America as a slang designation for Latin peoples, especially Italians.

"Why Italians?" Tullio asked. I couldn't say.

"I think Americans must feel about Italians like they feel about Jews and Negroes," Tullio said. "I think perhaps it is just as well I am not successful to go to America. I would always have fear they would lynch me."

Titto Gobbi sang *Falstaff* that afternoon and the performance was a memorable one. When we came out of the theater, evening mists covered the Arno. Gondolas slid silently under bridges; on the streets the carnival revelries continued. Confetti-covered, we walked through bombed ruins grown over with weeds and ferns. The moon lit it all like a ballet setting of decay by Eugene Berman. Tullio spoke of the cruel war years, of the longing in the mountains for the beautiful city, and, eventually when peace came, his return.

"It was all death," he said. "The people were dead and the city was dead. What was not dead was dying with despair."

Tullio's room was in a modest quarter beyond the Arno. We said good night at the Ponte Vecchio.

"When can we meet again?" I asked.

"Do you wish to see me again?" Tullio asked.

"Certainly. If we're to be friends we must see each other."

"You have already given me a great deal," he said. "Between friends there must be an exchange. What will I be able to do for you?"

"I should like you to think a little more kindly of Americans," I said.

Beneath the bridge some youths in a boat were singing a ribald Tuscan ballad. We listened until they passed by. "I think I must explain about Anna Magnani," Tullio said, "why it is so upsetting to sensitive and cultivated Italians that Americans like her. She is part of our postwar confusion. She has no dignity and is in rebellion against all formal life. For us this makes no enjoyment, only sadness, and we do not like Americans to think she is typical of Italy."

Every day of my two weeks in Florence was a rainy one. Frau Geisler, a German woman who ran the *pensione* in which I stayed, said it was the wettest winter of the twenty-seven she had lived in Italy. "Used to be ladies could go into the hills to pick anemone in January," she said. "Now the snow is melting in Siberia, and Florence is cold and foggy. Everything is *verkehrt*." Frau Geisler knew whom to blame. The Americans, naturally. "It's their atomic experiments have changed the weather. The rays Americans release make it rain."

Tullio and I lunched several times at Rosetti's. I became a family friend. This meant more generous portions and a visit with papa at the cash register. To eat at Rosetti's one had to make certain minor adjustments. Since there were no napkins it was advisable to carry Kleenex in one's pocket. It was best also not to wear one's best jacket, since the elbows were liable to soak up oil, wine, or most anything. In spite of these hazards, Rosetti's became one of my favorite eating places, and certainly the cheapest.

One day Tullio told me an American couple rushed into the American Express office to book immediate passage back to America. "They said that they will hurry home before the new world war starts," Tullio said. "Do American people really think there will be another war?" I said most Americans did not think so.

"I think they must," Tullio insisted. "It is sad. For many years in Italy we had nothing but war and poverty. In those years we think of America as a land where life is free and everyone is happy and working for peace. It is our only faith during the hard times. If America is not these things, then I am disappointed."

"America is these things," I said. "But ideals are useless without practical measures to defend them. Without the strength of America to oppose her, Russia might one day control Europe. If democracy continues in western Europe it is because America is ready to help defend it."

"You do not think what we have in Italy is democracy?" Tullio asked scornfully. "It is the ritual of democracy but it has not the heart of democracy."

"Remember that America does not govern Italy," I said. "The Italians are governing themselves. Even when it had the opportunity to govern, America preferred Italy to rule itself. Compare that with what Russia has made of Poland and Czechoslovakia and Hungary and you will see the difference."

"Like all Americans, you speak very logically," Tullio said. "But here in Italy head logic does not make converts. It is stomach logic that does."

Such arguments were long and exhaustive. To get out of the rain we entered Santa Croce and wandered among the tombs of Italy's immortals, Michelangelo, Galileo, Machiavelli, Rossini, Cherubini. The church was empty except for an old guide who slept with his head cradled on a little table of post cards and rosary beads.

Before the memorial to Leonardo da Vinci Tullio's eyes filled with tears. "We were once a great people," he said. "But we were also a foolish people and now we have only the memory of greatness. We are poorer than we know."

The next week-end was the last before Lent. I invited Tullio to go with me to Viareggio on the Riviera, where the *carnevale* was known to be the gayest in Italy. We took a train on Saturday afternoon, after he had finished at the American Express. The rain was pelting against the train windows, but Tullio assured me on the seacoast the weather would be clear. Sharing our compartment was a peroxided young woman reading *Ambra Eterna* by Kathleen Winsor and a brooding young man who was engrossed in *L'Enciclopedia Sessuale,* a book which he discreetly hid within a copy of the *National Geographic*. I was reading Aldington's biography of Michelangelo and Tullio studied a month-old copy of the *New Glarus Post,* the weekly journal of my Wisconsin home town. It carried the rather unusual story of a golden-wedding celebration in the church parlors at which twenty-five persons became sick with food poisoning. Tullio was incredulous. "Twenty-five *peoples* was poisoned," he exclaimed. "That is terrible!"

I said it was the sort of thing that happened now and then, and I went on reading.

"Those poor unhappy peoples," Tullio said. "Are none dead?"

"Apparently not," I said. He looked at the photograph of the hearty golden-wedding couple. "They don't look sorry at all," he said. "I think they'd be ashamed to smile."

"Why should they be ashamed?"

"For poisoning all those poor people!"

I said that they—the golden-wedding couple—hadn't poisoned the people, and anyhow, the photograph had been made before the poisoning.

"I suppose everyone made many excuses," Tullio said. He read the whole article again.

"But the journal says nothing at all about their feelings," he said.

"Whose?" I asked.

"The golden-wedding couple's," he said, and then added reflectively, "I suppose all those poor peoples that were poisoned felt badly in the stomach."

I said I was sure they did. He fell back into five minutes of thought. Then he asked, "If they—the golden-wedding couple—didn't poison all those poor peoples, who did?"

I tried to explain again that the poisoned food was an accident, that no one had deliberately contaminated it. This Tullio could not accept. In Italy poisonings were not accidental.

"It says the doctors were called to the church and some of the poor peoples went to the hospital in an ambulance. I suppose," he reflected, "there was a very great panic in the church."

I agreed there must have been. Tullio shook his head. "Too bad that none are dead," he said. "They could bury them under the floor of the church and the church would become a famous shrine."

Exactly, I said, as it would happen in Italy.

"Then they would all be Christian martyrs," Tullio said. "And perhaps one day saints." After much thought he arrived at a theory. "I suppose it was the Communists who poisoned them," he said. "Communists are against religion and against marriage. Naturally it was the Communists."

I said I doubted there were many Communists in New Glarus, Wisconsin. "You would not know," Tullio said. "Communists are everywhere, and you never know."

I thought that ended the discussion, but not quite. That evening in a Viareggio restaurant, Tullio ordered for my dinner a fish stew which he said was a specialty of the town. I seldom disdained an Italian dish, but the loathsome mess of octopus tentacles and tiny fish with their heads and viscera intact, challenged my stomach. I admitted to Tullio it didn't please me greatly. "Well, maybe you should go back to America," he said petulantly, "where they poison you in the church."

Despite Tullio's optimism about the weather, the rain continued to beat down. The night was cold and damp, with a wet wind lashing off the sea. The streets were deserted, so we went to a movie, *La Giungla d'asfalto* (*The Asphalt Jungle*). It was Tullio's favorite American film; he had already seen it twice.

"I think it is a true picture of American life," he said, "and not foolish fantasy like most American films." I tried to explain that *Asphalt Jungle*, *Naked City*, and the entire school of American pseudo-realistic cops-and-robbers films currently so popular in Italy were as distorted as the Esther Williams-José Iturbi technicolor daydreams he recognized as false. But he was not convinced. "In a materialist society like yours," he said, "there would naturally be much crime."

When we left the cinema we discovered the streets of the town had been roped off for the next day's *festa*. A *carabiniere* refused to let us cross and we were forced to walk several blocks out of our way to get to our hotel. There were no taxis and the rain poured down. My feet got wet and I began to sneeze. I cursed Italian inefficiency and the megalomania of petty officials.

Tullio listened politely, as he was accustomed to listening to complaining Americans at his desk every day. "It is true," he said when I finished, "Americans are accustomed to being efficient. It must be very hard for you to find happiness in Italy, where we have not learned the American efficiency."

I apologized. The rain, after all, was not his fault and neither was the idiocy of the policeman who had refused to let us walk the short route to the hotel.

Sunday dawned over the Mediterranean sunny and cold. Waves lashed green and foamy outside our window. The carnival was not to begin until the afternoon, so I suggested a morning visit to Pisa, five miles inland. It was a pleasant excursion. The day was wild and windy, the sky blue and cloudless. Pisa appeared badly bombed and dismally poor. The family crest of the rapacious Medici who once ruled the city still hung from her gates and palaces. Pisa's campanile, or leaning tower, is, even more than Rome's Colosseum, the most famous travel symbol of Italy. It stands on the Piazza dei Miracoli, "the square of the miracles," a green field of hardly ten acres, which it shares with the beautiful cathedral, a medieval cemetery known as the *camposanto,* and the majestic circular baptistry. Against the emerald grass and azure sky of this clean, wind-swept day, the white buildings of beautiful lace patterned from stone were an incomparable vision. Like tourists for seven hundred years, we avoided walking under the listing side of the tower, though the guide assured us it was not scheduled to fall for another three hundred years.

The terrible toll of the war on Italian art was heartbreakingly evident in the cemetery, which was almost completely bomb destroyed. A guide showed us prewar photographs of frescoes by Gozzoli, Memmi, and Lorenzetti and the graceful Gothic wall which enclosed them. What four centuries of wind and rain hadn't accomplished, bombs had. Much of the delicate wall still stood, but inside, the war had been as vengeful on the dead as it had been on the living. The slender arches, the noble sculpture, and the priceless frescoes were a pile of decaying rubble, and pools of water lay in the shattered marble sarcophagi. It was Tullio's first visit to Pisa since the war and he stood before the ruin in somber horror. "The world is very cruel to Italy," he said. I looked at it with a sickening guilt.

Workmen had begun the reconstruction of the *camposanto,* but as usual in Italy, it was moving very slowly for lack of money. "I am wondering if it will be finished before war destroys it again," Tullio said.

A guide demonstrated the remarkable acoustics of the baptistry by miming birdcalls. He described to us how on feast days a children's choir sang Bach fugues in the rotunda and how like paradise it sounded. In the cathedral we wandered through a Mass, looking at paintings by Del Sarto, a heartbreaking deposition by Sodoma, and the suspended bronze lamp which inspired Galileo's gravitation theory. Under the lamp were two chimney sweeps, a wisp of a man and his tiny beady-eyed son. Their eyes gleamed white out of faces black with soot. With their brooms and buckets they knelt to pray. Later on the street I saw the little one surveying a confectioner's stall with the hopelessness of one who knows he cannot buy. I told him to make his choice. He said nothing, but he hurried to scoop up what he could as if he feared the offer might be withdrawn. Then he followed his father down the street, clanging his bucket and brooms as he ran.

"No one knows where chimney sweeps sleep," Tullio said. "No one has ever seen one sleep. It is a national mystery."

"Perhaps they sleep in chimneys," I said, a flippancy which Tullio chuckled over for a quarter hour. We stepped into another bomb-damaged church. The Mass was just coming to an end. Among the sacred memorabilia inside was a horizontal statue of a dead child, a little girl saint in a nun's robe, with her hands crossed piously. Between her toes devout Pisans had tucked sprigs of yellow field flowers.

"She died defending her honor, no doubt," I said.

Tullio started to laugh and then quickly checked his mirth. "That is a terrible thing to say in a church," he scolded.

Like many educated Italians, Tullio talked for hours about the hypocrisy and social backwardness of the church, but like all of them, when he was in a church he was essentially devout. In the church and on the streets outside, I observed an unusual number of Negroid children, a startling sight in the Italian landscape. Often four or five played in a gang, or, as in the case of little girls, they walked home from church with gray grandmothers in black dresses. All were about six or seven years old.

"They are common war souvenirs in this part of Italy," Tullio said. "There was in Pisa an encampment of American Negro fliers, who planted their seed over the countryside and left a flourishing harvest. It was rumored the Negroes were exceptional in their manhood and the girls were crazy for them. A girl is proud to have a *bambino negro* and the children are very much loved."

I thought of young fathers returned to the racial confinements of American civilian life, and wondered if they ever gave a thought to their strikingly beautiful *bambini* playing their noisy games in the bombed ruins of Pisa and the Tyrrhenian coast.

In the morning, Viareggio had been cold and empty; when we returned, the city was alive with fantasy. The Italian's delight in the bizarre has its richest outlet in the spectacle of *carnevale*. In Viareggio a guild of artisans does nothing but prepare masks and *carri*—the American word "float" does not do these incredible carriages justice—for *carnevale*, and when *carnevale* is over they dismantle their creations and begin designs for the next year. On the Corso—a wide boulevard along the sea—hundreds of masked Pierrots and satyrs pursued screeching Columbines and nymphs; cloaked villains danced lewdly with daintily periwigged ladies, some of whom, Tullio said, were masked youths, though I would not have guessed it. Courts of masked knights rode steeds sagging with armor. Bands of hucksters sold wickered bottles of Chianti, sweets, sausages, bags of confetti, and garlands of roasted nuts which people wore around their necks like *leis*.

The *sfilata delle maschere* was just beginning. How can one describe this great parade of masks? A toy parade in which Ringling Brothers and the Sadler's Wells ballet have joined with Macy's parade? A Lewis Carroll spectacle by Rabelais? Neither does it justice. The *carri*, drawn by spans of six or eight white oxen, were populated with a shamelessly bawdy and dazzling papier-mâché zoo of animals and people, so large that human beings appear like insects beside them. Everything on them was in motion, like gargantuan wind-up toys in which the springs never run down. Eyes rolled, eyebrows leered, and red tongues smacked red lips. Some which might have been designed by *The New Yorker* magazine's Charles Addams were full of the sadism and cruelty which always make Italians laugh. Chickens ate human beings and mice ate cats, fish caught men on hooks, bears made women dance with whips, and dogs locked children in cages. A human Petruchio in a red silk shirt beat his mother-in-law with a rawhide whip, shouting obscenities at her until his voice was a rasp and feeding her finally to beasts which disdained her as too unpleasant to eat. The crowds in the street enjoyed even more the *carro* satirizing pregnancy, always a joke to a people who industriously keep themselves overpopulated. In this one a toothless old couple wearing long nightcaps swarmed with some thirty brawling *bambini* while a stork hovered sinisterly over their bed.

Americans were favored subjects. On one *carro*, the figure of a drunken American sailor guzzled huge bottles of rum while a monkey in the palm of his hand drank with equal thirst from a smaller bottle. A dozen voluptuous Negro women caressed both of them. The inference of this tableau was that American sailors reveled in Negro harems. It passed before a gray Italian grandmother who chortled richly, and the pretty dark-skinned little mulatto boy whose hand she held screamed with joy.

Animals and vegetables fifteen feet high strolled amiably through the crowd. Rabelaisian female figures adroitly flipped pumpkin breasts and buttocks and licked giant ice-cream cones. Tullio pointed to worn-out shoes and the tattered felt slippers which protruded from under the costumes and masks.

"You see, it is a sad merriment," he said. "The people of Viareggio are very poor. They live from tourists and from fishing. Since the war there have not been many tourists and they have had to fish more. A noble *carnevale* is their tradition and they will remain poor for a whole year to make it possible. Then for one week a year they can pretend they are not poor. That is why the old people seem sad today and only the young people have *lo spirito del carnevale*. The old people are not fooled."

The energies of the young gave no signs of abating. As the afternoon waned and the ribaldry increased with the wine consumption, it seemed only an intercession of the gods could save Viareggio from orgiastic self-destruction. The intercession came suddenly without warning, when the wind blew a salty gust of rain in from the sea. The parade stopped. Crowds tumbled pell-mell toward shelters. Hucksters pathetically gathered up their stock of melting candy and paper hats. From our hotel window we looked down on the Corso. Abandoned *carri* gleamed in the rain; grotesques leered obscenely as their sodden papier-mâché faces sagged. Unperturbed by the storm eight drunken youths square-danced lustily to a Gene Autry record broadcast from a sound truck.

I took a train to Rome, and Tullio returned to Florence. During the next three months, which I spent in Sicily and Naples, I received one letter from Tullio. It was written in English and said: "I have been missing your company very much. Girls are very rare. One of them, an American painter, has now an exhibit. Her paintings are so modern that they stand in the future; they don't enter history yet. She walks in a dreamy way, like a thick fluid. She once had eyes only for Enzo, who was a soldier in Africa. He is a painter and writer but mostly he is a bum. He cares not for her painting and to her he is as rude as a wolf can be to a kitten. I would like to have comforted her, but instead she chose to share an apartment with an American boy and the look of internal consuming pain is now gone from her face. There is a new bar called 'John's.' It is American, intellectual, sophisticated, and poor. The American students fluctuate in the atmosphere, drink *cappucini*, and stare at each other. So I now read *Mrs. Chatterly Loves*, but it is not very daring so I think it must be the washed one."

Early in May, Tullio and I met in Siena for a week-end, and I returned to Florence with him. It was still raining in the Arno valley. Rain fell every day that season until June. Frau Geisler's theory had grown in popularity as the weather continued bad. Shopkeepers, waiters, and priests were all certain America's atomic rays were causing it. "There was snow on Easter Sunday to prove it," a taxi driver told me. "There isn't a grandmother in all of Tuscany old enough to remember snow on Easter." In spite of the weather, Tullio and I went sight-seeing week-ends. His deep love for art and his sense of humor made him a most pleasant companion.

We went to the convent of San Marco to see the tranquil and serene art of Fra Angelico. The paintings were remote and cool; the nativities and assumptions, magnificent as Bach chorales and full of New Testament love and purity, lit the dark monks' cells with their own light. I loitered in the cubicles, pondering the brooding secrets of the generations of monks who prayed there and listened to the canaries singing in the larch trees in the convent garden.

Tullio was impatient. "Too sweet," he mumbled. "Too gentle."

He was preoccupied with two matrons wearing identical picture hats who were following us through the cells. "When rich ladies have dogs, the dogs always look like them, and I am thinking one of these ladies is the other lady's dog," he said.

"Which one is the dog?" I asked.

"It is hard to tell," Tullio said, "because they make change every day. One day one is lady and the other is dog and the next day it is reversed. This morning I think one say 'Today I will be lady' and the other say, 'No, today I wish to be lady,' so they decided that for today they will both be ladies. Tomorrow they will both have to be dogs."

Downstairs in the convent chapter house things were bustling despite the St. Peter with his finger to his lips which Angelico painted above the door to shush everyone who entered. A great nun bounced into the room, followed by a string of black-smocked little schoolboys at whom she boomed like an Old Testament prophet, "Look! Look at the sweet holy Virgin flying like an angel into paradise!"

"She did not shave this morning," Tullio said, reflecting on the nun's mustache. The nun herded her *bambini* to a Last Judgment and pointed with a lusty sort of triumph to the nude, writhing bodies in Angelico's inferno. "See the serpents eating the eyes of bad boys," she said. "Look at the devils carving them to pieces before the fire."

"Listen to the stories she tells!" Tullio exclaimed. "I am sure the little boys can't sleep at night. They will all grow up hysterically. I will never give *my* little boys for school to a nun."

The nun moved excitedly to the paradise side of the panel and pointed to angels flapping their wings like drunken butterflies as they embraced in warm welcome and then danced in ring-around-a-rosy formation on the shimmering golden stairs. Tullio's attitude toward the nun continued uncharitable. "She is hoping heaven is a place where someone more than Jesus will love her," he said. He had had enough of Fra Angelico. "It is very fine and it is very pretty," he said. "But now I am sick of gentle sweetness. I now need some flesh. Let us go to Michelangelo."

Across the piazza was the Galleria dell' Accademia, the home of Michelangelo's *David*. There is a copy of Florence's most famous statue in front of the Palazzo Vecchio; another overlooks the city from the Piazza Michelangelo beyond the Arno. Now for the first time, I saw the original. It is the statue of a boy upon whom manhood has begun to superimpose itself. There is something troublesome about it; perhaps it is too long on beauty and too short on strength, a Narcissus instead of a David. If, as many say, *David* is Michelangelo's most beautiful work, the four prisoners in the same gallery are his greatest. These remnants from the ill-fated tomb for Julius II are said to be *sbozzo*—unfinished—but if this is true, one can be grateful for the halting of Michelangelo's chisel. The powerful half-formed figures, straining to liberate themselves, are like embryos gasping for life in the terrible agony of birth, struggling with every bit of their human strength for freedom from the terrible stone.

"It is always so," Tullio said. "Men will never be free. We are prisoners in the stones when we are born. When God made man He didn't finish him; He left him to finish His creation himself. But man is not able. He has not the strength to do it."

"Every age, before and after Michelangelo, has had its poets and its prophets who look beyond the world and are free," I said.

"Poets understand their prisons," Tullio said. "They are prisoners even more than men, who do not."

"Perhaps that is the challenge of life. As long as there is one man in the world who can see beyond the stone, there is hope."

"There is no hope," Tullio said. "See how God made the stone stronger than man."

At the end of the gallery, bathed in white light like a pagan princeling, stood the *David*.

"He is very American," Tullio said, "so young and so sure of himself. The prisoners are us Europeans. We know very well the stone."

Looking at the *David*, I realized now why he disturbed me. It was his shining virtue, his calm and selfish aloofness. He held his freedom too lightly. "He could never have known Goliath," I said.

"He is too young to know about prisons," Tullio said. "But he looks upon the men in the stones, and perhaps one day he will understand their prison. Then perhaps he will help them."

"It will take a long time," I said.

"Perhaps not so long," Tullio said. "Have you noticed the sadness that is already in his eyes?"

It was enough art for one day. We crossed the Ponte Trinità to Camillo's, where we ate chicken. As I snapped a joint apart, Tullio winced. "If you please, do not do that," he said. "For I am thinking how the poor chicken must feel and I cannot eat him." Sharing our table were a white-haired old American lady and her Italian gigolo. The rouge glowed on the woman's parchment face, bracelets jangled on her plump arms, feathers nodded on her hat. She wanted it known she was a gay one, as she compared French mushrooms with Italian ones, and Santa Barbara, California, with Florence. She kept the youth's plate filled with food and his glass with wine. He was the traditional type, dark and handsome, probably twenty-five years old. He said not a word, only nodded dutifully. "One has comforts in Santa Barbara one does not have in Florence," she said coyly. "But in Florence the men are so heavenly." The youth lowered his eyes with becoming modesty. When they were gone, Tullio said sadly, "There are even worse things for poor young Italians than working for the American Express."

One Sunday we went to Lucca. This gloomy, restless town on a plain just north of Pisa is a curious anachronism. Its dark medievalism suggests it must be the least progressive of all Italian cities, a stagnation of the Middle Ages inside ponderous ramparts. Though it is little known to tourists, one hears more English spoken in Lucca than in any Tuscan city except Florence. Signs say "American Bar" and "American Restaurant"; monuments and landmarks carry explanatory plaques in perfect English. The town's sad pall of poverty is a curious deception. Lucca is prosperous. Her ninety thousand citizens possess more property than those of any other Tuscan town her size.

The prosperity and the familiarity with English are the result of Lucca's private relations with the United States. In Roman times Lucca was an important city, later she became overcrowded and poor. To improve their fortunes, Luccans became wanderers. In the early part of this century, young men went to America to work. There they lived frugally, saved their money, and when they had made their fortune, they returned to the town of their birth. The older men of Lucca either have been to the United States, or have relatives there. Those who returned were drawn back by a nostalgia for Lucca. Today it is their nostalgia for America which stirs them to speak English, to organize American *società*, to gather in the bars and cafés to spin tales of American triumphs.

The cloudy day was in keeping with the dismal sobriety of the town. The buildings were of a uniform grayness; no trees relieved the dreary landscape. It was two weeks until the provincial elections, and the walls were covered with political posters. As in other Tuscan cities most posters were Communistic and anti-American. The most frequent poster carried pictures of a loaf of bread and an atom bomb. "In 1948 they promised us bread," it shouted in bold black letters, "now they send us arms. Vote against the government of war." Other posters proclaimed "the scandal of the murder of innocents in Korea" and asked the citizenry to "Vote against the American party (Christian Democrats) and win freedom." Two nonpolitical posters appeared frequently about the town. One announced the football game that afternoon between Lucca and Bologna at Bologna, and another, black-bordered, announced the death of "the little pupil Giulio Rosada, twelve years old, torn away from the love of his parents by a very cruel disease, leaving in most profound grief which will never be comforted, his father, Alberto, his mother, Giorgia Renata Bernardini, his brother, Giovanni, his grandmother, Pia, and other relatives who are inconsolably grieved and who ask for your prayers."

Except for beggars, the streets were empty. It was the hour of Mass; women were worshiping in church and men in barbershops. In a provincial Italian town on a Sunday morning the busiest people are priests and barbers. An Italian man's hair is his pride and joy; in the Sunday barber ritual of laying on of hands in the cult of Narcissus, every man is a worshiper. We counted six barbershops in one block, all filled. Tullio, who worried over his own receding hairline, said, "A man's wife can be unfaithful. His children can die of plague. But nothing is so tragic as for a man to become bald. I think he would rather have a leg amputated than lose his hair." Barbershops also serve men as clubs and a refuge from women. Said Tullio, "In a barbershop men escape the prison of marriage and find romance with a mirror for a mistress."

Lucca has one artistic distinction. The façades of her churches, built in the Pisan manner, are a rich compound of columns, flutings, carvings, and graphite inlays. Because they have not always been kept in repair, they appear older than other Tuscan churches. Abundant rains sprout clumps of grass and shrubs in their walls and crevices so that they appear to be covered by a green mold. The gloomy interiors are disappointing. Only the cathedral has a shabby elegance, distinguished by a rose window which lights the nave with a wine glow. Unlike other cities of Tuscany and Umbria, Lucca never developed a school of painting, but she has some unusual sculpture. The cathedral has the celebrated tomb of Ilaria del Carretto, with the noble lady's effigy lying on a pair of marble cushions, her dog guarding her feet. In a small chapel we found an elegant black Christ with plaited hair and beard and a full-flowing mustache carefully curled. Of Byzantine origin, this shining ebony Jesus was as richly clothed and jeweled as a Romanov ruler. "To Luccans a black Jesus must seem quite natural," Tullio said. "For them black is a way of life."

Everyone we met was dressed in black. The beggars who followed us were like ravens. In every city beggars have their own methods. In Naples women carry infants; on Rome's Via Veneto they presumptuously pin a flower to your lapel. Here in Lucca there were two kinds: the blessing sellers who offered little slips of printed prayers; and the accordion players of whom we were never out of earshot. One escorted us to the Roman amphitheater. The great arena was a depressing symbol of Italian history. Having been in pre-Christian centuries a theater for chariot races, it was now a congested, unsanitary public market known as the Piazza del Mercato. A graceful white marble trough—for watering the horses of the ancient games no doubt—provided the communal waters. The old theater was like a giant insect colony, with every crevice a dwelling. Laundry flapped from ropes strung between cavelike cubicles; through open windows we caught the sights and sounds of crowded, impoverished living. In an archway, dank with urine, a ragged girl, hardly fifteen, tried to entice us inside. Tullio spoke with her. A hundred lire—sixteen cents—would have been enough. I gave it to her and we fled, the girl's eyes following us, full of consternation and wounded pride.

Hiding in a small piazza, called the Orange Tree, we found a restaurant with the name of Passeggero. Italians are master restaurateurs, but in the crowded tourist lanes the corruption of serving as little as possible for as much as possible has spread like a virus. This is based on the assumption that every tourist—especially if he is American—is a money-happy imbecile. The Passeggero was in the proud old tradition of superb food at moderate prices. Along its walls were shelves piled with wine bottles; in the center, tables were loaded with *antipasto*, cheeses, and fruit. After the *antipasto*, we had *scaloppine* in Marsala, tender asparagus picked in the morning, herb salad, and finally strawberries swimming in lemon juice. This with all the Chianti we could drink cost us six hundred lire, or just under a dollar. It was one of my most memorable Italian meals.

The Sunday guests were mostly family groups of prosperous bourgeois. We watched a party in which the women seemed to be related, probably sisters. There were three of them, a trio of overfed, overdressed, overloquacious matrons flashing diamonds and outshouting each other in their high-pitched excitement. Their dark-suited husbands meekly fed the children. Tullio was fascinated. Like all Italians, he loved children and spoke often of his misfortune at being twenty-seven and a childless bachelor. His plans were to give himself three more years of *libertà* to improve his fortunes, then, at thirty, no matter how poor, to marry.

Watching the elegant matrons, he said, "How will I ever be able to support one of those? And if I can support her, how will I be able to live with her." He pondered it for a moment and then said, "I think in America it is safer to marry. In America you divorce quite easily. In Italy marriage is for life, like an imprisonment."

After coffee and a smoke at an outdoor bar we crossed town to the church of San Francesco. The piazza outside the church reverberated with a pair of querulous male voices. They came from the amplified sound track of a movie, broadcast by the Francescan brothers to entice people into the movie theater they operated in the convent. According to the posters, the friars were showing *The Dangerous Widow* with Giovanni e Pinotto, as Abbott and Costello are known in Italy. The shouting was that of dubbers who had recorded the sound track in Italian. Outside the church a crowd of scolding women beat at the locked church door.

"Closed is the house of God! Open is the cinema!"

"We wish to pray to the saints, and they give us Giovanni e Pinotto!"

"Giovanni e Pinotto at fifty lire to fill their pockets and stomachs!"

"Come on out and face us, you eunuchs, frightened of women."

A woman explained the monks had locked their church to increase attendance at the movie. Believing in the omnipotence of Americans, she turned to me for help. I pulled on a bell cord they had been ringing without success. *"Un Americano,"* they shouted. "An American wishes to enter!"

In a moment a bald little brother looked worriedly through the peephole of the convent gate. It reminded me of when, as a schoolboy, I had been taken to a Chicago speak-easy.

"The American wishes to enter," the women clamored. "Let the American into the house of God!"

The monk was plainly agitated and the women burst into laughter.

"*Vedi*! Look at little Giovanni! Where is your brother Pinotto? Making water behind the bushes perhaps?"

He opened the gate a trifle and beckoned Tullio and me to hurry. We entered and he slammed the gate in the faces of the clamoring women. Through the peephole he told them the church would be open at four o'clock.

The convent garden was somewhat gone to seed. Two monks were playing at bowls, rolling wooden balls the size of croquet balls over the grass. Our man, bowing us into the church like an oriental butler, apologized for the *confusione* outside. "Habitual troublemakers, these women, not even communicants of the parish," he said. Like many Franciscan churches, this one was impressively expansive. Rich windows cast a warm light over the interior; a tablet decorated with *fasci* and dated 1927 announced that Luigi Boccherini, the composer, had been born in Lucca in 1745. The art and decoration were in a cluttered, baroque style. Tullio, a better art lover than a Catholic, passed quick judgment. "Too much detail," he said. "Catholicism becomes no more a religion of the spirit, but a worshiping of ugly idols. It is such things that will finally make a *protestante* of me." The confessionals for men and women were separated. "I have stopped some years going to confession," Tullio said. "You tell a priest you have fornicated and he say, 'My, my,' and give you a punishment of twenty-four paternosters to say, and then you are pure enough to go and fornicate again. I now confess straight to God and it works better."

Outside, the women were suddenly quiet. Looking out, we saw them bowed in prayer. Coming across the piazza was a disturbing apparition. A band of men in deep yellow robes and hoods, with slits for eyes and nose, carried flaming torches and chanted like fakirs at a city wall. It looked so much like a Ku Klux Klan rite, my flesh turned cold.

It was a funeral, Tullio explained, a special funeral for which the family had called in a professional society, the *misericordia*. Black horses drew a black and gold open hearse. The coffin in it was a small one. Behind it, school children chanted prayers under the direction of priests who walked backward like troop leaders in a boy-scout parade. The undersized coffin and the wailing children told the story. It was the funeral of the little pupil Giulio Rosada, torn away by a very cruel disease.

Behind the children marched the relatives, first the men, then the black-robed women, keening softly. We bowed our heads, and when it passed we fell into the procession and followed it across town, winding through narrow streets, past barbershops and bars, where men listened on the radio to the football game in Bologna, to the Piazza San Michele, where a crowd of men was gathered for a political speech. We dropped out to listen to the shouting young man on the platform. Behind him hung a canvas banner of the hammer and sickle.

"Do the workers of Lucca desire to go to war for imperialist America?" the speaker called out.

"No! No!" the men shouted back.

"Do the workers of Lucca desire *una vita di pace*, a life of peace?"

"*Si! Si!*" they chorused.

"Then vote against the Christian Democrats, *il partito Americano che vuole la guerra* [the American party of war]! Vote against *la casa bianca* [the White House]!"

The crowd cheered. Five old men sat silently at a sidewalk table. A bottle of wine stood before them. One of them asked if I was an American. When I said I was he stood up with much dignity and took my hand.

"My name is Franco Tocino," he said in English. "It's good to shake the hand of an American."

I asked if he had been in America.

"For fifteen years I was conductor on the New Haven Railroad to Boston," he said. "Mr. Morgan went to Boston on my train in his private *carrozza*, a palace on wheels, and rode back to New York the same night. He gave me ten dollars to keep strangers out of his car. I remember the students from Yale College, whole *carrozze* of jolly boys hiding gin under the cushions. Then Mr. Roosevelt is President and is no longer necessary to hide bottles. *Un bravissimo*, Signor Roosevelt, a noble man. Once when he take train in Boston I give him my arm to help him. He ask me my name. He smiles like I am his friend and say, '*Grazie, Franco!*' I am only man in Lucca who hold the hand of Roosevelt. There was great sorrowing in Lucca when Roosevelt died."

Signor Tocino introduced me to his cronies, each of whom shook my hand. One named Guiseppe Rossi said, "I work for Mr. Rockefeller in Jersey City. Is good to talk to American." Of the other three, one had been a miner in Wilkes-Barre, another a mason in Philadelphia, and the last a meat cutter in Chicago. "Is best country in world, America," the meat cutter said proudly. "I have grandson is student in Chicago University."

Why, I asked, had none of them become American citizens?

"We think is good for a man to die where he is born," Franco Tocino said. "We save our money and come back. Was great foolishness."

"Great foolishness," the meat cutter repeated. "Is best country in world, America."

On the piazza the speaker was bellowing about Wall Street dollar imperialism.

"He does not think America is best country in world," I said.

Franco Tocino's eyes flashed angrily. "Is great confusion!" he said. "In America I live in Bridgeport. I have house. Earn money six times what is possible in Lucca. My son is born in Bridgeport and goes to school in Bridgeport. On Memorial Day he speak the Gettysburg speech of Mr. Lincoln. I do not hear him for it is big day for railroad. But he speak the Gettysburg speech for me at home. I am very proud."

On the piazza the speaker shouted that a vote for De Gasperi was a vote for America and a vote for war; a vote for the Communists was a vote for peace and a vote for bread.

"My son still likes to make speeches," said Franco Tocino. "But I am no more proud. He has forgotten the Gettysburg speech of Mr. Lincoln. It is great confusion. A great confusion!"

It was time for the return train to Florence. We said good-by to the five American Italians. The political rally was behind us, now we heard the radios in the barbershops turned to the football game. Lucca was beating Bologna. An accordion wailed and a beggar tugged at my sleeve. Black-veiled women were returning from the funeral of the little pupil torn away. Death seemed everywhere in the gray town. As we passed the cathedral I thought of the black Jesus hanging inside. Near the station we were accosted by two flashy redheaded signorinas wearing tight plaid skirts. We extended our regrets and their derisive laughter followed us to the station.

The train pulled through acres of bombed ruins. It struck me as strange that Lucca, a town of gray people locked inside a gray wall, without industry and without soldiers, should have been bombed. I asked Tullio if he knew the reason.

It was the wrong thing to ask. He looked up from the *Time* magazine he had bought in the station. "That is for you to answer," he said sharply. "You are American."

I was taken back by his antagonism. His mood had been sullen since the political meeting.

"I do not know who bombed Lucca or why," I said.

"The Americans did," Tullio said. "The Americans bombed everything. They didn't need a reason." He gave me a bizarre account of the destruction of Empoli. "It was a small town without military objectives," he said. "The flying fortresses came on the day after Christmas, just as the peoples was eating their lunch. They destroyed Empoli and killed most of the peoples."

The story of bomb-happy American fliers on a destruction binge was a familiar one in Italy and I did not believe it. "Undoubtedly it was difficult in the early days of the war for bombardiers to know what was a military objective and what wasn't," I said.

"Of course, Americans with their high ideals were very careful where they dropped bombs," he said scornfully.

"How can you feel this way and yet plan to go to America?" I asked.

"To think of going to America is foolish," he said. "America doesn't want Italians. It doesn't want me. How can I be the friend of a country that doesn't wish me to be a friend?"

I looked into his magazine and saw what was upsetting him. He was reading a story on the McCarran Act, which limited the immigration of Italians in America to a pre-World War I ratio.

"If you want a world of peace, then you must share," Tullio said. "If America will not realize the world is changing and insists on keeping a standard of living as it was fifty or a hundred years ago, the world is not going to like it. You have everything in America. In Italy the peoples is poor and has nothing. But you tell us, 'Now be good and please stay home and have peace.' How can America speak of one world and yet close her own doors? What is the sense of saying, 'One world—but it must be *outside* our gates'? You tell peoples, 'We are Americans, and we are boss. We want you all to be good and have one world and *don't annoy us*!' That already makes two worlds, not one world!"

It was twilight. The train skimmed over fields of blood-red poppies which grow like clover in Italy. Tullio returned to *Time*. In a moment he exclaimed, "What foolish things they give for the American peoples to read!"

He read aloud a report that Italy, under the leadership of Premier de Gasperi, was behind America's struggle against Communism. "The Italian government says, 'Yes, if there is war, Italy will fight,' " Tullio said. "But did de Gasperi ask the Italian people? Doesn't he know that they are tired and they do not wish to fight? In Italy there is no democracy to fight for. The government which the Americans have supported is a government for the church and rich people who were the friends of Mussolini. Italians have nothing to lose, and people with nothing to lose do not fight. We care only for our home and to have food to eat. We care nothing about Russia. But the Russians speak with us about the struggle between rich people and poor people. How *they* got everything and they do not want *us* to have anything. I do not believe the Russians mean this, but many people believe them. They do not know what Communism will bring them, but they know it can be no worse than what they have now. So they think maybe they will take a chance and find out. It is a very little gamble. Is much better if the American journals listen to the heart of the Italian people than to Mr. de Gasperi. If there is another war I know the Italian people will not fight anyone but the Italian government, and Mr. de Gasperi knows it too."

I knew the government in Rome had little contact with Italy's lower-class majority. But in the matter of the people's loyalty to their government, I believed Tullio's pessimism as exaggerated as the Prime Minister's optimism. I had been wondering for several weeks how Tullio would vote in the forthcoming elections and now I asked him.

"It is very difficult to vote between Christian Democrats and Communists when you do not like both," he said. "If you were an Italian, which party would you vote for?"

It was a tough question and a fair one.

"I think I would vote for the Socialist party," I said. "I have two reasons to support my choice. First, in a country so overpopulated as Italy and so limited in its resources, Socialism is the only way to assure some reasonable distribution of goods. Second, it appears to me that of all the Italian parties, the Socialists come closest to the principles of American democracy as set forth by Thomas Jefferson and Abraham Lincoln."

"A vote for the Socialists serves Communism," Tullio said. "It is just like a vote for the Monarchists, neo-Fascists, or any other small party. It is a vote for Communism because it breaks up the anti-Communist vote."

I asked him again. "What party will you vote for?"

"I am not going to vote at all," he said.

Tullio's hostility to America was typical of the young and educated Italian. As he himself pointed out, it was based largely on personal frustrations. Obviously, the best way to overcome it would be for Tullio to make a trip to the United States. I decided to look into the possibilities of a scholarship in an American university for him. At the Fulbright office in Rome, I was told if I could arrange for a scholarship for him in America, the Fulbright committee would provide his transportation to and from America. I wrote a letter on Tullio's behalf to the president of my own university, which was known for its school of architecture. When I told Tullio I'd sent the letter, his attitude toward America began to mellow. He worried about his English and studied it evenings and on Sundays. He had no doubts that the scholarship would be granted, for he shared the Italian faith that every American is a miracle worker. He talked of his departure as if it were assured.

"I suppose the students at the university will call me a Dago," he said. I said I doubted it, that the term was generally applied to lower-class Italians and seldom used by university students.

"I shall not mind if they do," he said. "I know the American students will certainly make fun of me, but inside me, I shall perhaps secretly make fun of them. I should, however, be quite sad if the girls thought of me as a Dago."

I assured him beyond a doubt that he would have great success with coeds.

Late in the summer, Tullio and I made two more Sunday trips. The first was to San Gimignano, a town famous for its towers. There was no mistaking the town as we approached it on a bus. We were still miles away when its towers rose from the gray Tuscan mists like St. John's vision of paradise. As we came closer it looked remarkably like the silhouette of Manhattan. The spectacular sky line dates to the twelfth and thirteenth centuries when it was the fashion among the nobility of San Gimignano to build square towers beside their houses. At the peak of San Gimignano's prosperity there were sixty-five such towers. When they began to topple over and make life in the town perilous, most of them were dismantled. Today fifteen remain.

The towers bring many tourists to San Gimignano. In recent years they have also brought motion-picture companies, who use the town as a ready-made set for historical films. Much of the English film *Prince of Foxes* was shot in San Gimignano, and just before our visit an Italian company had made a film with Alida Valli and the French actor Jean Marais. The people are very proud of their film fame. Most of the town's wine growers and shopkeepers have acted as film supers.

It was, indeed, a town rich in atmosphere. Ivy, shrubs, and grass grew from the moist chinks and crevices of the towers, so that they seemed molded with age. This phenomenon, Tullio said, was attributed to the mystical powers of Fina, one of the town's more curious saints. He told me her story:

Fina was a beautiful thirteenth-century virgin. One day at the public well she was presented with an orange by a young man who loved her. She took the fruit home to her mother, who explained to Fina the facts of life and what terrible things could happen to a girl who accepted an orange from a man. She felt she must do penance for the sin of accepting the orange, so she lay down on an oak table, where she remained for five years with the most painful sufferings.

"Since San Gimignano has many orchards, Fina could easily have picked a liter or two of oranges for herself," Tullio commented on the tale. "It is very hard to believe that Fina could have been so innocent. It is my thought that the man must have given her something more than an orange at the well. And it is my opinion both Fina and her mother were somewhat hysterical."

The San Gimignano guidebook told us of Fina's end. It was written in the idiom so characteristic of English guidebooks in Italy. "The fifth year of her martyrdom she rendered her soul unto God," we read. "On this same day a great many violets of delicate and fine perfume sprang forth on the table on which the girl's body was lying; also the towers of the town were covered with flowers and the bells all ringing without that anybody had touched them."

The bells of San Gimignano were in the habit of carrying on in this manner; in the same book we read about the death of Vivaldo, another of the town's saints: "At the very moment when he breathed his last, the bells began to ring without that anybody had touched them."

San Gimignano is small—its population is less than ten thousand—but a walk down the narrow canyon of its Via San Giovanni was crowded even on Sunday. The men were at their Sunday rituals in the barbershops; the women were gathered in gossip clusters. In the cathedral square a man with a sound truck was making a speech on agricultural matters in an accent I could not understand. "Mostly about wine and cows," Tullio said. Pin-ups of American film stars hung on the walls of the shops, and posters called attention to a meeting of the *partito Communista*. It struck me that the people of San Gimignano couldn't make up their minds whether their allegiance belonged to Hollywood or Moscow.

In planning the trip, Tullio had promised to show me some of the most splendid paintings in Italy. He had not exaggerated. The cathedral, very old and not very large, was an unbelievable storehouse of riches. The walls were covered with frescoes by Bartolo, Barna da Siena, Taddeo, Gozzoli, and Ghirlandaio. A Gozzoli *Sebastian* covered the large wall over the entrance. Italians, fascinated by physical agonies, love Sebastian. They paint the youth and his arrows on their church walls more frequently than any other martyred saint. In Venice and Florence, Sebastians are wistful and feminine lads who wear their single arrow like a jewel over their heart. San Gimignano's was different; Gozzoli had peppered him with such an abundance of arrows he looked like a porcupine.

Where the walls of the cathedral had begun to flake, a second layer of frescoes peered from underneath, treasures even older than the five-hundred-year-old marvels on the surface. The walls were literally popping with excitement. Some of Taddeo's portrayals of sin were so lively they could successfully have been peddled as dirty post cards in America. When I pointed this out to Tullio he said starchily, "We pray to them. That is the difference between you and us."

High in the cathedral tower was an art museum. Here the most beautiful things were those from the town's Etruscan beginnings. The art of Etruria, like the clear-eyed portraits of Pompeii, is bright and buoyant. It sings of the freedom of the human soul before Rome taught men to worry about their salvation. Huntsmen chased boars around the bases of burial urns; graceful soaring birds seemed ready to wing into the landscape outside. Each tower window framed a serene composition of blue Tuscan orchards and vineyards and other towers. I was grateful for Italian genius that gave the world these lovely landscapes for the parched hills of Judea. A guide pointed out a tower, recently purchased by an American millionairess who, he said, already owned a villa in Assisi and a palace in Venice. What, I asked, will she do with it?

The guide shrugged. He did not know and neither, he suspected, did she. He drew me aside to point out some pornographic details on a series of frescoes portraying a bridal ceremony. "I show them only to men," he said. I asked how tourists reacted to having their attention called to the paintings. "The French and the English don't care," he said. "The Swedes laugh at them. But the Germans and the Americans! They like them very much and always make me a generous tip."

On Via San Matteo, the main artery of the town, shops were open to Sunday visitors. It was the time of the wine harvest, and everywhere pendulous clusters of multicolored grapes could be bought for a few cents a liter. In a dark little grotto frescoed with photographs of Greer Garson, Linda Darnell, and Lana Turner, a young shoemaker hammered on boots. At the edge of the town we climbed through a grove so biblical in feeling, it would hardly have surprised me to meet Jesus and his disciples discoursing in the shade of an olive tree. At the edge of the grove, closed tight, stood the old church of San Agostino. We circled it and pushed on a small door. It creaked open on a monastery kitchen, where our nostrils were filled with the scent of a savory dinner stew. A friar was watching the kettles. He nodded a greeting, then led us past long tables upon which plates and glasses were turned upside down and into a room filled with stuffed birds. There he left us. Musty cabinets held hundreds of dusty specimens, ranging in size from hummingbirds to hawks. I had a dismal picture of monks setting traps in the olive groves and clucking excitedly over their catches. We stepped from the gloomy bird morgue into a serene cloister garden with an old well, rows of pink hollyhocks, and cypress trees. From the labyrinth of corridors came the wails of men at prayer. A frail old monk grunted us in the direction of the chapel. On the way we met a group of brothers following their noses to the stew.

We found the wailers, eight novices, parroting a chant for a black-cowled friar. Their voices varied from soprano to baritone and in unison made a monotonous harmony. Our entrance distracted them so that they faltered in their prayers. Under their white robes, the boys wore heavy black stockings and shoes. They were from thirteen to eighteen years of age and had the coarse, heavy-eyed look of peasants. Their black hair was clipped to a brush. The younger faces were smooth as eggs; older faces were dark and bearded. Tullio said they were praying for intercession from the Virgin. "They have had no choice with their lives," he said. "They are from poor families who gave them to the friars when they were still *bambini* so they would have enough to eat. They have been sacrificed, like burning on a pyre or being thrown into the sea, sacrificed to poverty. In many ways they are fortunate, for in Italy there are no opportunities for poor young men. Here, there are no problems for them. No problems," Tullio added, "unless they begin to have thirst for women."

"Still," I said, "there must be things they would rather do than spend their lives praying and trapping birds."

"I'm sure they would all rather go to America," Tullio said.

With a lieutenant's alacrity, the friar snapped an order and the neophytes goose-stepped out of the church in the direction of dinner. At the door two of the younger ones turned back a second to look wistfully at us as if they wished they too might be free to wander about on a Sunday morning.

We stayed to look at the art. Martyred Sebastians hung everywhere. Above the altar of the church Gozzoli painted the life of St. Augustine, a panel full of medieval pageantry and bustle. Workmen had chipped away a corner of a fresco to make room for an electric-light switch. This aroused Tullio's aesthetic ire. "To destroy a masterpiece to make a switch for electricity," he said. "That is disgraceful!"

"I am surprised to see how easily Italians desecrate their art treasures," I said. "In Rome I have seen dirty words written on the inside walls of St. Peter's."

"Is more dangerous to give an Italian a pencil than a gun," Tullio said. "An Italian with a pencil will write on everything. With pencil we show how far we have fallen from the great people we once were. We take art for granted and don't have very much interest in it. We do not understand why the tourists make such a fuss about the churches and the paintings. We think that tourists who want to see paintings must be very foolish. The *turismo* people tell us there is economic value in paintings, but aesthetic appreciation we do not have. Italians do not care to look at paintings themselves. That is why there is never enough light where pictures are hung."

I told Tullio of Fanny, the maid in the Milan *pensione*, who lived three years within two blocks of Leonardo's *Last Supper* but had never bothered to go to see it.

"We are becoming more American than we think," Tullio replied sadly.

"Today is much more important to have the switches for electricity than Leonardo."

We walked back through the town past the barbershops, the festive fruit carts, and a cinema where posters announced a two-week festival of Russian films. Like most towns in the province of Siena, San Gimignano is strongly Communistic. I asked the theater manager if Russian films were popular. He shrugged. *"Così, così* [so, so]" he said. When I pressed him, he admitted they were not popular at all, that they were "too sober, not diverting as American films. When Linda Darnell and Jane Russell and Gary Cooper are the stars, then my house is filled and a line waits outside. These Russian films! One hardly hears any laughter during an entire evening."

Then why a festival of Russian films? I asked.

"Is necessary," the man shrugged. "One must please the Municipio (the municipal government) if one would be successful in business. Besides, there are profits to be made, even if the crowds are small, for the Russian films cost very little, or nothing at all. American films are *molto cari* [very dear]."

We found a terraced restaurant from which we could look over a valley soft with late summer haze. The walls were hung with life-sized posters of Lana Turner, Betty Grable, Errol Flynn, and Laurence Olivier. The food was only fair. The tomatoes, as usual, were green; ripe tomatoes are considered by Italians an Anglo-Saxon vulgarity. At the next table a husky young *giovane*, who carried with him the scent of the barbershop and wore a gold crucifix on a gold chain inside his open shirt, was eating a *chilo* or two of spaghetti. As he bent over the platter to shovel in the strands, the crucifix fell from his shirt and became caught in the spaghetti. If it hadn't been for the chain, he would have swallowed it.

The restaurant manager asked if we were associated with *il cinema*. "I will rent you one of my beautiful rooms," he said. "They are rooms worthy of film people. At this very moment I have rented a large and beautiful room to three film persons from Paris. Two men and a girl. Being French, they all sleep in one bed," he confided.

Interesting as his household must have been, we nevertheless departed from San Gimignano. An hour away we had to wait twenty minutes for another bus in a village called Poggibonsi. There was a warm and indolent lassitude over the town. On the piazza, protected by a glass frame, was a municipal bulletin board. I made a note of its total contents:

A large colored photograph of *Il Nuovo Stadio di Leningrado* (the new stadium at Leningrad).

A series of photographs of Soviet *atleti*—athletes—including beefy women in red tights.

Stalin's "outline for world peace."

Six pictures and a story on the life of *Alessandro Pushkin, il più grande poeta del mondo* (Alexander Pushkin, the greatest poet in the world).

A series of maps showing *Le basi dell' USA—strumenti di aggressione* (military bases of the USA, instruments of aggression).

That was it. Sitting around the bulletin board were shawled old ladies, nodding sleepily in the sun. A woman drained her *bambino* in the street, and *giovani* scratched their genitals and whistled at girls in windows. It was Sunday afternoon in Poggibonsi.

During the summer Tullio talked repeatedly of his year at an American university. He wished to visit Boston, "where you have much history," and he wanted to go South "to see for myself about the Negroes." He saw the film *Born Yesterday* and made plans to watch Congress in action and to visit the National Art Gallery. As the weeks passed and I received no reply from the university, he began to worry. His optimism turned to pessimism. I was not so discouraged. The president, a trustee of the Institute of International Education, was a man well known for his work in the education committees of UNESCO. I told Tullio that my letter, arriving in the summer vacation, had doubtless been delayed in getting to him. But Tullio, not reassured, sank into gloomy despair.

In September we made our last trip together, to Perugia for the annual sacred music festival of Umbria, and to see the Peruginos and Raphaels in the art gallery. Tullio offered to arrange for hotel and tickets. Against my better judgment I let him. We arrived in Perugia late on Saturday, an hour before a performance of Morlachi's great *Requiem* in the San Pietro church. Workmen were renovating the lobby of our hotel; the signora proprietress' desk was in the street. She assigned us a tiny cubicle without closets and joyfully informed us no other room in Perugia was available. We ate a quick supper and set out for the concert. When we arrived at the church it was the wrong one. We retraced our steps to the right one and found the concert had begun. The *carabinieri*, uncompromising as usual, refused to let us in.

The next day was no better. In the morning it rained and our room was damp as a cellar. We trudged through the wet to the Pinacoteca, only to find the gallery was "closed for repairs." It was as much frustration as I could bear. Tullio, to my amazement, burst into an angry diatribe at Italian inefficiency.

"It is a foolishness to close a gallery for repairs in the middle of a tourist season," he said. "We are very stupid about such matters. I think we have much to learn about efficiency from Americans."

That evening in San Pietro we heard a performance of Bach's *Second St. Matthew Passion,* conducted by Austria's Herbert von Karajan, with Austrian singers and musicians. It began at six o'clock, just as the twilight sun fell horizontally across the nave of the beautifully gilded basilica. When night fell, the light of hundreds of candles bathed the singers in gold like a heavenly choir in an *Angelico paradiso.* On the tier closest to heaven, apple-cheeked Vienna *Saengerknaben* in white lace robes sang like angels. It was music almost too beautiful for the human heart to bear.

We escaped the tumult of applause into the autumn night. Neither of us could speak. Tullio had missed the last express train to Florence; there was nothing for him to do but take a slow one with a long wait at Terontola, which would get him to Florence at six in the morning, two hours before he had to report for work at the American Express. I was staying in Perugia that night and going to Assisi the next day; after Assisi I was returning to Rome. We ate our supper together. Finishing a bowl of *minestrone,* fat with *pasta,* Tullio said, "Now I feel heavy, just like the basement of an American skyscraper." The soufflé which followed was more to his liking. He took a bite and said, "This is like kissing the lips of a lamb."

It was the last time I saw him. Before I left Italy, I invited him to Rome for a week-end. He did not answer my invitation. The letter from the university had not come and apparently he blamed me for shattering his hopes. The America he wanted to believe in had let him down.

CHAPTER 7

PULCINELLA AND A HAIR SHIRT

"It is impossible to be a day in Naples without discovering that it is the most depraved city in Europe"

—W. SOMERSET MAUGHAM

NAPLES IS THE GATE through which one should enter Italy and through which one should leave. Sights, sounds, and smells are strongest there. Naples is Italy distilled to its essence, the most Italian of Italian cities.

It is also the noisiest. The Neapolitan wears his emotions as brightly as Joseph's cloak. His life is an expression of laughter and tears, gaiety and sadness, birth and death. He is dynamic, cunning, corrupt, comic, warm, and wise. Many Americans are so intimidated by him they do not go to Naples. Even Italians from the north do not like to visit Naples.

This is a pity, for Naples is the most diverting of Italian cities. Pulcinella, traditional clown lover with a hunched back and grotesque nose, is a Neapolitan. So is the great film comic, Toto, Italy's modern Pulcinella. Built like a great amphitheater around her beautiful bay, Naples is an eternally unfolding play acted by a million of the best actors in the world. The comedy is broad, the tragedy violent. The curtain never rings down.

On my first visit the hotels were filled with an international medical convention, so a friend arranged for me to stay at a monastery. The order, my friend said, was dying out and the ten or so elderly friars that remained had taken to renting out rooms in order to maintain their handsome old building. It had two floors of monks' cells. The old friars lived on the first and their paying guests on the second. I had no contact with my pious hosts, but a guest in the next room, a traveling man from Milan, assured me they were congenial and would look with Christian forgiveness on venial sins providing the lady departed before dawn and I left an offering for the monastery Madonna, a plaster Virgin in the courtyard.

My room was designed for austerity. It had no decoration and the furnishings were limited to two rope chairs and a bed which was a two-inch-thick pallet on a wire spring. My first two nights on it were sleepless. The *comodità* was a kilometer of hallways away. A maddening jangle of bells reminded me each hour to pray. An inside window opened on the courtyard with the plaster Virgin, usually knee-deep in flowers. At any time of the day I could look out on women praying and lighting candles. What had once been a prayer chapel on the second floor was now a bar. The altar was laden with cognac, whisky, and wine, and in the center place of the Eucharist were two shining nickel taps.

Directly across the street was a five-story tenement of pink terra cotta from which each morning housewives did their marketing by letting down buckets on ropes from their iron balconies. Bargaining at the tops of their voices with vendors, the women drew up bread, milk, meat, and vegetables. In a poolroom around the corner an eerie green light shone on the life-sized statue of a saint bedecked with silver ornaments and flowers. Before the statue were prayer stools so the habitués could catch up between pool shots on their devotions.

My favorite walk was across the public gardens to the sweeping Via Caracciolo which follows the crescent of the sea to the fishermen's wharf. There at noon each day leathery barefooted fishermen docked their brightly painted boats and drew in their nets, three or four on a rope, with occasionally a woman helping, chanting as they pulled. If the weather was good, it was a gay time, attracting crowds of idlers, especially small children who came to feast on the tiny fishes discarded from the nets. As quickly as the fishermen tossed them, the children pounced on the wriggling fingerlings and threw them on a fire, roasting them alive, eating bones, heads, and entrails, covered with ashes and dirt. For a cigarette, boys would swallow them alive. The children, fortified with the oils and vitamins of the sea, appeared healthy. They lived their lives with primitive innocence, squatting on rocks like dogs to perform their functions. On warm days the boys bathed in the sea like schools of scaleless fish. Still naked, they clamored for cigarettes. Boys seven and eight years old inhaled deeply, releasing the smoke from their nostrils. One of the smaller ones invited me to look at some ugly scars which he said were "wounds of the war." I thought he was joking until he explained that he had been less than a year old when his house was bombed. Sometimes they asked for money, braying like devils their delirious singsong, *"Ho fame* [I am starving]," laughing merrily, making a joke of begging from tourists.

At night when the boats were lined up in neat rows, the wharf was a place of surreptitious activity, for here the poorer prostitutes, the girls without the luxury of a room, did a brisk business in and among the boats. On mellow nights one stumbled on lovers everywhere. Under the dim illumination of a street lamp I wrote a letter one night to Hollywood, U.S.A. I wrote it for a girl named Giulietta who was young, but not too young to have blondined her hair. She asked me if I'd ever met "Airin Donne." She had to explain that she was speaking of the "great and beautiful actress of the film *Life with Father*" before I understood. "Do you think Signora Donne can read Italian?" the girl asked me. I said I did not know. "I am sure she cannot and I wish greatly to write her a letter. Perhaps you will write it for me in English?"

She had stationery. "Dear Miss Dunne," she dictated in Italian. "I think you are the most beautiful actress in the world. If you would be my friend the ocean could not contain my happiness. In my heart you are enshrined forever. Each day I pray to the Holy Mother to bring you good fortune and good health. I have now only a picture from a journal and if you would send me a photograph, I would place it beside the Virgin and when I pray the holy candle will shine on you as the light of my heart will shine on you forever. Your everlasting friend, Giulietta."

I gave her the letter and said good night. She turned back to the beach. The sea had washed up some huge hairless dead rats, white and pink like baby pigs. In the dark they were luminous with decay.

Sicily had made me a puppet fancier. I wanted to visit a Neapolitan puppet theater, known as the Olympia. At the consulate I had been urged not to go. The theater was in a northwest corner of the old central section, a crowded and violent part of Naples said to be hostile to outsiders. "Americans are robbed and beaten," an official warned. "The police had to rescue four American sailors from a mob last week."

I found an American journalist to make the expedition with me. We climbed narrow crowded streets that rise from the heart of the town. It was an ordinary midweek night, but the streets were noisy and gay as a saint's feast. Neon light illuminated holy statues, and the smell of roasting chestnuts was in the air. Young women sold American cigarettes, not in packs, but singly, neatly laid out with American contraceptives, also sold singly. At a wineshop we drank a tumbler of extremely potent dark thick stuff. Many persons greeted us. "It's all in our psychology," the journalist explained. "If you reflect a feeling of confidence, don't appear nervous, and never get angry, you avoid trouble. It's only when you show fear, nervousness, or temperament that difficulties arise."

We moved deeper into the human jungle. Jagged walls of bombed and deserted buildings loomed up around us. On a bombed side street we found the Olympia. Tickets cost forty lire, about seven cents. It was a new cement structure, clean, whitewashed, and well illuminated; quite different from the dank smelly caves of the Palermo puppeteers. There were about one hundred and fifty chairs and all of them were occupied. Unlike Sicily, there were several shawled women in the audience. The stage was small, and the puppets were smaller than the brass and tin Sicilian warriors. A piano, violin, and horn played Neapolitan folk tunes. Like a movie house, the show, which began at five o'clock, was repeated until midnight. The melodrama upon which we entered ran the gamut from banditry, murder (by stabbing and shooting), and rape to kidnapings. This wide variety of carnage seemed to please the audience greatly. The wicked villain leered at the virtuous lady wearing a tiara and furs and demanded, "Be my mistress or be destroyed!" The virtuous lady screamed, but her husband did not hear her; she chose death and was immediately stabbed. "A scandal! A scandal!" were her dying words. The villain stole the dead woman's baby and took it to a cabin in the forest kept by a Shakespearean buffoon in pointed boots and a belled cap. The buffoon burned the villain in a furnace and reared the kidnaped child in the forest in the manner of *A Winter's Tale*. Twenty years and six scenes later, the child, full grown, was returned to his real father.

In an intermission boys hawked soft drinks, peanuts, and sweets, and members of the audience unpacked lunches from newspapers. The theater became pungent with garlic. The next part of the performance was a variety show, a burlesque with triple-jointed dancers, pumpkin-bosomed female puppets singing ribald songs, sailors paddling little boats across the stage, and a patriarchal fisherman in a candy-striped costume involved in a salty intrigue with some mermaids. I understood very little of the Neapolitan dialect, but the toy performers were wondrously agile and it was enough to watch. The dialogue was peppered with American idioms, G.I. contributions to the patois of Naples. Liberal use of Anglo-Saxon vulgarisms sent the audience into roars. Apparently we had been spotted behind stage as Americans, and the four-letter words were meant as a friendly gesture to us.

From the theater we walked to the Galleria Umberto, the geographical and spiritual heart of Naples. Under the great glass canopy of the arcade one can have his choice of a variety show or three motion pictures, do his banking, have a suit made, or get a syphilis cure. He can give away a small fortune in ten-lire scraps to beggars, get his corns pared, buy newspapers, Martini cocktails, a house in Posillipo, pornographic photographs, religious images, an excursion ticket to Sorrento, a hat, nylon stockings, and almost every other product and service used by mankind.

The beggars of the Galleria are the most pathetic in Italy. Mothers with babies at their breasts and ragged toddlers clinging to their skirts wailed for alms to buy food. It is a spectacle I could never take lightly, no matter how long I remained in Naples or how many Italians told me begging was a studied technique to snare sentimental tourists. Even more distressing were the "mice" of the Galleria, the scores of children, most of them silent little girls who appeared from nowhere, their hands outstretched, each looking more pathetic than the other. It was a mystery where they slept or when, for no matter when I appeared they were there. They came to know me, for a spotted giver was like a tooting Pied Piper. With me the most successful was a bright-eyed, thin girl of seven or eight, barefoot even when it was cold and wet, wearing always the same ragged shift. She had a genius for appearing tortured, wistful, and hungry. In any kind of weather, she crept quietly in and out of the Galleria, tugging at my sleeve and murmuring something inaudible, not letting go until she had her tithe of ten lire. I asked her questions and got only noncommittal answers. Her name was Teresa. She did not go to school. She wouldn't talk about her home or her mother and father. If I missed her on a walk through the Galleria, I would be worried. It was if we had a contract for her to appear and for me to give her ten lire. The feeling of familiarity between us grew into an attachment. Then one night we had a quarrel.

I was having an *apéritif* before the opera with some American friends. Teresa was there and I put the bit of ragged paper into her outstretched hand. Before a quarter hour had passed she was back, on the verge of tears, hand outstretched as before. I was annoyed and told her to leave. She did not go, but kept tugging at my sleeve, indicating with her other hand the small change which lay on the table.

"I have just given you ten lire. Once in an hour is certainly enough."

"No, signore, you have not."

"You were here only fifteen minutes ago."

"No, no." She shook her head.

I lost my temper. "You are lying, Teresa. Now leave me alone, or I will tell the police."

I thought the threat would send her away. It didn't. Still she stood there, shivering with cold, her palm hot and sweaty. A waiter came to my rescue. "*Vatene!*" he ordered, shoving her with his hand as he might a dog. She turned and ran away. I felt an unhappy twinge in my stomach and asked him to tell me what he knew of the child.

"Ah, it is a sad story. There are *two* of them, sisters, less than a year's difference between them and looking exactly alike. It is not always the same who comes. They are of a family of nine. The father is run away with another woman and the mother has trained all the *bambini* to beg. She is the *capitano,* the mother, she stands and watches them and if they do not collect enough lire, she beats them. It is a living, signore, a living." After that I gave ten lire to both Teresa and her sister and I never did know which was which.

One thing that is always for sale in the Galleria is *amore.* Poverty and vice are sisters and Naples is the home of both.

The flesh-peddlers' antiphony is sung loudest by the little pimps, the "Hey-Joe-wanna-woman" urchins ten or so years old. Their greatest success is with uniforms, but they consider civilians fair game. The girls themselves are less articulate and more subtle. One night over a *Cinzano* I watched their operations. They seemed to work co-operatively; their headquarters was a café flanked with a battery of public phones. From here they strolled, their arms around each other's waists, casually exploring the Galleria, returning to home base on the pretense of making a phone call, but really to discuss prospects. They held chatty conferences punctuated with arguments and giggles. The girls were of varying types and any age from eighteen to thirty-five. The ratio of pretty ones was discouragingly small. But there was one in this dismal sisterhood who stood out, a tall tawny creature dressed in some copper-colored stuff that matched her hair. She had style, and she seemed to enjoy herself.

I sensed that she was telling the others about me. She passed my table, each time a little closer, each time smiling more warmly. Finally she asked for the ritualistic light for her cigarette. In order to get it she sat on the other chair at my table. A waiter appeared, as if on cue, to take her order.

"American?" she asked.

At close range, she was somewhat less beautiful, but still striking in personality. She would drink anything at all, she said. "It doesn't matter. I am too sad to care."

"I'd guess you were the happiest girl in Naples," I said.

"Oh, signore. If only you could know me when I am not sad. You would really see how happy I can be."

"Why are you sad?"

She didn't want to talk about it, she said. "Why should I give you my sadness. You are a fine intellectual gentleman. When you walked into the Galleria I could see it. I only like intellectual gentlemen for friends. How long will you stay in Naples?"

The inevitable question. "I don't know," I said. "I am awaiting a letter which will determine my plans." It was a standard answer which gave no hint as to either the duration of my stay or my solvency.

"What is your name?" she asked. She was sipping vermouth the color of her lipstick.

"I am called Niccolò," I said.

"Niccolò. *Incredible!*" When excited she talked Italian. "Is my name too, Niccola. One can see fate brought us together."

"I do not believe it," I said. "That your name is Niccola."

"You do not believe me?" My doubt brought tears to her eyes.

"I have been in Naples too long to believe everything I am told," I said.

"I can understand it," she said. "Neapolitans are untruthful and insincere. They know nothing of honor."

"But you are Neapolitan?"

"Oh, no, Niccolò. How could you think it? I am of Ischia. On Ischia we are sincere and kind. We are not like the ugly Neapolitans always thinking of money. You do not believe I am from Ischia?" She took a document from her bag and handed it to me. It said that she was born on Porto D'Ischia and that her name was Niccola. I apologized.

"Americans understand love and friendship," Niccola said. "I had American friends in the war." Her voice trailed off into nostalgia and then returned. "Do you know Colonel ———?" I didn't know the colonel she named. "He was very young colonel and a fine intellectual gentleman. I am his secretary and live with him in hotel. Of course I am too young to make a secretary, but he says for friend he prefers girl who is too young for secretary. So I am friend and am paid for secretary. He is noble fine gentleman and I love him very much. Is happy time, the war. When is past the colonel went back to America. He did not send for me to marry him as he promised. He write once to say his father, who is very rich, will not permit it that he marry me. So I am left very sad, wishing again for the days of the war."

I commiserated as much as I could.

"Sir, you are kind and noble," Niccola said. "I will tell you my sadness. Is my home in Ischia. The *mamma* and the *papa* fight all the time, so I cannot listen any more and I come to Naples to leave behind the quarreling. Is *troppo triste*, my home."

Again her eyes glistened. I marveled at her facile tear ducts. "Is about my brother Bruno, all the quarreling," she said. "Bruno is just a *bambino*, only nineteen years. Bruno is seaman on merchant ship. So is *papa* seaman. His whole life *papa* is on merchant ship. *Papa* wishes Bruno to ship to Venezuela. To Venezuela Bruno does not wish to go. He desires to sail in the Mediterranean so he can come home to *mamma* and me and not forget Ischia and his home. *Mamma* does not wish for him to go to Venezuela. He would get homesick. So it is, *papa* says yes, *mamma* says no, and it is quarreling all the time. Today *papa* and Bruno fight and *mamma* cries. Is too ugly for a gentle heart, so I come to Naples to get for Bruno seaman's documents to get on ship in Mediterranean. Then he will not have to go to Venezuela."

"Aren't documents necessary for shipping to Venezuela?" I asked.

"For Venezuela *papa* will buy the documents. That is why I have come to Naples, to find a friend who will loan the money to buy documents without *papa*. You are kind and understanding. Americans are the kindest men in the world. . . ."

"How much do the documents cost?" I asked.

"I don't ask you to *give* me the money. It is only a loan until Saturday when I will pay it back. You will save poor Bruno from Venezuela and stop the *mamma's* tears. . . ."

"How much?"

"You do not think I would ask for money for love, signore?" She was beginning to cry again.

"*Mamma mia!*" I said. "The thought hadn't entered my mind."

"You don't think I am a common prostitute like the vulgar women of Naples who think only of money and know nothing of the heart. You don't think . . . ?"

"Anyone can see you are too well bred for that."

"Signor, you are a sensitive gentleman who understands love. I could never take money from you. But a loan, from a friend?"

"How much?"

"The documents cost twenty-five hundred lire, signore. I have five hundred lire and if you will loan me two thousand I shall return them on Saturday and the saints will bless you for your kindness."

"You will have the money to repay me on Saturday?"

"Sir, I swear it. On Saturday I have due some money." She took my hands gratefully and blinked through starry eyes.

"Then why not wait and buy Bruno's documents on Saturday?"

"But Saturday is too late. The boat for Venezuela sails in two days, and if the documents are not bought before, poor Bruno will be on it. It is because you are called Niccolò after San Niccolò, the patron of seamen, that you will help Bruno. It is the kindness of fate."

She was assuming I would loan her the money. It had been too easy. I hadn't put up the argument she expected, and for a Neapolitan—or an Ischian—what good is a triumph without a battle of wits? A new flood of tears came.

"Sir, I am sure you will loan me three thousand lire instead of two thousand. The seaman's documents cost twenty-five hundred lire and there are all the taxes and I will buy Bruno a warm sweater for the sea. He is not strong and has a weakness in the chest. I will return the money Saturday, before the Holy Mother I will."

She leaned across the table and kissed me. It was a heady gesture. "My San Niccolò," she said. "Tonight Niccolò will see what it means when Niccola is a good friend."

"But there is not going to be a tonight," I said. "You see, Saint Nicholas wears a hair shirt. He lives in a monastery."

"Is good joke. Americans are always joking. But no American ever live in a *convento*."

"You are wrong. This one does."

"How is it possible, an American in a *convento*?" Niccola asked. Her hands pressed mine. I was thinking of the Madonna in the monastery grotto, surrounded by candles, rising from her sea of flowers, radiating her blessings and tolerance for an offering. "I know a hotel, clean and polite, is a *buon mercato*," Niccola said.

"No, Niccola, I am going to my monastery."

I was sick of tears and I got up to leave. "Niccolò, the money you have promised for Bruno, the three thousand lire."

"Not three thousand," I said. "Two thousand. I will be here at nine o'clock the day after tomorrow. If you meet me with Bruno I will go along to the seaman's office to buy the documents."

In the doorway of the café the sisterhood was watching us with hostile interest. "Sir, *papa* won't permit Bruno to come to Naples. I must get the papers tomorrow."

"On Friday," I said. "Bruno will have a full day to get on a Mediterranean boat."

"Niccolò, where will I sleep tonight? I have no place to sleep."

I said good night. The girls came from the café to comfort her. I heard Niccola's voice, not pleading or tender, but fierce and full of fire.

"God-damned stingy American!"

It was more to my liking than tears.

I left the Galleria and climbed a winding road into the hills. In a tiny pizzeria I came on a scene right out of a *commedia dell' arte*. The leading character was a ruddy white-haired old man in a white apron and a flat baker's cap, a kindly gnome beaming with warmth and good will. He stood behind a counter of cheeses and smoked meats, red chops and steaks, a beef liver, and a ham. He was making pizzas, shaping each pie carefully on a huge wooden shovel and extending it deep into an open hearth. There were only two customers, a Neapolitan Jack Sprat and his *fidanzata* who sat at a table under the bouquet of meats. They were young. The woman had a wisp of a beard from a wen in her chin; her bulging body was encased in black satin and laden with artificial gold jewelry. Jack was pale and frail. His hair glistened with oil, he wore a pin-stripe suit, and his adoring eyes rested glassily on the great mound of woman that was his, all his. Occasionally he pinched her varying melons of flesh while she quaffed wine and giggled with amiable coquetry. The gnome at the hearth watched with irritation; he was ill-accustomed to such an indifferent audience.

"You are a stranger," he said to me.

"Yes, signore. I have not been long in Naples."

"*Americano?*"

"Yes."

"Maybe you live in Boston, yes?" He spoke fairly good English. "I am from Boston. Many years ago I make chef in Hotel Copley. You know where is Pigeon Cove? I am greatly loved by a lady professor in her *grande villa* by the sea." He looked into the hearth to his shovel. The smoldering pizzas were for the Sprats, who were paying no attention to their creation. The gnome thrust his shovel angrily into the flames.

The front door opened and the flour man entered, carrying a white bag on his shoulder. He was a Pulcinella in white, his shoes were white, his face and hands were white, his hair was white. He leaned forward to empty his sack into the bin by the oven and as he did so a gust of wind swept in like a poltergeist, billowing a cloud of flour through the room. The old man felt his way to shut the door. In the fog I could hear the fat woman cough and Jack Sprat choking. When the flour settled at last, everything was covered with it. The Sprats and I were as white as the flour man. The woman's dress had turned from shining black to a dull gray; the rouge on her face was no longer visible. She began to sob, and the rivulets of her tears made paste on her cheeks.

Jack Sprat scolded like an angry bird. "You fool! You cretin!" he railed at the flour man. "You have ruined my suit. You have insulted a lady. See, she is weeping. You will apologize."

"He did not blow the wind," said the old pizza maker.

Jack Sprat turned on the pizza maker. "You will pay! You will pay for the lady's dress, you will pay for my suit. You will pay, or I will bring the police."

"Wind is the invention of God," said the pizza maker. "You must speak to God about payment." He bid the flour man a courtly farewell. The flour man departed like a ghost into the night. "What are you going to do?" demanded Jack Sprat.

"Nothing," the pizza maker said calmly. "These things happen." The woman's sobs grew louder, she shook like a ship on a swell. "But the signorina is not happy here. If you are a gentleman you will take her home."

"You will pay," Jack Sprat sputtered. "Law protects the dignity of a lady." He hoisted the woman to her feet and led her like a blind one to the door. "Pay! Police . . . !" he shouted. Their feet made prints as if in snow.

The pizza maker shook his head. "He is Neapolitan. He has no control of himself," he said. He went to the door and bolted it. Then he came to me and gently brushed the flour from my jacket. When this was done he placed a bottle of Chianti on a table and brought the pizza prepared for the Sprats, sizzling with melted provoloni, covered with anchovies and bits of salami. He sat down with me and poured some wine.

"Now we will eat," he said. "You are my guest."

The pizza was a masterpiece, dry and crisp and strong with garlic. "You eat pizza like this in America?" he asked. I never had.

"To the lady of Pigeon Cove," I toasted. We drank.

"In America is always tomato on pizza," my friend said. "Is no real pizza with tomato. In America is everything tomato. Tomato, tomato, tomato!" We ate to the end and washed it down with wine. "In Pigeon Cove I make pizza like this," he said. "She like everything that I cook for her." The man's dreamy eyes looked beyond me into the past. He looked a century old. "She like even better the love that I make for her. 'Alfredo,' she said, giving me the name from the beautiful opera of Verdi, 'for you I will die.' We would lie on the sand by the sea in the evening to watch the birds hunting the fish, and each time a bird would catch a fish she would wish me to bite her ear. I was a young man, very handsome, and performed *bravissimo* in the arts of love. Of course she was not Violetta, for she was older, but for love, a woman, like the wine, must be aged if it will please."

"Of what was she a professor?" I asked.

"Of the language French in a college for girls," he said. "When I return to Napoli she came every summer to see me. She wished to marry me, but in Boston is not possible for a lady professor to marry with a foreigner. Neither do I wish. In Napoli when a young man marries an older woman it is said he cannot please young women. So we do not marry. Comes the war and it is not possible for her to come back to Napoli in the summer. Is the end. I never see her again."

"Which war?" I asked.

"The war of 1914," he said. "No doubt is dead many years, this lady." There was a mist in his eye. We drank quietly. Then he said, "You are young man. Is one thing you must know. Is good for young man to pick roses in June, for memories are necessary in December."

CHAPTER 8

THE GROTTOES

THE HILLS of Naples are lava rock. For centuries men have mined stone from under the cliffs to build palaces and cathedrals on the surface, leaving caverns as sprawling as Kentucky caves. During the war these grottoes were bomb shelters for the people of the city. After the war Naples' displaced and homeless lived in four of them like colonies of moles. For a time the Medical Nutritional Commission of the Allied High Command studied these people to document their reports on the nutritional effects of war. Then officialdom abandoned them and the Congregational Services Mission of New York reached a hand into the darkness, sending to Naples three volunteers freshly graduated from Oberlin College in Ohio. When I met them, these three young people—two young men and a girl—had been in Naples eight months. To them, Americans of conscience are deeply indebted. The sins of Americans abroad—military, diplomatic, and tourist—are great, but the youthful selflessness and Christian idealism of these three volunteers won a bit of absolution for all of us.

Their leader was Belden Paulson of Chicago, only son of a lawyer father and a social-worker mother. Lean with a Scandinavian ruggedness, he had a quality rare in youth, that of complete self-abnegation.

The girl's name was Jane Weed. She was the handsome daughter of a New York city engineer and had majored in sociology. She was shy, modest, and courageous.

The third member of the trio, Paul Rusby, had a perfectly shaped diamond branded into his cheek. It was the first thing I noticed about him. He had two more on his hand and arm. Later I learned that when he was a year old he had fallen against a hot radiator which burned into his flesh. The son of a Lehigh University economics professor, he was twenty-five when I met him and the oldest of the trio. He seemed the youngest. In appearance he was a smooth-faced, apple-cheeked adolescent. He had come to Naples from a disappointment, his failure to get into medical school. In Naples he proved he would have made an excellent doctor.

When I met the three workers, they were in the midst of a crisis. Belden Paulson had been summoned by his Chicago draft board. He had gone to Rome to enlist diplomatic aid toward a deferment, but had been unsuccessful. Now he was arranging for a boat to America. He who had done as much toward international good will as any American I met in Italy was being called to prepare for war.

Jane Weed and Paul Rusby, who had served three years in the army, decided to go it alone. The day Paulson sailed Rusby was depressed and lonely. I invited him to dinner. "You'll find me an awful chiseler," he said. "When I'm offered a good meal I take it." We went to Stampa, the Neapolitan press club in the public gardens to which I had an honorary membership. We ate American-style steaks. He told me his daily budget permitted him a thirty-five-cent lunch, and two hamburgers and a beer for dinner providing he bought them at the cheap Seamen's Service Club.

The mission—which was operating on a budget of six hundred dollars a month—paid each of the three workers eighteen thousand lire, or about twenty-six dollars a month. Jane Weed lodged in an orphanage operated by nuns; the two boys set up mattresses in part of a two-room outbuilding by a villa on a hill above Naples. In the other room the owner kept nine pigs, two of which died from overcrowded, unhealthful conditions. Mostly the three workers ate cheap, starchy meals of *pasta* and worked from sixteen to twenty hours a day. Their work was of a medical and social nature. Rusby told me, "We distribute Care food packages sent from the United States. Occasionally we are able to buy milk for sick children. Janie distributes clothing sent from America and organizes sewing classes to teach women how to repair them. We distribute drugs and medicines contributed by American firms. Much of it is outdated and some is too old to be effective. Some is experimental stuff and is sent us on the condition that we send reports of the results to the American manufacturers. We try to arrrange hospitalization for the seriously ill and the dying. Almost all of our people are sick, mostly with tuberculosis.

"All this is stopgap activity. Our real purpose is to get them out of the caves into the sunlight. We spend hours getting working permits and jobs for the men and above-surface housing for families with children. Or if not that, at least some rudimentary sanitation and electric lights for the caves. These are interminable processes. We are opposed everywhere by municipal and church authorities, neither of which do anything to help the cave dwellers. Because we are Protestant we naturally do no religious teaching. All our work is service. Still, half our time is taken up fighting the hostile Catholic authorities and hostile Catholic press. Italian bureaucracy is infatuated with documents. Every official act of a man requires a handful of paper. For us documents which ordinarily are procurable in a matter of days are delayed for months. Our doctor is an Italian volunteer and he is constantly harassed by functionaries demanding to see documentary permission to treat people, even the dying ones. When Janie took some coughing children out of the caves into the public park for a few hours of sunlight each day, the police protested because the ugly sight of them offended the sensibilities of aristocratic Neapolitans. Even American diplomats are against us. Their attitude is that Protestant 'missionaries' are bad public relations in a Catholic country."

The American diplomats could hardly know how shortsighted they were. The cave dwellers were a stormy, rebellious lot and hostile to Americans. They could not forget a band of zealous American "Youths for Christ" who, speaking not a word of Italian, one day came through the caves distributing Italian translations of the New Testament. The police had to come and rescue them. When Paulson, Rusby, and Jane Weed arrived in Naples they knew no Italian. Their first attempts to deal with the cave dwellers were abortive and even dangerous. But within weeks they had won the trust and respect of even the most recalcitrant. Now when there was trouble in the caves the police counted on the three volunteers to keep it under control. The cave dwellers called the trio of volunteers "the three American saints."

On Paulson's departure Rusby had been offered a ten-thousand-lire monthly increase in salary which he had declined with the request that it be divided among the Italian staff, including a schoolteacher with a family and a cleaning woman who was struggling to support three children on five thousand lire, or about eight dollars, a month.

The morning after our dinner together Paul Rusby took me to two of the grottoes, the Mergellina and the Capodimonte, named after the sections in which they are located. In the Mergellina grotto there were sixty-four families averaging five people; at the Capodimonte, thirty-six families. Rusby made it a point to visit the five hundred persons in the two caves every day. "We will go to the Mergellina first," he said. "It is somewhat higher class. As far as cave dwellers go, the Mergellina are a moderately healthy group. They spend much of their time in the sun, and some enterprising ones even live in shacks which they have built outside the caves. These are known as villas. There will be a crisis, of course. There is always a crisis when I arrive. If there isn't, one is quickly manufactured."

We climbed on foot up a steep rocky path in the north section of the city, arriving on a plateau with a view of the sea and the most beautiful bay in the world. In front of us was a cliff with a dismal dark hole in its side.

Most of the inhabitants were taking the morning sun. A scolding woman was delousing a screaming child; others were doing laundry outside the cave and wailing as they worked; an adolescent girl, dirty and beautiful, was sitting on a rock languidly combing her hair like a Lorelei. The moment we were spied a crowd surged toward us. "Paolo!" was the cry, "*Il buon Americano*! [the good American]." The children sang, "Paolo! Paolo! Paolo!"

There were two crises. The day before, a "villa" had been ignited by one of the charcoal buckets over which cave dwellers cook their food, and the trousseaux of two sisters about to be married were destroyed. We went to look at the ashes. Near by the family already had walls up for a new villa. Only the trousseaux were irreplaceable, and the mother of the brides lamented them loudly. "A tragedy! A catastrophe!" she mourned. "Cecilia would marry a soldier and Adelina an apprentice shoemaker and now there are no dresses!" She had a hopeful idea. "Do marriage dresses come in the boxes from America?" she asked Rusby. He promised to have Jane Weed look into it.

I saw a red rose growing from a tin pail by the door of a shack which was the community "Hospital." It had one small room with a dirty lumpy cot and a first-aid medical cabinet.

The second crisis affected the dwellers inside the caves. Women waved legal-looking documents which the mailman had brought that morning. They were orders from city authorities to leave the caves at once. The forms said they were dangerous to human life. "Where will we go? What will we do?" the women clamored.

"Oh, God!" Rusby sighed in despair.

"*Che c'è*, 'God'? [What means 'God'?]" a woman asked, and another wailed, "What will happen to us now?" Rusby told me that several days before a chunk of stone had fallen from the ceiling of the cave, almost killing several people. With this as a point of attack Rusby had gone to the city authorities to renew his plea for proper housing for the cave dwellers. The result of his efforts was the moving orders. "Actually it means nothing," Rusby said. "No police would move the people out because they know it would mean a nasty riot. But officials keep sending notices and they keep getting excited." To the women crowding around he said, "You will not be moved out. I will go to the office of the mayor this afternoon."

The cave's high mouth permitted a shaft of sunlight to penetrate a short distance inside. White fragments of laundry were strung across like semaphores. Looking into the darkness I saw, glowing like red eyes, the devotional candles of holy shrines, one in each cell, a statue of the Virgin, or perhaps only a picture. Between the candles and the images there were wilting handfuls of flowers, and beside the Virgins garish pin-ups of American movie stars. The cave was probably five hundred feet deep. We penetrated it in the company of dogs, children chewing chunks of dirty bread, and garrulous women, pregnant or carrying children. Where a sliver of sunlight flashed through a crack in the ceiling, flies swarmed in the warmth.

The stench was monstrous, the noise worse. Women screamed, infants wailed, chickens cackled, dogs barked. All of it echoed in a frightful din. Family enclosures were built on a sort of street winding along the natural convolutions of the cave. Cells were fashioned from old packing crates and tin billboards. A few attempted privacy with paper ceilings; others were open to the black roof of the cave seventy feet above. Some of the rooms had a mattress; others only a bundle of rags. Rusby pointed to one which was the home of a couple and eight children. The bed was a pile of matted straw in the corner.

One man was in high spirits. Rusby had succeeded in getting him a work permit. He had made a sort of tailor shop of the box, which he shared with three children, a pregnant wife, and a sewing machine. In a cell farther back a woman offered Rusby a bite from a soiled piece of bread which she was munching. He bit into it and thanked her. The deed was more than a breaking of bread, it was an act of Christian compassion. In still another cell an old lady lay dying on a mat. In a voice that was little more than a whisper, she called *"Americano! Americano!"* We went to her. She reached out for Rusby's hand and kissed it, murmuring *"Paolo, un buon Americano!"* Then she took my hand and drew it to her lips.

As we were leaving, a dirty child caught sight of the thick crepe soles on my shoes. *"Oh, mamma mia!"* she shrieked, and called for everyone to come and look. *"Vedi! Formaggio!* The American walks on cheese!"

Capodimonte is in the heart of the town, a crowded section not far from the Cathedral of San Gennaro and the National Museum. On the way there Rusby asked me if I felt strong enough for it. I wondered if he were joking. He wasn't. He said, "Officials do not want tourists to know Capodimonte exists, so the people are not permitted out of their caves. They never get into the sunlight, consequently eighty per cent of them have tuberculosis. They call it 'teepeech' from the American 'T.B.' Since they all have a fever, they are hysterical people very much excited by visitors. There is always trouble when a stranger comes. One day I brought two American sailors. The sailors were so upset by what they saw they gave away their money and cigarettes to the grownups and their candy to the children. But their gifts reached only a few. A riot started and the sailors had to be rescued by the police. It will be necessary for you to be very careful."

The entrance to Capodimonte is a small black hole in a cliff that rises from a busy intersection. It exhaled formidable vapors of cooking and urine. I had to wait a moment for my stomach to settle before I could enter. Inside I heard a fugue of coughing, worse than any hospital ward, deep wracking coughs coming from the bowels and rising out of the darkness like the baying of jackals. We descended wet slippery steps into an empty space that looked like an abandoned coal mine. I buttoned my coat, for I was chilled by the damp as well as a fear of the unknown. Here was something as terrifying as Dante's purgatory. Around us I saw eyes, then white fungus faces shining like phosphorescent deaths-heads. There was a stampede toward us and cries of *"Americano! Paolo!"* Hands grabbed us, angry hands supplicating, feverish, nervous, spastic as puppets! Voices screamed curses against policemen, priests, mayors, and all men of authority. I could see why police guarded the narrow entrance. No less than cholera, rampant rebellion had to be kept from infecting a city. "They are people in body only," Rusby said. "Spiritually they have returned to the beasts." Moving deeper into the pit I saw deep in the heart of the cave a flickering shrine of the Virgin.

Around me, I could distinguish the outlines of a community, the tiny cells of slats and tin and the pasteboard ceilings. Suspended over the doors of many were oxhorns, a phallic symbol of fertility. They had a diabolical appropriateness, for most women of childbearing age were pregnant.

"Tuberculosis heats the blood," Rusby said. "Sex is all that is left these people. They have nothing to do but cough and breed. Women average a baby a year and the paternity is often ambiguous. It doesn't matter much who the father is since most babies that aren't stillborn die of tuberculosis within two or three years."

Rusby pointed out a cubicle with a mound of putrid bedclothing in a corner. "Stefano Rocco lives here with his wife and her sister, both of whom he makes pregnant," he said. In the corner of the room was a crude sort of box. "That is for the *bambini* to sleep in, those that don't die. Stefano has just finished a three-months' jail sentence for starting a riot in the cave. Today I am going to tell him he has a job and is to report for work at once. It took me three days to get him the job. First it was necessary to get him work documents. Stefano is illiterate so I spent an hour teaching him to sign his name. Then I filled out the rest of the documents and had them approved in the labor office. Yesterday I got a street contractor to agree to employ him." Above the coughing and shouting Rusby asked, *"Dov'è Stefano?* Where is Stefano? I have news for him."

Two bloated women began to sob. Wailing children clung to their dark skirts and the damned gathered around, all talking at once.

"Stefano is in jail," the sisters cried.

Slowly, with God beseeched and policemen cursed, the story came out. Stefano had been arrested the night before for begging in the streets. This time his fine was four thousand lire; unless he paid, he would remain in jail.

"Who has four thousand lire?" one of the sisters wailed. "What will happen to us? What will happen to me? What will happen to my poor sister?"

Rusby promised to tell the police Stefano had a job. The sisters became somewhat calmer, but the hysteria did not subside. The cave dwellers fanned each other's excitement. The noise they made was like a panic in a zoo. A heavy old woman pushed angrily up to me and shouted, "This is beautiful, isn't it? Just like America!" I could not answer her. Rusby told me her husband was dead of the "teepeech," that she had six children living in the cave. "Almost all the residents of Capodimonte are related one way or another," he said. The woman insisted I look at her cell where she lived with three unmarried children. Next door three women slept together on a bit of straw in a corner. "Does it remind you of America?" the old woman demanded. A woman who had borne twenty children of whom three were living was carrying the youngest, a sick thing, in her arms. She asked me to look at it. *Il bravo Americano*—she meant Belden Paulson—had arranged a daily supply of chocolate milk. The child was a listless doll with glassy blue eyes, fair soft curls, and feverishly pink cheeks. It was too feeble to cry.

"*Teepeech!*" the woman said, and added that her two other children were in a hospital with "teepeech." She raised the arm of the infant and let it drop. It fell like old rope. "*No buono,*" she said. "*Kaputt! Finito!* [No good. Finished]."

Beside me the angry old woman stormed. "Will you come and live here? It is cheaper than a hotel." A youngish man tried to silence her. "I will speak," she shouted. "I will not be quiet." Rusby said the young fellow was one of her sons; he was twenty-one years old and his name was Alberto. He was haggard and nervous and looked considerably older. He was coughing. "My *mamma* is very exciting," he said to me in Neapolitan street English. "You give me cigarette?" I slipped him several cigarettes. He lit one, shaking like an aspen. It doubled him with coughing, but he drew hungrily on it. Alberto attached himself to me as a sort of protector, inviting me to come to see his *casa*, which he said was the "nicest house in Capodimonte."

I went with him to a large room closed off from the other cells. Inside it was brightly illuminated, a bizarre island of electricity in a sea of darkness. Here Alberto lived with his wife, a brother and a sister, and their mates. The men, by holding intermittent laboring jobs and pooling their resources, had gathered together some scraps of human domesticity. The room was clean and almost grotesquely cheerful. Three large beds, covered with pink satin spreads, nearly filled it. There were several chairs and a phonograph, all bought on the installment plan, Alberto proudly informed me. The walls were covered with the usual confusion of saints and Hollywood stars. The occupants were there in the room, the brother, the sister's consort, and the three girls, two of them pregnant. All six appeared to be around twenty years of age. Alberto gave the two boys cigarettes; they lit them then began to cough. The sister's consort, a thin adolescent in a turtle-neck sweater, muffler, and beret, put a record on the phonograph. It was an old Glenn Miller recording, "A String of Pearls." The garish music echoed through the cave, drowning out the coughing. The sweatered youth became tense. He planted his feet solidly, spread his knees, and began moving his body to the rhythm. He reached for his wife and whirled her about, hardly moving himself. The other two couples, Alberto and his brother and their wives, joined them, dancing, puffing their cigarettes, and coughing.

Their pale faces glowed with color, beads of perspiration formed on their brows. The men crouched low, doing a sort of American jitterbug. At the open door the citizens of Capodimonte, the sick children and wheezing men, the women carrying babies inside and outside their bellies, gathered to watch, enjoying a moment's release from the ennui of the endless night. In the center of them the angry old mother beamed and forgot her rancor as she looked proudly on her brood.

Then an unearthly grinding shook the cave, a racket which sickened the stomach and set the teeth on edge. "*I compressori* [the drills]!" the cave dwellers said. Rusby explained that pneumatic drills on the stone roof of Capodimonte were sinking pylons for a new church to be built by the Neapolitan diocese.

It was more than I could bear. I started for the round hole of light by which we had entered. The cave dwellers followed, laughing at me, the weak *Americano* who could not endure their reality. "*Vedi!* Look at him! See him go!" they bayed, following me past the glowing shrine of the Virgin, as far as the police permitted them, taunting, laughing, and coughing. Between spasms of the drill, I could hear faintly in the background "A String of Pearls."

Outside, the sun was shining. I felt as though I had been spewed up from hell and was unworthy of my redemption. From the dark hole those for whom there was no redemption watched, bright eyes glowing in pale faces. Above, the drills ground, planting roots for yet one more temple of stone to a poor carpenter's son.

CHAPTER 9

THE DAUGHTER OF SAN CARLO

As THE YANKEES and the Dodgers split Americans into rival camps, La Scala and San Carlo divide Italians.

Both opera houses were built in the eighteenth century, both were bombed in the war, and both have been restored. Of the two, Milan's La Scala is the grander and more elegant. Its association with Verdi and Puccini and the career of Arturo Toscanini have made it the most famous opera house in the world. San Carlo is a smaller, lovelier house with an intimate spirit more conducive to the enjoyment of music. Productions at La Scala are elaborate and spectacular. At San Carlo they are more fun.

I went to Naples to hear Renata Tebaldi in *La Traviata*. Prima donnas are a common commodity in Italy, and debuts are frequent, but Tebaldi's had aroused a musical tempest.

The Junoesque young singer was a home-town girl, called by the journals "the daughter of San Carlo." She had been to America and failed to make an impression. Earlier in the season she had sung the role of Violetta at La Scala. It had been an unfortunate debut; both the press and audience were hostile. The American failure had disappointed Miss Tebaldi's Neapolitan admirers, but the Milan debacle infuriated them. The newspapers fanned the old rivalry. A Naples columnist wrote, "What did they do to our dear girl up there in the north? Did they really have the bad manners to make her weep? Neapolitans will be happy to protect her and give her back the faith she needs." One journal accused La Scala's conductor, Victor De Sabata, of sabotaging the performance, a charge which Miss Tebaldi hastily refuted. During the fuss and feathers, the singer quietly returned home and continued to study *La Traviata* for San Carlo.

The Ministro degli Spettacoli in Rome had given me letters entitling me to free entrance to Italy's opera houses. The letters brought me a variety of receptions, depending on the politics of the local managements. In Milan the letter was greeted with stiff politeness; in Rome it was ignored; in Catania it unlocked the royal box; in Florence, where anti-American feeling was high, it aroused hostility. In monarchist Naples my welcome was the most cordial. I was received as if I had been a visiting prince.

It was the day before Tebaldi's *La Traviata* and tensions were high at the opera house. I presented my letter to the secretary, Dr. Rogreni Ferucco, a small bubbling man of middle years, with flashing eyes and black hair. The fact that I was American sent Dr. Ferucco into a fever of excitement. *"Americano!"* he cried out. "The most wonderful people in the world, the Americans. So sweet! So sincere! So honest! So noble! So beautiful!" Then he kissed his fingers with ecstasy and started to sing "The Star-Spangled Banner" in a cracking tenor. To his colleagues he introduced me as *"Un maestro Americano."* Conversation between the doctor and me was difficult. He had no patience to hear out my labored Italian and his own Neapolitan was so furiously paced that I understood only part of it. Now he was telling me that I must move at once into the fashionable seaside Excelsior Hotel as a guest of the opera company. I tried to make him understand that he had greatly magnified my importance and refused the invitation. This almost brought tears to his eyes. How could I think of it, coming all the way from America to visit the opera and not accepting such a slight courtesy? "I will arrange for you to meet beautiful girls, as many as you desire," he promised. "Do you prefer sopranos or ballerinas?"

It was a decision I was not often called upon to make, and I deliberated. "Sopranos run somewhat large for my tastes," I said.

"But they need bellows. How can they sing *Aïda* without bellows?"

"I know."

"Of course, if you want a puny little Musetta?"

"Not too puny," I said. "And she would have to sing well."

"I think you would prefer a ballerina," said the doctor.

"But I have never seen an Italian ballerina whose dancing I liked," I said.

"How can you know without seeing, Maestro?" the doctor said. "Come, I will show you the ballerinas!"

He led me through the opera house. I tried to explain that "Maestro" was hardly a title I deserved. He embraced me. "Ah, Maestro," he protested. "Such modesty! Such sensibility! Only an American would have it. Neapolitans love Americans. In Naples there were no Fascists, just four or five wicked men who led the people astray. You cannot imagine the joy when the Germans are gone. How the people of Naples danced when the Americans freed them from the Nazi oppressors! Americans were angels from heaven sent by God to save us. Maestro, how fortunate you are to be American and live in such a noble land." He started to sing the United States Marine Hymn.

In the grand tier promenade Dr. Ferucco unlocked a door. I followed him into darkness. Not until the door was shut did he turn on the lights. *"Veda! Bellisimo!"* He spoke with soft reverance. We were in the royal box, directly facing the stage. Of all the royal opera boxes I had seen, it was the most regal. Suspended over it and covering the full width of the box was a great gold crown; from it was draped a stone canopy fashioned like folds of cloth. The doctor called for the house lights; in a moment the theater glimmered like a rich gold and ruby jewel, a true flowering of the baroque style. Almost round, it had six tiers reaching to a magnificently frescoed ceiling. Over the stage hung the crest of the House of Savoy and a great gilded clock, the hands of which were the arms of gold Venuses. Passing his finger over the red and gold chairs, the doctor brushed away the dust. "A sin!" he muttered. "Dust on the seat of a king."

"Apparently the box hasn't been recently occupied," I said.

"The box of the King is never occupied," the doctor said.

I replied that it was a pity, since the opera house was always sold out, to waste so many seats. La Scala used its royal box. I had sat in it myself. The information brought a curious reaction from the doctor.

"I am aware," he said, "that La Scala uses its royal box. Here at San Carlo it is kept sacred to the name of Savoy. No one has sat here since Mussolini." Then, thinking I might be offended at the mention of the Duce, the doctor burst into vehement epithets. "Uncultured brute! Boorish peasant! Primitive beast! Hitler pig!" His voice rose; he was protesting, I thought, too much.

The ballet school which the opera company conducts was at the top of the house. We crossed the stage, set with Violetta Valery's salon for the first act of *La Traviata*. "This is the stage from which Enrico Caruso was hissed," the doctor said. At the right of the stage an elevator squeaked precariously down from the flies. It was a cage of open grillwork suspended only by ropes. When the doctor opened the door for me, I expressed some apprehension about its safety. He laughed. "It is as safe as a bed," he said. "With Ferucco there is nothing to fear." Looking back over my shoulder, I noticed him gravely making the sign of the cross and muttering a paternoster before he stepped in behind me. As we started to jerk upward, two black cats crossed the stage. "We have many black cats to keep the house free of rodents," the doctor said. "For rats and mice, black cats are best."

We made the unnerving ascension without mishap. The upstairs area was a vast barnlike room whose ceiling billowed like a blimp hangar. We passed through some scenery studios, the walls of which were decorated with designs for opera sets. "Ah, *Il Mosè*," said Ferucco, looking at one and kissing his fingertips. "*Bellissima!*" He sang several bars from an aria of the opera. We reached the next design. "*Tosca!*" Another kiss and the doctor burst into "*È lucevan le stelle.*" Next came *Falstaff*. "*Formidabile!*" he shouted and sang "*Dal labbro il canto estasiato vola.*" He bellowed through the gallery to a sunlit ballet studio. The ballet mistress, a buxom blonde woman, sat on a high stool, thudding her Aaron's rod on the floor. "*Sur les pointes! Sur les pointes!*" she cried.

"*Bambini*," Dr. Ferucco whispered, "beginners." They were, indeed, children from twelve to fifteen years of age; thirteen pretty girls, some astonishingly plump, and four slender boys, haughty and superior, with gold bracelets on their ankles. They were chewing gum. "*Il maestro Americano*," Dr. Ferucco introduced me to the mistress. "Maestro" I was to remain. The mistress, a retired ballerina, dropped from her stool to the floor, bowed, and insisted that I take her place. I felt like a dunce in an arithmetic class as she clapped her hands sharply and signaled to the lady at the piano. The pianist beat out a spirited *Dance of the Hours*, to which I had hurled myself about with more abandon than skill in a dancing class almost twenty years ago. While her students whirled on their toes, the mistress explained that dancers were selected very young and were required to study at least five years before they were permitted on stage. Dr. Ferucco asked me wickedly if I was finding any of the little ballerinas delectable. I turned to see if he was joking. He was. "It would be difficult to arrange with their *mamme*," he said. "We will have to wait for a real ballerina."

We took our leave. Behind us I heard the mistress thump her crook. "*Sur les pointes!* This is a swan lake; not a duck pond!" she scolded. Singing "*La donna è mobile*" and "*Celeste Aïda*," the doctor took me on a walk of the king's promenade which connects the opera house to the

royal palace. Remembering his love for democracy, he bubbled the praises
of Abraham Lincoln and Franklin Roosevelt. Back in his office he handed
me a white pasteboard box, the kind in which pastry shops pack fancy
cakes. He said it was an "Easter sweet" for me and that I should open it
at once. It contained a chalk-white death mask. My shock sent the doctor
into uncontrolled laughter. The mask was a copy of one made of Francesco
Cilea, recently deceased composer whose opera *Gloria* was being prepared for production. "Note the serenity and tranquillity," said the doctor, gently stroking the dead features. "It is a beautiful thing."

He showed me pictures of sopranos, pointing out those who would be
happy to meet an American maestro. He invited me to dinner and assured
me that during my stay in Naples my every wish was his command. I had
to remind him that what I really wanted was tickets for the operas, particularly the performances of Renata Tebaldi. "Tebaldi!" He kissed his
fingers. "When she sings Violetta she will make the whole world forget the
terrible scandal of La Scala. For tonight, I must apologize, the tickets will
not be the best in the house. Tonight you must sit in the manager's box.
But after tonight you will have armchairs, the best in the house."

I invited an American composer, a Fulbright scholar in Naples, to go
with me that night. When we presented our tickets, the sword-bearing
gendarmes at the door would not permit us to pass. We were, he said, not
properly dressed. It was my companion's necktie. Not only was it not a
black bow, it was rather a flashy flowered affair. I said that I was sure
Dr. Ferucco would wish us to be admitted. The officer was adamant, as
uniformed Italians are apt to be. Soon a score of brightly uniformed ushers,
doormen, and policemen gathered round like a *Student Prince* chorus.
After a frantic consultation, they decided that I might enter, but not my
friend. I refused, and the stalemate continued. A crowd collected to await
the outcome. Finally a desperate doorman telephoned the director's office.
He came back with orders that we were to be taken to our seats at once.
"*Uno scandalo!*" snorted the head usher. A guard in a tricornered hat
and a sword quickly ushered us to the box. When he had hidden us from
the public eye, he carefully locked the door from the outside.

Within five minutes the key rattled in the lock and Dr. Ferucco flew in.
He was a startling sight. His face was hot with excitement. With his evening dress he was wearing a bright green tie, which he had obviously just
put on as a democratic gesture to us. He took us in his arms, both at the
same time, and sputtered his apologies for the indignities to which we

had been subjected. "Forgive me for the ignorance of those stupid cretins," he begged. "What do they know about democracy? Fascisti! Every one of them! For my very life I would not have had this happen. Americans are the most democratic people in the world. Oh, I wish I were in America this minute! Such a brave country! Such a noble people! The saviors of the world!" I assured him the matter was forgotten. He praised our understanding, our compassion, our kindness, and then popped out to attend to other matters.

The lights dimmed. People were quiet, quieter than they would have been in church. Someone whispered and was shushed with angry hisses. The curtain parted on Violetta and her friends. Unhappily, we were too close for a perfect illusion. The drawing room set was tacky. The tall Tebaldi looked more like a blooming Valkyrie than the frail consumptive Violetta. The audience applauded, sending its warmth to the stage. Tebaldi started to sing, filling the house with her opening, "I bid you all welcome." Her voice was sweet, strong, and well controlled, effortless and pure as a bird's. The house settled back; everything was fine. Between singer and audience there was complete rapport. The audience participation is what makes the difference between hearing opera at San Carlo and, say, New York's Metropolitan. In America opera is for musical connoisseurs to whom the libretti of Verdi, Puccini, and Bellini often seem lurid, hysterical, or downright silly. In Italy the stories are part of life; arias are the popular music of the people.

The act moved on; the performance grew and bloomed. Tebaldi lost herself in the opera's sweet sadness. Her performance cast a glow over the whole company; other singers responded and sang the better. When the curtain fell on *"Sempre libera,"* the house burst into cheers. Tebaldi took seven curtain calls.

At each intermission the salons and corridors were a delirium of excitement. Students ran from the galleries into the streets to buy roses. Crowds of people were gathered outside to participate vicariously in the excitement. The word spread that Tebaldi was as great as Claudia Muzio in her prime. Flying through the crowd, Dr. Ferucco shouted, "Ah, Tebaldi! Ah, Verdi!" I noticed that he had changed back to his black bow tie. During the second-act duet I could hear weeping. When it was over cries for an encore went up, *"Bis! Bis!"* Tebaldi and the baritone, who had left the stage, returned to the garden to repeat the duet.

Neapolitans live in constant intimacy with death; one has only to see the daily parades of hearses to know it is never far from their minds. The death of Violetta was so real to this audience that there was sobbing in the theater even before the last act began. Tebaldi started gently, rising in emotion and voice. As she died, she seemed to grow in spirituality. Her final cry, "'Tis life returning! Oh, rapture!" was a jubilant expiation.

The house turned into bedlam. The curtain rose and fell on a score of curtain calls. The crowd surged down through the orchestra toward the stage where Tebaldi was throwing kisses into the theater. From the balconies and boxes, students pelted her with roses, great bundles of them flying through the theater, until she was knee-deep in them. Lackeys in pink satin pantaloons and buckled shoes swept them up and carried them off. Still they came, like rain, while three ushers struggled to keep the stage clear. The demonstration was a vindication of the indifference of America, the injustice of Milan. The ovation did not stop until Tebaldi, spent and clinging to the curtain, begged for release. The hour was one-thirty A.M.

The singer's triumph swept the city like a fire. The next performance two days later was a popular-priced one beginning at six o'clock. All day students and workers stood in line for admission. Inside they chanted "Tebaldi! Tebaldi!" as if the name belonged to a football hero. When the house lights dimmed and the orchestra began the prelude, sobs burst out in the darkened theater even before the curtains were raised. It was an even better show than the first. Each time Tebaldi cleared a high note she was cheered as if she'd made a touchdown. There were encores during the opera, and by the third act everyone was so spent with weeping and shouting that a sort of peace settled over the house. But in the end the eruption was more tumultuous than before. Students leaped onto the stage in an attempt to capture the soprano and carry her in triumph to the streets. The battle of roses continued a half hour until Tebaldi herself was quite hysterical from laughing and weeping. I made a trip backstage and discovered that what I had suspected was true; ushers were carrying the roses from the stage into the lofts where students threw them a second, even a third, time. The matinee which began at six P.M. finished at eleven o'clock.

For a fortnight the daughter of San Carlo was the toast of the town. Performances of Cilea's *Gloria* and Beethoven's *Fidelio* were canceled so that more *Traviatas* might be scheduled, as many as two or three a week.

Seats were sold out as soon as they went on sale, and one saw the same people at each performance. Finally, Tebaldi, exhausted, had to stop. Naples settled back to normalcy.

Before I sailed for America I went to say good-by to Dr. Ferucco. He was sorry, he said, that I hadn't found a wife among the ballerinas. "Italian girls are obedient, sympathetic, and understanding," he said. "They make perfect wives for artists. A young man without a wife is a sadness. When you come back if you do not have a wife I will find one for you, a beautiful young Tosca. I think perhaps it is sopranos you prefer after all."

I promised to return, whether it was for a wife or not.

"When you are in America, you will forget us and never return," the doctor said.

"I will be back," I said.

"We will welcome you," he said. "San Carlo is your home in Naples."

CHAPTER 10

CITIZENS OF THE WORLD

Is CAPRI or Taormina more beautiful?

In all gathering places of international bohemians, those migratory birds of passage who follow the seasons, one hears the question argued. Hostility between the two resorts is traditional. Both were playgrounds of antiquity, Taormina first of the Greeks and later of the Romans; Capri of the Romans. Shopwindows in both communities display photographs of contemporary celebrities who have indicated a preference. In Taormina I saw the faces of Orson Welles, Gayelord Hauser, Truman Capote, Alan Ladd, and the late André Gide; in Capri those of Ronald Coleman, Greta Garbo, and Barbara Stanwyck. "Sicilians are primitive peasants, uncultured sheepherders," a Capri vintner said when I told him I had recently been in Taormina. A young Taorminese told me, "Capri is jazz. Taormina is Mozart."

One Saturday noon, I went down to the Naples harbor and bought a ticket for the little Capri boat. Everyone but me seemed to be traveling with friends. As the boat pulled out of the harbor, I fell into a brooding loneliness. On deck it was windy and cold, so I spent the two hours writing letters and drinking vermouth in the boat's tiny bar. At Capri's Marina Grande we got a noisy reception from hucksters and guides. I rode the funicular to the town above. The village square, like a diminutive opera setting, was just awakening from its afternoon siesta. I found my way through a labyrinth of tunneled alleys to the Albergo Bel Soggiorno, the Beautiful Visit Hotel, where a room was reserved for me. Here I was greeted by an amply built, handsome girl about twenty years old. Her name was Maria and she was overjoyed that I was American, for her happiest memories were of the war years when the Beautiful Visit was a convalescent home for American fliers. She showed me to a large, clean room with two beds and a veranda looking out on the sea. Under the veranda an orange tree bore ripe fruit. She gave me a front-door key, a medieval iron affair that filled my pocket.

I began an explorative walk through streets three feet wide covered with roofs and arches. As the crowds came out of the network of tunnels onto the piazza, the operatic illusion was greater than ever, for the costumes were as colorful and varied as those of a *Rigoletto* mob. There were more men than women, and like birds, the males were more brilliantly plumaged. I saw chartreuse corduroy trousers, black velvet bullfighters' pants, an assortment of embroidered shirts, fringed and tasseled headgear and an Inverness cape of bright orange. Some of the men had beards which they'd trimmed to look like D. H. Lawrence or Ernest Hemingway, depending on how much they weighed. The two languages most spoken were the two I best understood, English and German. A majority of the men seemed to be American and English, but many Swiss women moved in and out of the crowds like gray chirping sparrows.

In the assortment of people, I began to recognize some faces; a student from Boston named Tom, an artist who had worked on a magazine with me in New York, and several I remembered seeing in Taormina, but whose names I did not know. One of them, an arty aesthete with a fashionably lean face and wavy blond hair, joined me under an awning for a drink. He was wearing carefully faded blue denims. His name was Alexander and he said he was Scottish. I suspected he was really American. I had observed that aesthetic young Americans frequently invent other nationalities for themselves.

"You're that writer chap," he said. "I'm doing a little writing too, but nothing really serious. It's just too boring here and I don't know where to turn. Where can one go? I've been living in Paris but I hate it, and really, you know, one must live someplace and where can one live but Paris even if one does just *loathe* it."

I tried to muster up some compassion for his plight. In turn he commiserated with me. "The Beautiful Visit is a distinctly third-rate hotel," he said. "Living there you simply won't meet anyone. To get into Capri society you must rent a villa or at least live at the Grand Hotel Quisisana. Too bad you didn't know that. Countess Mondschein is having a dinner tomorrow night for Tom. . . . You know he's the ambassador's cousin. I might have arranged an invitation, but living at the Bel Soggiorno makes that quite impossible." I said I was only staying two days and had no social ambitions. "Of course you can always take up with people you run into. Everyone eats at the Gemma, and afterward the only place to go is Tabu."

Alexander excused himself for a cocktail date. I walked into the open country where the long shadows of the hills fell like chilling blankets. On all sides the sea was glimmering through evening mists. It was the eve of the Sabbath, and in the hills I heard men singing a Neapolitan *canzone*, and farther on a hymn to the Virgin. Through centuries of invasion by strangers, the Caprese has receded into the landscape; to the visitors who bring him prosperity, he is aloof and diffident. Foreigners are rarely on intimate terms with a native of Capri. One meets instead Swiss, English, Scandinavians, and Americans. Visitors do not remain long; a visit of two or three days is average.

On every side I faced breathtaking post-card scenery which seemed no more real than the operatic village. Capri, "the pearl of the bay of Naples," is a toy island with a toy enchantment, a miniature world all within walking distance. Because it is so small and so many people visit it, it is always crowded.

The Capresi are a prosperous and happy people. I could hear them coming home from the hills, singing everywhere. The brown, barefoot vintners and fishermen I met were cordial but not overfriendly. Compared to the tourists' costumes, their twisted berets, old patched denims and blue turtle-neck shirts seemed like protective coloring. Above me, carved into a perilous precipice on a ledge over the sea, was a shrine to the Virgin. There She was, challenging stalwart youths to scale Her wall and place a lighted candle at Her feet. Many succeeded, for the candles in the deepening shadows stood out like stars.

It was dark when I returned to the village. I went to the Gemma, a series of connected caves with whitewashed walls which set off the bright costumes of the diners. In one room some youths were singing "Roll Me Over Again" to the accompaniment of a hunchbacked guitarist. I took a table in an adjoining room hoping to absorb some of the merriment. But lonely ones are not welcomed by the group and even the waiter was hostile because I had a table which ordinarily seated four. I ordered a bottle of wine and a steak. When I had drunk and eaten, I left. In the room of the hunchback they were singing "Loch Lomond." Outside I heard another tune, "Alexander's Ragtime Band," ringing through the town. I followed it through several tunnels to the night club Tabu. Inside they were dancing the Charleston. Disembodied legs and arms seemed to be flying through the room. I joined the bar stag line and watched them dance by, an American college girl in a white blouse with a supercilious Neapolitan escort, a French blonde in slacks with a German man in satin trousers. Men and women appeared to be engaged in an extravagant sartorial race, with the men in the lead. The musicians blew police whistles and made a devil of a racket. For an encore they played "Nola." An elderly Swedish couple, rich and handsome, stood up and danced through the melee with old-world dignity. Two youths arrived and ordered "parliamentaries." The bartender emptied some gin and squeezed some lemon into a glass of beer and added two straws. "No, darling, you should know never to put *two* straws in a parliamentary. Take one out please!" one youth addressed the bartender. Then he turned to me. "My name's Algy. I never associate with geniuses, so if you're a genius you might as well tell me at once and we'll drop the whole thing."

I was saved by the arrival of Alexander and Boston Tom, who joined Algy and his pal. On a small pad I made shorthand jottings of their conversation. It went like this:

Boston: "I'm getting drunk. Where are we? In Italy or in Paris?"

Algy: "In Tabu, darling. Don't you remember?"

Alexander: "Perhaps we should all go to Paris."

Algy: "But we can't. My villa in Paris hasn't any heat and I've got to stay here at least another month."

The Nameless One: "How is the Comtesse de Courville? She's my oldest enemy. We love each other madly. Does she look as green as ever?"

Alexander: "You know we really should all go to Cannes to be with Rita for the divorce. That bastard Ali's going to make it beastly for her."

Algy: "Rita and I have worked the whole thing out together."

Boston: "What, darling?"

Algy: "When to be foolish and when not to be foolish, of course."

A cowboy entered—at least he was dressed like one—in boots, a Stetson, tight pants, and a beige buckskin shirt with six-inch fringes. He was a lean boy, blond, blue-eyed, with a smile as big as his hat.

"Stirrup!" So he was greeted along the bar. He strolled to the end and took a place beside me. Without waiting for an order, the barkeep served him a double Haig-and-Haig. Stirrup took it in one gulp and the barkeep poured another. With the second Stirrup took his time. He turned his open face to me. "I met Orson Welles in here once," he said."You know, Orson Welles is a great guy. He's the leader of the international set." He spoke slowly, gently, as if he were talking to a child, but with a masculine vigor. "I'm bored," he said. "You see, the Riviera isn't warm until May first, so I got to stay here until then. I'm bored as hell."

"That's tough luck about the Riviera," I said.

"Yeah. April is a bad time. I got no place to go. In June I go to Paris and in July to Scotland. But where is there to go in April? I wanted to go to India, but they wouldn't let me drive my car through the Khyber Pass."

"Life is all complicated by red tape," I said, "like not letting you drive your car through the Khyber Pass."

"Yeah," he said gratefully. He bought me a drink. "You know there aren't many places left a man can go. I spent most of the winter at Casablanca and Cyprus. But man, it got to be a drag. I'm getting sick of the Mediterranean circuit. In here, for instance, it's the same thing every night. Same people. I'm bored."

"Maybe you ought to have a hobby," I said.

"That's what everyone says. I got three. I collect old coins. I take pictures of dirty statues. You'd be surprised how many dirty statues there are to take pictures of. My favorite hobby is racing my MG. I'm trying to fix up a race from Cairo to Alexandria with a guy that's got a Porsche. If he'll race, we'll go to Egypt next week. Man, it's something to do."

"Haven't you got any ambition in life?" I asked.

"Yeah. I got one. It's never to go back to Boulder. I was born in Boulder and I got a strong ambition never to go back there again. It's not that I don't like my people. I like them fine as long as they keep sending me those little blue slips of paper every month. There's enough of those blue slips back in Boulder. You oughtta know my old man. He's eighty-three years old and he rips around in a convertible. He's just got married the third time and I got a new mother that's twenty-two, which is two years younger than I am, and I'll bet the old bastard knocks her up. That's *his* ambition. You see, he never had any other kids. I'm the only one. My mom was thirty-five years younger than my old man when *she* married him. They got divorced when I was a year old. Her score is higher than his. She's been married six times. I got an aunt just got married the fifth time to the onion king of California. I had four fathers before I was ten years old. I got kicked around. The old man's in fire insurance and mom's in real estate. See what

I mean about the dough? I ain't the insurance or real-estate type. So all they gotta do is keep sending me those slips.

"I got another ambition. I want to play boogie piano in the Rue Pigalle. Used to play boogie in the village when I went to NYU. I went to NYU because my grades were so bad it was the only school that would take me. Went to Eddie Condon's or Nick's every night. Flunked out in my sophomore year. Modern history and economics. Got a B in philosophy. Now that's the sort of course I like. You just sling a lot of bull the professor doesn't understand and you're okay. The world situation? Listen, pal, I figure I'll drink myself to death by the time I'm thirty-five, so the next eleven years in the history of the world ain't going to make much difference one way or the other. Haven't looked at a newspaper in two months. They depress me. So don't tell me what's going on. I don't want to know. All I want to know is, will that blue slip catch up with me by the first of the month. That's all. As long as I keep needing it, I figure it will."

The police whistles blew and the orchestra started a frenetic samba. I asked for my check.

"Where you going?" Stirrup asked.

"I need air!" I said.

"Me too." Stirrup followed me out. It was raining softly. The piazza was empty. The moon broke through a layer of clouds over Naples; the lights of the city flickered like a diadem.

"You happy?" Stirrup asked.

"It's enough not to be unhappy," I said.

"I was happy once. It was the three years I was in the Marines. Had lots of friends then."

"Maybe you should go back into the Marines."

"The way I figure, why? If there's a place in life for me I'm waiting for it to find me. If it doesn't then I'll drink myself to death. I like the International Set. I like to go where Orson Welles goes."

"Be seeing you," I said.

"I get lonely," Stirrup said. "Don't you?"

"Sure," I said.

"I get lonely as hell," he said.

Sunday began badly with a headache and not an aspirin in the Beautiful Visit. I ordered orange juice and got two ounces in a glass, though an acre of oranges was growing right outside my window. The weather was dreary, but later the sun came through and I set off with a group of tourists for the Blue Grotto. The four men, including a priest, and one woman in my boat talked German, so I concluded I was with Germans. I couldn't have been more mistaken. The woman and her husband were an American military couple on vacation from Frankfurt. Two men appearing to be about thirty years of age and wearing splendid brown tweeds were the captain and first mate of a British world-cruise vessel docked at Naples. The priest was Father Sepp Diesbach, teacher in a parochial boys' school in Canton Zug, Switzerland. He was the most animated passenger in the group and kept the boat rocking precariously. To enter the small mouth of the grotto we had to lie flat on our backs. As our boatsman paddled us into the silver azure underworld, he said, "Here Tiberius kept as prisoners the most beautiful youths and maidens of the Roman Empire, as nude as the day they were born. . . ." Father Diesbach sat up and bumped his head on the ceiling.

At the end of the expedition the priest, the two seamen, and I banded together for lunch. The three were on Capri just for the day, so they were anxious to see as much of the island as possible. We heard that lobsters were a specialty at a restaurant in the Little Marina across the island, so we took the funicular up into the village and walked down the other side. As we snaked along the cliffs, Father Diesbach chattered away; the tight-lipped seamen listened silently. On a ledge above us the priest spotted something that looked like edelweiss and made a perilous little climb to investigate it. While he was gone I learned that the sea captain was named Bob Robinson. He was a robust man with an air of mystery about him, a sort of Joseph Conrad character. I judged him to be about thirty-five years of age and was startled when he said he was fifty-one. He was a widower with two grown sons and, as he casually put it, "several bastards." The first mate, whose name was Paul Cox, had the same bronzed hardness that marks professional seagoing men. He was twenty-nine years old, lean and rangy, and had a wife in Liverpool whom he ironically referred to as "a little homemaker."

We passed signs announcing meetings of the *Partito Nazionale Monarchico* and another for the *Partito Communista di Capri*. Under a cliff by the sea we came upon an outdoor pavilion which was the restaurant we sought. Below us the waves broke angrily against the rocks. Settled at a table in the sun we ordered a gallon of wine, Capri's regular. It was strong. Very quickly it unclammed the seamen, who began talking as freely as the priest. Father Diesbach did not speak English, so I interpreted from Swiss into English and back into Swiss. The priest, it turned out, was two weeks older than the captain. The coincidence made them pals. Captain Robinson confided to the priest that he had a "lady friend" in each of six cities, London, Paris, Lisbon, Dublin, New York, and Capetown, but that most of all he was partial to South Sea Island ladies. "When I retire in another five years I'm going to get myself a little piece of land on the Fiji Islands and settle down with a little brown girl," he said. "You ought to come along, Father."

Father Diesbach roared with laughter. "I will ask the permission of my bishop," he said.

We ate prodigiously, Paul Cox and I dividing a lobster the size of a rabbit. At a table several yards away the restaurant's only other guest, a little pink man wearing a blue beret from under which wisps of white hair protruded, watched us with interest. Captain Robinson was telling the priest he had a date in Naples that night with a girl named Angelina. "Spend the night in Naples, Father," the captain said. "I'll get you a little girl." Shaking with mirth, the priest said he'd like to but he had an appointment in Rome the next day to meet the Pope. While I was translating, the little man at the other table bustled over to us. *"Ihr sind doch Schwyzer,"* he said to the priest and myself. Amid a flood of high Swiss spirits he introduced himself as Rudi Troelsch of Glarus, Switzerland. I said I had a great grandmother who had come from Glarus. As simply as that I became his cousin. He called me Klaus, the Swiss diminutive for Nicholas. "This wine's not fit for a cousin of mine," he said in Swiss. He reprimanded the waiter for serving such an inferior wine, ordered it removed, and demanded several bottles of a pale canary-colored wine labeled "Angels' Tears." He polished the cut-glass goblets himself. Then. he tested the bottle for temperature. Handling the wine with loving care, he ceremoniously poured a glass for each. The Angels' Tears were light and dry with a cool bouquet and an excellent flavor. Herr Troelsch told us that he was the leading vintner of Capri and that the Tears had come from his own presses. We toasted him and he beamed with pleasure.

"There is a terrible sorrow in Heaven," Father Diesbach said. "All the angels are crying because the Heavenly Father has sent Dionysius to hell. Our good and sainted friend, Herr Troelsch, has bottled their sorrow."

Offering his glass to be refilled, Paul Cox said, "Bloody sad, these angels."

The sturdy little Swiss, about five feet, five inches tall, was a fountain of energy. In 1912 when he was about thirty years old he had traveled to Italy on a visit, liked Naples, married a Neapolitan girl, and stayed there. Like most Swiss who put down roots away from the homeland, he had prospered. He owned a popular German *bierstube* next to the USIS on Naples' Via Medina, a mountain-side vineyard, a wine press, an olive grove, several houses on Capri, a villa in Anacapri, and an old palace in the vicinity of Positano on the Italian mainland. And like most wandering Swiss he had never given up his Swiss citizenship; once a year he made a pilgrimage "home" to Glarus.

Father Diesbach, bubbling with high spirits, swore he'd never had such a holiday since he'd taken holy orders. He and Rudi Troelsch started to yodel a ballad of a mountain girl known as Vreneli von Guggisbärg, and her lover, Hans-Joggeli. "In my lover's garden there are two bushes," warbled the priest, "the one bears muscats and the other cloves," and Rudi Troelsch responded, "The muscats are sweet and bitter are the cloves." The captain took out his watch and saw it was time to start across the island for the Naples boat. Waving good-by to Rudi Troelsch, we set out in an open cab, careening wildly back and forth across the face of the cliff, taking the curves in true *Italiante* fashion. The priest, holding greater trust in God than the rest of us, remained unperturbed during the wild ride. Louder than ever he yodeled, "Down in the hollow there is a water mill," and from far below came the piercing voice of Rudi Troelsch, "It mills nothing but love, all night and all day."

The next day I walked two miles to the west Capri village of Anacapri to lunch with my new cousin, Rudi Troelsch. I arrived early enough to visit the church of San Michele, famous for its majolica pavements portraying the garden of Eden. The doors were locked, so I found the caretaker, a sharp-eyed little man who talked English. He took me up a corkscrew stair-case into a tiny organ loft. From there the pavements were incredibly beautiful, three thousand tiles in greens, yellows, and blues, covering the floor of the church. Against a rich background of flora was a tile menagerie of animals from the real and mythological world, lambs and crocodiles, leopards and unicorns. In the center of the floor an angel of the Lord cast forth Adam and Eve while the serpent coiled triumphantly about an oak. As I was looking down on this magnificence my guide started speaking of

New York. His name was Domenico Guida, he told me; in the 1920's he had been a New York bootlegger known as "Mingo."

"I know New York like a copper," he said. "Jimmy Walker and Babe Ruth were my friends. They knew they could trust Mingo for good stuff. Imported from Canada. No bad moonshine for Mingo's friends. Babe Ruth invited me to his box to see the ball games. I was there for the first game after his wedding. . . ."

Mingo acted out the game, taking a batting stance, swinging a bat, and imitating the excitement of the crowd all at the same time. The rickety little organ loft trembled.

". . . There is three men on bases, and Babe, he hits a homer, knocks the three men in and between third base and home plate he runs to the box to kiss his wife and then finishes his home run. The crowd is crazy. People jump into the field to mob the Babe. His wife is crying. Is biggest thing I ever saw."

After prohibition Mingo returned to Capri with his savings. "I am rich man in America," he said. "Is nothing to make five hundred dollars a week." Times had apparently changed; when I left, Mingo graciously accepted a hundred-lire tip for showing me the church.

Rudi Troelsch dined me in the sun, under a canopy of wisteria and lemon trees, overlooking the blue sea below. We ate thick steaks covered with fried eggs and washed them down with more Angels' Tears. Also present was Rudi's dog, a white woolly terrier, who on his own plate was served identical fare minus the Angels' Tears. "He's getting married tonight and he's going to need the steak," Rudi said. The bouncing little man talked endlessly, drawing all the elements of his bustling life into the conversation. Like a factory foreman in Zurich he complained of the shiftlessness of Italian laborers. "Poor workmen, these Italians. Irresponsible, lazy, not to be trusted. In thirty-nine years my troubles with them have never ended. It's a wonder I managed. Many times I thought of giving it all up and returning to Switzerland where men are honest and willing to work for their wages."

Lunch finished, Rudi took me on a tour of his orchards, vineyards, and houses he rented to his laborers. With the canine bridegroom yapping at our heels, he went on about his troubles with the natives, and wherever we went, the natives bowed graciously to the lord of Anacapri. "*Buon giorno, Signor Troelsch,*" they said, but there was no friendliness in it, only the servitude of the kulak for the landlord. It saddened me. When I said good-by, Rudi invited me to come to his *bierstube* in Naples. "Always some Swiss there," he said. "But business isn't what it was during the war. During the German occupation it was *lustig*, I tell you. Always full of soldiers singing and drinking and eating pigs' feet. The Americans also like my beer. Americans are *herrlich* boys, almost as *herrlich* as the Germans. But the English! *Schweinehunde!* You come, we will have a *yass* game and some *echtes Schweizer Bier*. But it will not be so *lustig* as in the war. You would have liked it then."

The lunch with my new cousin, despite its abundance of Angels' Tears, sank me back into the lonely despair that hung over my visit to Capri. I turned into the open country, going to the easternmost tip of the island toward the Villa Jovis, the most lavish of Tiberius' twelve Capri villas. It was a long steep climb up a rocky path. I started fast and was soon breathless and giddy. Below me the shadows of the mountains covered the chilling village; the Capri square looked like an insect colony crawling with brightly colored bugs. Above, the afternoon sun was still on the peaks. The higher I climbed the steeper it became. Except for some scraggly scrub pine and wild olive trees, life was behind me. My head swam. Some strange instinct urged me toward the top as if it were my soul that was imprisoned up there waiting for me to set it free.

The view was Olympic. From the summit of the island where, legends say, Tiberius threw his victims a thousand feet into the sapphire sea, the whole of the Neapolitan bay spread out. Naples was a soft coral cloud to the east; Ischia an indigo meadow to the north. Below, a pair of soaring seabirds cried to each other; otherwise it was silent. At the highest point was the church of Santa Maria del Soccorso, the Madonna of Succor. I climbed up through the crumbling walls of the villa, struggling on toward the benediction my spirit sought. When my legs buckled and would no longer carry me, I pulled myself with my hands. Reaching up to draw myself to the flat meadow at the top, a jaw closed on my hand.

I could go no farther. My legs were rubber and my head reeled. Like a hurt animal I gasped and whimpered. Time passed, how much I do not know. Then I felt a presence. Above me a young woman, strong and dark from the wind and sun, was looking down at me with a wondrous blend of laughter and pity. I pointed to my ensnared hand.

"*I lucertoli* [The lizards]," she said. She freed my hand from the coils of a small trap. "But you are not a lizard."

She helped me to my feet. I leaned against her and we walked across the plateau, stepping carefully so as not to spring any more lizard traps, toward Santa Maria del Soccorso and down the ledge to one of the rooms of Tiberius, a dark cool grotto where I lay on some wool, facing the door which looked on the sea and sky. There she cared for me, gave me some rice and bits of lamb to eat and some rich dark wine to drink, and I slept so that I did not know when the day turned into night, or where the world ended and the dream began. In sweet warmth I slept away the Angels' Tears.

In the morning we went together into the church and knelt before the Madonna of Succor. Then in the crisp sunlight outside we clasped hands. "*Arrivederci*," she said. "Until we meet again." I started down the path. The Capresi were singing with the birds as they went up into the hills to their vineyards and gardens. I felt whole and strong, my head was clear, my heart light.

I went to the Beautiful Visit to wash and change, and then I took the boat to Naples. There was a wind on the sea and the air was cold. Reno was on the boat with the Englishman, Algy. We exchanged greetings; they were going to Rome together. "I hear Orson Welles is making a movie," Reno said.

Algy turned to me. "Reno is so bloody manly. That's what's so refreshing about you Americans."

I went to the stern. Behind me Capri was fading into the mists. Still visible was the jutting tip of the island, the cliffs of Tiberius, and on top, the church of the Madonna of Succor and the grotto chambers of the Villa Jovis, looked no larger than swallows' nests under a cliff.

CHAPTER 11

THE VIRGIN'S CITY

"Sena Vetus Civitas Virginis"

I

I HAD SEEN THE WORDS engraved on a coin in a Rome museum: "Siena is the ancient City of the Virgin." Now, on a soft Friday in May, I was on my way to the Virgin's city.

The bus snaked gently through Tuscany. In the distance three hills formed a three-pointed star rising from the mists of the green Chianti plains. Originally Etruscan, the most medieval of all Italian cities was later colonized by Senus, the son of Remus, who gave it his name and the Roman symbol of the wolf suckling the twins. The Sienese had a stormy history. Their most hated enemies were the Florentines. For three centuries they fought their rivals until Florence bred the ruthless Medici geniuses, under whose leadership she rose brilliantly to Tuscan supremacy.

The wars with Florence were responsible for Siena's intimacy with the Virgin. On September 2, 1260, the austere councilors of the Siena republic sat in meeting in the Church of San Cristofano to consider the factional squabbles of their quarrelsome citizens. The night before, two hostile parishes had come to blows over a donkey and blood had flowed in the gutters. In the morning, wives bolted their doors in fear. While the councilors in the church were considering reprisals, and the malefactors were brawling in the piazza, two horses galloped through the unguarded gates. Women and old men peered fearfully from behind closed shutters to see riders bearing the hateful Guelph banners of Florence. At San Cristofano the horsemen presented a cruel ultimatum. The Republic of Siena must surrender at once to Florence, or the city would be annihilated. To make good the threat, armies were already riding in eastern Tuscany. The canny Florentines knew the time was propitious, that the strength of the

Sienese had been sapped by thirty years of internal fights. It was a black moment for the Sienese.

The councilors ordered bells tolled to stop the squabbling in the streets. From every quarter the people converged on the cathedral square, singing litanies and shouting prayers. Before the altar, the bishop and the governor prostrated themselves to make a pact with the Holy Virgin.

"We offer ourselves, our goods, and our city," they said. "Pray thee, Mother of Heaven, that thou wilt be pleased to accept it, though it is but a little gift. . . ."

"*Ave, ave!*" the people shouted.

"Likewise we pray and supplicate thee to defeat these accursed dogs, the iniquitous Florentines who wish to devour us."

"Amen," the people chorused.

Then, so history tells us, the people confessed their sins, made peace with each other, kissed their enemies, and received the Sacrament.

The Virgin accepted the challenge; she indicated as much that night by laying her mantle in the form of a white cloud over the city. With this miracle the Mother of the Prince of Peace annexed as her personal domain the most turbulent and bloodstained city in Tuscany.

Spurred with confidence, the Sienese marched to battle in the morning, meeting the enemy at Montaperti on the Arbia River. An eyewitness (quoted in *Palio and Ponte*, by William Heywood, Siena, 1904) tells what happened:

"It was astonishing to see the great butchery that they made of these dogs of Florentines. The slaughter ever increased, and so furious was the onslaught that if one fell to earth, he might by no means regain his feet and was trampled to death. And so great were the piles of slaughtered men, and horses, that it was difficult to pass them to smite what remained of the enemy. The blood stood ankle-deep, as if it were a lake, and flowed so strongly it would have sufficed to turn four great water mills. And the valorous people of Siena ever followed the Florentines, butchering them as a butcher slays the animals in a slaughterhouse. The number was incredible; there were ten thousand dead, besides the horses, which were slaughtered to the number of eighteen thousand. By reason of the great stench from the rotting corpses, for much time no one dwelt there, neither did any living thing come nigh it, save only wild and savage beasts."

The next day—Sunday, September 4—the victorious Sienese warriors returned to their city. To bring the captured *carroccio*—the Florentine battle chariot—into the city without lowering the Sienese banner, it was necessary to break a hole in the wall. The flag of Florence was dragged through the streets on the tail of an ass. For her decisive assistance in slaughtering Florentines, the Virgin was duly celebrated. In the cathedral the warriors laid the keys to their city before her image. It was a symbolic deed, making Siena forever the personal property of the Virgin. To proclaim her proprietorship, they struck new money with the words, "*Sena Vetus Civitas Virginis.*" The phrase was no idle one. Ever since, the Sienese have lived in intimate closeness with the Virgin. She is their advocate, defender, and mother. Her image was placed not only in churches, but in streets and houses. The Sienese performed every act of their lives in her name. They honored her with endless *feste*, including horse races known as *palios*, which still are the most spectacular celebrations in Tuscany.

Despite the patronage of the Mother of the Prince of Peace, the Sienese continued a quarrelsome lot. For three centuries blood flowed in the name of the Virgin. In the end she must have tired of being a goddess of war, for she punished them terribly with defeat. In 1554, German and Spanish troops joined Cosimo de' Medici for a final attack on Siena. On a hill outside the Porta Camollia, the foam-flecked cavalries of the two enemies hurled themselves at each other, and their infantries butchered one another until the ground was strewn with corpses. For eight anguished months Sienese soldiers resisted at the gate, while the citizens starved inside. The conquerors showed no mercy. Peasants who attempted to bring supplies to the starving city were hanged. In desperation, the Sienese thrust to a lingering death outside the gate the lame, the halt and the blind, the aged and the helpless young; all who were not useful to the defense were expended. In the cathedral the Sienese, by rededicating their city to her, reminded the Virgin of their pact, but the Virgin, distressed perhaps by the cruelty to children and aged, failed them. After eight months of starvation and with half the population dead, the enemy entered the town; the four-hundred-year-old Republic of Siena was finished. She lay dormant in history until 1859, when she made the first move toward a unified modern Italy by voting annexation to Piedmont and the monarchy of Victor Emmanuel II.

II

As the bus climbed the hill to the Camollia gate, I could see women cultivating their beans between rows of vines and white oxen pulling wooden plows across the slopes. There was a biblical languor over the land; it was hard to believe that the black, freshly turned furrows were once rich with human blood. Over the historic gate were carved the words, *"Cor Magis tibi Sena pandit"*—"Siena opens her heart to you wider than this gate." The gate was hardly wide enough for the bus to pass through.

It was the siesta hour and the city was asleep. We drove through a modern quarter and a public park, past the inevitable Excelsior Hotel, and stopped on the sweeping Piazza Matteotti. I left my baggage with the driver and went to find a room. This turned out to be difficult, for Siena has few hotels. Visitors to Siena usually come for the day on American Express or CIT tour buses from Florence, where hotelkeeping is a major industry. A clerk in a filled-up hotel made a phone call and found a room in the Pensione Ferrari. He gave me directions to get there. I walked through a maze of streets and found the right one, but I could see nothing that looked like a *pensione*. From a dank doorway a billowy, peroxided blonde woman in a red chenille bathrobe signaled me to come in. I ignored her and continued on my search for the Pensione Ferrari. The woman started to follow. I increased my pace. It was, I thought, hardly the time for such games. She caught up with me. Was I the American looking for a room? she asked; if so, she was Signora Ferrari.

Outside the signora's door there was a public urinal. The long dark entrance corridor was pungent with the acids of centuries. We passed through several rooms to one which was spacious and shabbily elegant. It was crowded with furniture; one of the two beds would do for my friend, Tullio Vacini, who was coming from Florence the next day. To my question about hot water, the signora smiled; the idea amused her. When I mentioned a bath, she laughed in my face. Yes, there was a bathroom, but the pipes were rusted and she'd never had them fixed. No point to it, since Siena was short of water. Then I remembered that water had always been a problem because the Sienese had built their city on ledges of arid tuffa rock.

"Don't the Sienese bathe?" I asked.

She shrugged. *"Si,"* she said, *"di tempo in tempo* [from time to time]."

The signora was the widow of a Mussolini colonel killed in the war. She

had a ten-year-old son, Umberto, a polite fat boy. There was also a lusty
young stonemason who, I found out later, shared not only the signora's
board, but also her bed.

I asked for a porter to carry my bags from the piazza. The signora
called her chambermaid, a slight peasant girl. I protested; the bags were
too heavy. Because of a back injury I could not carry them myself. The
signora assured me that peasant women were strong and Maria could
carry them. The girl could hardly lift the bags from the pavement. I followed her in shame, but my blushes were ignored. None of the men on the
streets even noticed. What, after all, was a woman but a beast of burden?

The town was coming to life, for now it was the hour of the *passeggiata*.
Bicycles swerved around corners; women shouted to each other from windows. I couldn't wait to explore the town. The tiny streets coiled gracefully about beautifully curved palaces. From a butcher's window the
heads of pigs grinned at me and the wide, brown eyes of calves stared in
amazement. The open bellies of cows were filled with flowers, wisteria
and ivy twined into an image of the Virgin. No Italian tradesman takes
more pains with his windows than the slaughterer; the pagan fascination
for blood and flesh is traditional.

One of the mysteries of Siena is its hunchbacks. Deformed men are as
common as one-legged men in German and Austrian towns. There is a
reason for the German cripples: German wartime surgery seems to have
consisted largely of amputations. But one wonders at the monsters of
Siena tottering through the dark alleys or sitting by the fountains taking
the sun. Centuries of crippling warfare, malnutrition, and disease must
have left their stamp on the genes of a prolific people.

Then there are the cats. Siena has more cats than any other city in Italy,
with the exception of Venice. Sienese cats have their own well-organized
municipality; different species maintain independent social lives. There
are great black panthers of cats, spotted tiger cats, aristocratic white cats,
scrubby gray ones, and puny cats with sick eyes. One sees them during
the siesta hour on roof tops, languishing in the sun, and when the sun is
low, hurrying through the shadows to and from appointments.

The kinship of the ark, fellowship between man and beast, is everywhere apparent. Like the animal sculptures in German cities, Siena has
horses, lions, griffins, and steers of stone leaping from the cornices of
buildings and iron ones serving as door knockers and banner holders. In
the north, the animals are placid, as if they had just been fed. Siena's are

either angry or on a stealthy prowl; their manner is as restless as the people's.

The heart of the town is the Piazza del Campo, a shell-shaped hollow where the three hills meet. From the Via Cavour, the main artery of business and society, you descend a broad flight of stairs known as the Costarella dei Barbieri, the little hill of the barbers. It is best to come upon the campo suddenly, to be swept at once into its elegant beauty. It has the shape of the graceful shell from which Botticelli's *Venus* rises. Its edge is bordered by a *corso*, or track, upon which the Virgin's *palio* is run. A stranger race track it would be hard to imagine. It rolls up and down and has two right-angle corners. At its elbows fourteenth-century palaces curve graciously along with it.

In the deep center of the campo stands the Palazzo Pubblico, the city hall, built for governing aristocrats, known as the *Signorie*. Vines and grass tufts grow like green hair in its ancient crevices; from its cornices, sleek stone dogs leap into mid-air. The *palazzo* is not so noble as Florence's Palazzo delle Signorie, but its Torre del Mangia is the fairest tower in Italy. It soars like no tower in the world, a graceful flight of fancy caught in brick and stone. It has borne witness to six centuries of Siena's history. Whenever people assembled to do good or evil, they did so in the piazza below. Armies gathered here on their way to battle and here they returned their prisoners for mutilation and execution. At the foot of the tower, the great preacher San Bernardino railed against gambling, lasciviousness, and the immodest dress of Sienese women and built a bonfire of cards, dice, false hair, cosmetics, and obscene books. Here in 1799 a mob sang *Ave Maria* while nineteen Jews were burned for the glory of the Virgin!

Today the campo is Siena's civic center. The religious center is the Piazza del Duomo. I came upon it from the rear, through a winding alley which brought me to the baptistery of the cathedral, also known as the Church of San Giovanni. In the darkness inside a figure glittered. It was a simpering statue of Jesus. Strands of pearls were looped from the neck, and the arms shone with jeweled bracelets and watches, all gifts of the devout. I thought of the power dams and factories that could be built, swamps drained, and land restored to feed the poor millions if all the money spent on expensive baubles, shrines, and statues in Italy were put to the common good. But mine was the Calvinist view; I had not yet learned to understand the Latin Catholic's spiritual hunger which is fed by the glitter of saints.

From the baptistery it was a few steps up to the highest plateau of the town, the summit on which the Sienese chose to place their cathedral, one of two great achievements of Gothic builders in Italy. They began it in 1229 and took one hundred and fifty years to finish it. Only a remarkable people could live so intimately with heaven and with hell; could think so lightly of life as to seek death in battle, and so profoundly of immortality as to embroider lace from marble, flute pillars from rock, and fit stone upon stone for six generations in order to raise toward heaven such a tribute to their Virgin patroness.

The Virgin must have been well pleased, for she brought them a blessing to which they were ill-accustomed. It was peace. The wars ceased, and for almost thirty years there was prosperity under the republican government. The borders of the state were enlarged. Siena was—finally— the equal of Florence, and the two states maintained a friendly alliance. Trade flourished, and everywhere there was building. On the Piazza del Campo the lordly Palazzo Pubblico was finished, and beside it the Torre del Mangio soared into the air. New city gates were opened and fountains were built. When word came that the Florentines were building a grandiose cathedral to the Virgin, the Sienese got the notion that their half-finished one was too small. They would build one much greater. They made new plans for a cathedral so monumental that the one they were already building would serve it as a transept. It would be the temple of the world, to remain forever the most majestic tribute to the Virgin on earth!

Something went wrong with the dream. Perhaps the Virgin herself questioned the motives of her self-appointed subjects. For in 1348 the great plague struck Siena. Everyone became sick and four out of five died. The ring of the hammer and chisel turned into the thud of the gravedigger's spade and the wail of the coffinmaker's saw. The splendid city of one hundred thousand dwindled to a haunted village of twenty thousand wretched souls. In the common misery old hatreds also died. A survivor wrote: "All those who remained alive lived as if they were brethren; and every man was familiar and jested with his neighbor, as if they were kinsmen; for to each of them it seemed he had regained the world."

The new temple was abandoned for lack of builders and money. The original cathedral was brought to completion, its lacy façade alone, with mosaics by Giovanni Pisano, marble saints, and animal statues, taking thirty more years. The outer shell of the great dream is still there, graceful high walls without a ceiling which frame patches of blue sky by day and shimmer at night like the white husk of a bombed city. Inside these walls, the finished building stands like a doll cathedral. The Siena police station is also there.

III

The piazza has the feel of eternity. I felt it most the next day at noon when I walked into it and saw the cathedral looking exactly as it does on the fifteenth-century paintings in the museums. Its walls and campanile are striped like a prisoner's suit, the strata of black and white marble representing the joys and sorrows in the life of the Virgin. The inside of the cathedral is disquieting and gloomy; its striped columns of black and white agitate rather than soothe the spirit. The too-rich collection of sculpture and painting clutter it like a museum; the wooden planks which cover the marble graphite floors add to the disorder. Worst of all is the veneer of baroque which threatens to strangle it like a multi-tentacled monster.

Such crimes against taste were committed in all Siena's great churches in the seventeenth century by Pope Alexander VII, a member of Siena's patrician Chigi family. The pontiff wished to bring to Siena the current fashions of Rome. Frescoes were covered with lime and painted over. Great paintings of the Sienese school were taken from the altars to make room for imitators of the florid Venetian and Bolognese schools. Their sprawling pictures are as tasteless as those which they imitated in St. Peter's of Rome. Rome's stylish sculptor Bernini fashioned gilded angels for the altar, and his pupils continued the travesty with statues of saints. One wonders how the Sienese, always so positive in their views, tolerated it.

But to enter the churches of Italy, indeed to enter Italy itself, one must leave his sense of order at the door. The whole is never so beautiful as its parts. In the Siena cathedral there is the library with its walls covered by ten frescoes from the life of Pope Pius II. The artist, Pinturicchio, was a Perugian. In all Italy there is nothing quite like these dazzling jewels of the Renaissance for decoration and pageantry. Each is a stage setting, teeming with the color of courtly life. In one of them, there is a mystery. Two figures stand facing front, utterly aloof from the regal bustlings about them. The older is a jaded, aging cynic; the younger a dreaming, fair-faced adolescent.

"Signore, do you know who are the two friends?"

The speaker was a bright little man, wearing a cap pushed back on his head, certainly the only male head covering in the cathedral. On it was printed *Sacristano*.

I said I didn't.

"They are the artist and his protégé," the sacristan said. "The boy is Raphael."

"Why is Pinturicchio so dour?" I asked.

"Ah, signore, he is very discontented. The pupil is young and he is not and he knows the boy will one day be an artist greater than himself. Is it not enough to be sad?"

The situation was perhaps more romantic than true. Still, it was possible. When Raphael was twenty, he came to Siena to assist Pinturicchio with the sketches for the frescoes.

The sacristan introduced himself. His name was Miro. "You are *molto serio, signore*," he said. "It gives me pleasure to watch people look at paintings when they are serious. You must be English."

I said I was American.

"You must forgive me," he apologized. "It is not always easy to know Americans from English. Would you like to see *La Madonna del Voto*?"

He was speaking of the Madonna of the Vows, the most venerated in Siena, the one to whom the victorious warriors of Montaperti brought the keys of their city when they made the Queen of Heaven the Queen of Siena.

"One moment," he said. He unlocked an iron door and pushed me into a small chapel with frescoes by Pinturicchio and Sodoma. Outside I heard him shout, "The cathedral is closed! Everybody out at midday!" When the cathedral was empty of nuns and tourists, Miro called me. We climbed the altar steps to a small locked box. Miro turned a key and the door swung open. I focused my eyes on the darkness inside. The wood, painted seven hundred years ago, was dark and stained; the images of the Virgin and her *bambino* were faded to shadows. Both wore gold crowns set in relief over the painting and both were covered with watches and Ex-voto jewelry. The gold only seemed to push them deeper into the seasoned wood. The faded *bambino* was less an infant than a dwarfed adult stiffly detached. The face of the Mother was bland and expressionless, the nose was long and straight. The eyes were large and intent like the eyes of a cat lurking in shadows.

I told Miro I remembered a Madonna with the same expression in the Uffizi Gallery in Florence. It was the wrong thing to say.

"*Rubata*! Stolen, no doubt. The dogs of Florence stole everything." So the ancient hatreds still raged hot. With an angry little click, Miro locked the cover on the Madonna. "Blasphemous enemies of the Almighty! Heathen devil-followers who made themselves rich robbing Christians! Murderers! Bloodthirsty dogs who killed for pleasure!" Miro, working himself into a sweat, was giving off the stale, unwashed odor of the Sienese. I was thinking of the rivers of Florentine blood at Montaperti. "When Florentines made prisoners of women, they took them to Florence for whores," Miro said. "But when Sienese captured women, it was another story. They were bound with ropes and brought here. The widows of Florence were presented to the Virgin and then set free!" He took me into the sacristy to see state archives, which were preserved in glass cases. There were medieval illustrations of the warriors of Montaperti presenting the keys to the Virgin, the Virgin recommending the city of Siena to the crucified Christ, an allegory of the Virgin guiding the ship of state into port, and another of the Virgin protecting Siena through an earthquake. For the Sienese, no event, whether wrought by God or man, was unattended by the Mother of Heaven.

Miro showed me pictures of his children, a sharp-eyed boy of twelve, a pretty girl of eight. "You will see them," he said. "Tomorrow you must come to my house for supper."

I said I was expecting a friend on the evening train.

"An American?"

"No, an Italian."

"The evening train comes from Florence," he said.

"Yes," I said, "my friend is a Florentine."

"Perhaps after your friend will leave you will come to my house," Miro said.

"I am leaving with him."

"To Florence?"

"Yes, to Florence."

Miro opened the door to let me out. "Have you already been to Florence?" he asked.

"Yes. Several times."

"Then you have seen the ruins of the bombs." He waved his hand over the panorama below us. "Have you seen any ruins in Siena? No! Of course not! Siena was made invisible to the eyes of the aviators by a miracle of the Queen of Heaven."

From the cathedral I went to the picture gallery. They say that the language of the Sienese is the purest Italian spoken in Italy; it is also true that the art in Siena is the purest in Italy. The great galleries of Florence and Rome overflow with many styles and schools, reflecting the sophisticated tastes of acquisitive popes and noble families. With few exceptions, paintings in Siena are of the Sienese school. To see the great works of Duccio, the brothers Lorenzetti, Simone Martini, Lippo Memmi, Matteo di Giovanni, and Sodoma, one must seek them at home in the churches and galleries of Siena. Few schools are so easy to identify. It was part of the contradiction of these stormy people that they should demand of their artists only religious paintings. Portraits and mythology interested them little; anatomy and movement even less. What they painted were saints, and with persistent monotony, usually with poker faces in an extravagance of colors and a great deal of gold. Gold leaf is the trade-mark of early Sienese painting. More than to any other people, painting was worship to the Sienese, the expending of gold in sacrifice. Their favorite subject was naturally their good friend the Virgin. The Sienese Virgin is young and pretty, with a bland spirituality. It is hard to believe that such a tranquil and innocent child-mother's face could rally her people to such bacchanalia of death.

Art, like everything else, came to a halt in the great plague. Ambrogio and Pietro Lorenzetti died while they were still young men. Out of the death orgy came a new subject, *La strage degli Innocenti*, King Herod's massacre of the innocents. No matter where one goes in Siena, one is confronted with this terrible spectacle of infanticide. There is at least one *strage* in every church. In the cathedral it is in sculptured relief on the pulpit and in the graphite pavements on the floor. Matteo di Giovanni painted it no less than five times—broad canvases filled with a harvest of slain babies stacked like sheaves in the field while anguished mothers flail at soldiers' bloody swords. It would be hard to imagine a subject more different from the Virgin and saints. Still, a people for whom death was never moderate must have understood it well.

IV

Tullio Vacini came from Florence in a spirit of tolerance. He was not pleased, however, to find me so enthusiastic about Siena. "It's true," he said somewhat stiffly, "in Florence we are not mystics. You must not say to the Sienese that I am a Florentine or they will have me in the middle of the campo and burn a fire under me."

Siena was in an uproar, though hardly because of the arrival of a Florentine. One of the most militant wards of the town was having a rally. Siena is divided into wards called *contrade,* known by the names of the animals they have taken as mascots. *Contrade* rivalry is the dominating element in Sienese social and political life. A citizen is loyal a lifetime to the *contrada* into which he is born. Each *contrada* has its own churches, battle uniforms, and banners. The ancient rivalries expiate themselves with *palios,* which are held twice a year, on July 2 and August 16. The rivalry of a *palio* was for the favors of the Virgin. Whichever *contrada* she assisted to victory in the *palio* was considered in the best graces of the Mother of Heaven. *Palio* preparations begin on spring week-ends with *contrade* pep rallies, not unlike those sponsored by the home team before an American football game, except that in Siena, they run longer and are noisier. We were caught in the first rally of the season, that of the *oci,* or geese, Siena's most powerful *contrada.* Goose boundaries enclose the house of Italy's patroness, St. Catherine, the great church of San Domenico, and a good part of Siena's business section. They also take in the Pensione Brusoni.

Geese were everywhere! Geese brocaded on silk banners were carried through the streets by youths in velvet doublets. Porcelain geese hung from lampposts and houses. On the streets, flocks of live tethered geese honked angrily.

On the Via San Catarina, old ladies roasted sausages and chestnuts in charcoal burners; tables were stacked with pastries and barrels of Chianti. The lower end of the steep street was blocked by a flower-covered altar, supporting a life-sized silver statue of Catherine. Before the altar a brassy, dissonant band played for dancing.

The night was chilly and people crowded into the house of Catherine for warmth. According to my guidebook, St. Catherine was the twenty-fourth of twenty-five children born in wedlock to Jacopo Benincasa. The dyer Jacopo would hardly have recognized his house, which the Geese had taken over for their official headquarters. The rooms inside were richly frescoed by Sodoma and other painters. There is a chapel to which women kept coming to pray and museum rooms filled with *bibelots* of the saint and *palio* trophies. The Geese have won more *palios* than any other *contrada.* In addition to prize banners, they displayed saddles and bridles, the dust-laden tails and hides of winning horses, jockeys' costumes mounted on wooden dummies, and *nerbi,* the ferocious-looking truncheons used by jockeys to beat each other during the race. Walls were covered with paintings of winning horses and photographs of the more recent ones. Shelves were loaded with vellum volumes of *contrade* history and the detailed records of centuries of *palios*. In these rooms, men talked of nothing but *palio*.

"Forty-six was the year the dog of a panther jockey pushed our jockey from the horse."

"In thirty-three the Ostriches and Rams tried to roll our horse into the Cappella di Piazza."

"Slovenly people, the Ostriches. How dirty they keep their streets!"

"The Rams are all drunkards and blasphemers of the Virgin. Their women are *puttane* [whores]."

"They say Leopoldo is planting his sword these nights in the scabbard of a signorina of the Snails."

"He will pay dearly for his folly. She will keep a dirty house for him and his *bambini* will beg in the streets."

"Such a marriage cannot be successful. She will always remain a Snail."

At six the next morning I was awakened by a din of drums. I got up and opened the shutters on a bright blue morning. In the towers of the San Domenico church the bells were ringing vigorously. "*Questi Sienesi,*" Tullio muttered sleepily. "You are correct. Siena is very mystic indeed."

The signora, wearing her pink chenille robe, brought us bread, jam, and coffee. We ate and then set out on a tour of Siena's great churches. The Geese, wearing medieval livery, were already parading. Flag throwers wove their banners through the air with cock-and-shuttle synchronization. In other *contrade,* the streets were empty, but the Geese din of drums and horns rolled like thunder over the three hills of the city.

The Church of Santa Maria dei Servi is a sanctuary to the Virgin, second in importance only to the cathedral. "You have come to the Servi on a most important occasion," the sexton said. "It is the six hundred and fifty-first anniversary of the death of Beato Francisco Patrizzi. Today we will show you his body so miraculously preserved." We followed him into a chapel where he turned a fluorescent light on the mummy of the thirteenth-century religious. It was indeed a necrophilic treasure. The face was the color of Tuscan leather. Its perfect teeth grinned ludicrously; its fingers, dried into lacy claws, clutched at the air.

"*È bellissimo?*" the sexton asked. "No?"

The mummy was as unbeautiful as anything I have ever seen.

In the Servi, gold was everywhere. The church is so brightly burnished that a flash of sun through a window was magnified to a blinding luminosity. Certainly one of the sicknesses of Siena during the stormy centuries was the idolatry of gold. To cover the Virgin with gold, they hungered for centuries in damp cellars and slaughtered men in battle. Tullio read my thoughts.

"When you understand that," he said, "then at last you will understand the Italian people."

A short walk by the Loggia del Papa, the monument built to himself by the Sienese Pius II, brought us to the Church of San Agostino. Here workmen were busy ripping away the baroque interior. Having tolerated for three hundred years the artistic sins of the seventeenth century, the Sienese passion for wiping them out was suddenly so great the men even worked on Sundays. Their clothes and shoes were so caked with lime they looked like white statues. They were returning to the light a beautiful *Adoration* by Ambrogio Lorenzetti. Unharmed by his ignominious three-century interment, the greatest of the *trecento* masters was emerging radiant and fresh. His *Adoration* lit up the dark room like a miraculous resurrection and brought tears to Tullio's eyes.

"I sorrow for all Italians," he said. "We were once a very great people."

A bespectacled little monk offered himself as a guide. He showed us massacres of the innocent by Lorenzetti and Matteo di Giovanni, shocking canvases of tiny dead bodies similar to those which also hung in the Servi. Then he directed us to San Agostino's finest painting, not by a Sienese at all, *The Crucifixion* of Perugino, and pointed out the faked marble columns painted on the church wall to frame the painting.

"The robber Napoleon stole the true marble," the monk muttered angrily as if the incident had happened only a week ago. "He stole it for Paris."

San Francesco, the most austere of the old Gothic churches, is outside the city gates. Its paintings are largely by Ambrogio Lorenzetti, for whom it is almost a museum. A priest drew us aside to show us his own treasures, a candle thick as a log which he said would burn for a decade, a wooden image of Christ crucified, with glass eyes, a dusty tangle of long black hair, and a branch of hawthorn bramble which the priest said was Christ's crown of thorns. He fingered it lovingly as if he would have liked to press it into his own brow.

One more station remained in our pilgrimage, the great Church of San

Domenico. Since it is in the heart of the Goose *contrada*, it was not hard to find our way back. We had only to follow our ears. This church, so intimately associated with St. Catherine, is on one of the highest hills of Siena. From there, on a bright day, you can see far over the land of Tuscany. Inside, a Mass was underway. A Gregorian choir chanted litanies which resounded from the ceilings like ancient echoes. In a case of silver and glass above the altar was an onyx-black mummified head which through dried slits of eyes was keeping a grisly vigil over the sanctuary. Italians can make a corpse go a long way. The body of St. Paul is in one section of Rome, his head in another, and scores of churches in Italy profess to have fragments of his bones. In Rome's Church of Santa Maria Sopra Minerva I have seen the tomb which contains the body of St. Catherine. Now in San Domenico I was seeing the head of Catherine. It was dressed as if for a *festa* in a freshly starched white cowl and ruff. Tullio was dubious.

"It is probably a reproduction," he said in Italian.

He had hardly spoken when a crone of a woman tugged at his elbow and scolded him shrilly for having such blasphemous doubts. The woman was dressed in black; she seemed as aged and shrunken as the head. "*Guarda i suoi denti,*" she shrieked. "Look at the teeth; see how perfectly they are preserved. It is a miracle, certainly."

The teeth did, indeed, look faultless. To the old woman they were perfect proof of authenticity. "The sainted Catherine was only thirty-three years old when she died," the woman rattled. "She had the same years as Jesus Christ. Thirty years after her death, a procession from Rome brought her head to Siena. The *mamma* of Catherine, who had more than ninety years, walked twenty-five kilometers on the road to meet it." The woman crooked her finger for us to follow her to a transept which was almost as large as the nave. The walls were lined with scaffolding; here, too, workmen were chipping away cherubs and curlicues. "*Il barocco è brutto,*" the old lady muttered to herself. "Baroque is ugly, ugly, ugly." She told us that the frescoed walls had been splashed with lime as an antiseptic during the plague; it was believed that everything must be made white to control the pestilence. In their zeal, the desperate Sienese had covered even their noblest art. Actually the lime had preserved the paintings; wherever the workmen reached bottom, the noble figures of Lorenzetti and Sodoma shone through the dust.

Our guide unlocked an iron gate and ushered us into a St. Catherine chapel. The walls of this exquisite little room were covered with paintings by Sodoma showing the saint in ecstasy and receiving the stigmata. Our little lady told us about the stigmata: "When the word spread that Catherine of Siena had been honored by heaven, the Franciscans in Assisi were very jealous. The Franciscans would permit only St. Francis to have the stigmata. Even the Pope [Sixtus IV, who was himself a Franciscan] said Catherine could have no stigmata. Siena had to fight with Rome for one hundred and fifty years before it finally permitted poor Catherine her stigmata." Our guide chattered on. "The blessed Catherine healed the sick with a miraculous potion of honey, milk, and herbs. She pressed wine from strawberries, and everyone said it was wine which angels drink in heaven. The holy sisters still press strawberries into wine. If you wish you can buy some in the cloister."

On a wall of the transept we saw a portrait of Catherine painted by her friend Andrea Vanni. Against a background as fresh and green as spring, the saint wears a black cloak; her head is wrapped in white. In one hand she holds a slender stalk with four white lilies; with the other she receives a kiss from a devoted follower. It is a regal painting, haunting and perfect. In its presence I could feel the power of the saint. Modern psychologists speak of Catherine as hysterical, or possibly epileptic. She lived in a male world where the female was man's chattel, the same as his donkey and his cow. Small in stature, Catherine was able to rise in such a world to a position from which she could persuade Pope Gregory XI to return the Papal See from Avignon to Rome. Modern Italy has done well to make Catherine its patroness, for Italy's debt to her is great. It was Catherine who made Italy the religious capital of the world.

Three steps of stone led to a simple altar. The steps were worn in two places. Our guide fell to the floor and kissed the imprints. "The stone was worn by St. Catherine as she crawled to the altar to pray," she said, kissing mineral stains in the rock. "Here is the blood which flowed from her knees." The old woman lay crumpled on the floor. Tears flowed down the little ruts of her face; inarticulate Latin phrases poured from her lips.

"She believes," Tullio whispered wonderingly. "She believes."

The air was heavy with the incense of the Mass; the song of the choir filled the church and the bells rang above. First Tullio, then I, kneeled on the dusty floor.

As we left the church a pink-cheeked nun sold us a bottle of rose-colored wine. We took it to the grassy slope outside the church. From the tower a spirited country tune was amplified over the town. Below us four couples whirled through a peasant dance. A pair of bearded monks greeted us. The Tuscan sun was in our eyes, Catherine's strawberry wine on our lips. I tried to think of another moment in my life so filled with contentment.

Tullio was thoughtful. "Florence was sophisticated," he said. "In Florence we knew too much. That is why we made our triumph over the Sienese. But in Siena, they understand things we in Florence do not understand. It is a triumph they now have over us, this understanding."

We returned to the quiet heart of the town. The beautiful campo had a Sunday afternoon calm over it. At a café table facing the Palazzo Pubblico, we ordered some steaks and Chianti. The *festa* of the Geese was an echo on the other side of town. A flock of pigeons soared like a storm cloud to the slate roof of a little chapel which the Sienese built as a tribute to the Virgin when she lifted the plague from their city. The slate shone brightly, reflecting the sun like a mirror, and the pigeons slid nervously over it.

"Do you know how the roof has become so polished?" Tullio asked.

I didn't.

"It has been polished by the feet of the pigeons," he said.

He was no doubt right.

"How old is a pigeon when it has little pigeons?" he asked.

"Less than a year," I said.

Tullio wrote some numbers on the tablecloth. "It is more than six hundred and three generations of pigeons that has polished the roof," he said.

Six hundred and three generations of pigeons. Pigeons at the executions, pigeons at the revolution. Pigeons that heard San Bernardino scold the Sienese for their sins, pigeons that soared over the flames that burned the Jews and pecked at the charred bones in the morning. Six hundred and three grandfathers and grandmothers of the pigeons cooing around my feet.

"Pigeons have a short life," Tullio said, and then he added, "so do men."

The sun crossed behind the tower; we still had an hour until the bus left for Florence. At the Pensione Ferrari, the signora greeted us in her robe. She took us into her parlor and showed us the portrait of her husband in a dashing uniform. Over it she had hung a fertility symbol, a small sheaf of wheat. She began to weep. "Ah, signore, the cruelty of war, destroying men in the vigor of life, leaving me a poor widow, my *bambino* an orphan.

What does it all come to? Still life is sorrow, and the world so full of troubles for a poor woman whose life ended when her husband was taken. Where does it flow, this river of blood? Where, signore?"

Tullio and I were so affected by her tears that we were too embarrassed to protest when she overcharged us for the room. On our way out we met the stonemason coming down the hall.

The Geese were not yet at rest. As we climbed up the hill, they came down, a noisy crew in tunics and doublets, first the drummers and then the flag boys, throwing their banners like rockets into the sky. Behind them Geese carried the great cathedral banner of the Virgin. Several Snails challenged the right of the Geese to carry the Mother of Heaven; she was, they argued, protectress not only of Geese but of the entire commune of Siena.

A fight started and the Virgin crumpled to the street while the crowds gathered for battle. Men cursed and women screamed. *"Evviva la Vergine!"* they cried. It went on for a half hour, and when it was over, two Snails and a Goose lay groaning in the gutter. One of them rolled onto the silken banner and his blood stained the Mother of Heaven. An amiable cat and dog jogged by together. "See how mystic Siena is?" Tullio said. "The cats and the dogs do not fight."

"Viva Maria," we heard behind us. *"Viva Maria!"*

v

In August I returned for the *palio*. The weather was crisp and cool; the sky blue and cloudless. After the debilitating heat and humidity of Florence, the vigor of Siena was like adrenalin in the veins.

My room—reserved this time—in the Hotel Chiusarelli on the piazza of the San Domenico Church was light and sunny; it had a red-tiled floor and a high ceiling decorated with delicate Pompeian friezes. The windows opened on an athletic field similar in size and shape to an American football stadium. Beyond it was the Fortezza di Santa Barbara. From over the walls of the turtle-shaped medieval citadel, I heard the recorded voice of Gene Autry singing "Deep in the Heart of Texas." The porter, whose name was Rico, explained that the *Mostra del Vino*—a wine fair—was being held in the fort. Since Siena is in the heart of the Chianti vineyards, the *mostra* was an important affair.

The climax in the two-week Festival of Our Lady of August was, of course, the *palio* on August 16, the day after the Feast of the Assumption.

Literally, a *palio* is a brocaded banner, but in Siena the word had come to mean the horse race for which the banner is a trophy. Rico told me that the *contrada* of the Panthers had won the July *palio* and it was determined to win again in August, thus to *"fare un cappotto."* The idiom literally means to "make a winter overcoat," but in Sienese parlance, it meant winning both *palios* in one season. Rival *contrade* were as determined to defeat the Panthers as the Panthers were to win, for the Panthers, both rich and strong, were the most unpopular *contrada* in Siena. "In Siena, we are very *Communisti,*" Rico said. "Many Panthers are aristocrats. Naturally they vote for the Christian Democrats and they are pro-American." It was also true that the Panther colors are red, white, and blue, the colors of the American flag. In 1945 thousands of American soldiers came to Siena for the first *palio* after the war, known as the *palio della pace.* One of the most heated *palios* in history, it was won by the Panthers with American financial and moral support. "Ever since, the Panthers have been especially unpopular," Rico said. "They are known as *la contrada Americana.*"

It promised to be a good *palio.* To prepare myself for it I spent a day studying the old archives. I learned that *palio* is a corruption of the Latin *pallium,* which in English means a cloak. Prizes for the medieval horse races were bolts of silk or woolen stuff, later made into a banner. The *palio* races are not a Sienese invention; in the thirteenth century they were common in Italy. Florence ran several, one in honor of St. John the Baptist, another to glorify St. Onofrio, the patron saint of the Dyers' Guild. Dante in the *Divine Comedy* speaks of a *palio* at Verona; there were others at Ferrara, Lucca, and Padua. In Bologna the second prize was a suckling pig. When the Perugians captured Arezzo in 1335, they held a mass of thanksgiving in the captured cathedral, and then ran a *palio* of naked prostitutes on the square. The Pisans also honored saints by racing *le femine mundane.*

Ever since their dedication to the Virgin, the Sienese have celebrated her Assumption with an annual fair. To call a *palio* a horse race is a misnomer; one might more accurately call Nero's colosseum circuses a lion act as to label what happens in Siena a horse race. Both *contrade,* as military divisions, and *palios* are mentioned for the first time in the thirteenth century, but the two were not associated until 1482 when the *contrade* competed in a *palio* honoring St. Mary Magdalene. In the early centuries, there were several *palios* a year; almost any church holiday was an excuse for one. They were run outside the city gates. In those days the campo was a foul place, a community privy and a commons for swine. The *palio* horses were often nags mounted by kitchen knaves who egged on their mangy mounts by thrusting thistles under their tails.

Nor was the *palio* always a horse race. Occasionally the ingenious Sienese devised curious substitutes to glorify the Mother of Heaven. They raced mules and donkeys and fought bulls. One of the most memorable assumptions was in 1546, when naked gladiators battled boars, bulls, stags, porcupines, badgers, and foxes in an amphitheater on the campo. For this event the Sienese built three *grandi carri*, or floats. On the first the Virgin, surrounded by fluttering angels, was propelled to heaven by hidden mechanisms; on the second rode God the Father with "many fair adornments"; the third carried prophets and sibyls. At midnight a buffalo whose hide had been stuck full of fireworks was ignited. The bombs bursting in the crazed beast's flesh cast a lovely glow on the face of the Virgin, and the buffalo's glorious death for the Mother of Heaven caused long and hearty merriment in the galleries.

During her pre-plague affluence, Siena had some sixty *contrade*. In the eighteenth century there were forty-two; for the past two centuries there have been seventeen. They are the *Tartuca* (turtle), *Chiocciola* (snail), *Selva* (forest with a rhinoceros as symbol), *Aquila* (eagle), *Onda* (wave with fish as symbol), *Pantera* (panther), *Montone* (ram), *Torre* (tower with elephant as symbol), *Leocorna* (unicorn), *Civetta* (owl), *Nicchio* (shell fish), *Drago* (dragon), *Oca* (goose), *Giraffa* (giraffe), *Bruco* (caterpillar), *Lupa* (wolf), and *Istrice* (porcupine). In the old days, all seventeen *contrade* entered a horse in the race, but after July 2, 1702, when some spectators were killed, a system of rotation was inaugurated which limits the horses in each race to ten. The banner awarded in the July *palio* contains a picture of Our Lady of Provenzano; the one for August, a picture of the Assumption of the Virgin.

In the endless cycle of *palios*, some, for one reason or another, have stood out in history. In August, 1492, the *palio* was won by a horse owned by Cesare Borgia, but the deputies of the race questioned his right to the banner because of the dubious tactics of his jockey. At the Assumption of 1581, the horse of the Dragons was ridden by a peasant girl named Virginia. This unprecedented event almost brought on one of Siena's revolutions. All the gallants of the town became enamored of the fair *contadinella*; endless verses were written to her. Even the governor, a goaty old character, was stricken. He presented Virginia with a thoroughbred horse and asked her if she liked to ride old horses as well as break young and unruly colts. The race was ungallantly won by a male jockey riding for a rival *contrada*.

In July, 1788, the Wolves were the favorite, but the Giraffes and Panthers were so determined to prevent a Wolf victory, their two jockeys dismounted and beat the Wolf jockey senseless with their *nerbi*. Only seven horses ran out the race, which was won by the Snails, a weak contender. The Elephant and Ram horses led in the Assumption race of 1864. When they rounded the abrupt San Martino corner, a lady Elephant reached onto the tracks and dismounted the Ram jockey. He lay waiting until the next time around when he dismounted the Elephant jockey. The riderless horses finished the race, which the Elephant horse won. The same thing happened in July, 1947, when a horse known as Duchess Salome finished first without a jockey.

The *palio* of July 2, one of the two still run today, dates back to the late sixteenth century, when a modest and uncelebrated Madonna mounted between two windows of a humble dwelling on the Via di Provenzano acquired a curious reputation for curing the occupational diseases of prostitutes. As the story is told in Siena, a woman of notoriously evil reputation named Giulia di Orazio scoffed at the image during a Feast of the Visitation on July 2. At dusk that evening she was driven by a mysterious force to return and kneel before the Madonna she had blasphemed. The next day her astonished doctor found her sores healed, and every trace of her ailment gone. Word of the miraculous cure quickly spread, and that night the whole population thronged to Our Lady of Provenzano to pray. The Sienese were quick to recognize the advantages of such a specialized miracle worker. They built the Church of Santa Maria di Provenzano and with great pomp transported the image into the sanctuary where she has been performing her miracles ever since. The character of the neighborhood was not greatly changed by the new temple. On each feast of Santa Maria di Provenzano, respectable people were compelled to draw their shutters tight so as not to see or hear "the execrable and shameful things" that were done for the glory of the Virgin. A historian who peeked through his shutters described the revelries: "Copious streams of wine spouted from the mouths of the wolves of the fountain, while the populace splashed and struggled in the basin below, a merry and delightful spectacle. A fierce and terrible battle was fought between squadrons of ten men each, armed with swords filled with fireworks." The Feast of Our Lady of Provenzano became the second most important holiday on the Sienese calendar.

VI

The most decisive day of the *palio* week is that upon which horses are assigned and jockeys hired. It also begins the complicated series of intrigues and negotiations that eventually determine the *palio* winner. The skulduggery and behind-the-scenes maneuvering would make an American race track tout blush with shame. The day came on a Monday. Over the week-end workmen covered the campo cobblestones with sand, which was subsequently packed by rain into a hard track. To protect horses and jockeys, they lined the track's sharp corners with mattresses. In front of the shops they built bleachers reaching to the balconies of the palaces above. I arrived about ten o'clock in the company of a Sienese law student named Giovanni Grottanelli. Both campo and bleachers were filled with people. Any large gathering of Italians is a tumultuous affair, but this was stormier than most. *Contrade* representatives shouted ribald insults at each other.

A lady Goose: "No decent citizen could live with Porcupines. A Porcupine never heard of cleanliness, honesty and Godliness."

A lady Porcupine: "The Geese keep the *Fontebranda* so putrid even the carp are poisoned."

A young Owl: "Every Giraffe husband wears horns. I've put a number of horns on Giraffes myself."

A lady Giraffe: "One has only to look at Owl women to see why Owl men have no horns on their heads."

The young Owl: "Owls wear their horns in their pants, not on their heads."

A male Giraffe (to the young Owl): "Perhaps you should have a jockey to ride on your back."

A ruffle of drums turned their attention to the city hall. "*I cavalli,*" the cries went up. "The horses!" They trotted out of the building, sixteen of them, each with a large number painted on his rump and a jockey riding bareback. They were a heterogeneous group of beasts, varying in age, size, and color. A few of the young ones were nervous. More were *palio* veterans, at home on the campo and less excited by the crowd than the crowd was excited by them. Five lined up at the *Costarella*, or Barbers'

Stairs, for the first rehearsal race. The purpose of the rehearsal races was to select from sixteen the ten horses most evenly matched. Since the *contrade* still did not know which horse would be theirs, they cheered and jeered them all, with disarming impartiality. The horses were as anxious as the crowd to get underway; they pranced and reared at the starting rope. The man on my left took paper and pencil from his pocket and worked on his own dope sheet. The starter raised a torch to a charge of powder in a wicker cage; when it exploded, the seasoned horses leaped over the rope before it could drop to the tracks. "It is how they are trained," said Giovanni. "The start of the race is important. Often a lead at the rope continues to the end of the race."

The crowd went wild. A race was three times around the track. The hysteria increased with each lap. The man beside me said number eight would not make the corner, and number eight didn't. A horse parted company with his jockey at the mattresses and came in second. The crowd cheered him. The horse they cheered most was the smallest, a dapple-gray mare which carried the number "1" and came in second in the third race. "*Evviva Duchessa,*" they shouted, "*Evviva Salome.*" It was the same Duchess Salome who rode to victory without a rider in 1947. She was old, twelve years to be exact, a veteran of many *palios.* "She is still very fast," said Giovanni. "She is able to stay ahead for two times around, but being old, she has no longer the air to stay ahead three times."

"*Una brava vecchia* [a fine old lady]," the crowd cooed.

In the fourth and final run-off, number "15" came in first and "3" crowded "12" into the mattress and ran second. These three, said the dopester, were the most impressive horses, with "15" the best of all. "Look at him, *bellissimo!* The most noble *palio* horse in twenty years! Watch his gait, the grace of his head. A Pegasus for certain!" The captains of the *contrade* gathered on the *Costarella* to select ten horses.

The next step was the assigning of horses to the *contrade.* No matter how many factors contribute to winning a *palio,* the horse is still important. Its selection is a solemn *contrade* event. Two glass bowls were brought to a table on the steps of the city hall. The crowd waited silently as an official drew a paper from a bowl. It was number "7," a horse which did not distinguish itself in the races. The crowd howled derisively. "*Una capra,*" someone shouted. "A goat!" "Three legs!" Each gibe was followed by a roar of laughter. A *contrada* was drawn from a second bowl. It was the Giraffes. Immediately the Giraffes worked up an enthusiasm for the horse. "It is a young, a noble beast," they said. "Properly ridden, it will run a good race." Men of the Giraffes led the horse away to a stable already prepared for it. Women Giraffes followed; they were quite taken with the horse's beauty. "*Ah, che carina,*" they sighed. "A dear one. Look at the sweet beast."

The next horse drawn was number "15," the handsome chestnut gelding so highly praised by the dopester beside me. The crowd could hardly wait to know the *contrada*. Number "15" went to the Worms. Immediately the dopester—he was an Eagle—said it was a sorry beast given to spavin and distemper and should never have been entered in the race at all. The Worms were of a different opinion. There was wild celebration as they triumphantly paraded their prize home. The drawing continued. Number "12" went to the Turtles, a small *contrada* which hadn't won a *palio* for fifteen years; number "3," another favorite, to the Panthers. Panthers started to sing, "*Giovedi si fa cappotto* [on Thursday we make an overcoat]." The crowd yowled its displeasure at this possibility which the Worms immediately promised to prevent. The two delegations began to slug it out, a platoon of *carabinieri* came to break it up, and the Panthers led their horse home amid a storm of cursing. The old gray Duchess Salome waited patiently while the other horses charged spiritedly away. She was the last to be drawn; she went to the Foresters, the *contrada* whose mascot is the rhinoceros. Her departure was a sad affair. A couple of old Foresters led her off disconsolately; two small boys followed beating her with sticks. The crowd rocked with laughter over the old horse. "*Guarda, la vecchia,*" the woman taunted. "Pity the poor old wretch having to walk without a crutch." The man beside me lewdly observed, "An old woman is good for nothing."

As far as I could determine the horses had been honorably assigned, but it was the last time honor was done that week. The hiring of *fantini* was left to the *contrade*. Jockeys are considered more important than horses to the winning of a *palio*. Some jockeys are Sienese; others come from the horse ranches of western Tuscany. Some have ridden several years for the same *contrada*, but this is unusual. Most jockeys seldom ride two consecutive races for the same employers. No *contrada* wants to rehire a losing jockey, and a jockey who has recently won a race demands so much money that no *contrada* can afford to pay him twice in a row. The current favorite was a jockey named Gentili, popularly called "Ciancione"—"the Swaggerer." Ciancione had been paid a million lire to win the July race for the Panthers; his price for August was a million and a half lire. A shrewd jockey will make enough in one *palio* to live a year. If he feels he is not being paid his worth by his *contrada*, or if he knows that his horse is a hopeless contender, he will accept payment from other *contrade* to help prevent a favorite from winning. For this, jockeys are equipped with *nerbi*, wicked-looking truncheons of leather and wood with which they beat each other during a race. When the race is over, the winning jockey's blood-streaked *nerba* is carried to an image of the Virgin. No *palio* winners have ever doubted that the Mother of Heaven made their victory possible.

From the time he is hired until the race is over, a jockey is never left alone. Strong men even guard his sleep to prevent his contamination by rival gold. But guards are susceptible and corruption occurs just the same. Horses are also carefully guarded. Horses have been injured and stolen, or even dosed with powerful cathartics to put them out of the running. The overseers in all this are the *contrade* captains, the most harassed souls at a *palio*. Captains raise money to hire the jockeys. They arrange *l'ultima cena*, the "last supper," which takes place in each *contrada* the night before the race, and they supervise the building of the *carri*, floats with which *contrade* compete in the *palio* procession. For weeks before a *palio*, *contrade* citizens saw, hammer, and paint to outdo each other in the splendor of their *carri*.

The first rehearsal race was the same evening. Everyone came to see the jockeys which the *contrade* had hired. Streams of humanity poured into the campo an hour early. *Bambini* rode astride their fathers' necks and fat nuns sailed in at full mast. Two men pulling a coffin on a cart had to pull to the side until the crowd passed. Buildings were draped with banners and tapestries. *Contrade* flags flew from the city halls. Clouds of pigeons soared nervously over the campo. On a palace roof a band of little orphan boys in identical blue pinafores stood primly in a row.

At six-thirty, the gates were closed. A moving fence of thirty *carabinieri*, looped arm in arm, walked around the track in order to clear it of people. Behind them, gnomelike little men with black brooms swept the tracks smooth. The starting rope, three inches thick, was tightened on the windlass. Promptly at seven o'clock, ten horses pranced out of the city hall. They had no numbers. People knew the *contrade* from the colors of the jockeys' livery. The Swaggerer, the one-and-a-half-million-lire jockey who had won in July for the Panthers, now wore the blue and gold livery of the Turtles. The crowd went into an uproar. How could the Turtles afford him? Such a small *contrada* and of such modest means? Even if the horse was worthy of such talent, who was paying the Swaggerer?

Giovanni knew the answer. The powerful Geese, who because of rotation were not eligible for this race, were so determined to prevent a second *contrada Americana* victory that they had thrown their support and money to the Turtles. The Turtles were a natural choice for Goose support: they had drawn a strong horse; they were geographic neighbors to the Panthers, and, consequently, of great nuisance value; and they were so small they could not object to Goose domination. "It is a situation where the Geese may win the *palio* even though they cannot run in it," Giovanni said.

The Unicorn jockey was greeted with hisses. "The most criminal man in town," Giovanni said. "When he is in a *palio* there is always trouble." A jockey riding for the Worms on the horse that had looked so good in the morning caused no great stir. "He is a very ordinary jockey," Giovanni explained. "The poor Worms have not much money." As usual, poor gray Duchess Salome was one of the last to appear. She also had a new jockey, a sixteen-year-old who looked like a boy of ten. The crowd broke into gales of laughter and named him on the spot. "Mezzetto!" the cry went up. "Mezzetto-half-a-hundred-grams!" It was Mezzetto's first race; the Foresters had selected him because he was so small. "They think the old lady will run easier with a small boy on her back," Giovanni said.

"Look!" It was the women ecstatically greeting the jockey in red, white, and blue. "*È il Lampone!*" they squealed. "*Com' è bello!*" It was Renzo Mellini, the handsomest of the jockeys. Because he blushed so charmingly in their presence, the ladies had named him "Lampone,"—"the Raspberry." Giovanni said he had ridden for the Panthers four times before and once had won the *palio* for them. He was small, but a commanding sight as he rode high like a toy general. His hair glistened like ebony, his eyes flashed black and his teeth white. He paid no attention to the women swooning on the railings. "Isn't he beautiful?" they sobbed. "Oh, such a wicked little god!"

The horses leaped about. Lining up at the rope, the Raspberry and the Worm jockey began a fight for the inside place. They beat each other with their *nerbi*. The Swaggerer held his horse in the background, not taking a place at the rope. The crowd suspected a trick. They were right. When the starter raised his torch to the powder, the Turtle horse leaped into the rope. He was already over it when the powder exploded on the campo. The Worm jockey refused to run. He was protesting; so the committee of captains ordered a new start. This time the Swaggerer joined the Raspberry in beating the Worm jockey, and the excited Giraffe horse leaped over the rope. A third start was ordered. Then the Turtle and Panther jockeys beat the Worm jockey and all three missed the start. Seven horses leaped into the race, leaving the three favorites trailing behind.

Old Duchess Salome pulled slowly ahead. Little Mezzetto seemed to be flying on top of her. His head was on the horse's neck, and his buttocks were higher than his head. The *contrade* members forgot their loyalties. The old horse and the small boy especially aroused the women. "*Il piccioncino,*" they shouted like a chorus of crazed sirens, after Salome and Mezzetto. "Look at the little pigeon fly!" At the end of the first lap, Mezzetto was still ahead. Turtle, Panther, and Worm jockeys, flailing each other like furies, pulled into the knot of horses. Second time around, the Swaggerer and the Raspberry threw the Worm jockey and tripped his horse. It kicked the air like an overturned beetle. "*È ferito,*" women shouted. "The poor dear is injured." Turtle and Panther horses pulled into the thick of the race. Mezzetto's lead became narrower, then exactly as Giovanni had said she would, Salome began to lose speed the second time around. "It is possible Mezzetto is deliberately holding her back," Giovanni now said without conviction. "This race has no significance at all and it is common for a jockey to save his horse for the big race." He may have been right and he may not. In any case, Salome was quickly absorbed in the cluster. The third time around, the Turtle and Panther horses, now side by side, pulled ahead of her. As they passed the Worm horse, the stricken beast, in the best *palio* tradition, stumbled to its feet and hobbled riderless after them. The Raspberry on his Panther horse crossed the finish line first, the Swaggerer on his Turtle mount second, and Salome and Mezzetto came in third. The riderless horse of the Worms, with half a lap to go, limped painfully to the end of the race.

A riot broke out on the campo. Men hurdled railings to get onto the track and women crawled under them. Panther ladies kissed the Raspberry; Panther men kissed their horse and then carried the Raspberry in triumph on their shoulders. The Swaggerer also rode the backs of his employers. The Foresters tossed their little Mezzetto back and forth like a medicine ball. "It's going to be a great *palio,*" Giovanni said. We sat in our seats, waiting for the tumult to subside so we could venture into the streets. I looked up at the tower clock. It had all happened in less than ten minutes.

A lull soon settled over Siena for it was the hour of the Virgin's novena and everyone was in the cathedral. It was, however, a false peace. Only the women went home after the praying and not all of them. In every wine cellar in town men gathered to fan their hatreds. The night rang with toasts to horses, to jockeys and to the Virgin Mary and with curses on the villains of other *contrade*. From the wine fair in the old fort on the other side of town, the "Pennsylvania Polka" and the "Anvil Chorus" from *Il Trovatore* rang out over the town.

The endurance the Sienese displayed that week was formidable. I took it as casually as posssible, but it was an exhausting experience. Even in my pleasantly detached room life was circumscribed by the Sienese schedule. It began before seven A.M. with a wild pealing of bells ringing the Sienese to the cathedral to celebrate the Virgin in holy Mass. It was possible that a Sienese might sleep through this, but not many did. At nine o'clock each day the *contrade* gathered on the campo for a rehearsal race. I passed up these morning races, but not for sleep. At eight o'clock I had already been aroused by a sports event of a different sort. In the stadium outside my window the Siena football team met mornings for a three-hour workout. The practice drew an exuberant crowd of sporting fans to the foot of my window, including all the priests of San Domenico. It was a fine show to watch over a pot of coffee. There were about thirty of them, splendid young animals with remarkable grace and agility. Their routines struck me as more fitting to the training of a *corps de ballet* than a champion *calcio* team. They played leapfrog, pedaled bicycles in the air, did stretches and splits, and tumbled over each other like bear cubs. Not until the last hour were they permitted a swift workout with the ball.

About noon the wine fair in the *fortezza* began blaring out its amplified music. From then until three A.M., operatic arias, Neapolitan love songs, and American cowboy ballads screamed over the town. At five o'clock the *passeggiata* commenced. In Siena this is a back-and-forth marathon on the Via Cavour from the Piazza Matteotti to the campo, a mysterious pursuit which continues, with an occasional time out for a *Cinzano* or a *caffe*, until midnight. At seven o'clock Siena converged a second time on the campo for the evening rehearsal race. These I attended. They did not vary greatly from the first. As the week progressed, tempers were shorter and tensions mounted. Only nine horses ran these races, the Worms reporting their horse too injured to compete. Most Sienese did not believe this; it was typical of the Worm knaves, they said, to offer some lie to stay out of the rehearsals. Rehearsal races were usually won by the Swaggerer or the Raspberry for the Turtles or Panthers. Mezzetto permitted Duchess Salome to lag behind. It was said he was saving her for the final race. When the rehearsals were over, and before their blood had a chance to cool, the Sienese went to their Virgin novena and then resumed their *passeggiata* or went to the wine fair.

Ordinarily Italians take a dim view of alcoholism. Even though they produce and consume more wine than any people in the world, their drinking is the most temperate in Europe. A wine fair is an exception. Siena is in the heart of the Tuscan vineyards, and the traditional spirit of the Virgin's city includes a hearty seasonal obeisance to Bacchus. The fair's setting was in the neoclassic Mussolini style, recalling the dictator's athletic forum in Rome, or his pavilion at the New York World's Fair. On top of the *fortezza* walls were some thirty wine booths in which girls, wearing native peasant dress, offered for sampling the wines of Sicily, Sardinia, and Calabria, as well as Tuscany, Umbria, Lombardy, and the Abruzzi. The challenge of the fair was to circumscribe the fort completely, sampling every wine on the way. There were the smiles of the girls to encourage you. Apparently it was no problem to a young Sienese. Many boasted of making the rounds nightly for two weeks. It was a problem for me, however. On the night I accompanied a band of *giovani*, they misinterpreted my presence as a signal for a drinking contest between Italy and America. Unfortunately for American prestige, I got no more than one third of the way around; the succession of sweet, dry, light, heavy, red, and white wines affected my stomach quicker than my head.

The ten-acre space inside the fort was bizarrely illuminated with green and red lights. Fountains flowed, not with water, but with red wine. The greatest of the fountains in the center had a stone bowl perhaps a dozen feet across, from the center of which a red column of wine spurted twenty feet into the air and then cascaded like liquid rubies down into the basin. A French ballet company performed before an amphitheater, and a group of musicians, billing themselves in English as "The Jolly Swing Band," played for dancing. Their reasonable facsimile of Louis Armstrong and Bob Crosby Dixieland was a wild success with the younger set, which jittered orgiastically. There were, for Italy, a surprising number of girls on the dance floor, most with mammas watching in the bleachers. When there were not enough girls, the boys danced with each other. For my companions the climax to the night's games came well after midnight when the mammas and papas had gone home. It was a bath in the great fountain of wine. My Anglo-Saxon modesty did not permit me to participate in this revelry. It was enough to watch the lithe sun-browned Pans sporting like seals in the wine.

VII

Early on the morning of the Assumption the bells rang out. Masses and prayers occupied the Sienese until noon. After church, they breakfasted on roasted meats, their only meal before nightfall. A tension hung over the city, like the moment between a lightning flash and the clap of thunder. The weather was humid; the sour smell of Sienese bodies assailed the nose everywhere. Though no rooms had been available for two days, tourists kept pouring into the town. In the afternoon I found peace and solitude in the *pinacoteca*. During the Assumption madness, no one was interested in art, so I had two hours completely to myself with the pictures. The gallery windows, looking out on red tile roofs and medieval towers, framed landscapes exactly like those in the five- and six-hundred-year-old paintings. The past merged with the present; the pictures came to life. Some excitement in the street summoned me from the gallery. Outside, it was dark and ominous. The streets were filled with black-robed people carrying candles and chanting litanies. It was the annual procession of candles, the gift of wax on its way to the cathedral Virgin. The parade was divided into fourteen sections, one for each of the fourteen parishes in the Sienese diocese. Small boys carried the parish banners with signs announcing the money presented, along with wax, to the Virgin. "San Spirito, fifteen thousand lire," they said; "San Agostino, eighteen thousand lire," etc. Little girls followed the boys, tiny white-robed and veiled brides, carrying candles, one lit in their outer hands, and a hamper of candles between them. The candles were from two to four feet long. Then came the priests and nuns, chanting canticles, followed by trumpet choirs and drum corps, aristocrats in black gloves and top hats, and *contrade* representatives in *palio* livery. Finally, four white oxen in golden livery pulled the *carroccio*, a great gold-gilded, hand-carved wagon hauling thousands of candles and with a huge flaming candle rising from its center like a telegraph pole. An escort of armored knights carrying spears followed it to the cathedral.

The cathedral flickered with lighted candles. I saw Miro, bustling about with a stubby flame between thumb and forefinger, lighting those that kept going out. In booths, priests and nuns sold religious medals, post cards, and candles. Walls were covered with *palio* flags and *contrade* banners; hanging in the nave was a scoreboard listing donations to the Virgin. "*La famiglia di Giovanni Martino*, five hundred lire"; "*La scuola Ognisanti*, five thousand lire . . ." The listings were endless. A large gift like that of the School of All Saints was approximately eight dollars; the average gift, such as that of the Martino family, was less than I usually spent for a meal.

On the floor the graphite mosaics, covered the rest of the year by planks, were exposed for the Assumption. Were there nothing else in Siena, these fifty designs, covering twenty-five thousand square feet, would bring the Sienese everlasting fame. As usual carnage and death are conspicuous motifs. There is a sickening massacre of the innocents by Matteo di Giovanni, the hanging of Absalom and five Amorite kings, the blood sacrifices of Abraham, Isaac, and Elijah. But not all are violent. A calm section by Antonio Federighi portrays with sublime beauty the seven ages of man. The first four ages are identified in Latin as *infantia, pueritia, adolescentia* (a boy in a field of flowers), and *juvenus* (a young huntsman with a falcon). To this point the cycle has sweetness. Maturity, decline and senility, a decrepit figure hobbling on sticks to the tomb, are shown with gentle irony. Obviously Federighi knew the difference between the actual and the natural span. Life in Siena was short; a man of twenty had spent more than half his years. Violence struck early and few walking over the pavements during the stormy centuries could hope to live out their span.

The Virgin in custody of her wax, Siena returned to the campo for the last rehearsal race. The crowd was the largest of the week and the race the dullest. The Panthers won by default. When it was finished, *contrade* members hurried off to their *cene*. These suppers have both a business and a social function. If the *contrada* hopes to win the next day, a final attempt is made to raise money to pay for the help of those that have no chance of winning. The price is usually fifty thousand lire to a *contrada*, plus a bonus for its jockey. For this, jockeys will committ any sort of foul play to prevent the paying *contrada* from losing. A *contrada* that has no illusions about winning will decide at supper with which faction to align itself and for what price. Socially, a *cena* is the final rousing of *contrade* spirit, accompanied by toasts to the Virgin and the jockey on the chance that such last-minute ministrations will stimulate them to greater efforts on the track the next day.

Being an American, I was invited to the banquet of the *Contrada Americana,* the Panthers with the red, white, and blue livery. It was held in a baker's garden. The setting was perfect. On one side rose the back wall of the baker's house; on three sides the garden was enclosed by low stone walls over which we saw the hills of Tuscany in the silver moonlight. Over us was a canopy of fig trees and ripening grapes; Japanese lanterns hung on electric-light bulbs. There were flowers on the long tables. The *cena* was predominantly a stag affair; only a few women were present. One, a tall, haughty, blue-eyed blonde was extraordinarily beautiful. Apparently she was someone of position. Her clothes were Paris chic; her jewels rich. I was seated directly across the table from her. Lampone, the Raspberry, sat beside her, a roguish Pierrot in his red, white, and blue clown suit, and, beside him, the Panther captain, a distinguished, kindly man who was the jockey guard. Beyond the captain an upper bourgeois gentleman exuded affluence and well-being. He was introduced as *Professore Dottore* Franco Lenzi, a well-known heart specialist and member of the university staff. The ice lady across from me was Signora Lenzi; they were the most distinguished couple in Panther land. On my left was a large blustering man in pin stripes, a bush-league operatic basso named Bastianini. On my right was the *contrada* chaplain, a twinkling white-haired priest with thick lenses who smiled benignly whenever he caught my glance but who was too preoccupied with food and wine to speak. The bowls of spaghetti, trays of ham and chicken, salad, potatoes, cheese, and fruit reminded me of a bountiful American church supper, with one exception—the wineglasses were never empty. The result was an increasing loquaciousness on the part of everyone except the jockey, who had not the social gift of conversation, and the priest, who, after dedicating the occasion to the Mother of Heaven, sat down and enjoyed it in happy silence. He seldom let the wine bottles get out of reach and each time he caught my eye he bowed his head graciously. The Raspberry blushed and his eyes danced wickedly at the golden signora who poured his wine and served him sweets.

Around the table, the affairs of the *contrade* were under heated discussion. The question was whether money should be raised to attempt another victory. Goose support of the Turtles had skyrocketed the price, and there were those who thought the chance for victory should be by-passed. Suddenly, the golden signora spoke to me in English.

"Everyone here is very nice except the priest," she said. "He drinks too much."

The padre, knowing she spoke of him, nodded and raised his glass in a toast to her. She continued coolly: "You are fortunate in having an invitation from the *Pantera*. It is the most cultured and high-bred *contrada* in Siena. I am happy that my husband and I live in it, because it is the only *contrada* we could possibly attend. All the other *contrade* are very low people."

She took a delicate swallow of wine. "You see, we are just like a happy family," she said. "Not like the Worms and the Geese, who are fighting all the time."

I complimented the signora on her English, which was the best I had heard in Siena.

"I have been in England much," she said. "You see, my husband has studied at the University of Edinburgh. I loved Scotland much. Of course, I am not from Siena," she said, making her point strongly. "I am from Grosseto, which is one hundred and fifty kilometers to the west. It is a very agricultural place, a land of cowboys and horses and cattle, very like Scotland. It is also the home of Lampone. He is *my* friend."

At the sound of his name the Raspberry grinned and drank his wine. His connection with the Panthers was now clear. He was the friend of the signora, whose husband was the largest contributor to the Panthers' *palio* fund. Of the five *palios* in which Lampone rode, four had been for the Panthers. In July, when the Panthers hired the winning Swaggerer, the Raspberry had ridden for the Giraffes. "Gentile [the Swaggerer] is the best jockey, of course," said the signora, "but he did not prove very compatible or affectionate with us. We are very anxious that he does not win the race for the Turtles tomorrow. It is very bad morale for a jockey to win many races. But the Geese wish so much to defeat us that they have hired Gentile for the Turtles. The Geese are very ill-bred, vulgar people. They are *Comunisti*."

The Panthers were not *Comunisti*; this was evident by the presence at their *cena* of two Christian Democrat government ministers from Rome. "No one knows their names or what they are ministers of," the signora said languidly. "Ministers change every month and maybe they will find they are no longer ministers when they return to Rome, so I do not try to remember. It is much too difficult."

A cry went up for Signor Bastianini to sing. The basso declined modestly: it was not the occasion, he was not in good voice. *"Il Barbiere di Siviglia,"* someone shouted, and the cry went up, *"Il Barbiere!"* The singer blushed; across the table the Raspberry also blushed, but with anger because attention was shifting to the basso. *"Senza musica?"* the basso roared. "Without accompaniment? Impossible!"

"Si! Without music!" the Panthers cried. The signora leaned toward the basso and suggested perhaps the two ministers would be so impressed with his singing they would get him a contract for La Scala. That did it. Signor Bastianini sang as everyone knew he would. Once started he wouldn't stop. Before each aria the signora turned to enlighten me, an uncultured American, with the name of the song, the opera it came from, and its composer. The audience applauded wildly and *contrada* officials, anxious to get on with their business, were at a loss.

It took the priest to bring him to a halt. Without warning, in the middle of Boris Godunov's death scene, the drunken cleric let out a series of shattering "yippees"; and then, his eyes very glassy, he subsided into silence like a child caught saying a dirty word. The crowd burst into raucous laughter. The basso was finished, and the Raspberry, happy at his fall, smiled again. The officers turned to their agenda, the first item of which was to make a Panther of *Il Americano*. After pledging never to marry a Goose or a Turtle, I was decorated with the Panther insignia, a gold button on which a fierce panther bristled on his hind legs, ready for battle. The button was clipped firmly to my lapel. I was blessed by the priest, who remained seated. The occasion called for more *vino*. I was toasted, along with the Virgin, the Raspberry, and the ministers from Rome. The next, and considerably more important, business was the raising of funds. A chorus of young men sang improvised testimonials to the priest, the captain, the ministers from Rome (with a suggestion that they appropriate government funds for the Panthers to win the *palio*), the *dottore* and his signora, and all the humbler Panthers at the supper. While they sang the captain circled the table taking pledges of money and the signora made a confession. "My husband and I paid sixty thousand lire to win in July," she said. "It costs too much to win. I want to lose this time." The fund-raising technique was exactly like that of organizations whose dinners I remembered attending in the Astor and Waldorf-Astoria Hotels, except that in New York the extortions were accomplished without the charms of song. His collections finished, the captain slipped away to those mysterious all-night negotiations which precede a *palio* and which determine the winning horse. The singing serenade concluded with an ode to the Raspberry. He smiled coyly, his face the color of the fruit for which he was named.

By this time, the Panthers were as punchy as the bristling panthers clipped on their lapels. It was the custom, the signora explained, on the night of the Virgin's Assumption, for all men to go and do battle in the streets. *Contrade* warriors invaded enemy territory, engaging each other in warfare for the glory of the Mother of Peace. I was now an initiated Panther and could not easily escape this ritual. We organized our forces and marched forth. Basso Bastianini stalked bravely ahead, waving his arms like a windmill to lead us in our battle cry, *"Domani si fa cappotto* [Tomorrow we make an overcoat]." After him came the Raspberry with an escort, and then the rank-and-file Panthers in rows of four, arms locked on each other's shoulders. Our padre, hobbled by his tight black skirt, trotted happily with dainty steps between two brother Panthers.

Over and over we sang our overcoat song. In our own province we were safe to make as much noise as we liked. But we were approaching the center of the town and we could hear the battle cries of enemy *contrade*. We tightened arms. Above the dark streets, old men closed the shutters and watched us through cracks. We passed into Eagle territory and crossed without mishap into Owl land. Small *contrade* did not challenge us. We even passed through Goose land unattacked, but this was by default, for the Geese were at the moment engaged by Dragons. A brief and bloodless skirmish took care of the Giraffes. Our only casualty in this was the natty appearance of our basso. His shirt was torn and his necktie jutted rakishly, but the rubbing of his fur only whetted his Panther lust for adventure and he sang louder than ever, *"Domani si fa cappotto."* When we were still in Giraffe land, a delegation of Wolves came to warn us we were approaching their territory and if we valued our Panther hides, we would stop at once. "Haw, haw!" our basso roared, and led us on. We followed him like sheep, baaing about the overcoat. Our Boccaccian padre, dropping into a rear position, punctuated our song with his falsetto "Yippees." Hypertension was pink on his face as he stumbled along, but his spirit continued strong. The enemy, waiting at the border, ordered us to turn back. "Haw, haw," our basso thundered. "They are telling Panthers to turn back!"

Female Wolves hung ragged old overcoats from their windows to insult us. We ripped them down and started fighting. In the hand-to-hand combat, we quickly discovered we were outnumbered. The Wolves had secretly joined forces with Worms and Giraffes. Two young Worm priests, their flat fur hats at rakish angles, began to manhandle me. It was the first time I ever fought a man of God, but for the glory of the Mother of Heaven, I swung. Behind me our own myopic padre flailed blindly to the right and the left, hitting no one, until he swung himself off balance and fell on his posterior. Brother Panthers returned him to a vertical position; with a blood-curdling "Yippee!" he swung himself off balance again. Lady Wolves threw tomatoes from windows. A ripe and juicy one spattered a little old lady in black who had joined up with us for the fun of it. *"Mamma mia,"* she moaned, rubbing the pulp out of her eyes, "Holy Mother. Oh, Holy Mother!"

We would have been beaten had not the Virgin—as my brothers explained to me—interceded divinely in our behalf. A truck of policemen careened into the piazza. The fighting stopped. Panthers, Worms, and Wolves scattered like chickens. A few minutes later, we were bravely reunited in Goose land, searching out Geese who, it was rumored, had felled the Dragons. Our basso, his face streaked either with tomatoes or blood, resumed his brayings about the overcoat. I noticed that the Raspberry was no longer with us. Someone apparently had decided he would be safer under cover. It seemed like a wise course to follow. Stepping into an outside line, I was able to slip unnoticed into a dark doorway.

I tried to remove my Panther button, but it was clamped solid on my coat. Carefully folding under the lapel, I wandered about for an hour. The night was filled with warriors. Each time two bands met there was a fight. Every battle had a priest or two with torn robes and streaked faces. Vans of *carabinieri,* their sirens yowling, raced about breaking up skirmishes. The Virgin, freshly assumed into heaven, must be shown that her Sienese subjects adored her. They were still adoring her when I went to bed at three o'clock.

VIII

In the morning mail I received a post card from Tullio in Florence. "You'll be delighted to know," he wrote, "that the hills where Siena stands are almost empty inside. It's a type of soft stone, and so Siena stands on a precipice into which she may fall to ruin at any minute. I am in great fear that it will happen in the middle of the *palio* excitement and that you will be consumed."

I wouldn't have been surprised.

At last it was the day of the *palio*. At six o'clock the church bells began to ring. At nine o'clock the football boys were doing their eurythmics in my back yard; an hour later the "Pennsylvania Polka" boomed out of the *fortezza*. I worked on my *palio* dope sheet. This is what I wrote:

Turtles—Best chance to win. Strongest jockey. With Goose support, most money. Horse has won three rehearsal races. A point in Turtles' favor is unpopularity of Panthers.

Worms—Mystery. Excellent horse. Does or does it not have a ripped tendon?

Panthers—Powerful contrada, good horse, good jockey. Because public opinion is so strongly against them, victory will be difficult.

Foresters—Mezzetto and Duchess Salome have much support, especially among *contrade* which are not in race, or which haven't a chance themselves. Turtle-Goose enemies think it would be a good joke if the old horse and the young jockey won. Situation still very cloudy. They say the Virgin knows!

All morning country folk poured through the city gates; slow-moving buses waiting their turn to unload bore the signs of Pisa, Leghorn, Volterra, Florence, Lucca, and other cities as far south as Rome and as far north as Genoa and Milan. By noon the Siena population had tripled and still they came, carrying their food parcels and wine bottles, choking the streets and piazzas and jamming the caves and wine cellars.

At two o'clock, deafening drums sounded the call to arms. In each *contrada* the landscape was alive with knights in armor and pages in velvets and silks, wearing long blond wigs. It looked like a comedy, but it was all frighteningly serious. In front of their clubhouse, Panthers were conditioning their horse by waving a banner before its eyes, beating drums, and shooting guns until the beast quivered from terror. At three o'clock each *contrada* took its horse to church for holy consecration and a victory prayer. It did not seem incongruous to a Sienese that the Virgin should be petitioned to guide ten horses to victory. Though they are fully aware of the political and financial maneuvering that makes a *palio* winner, the people of Siena still participate in the prayers with utter sincerity; they never appear to doubt that the Virgin is partial to their own *contrada*. On record is the case of a Madonna who did not fulfill her responsibility to bring her *contrada* victory. Tried by a jury, the Madonna was found guilty of accepting a bribe of silver from another *contrada*. For punishment she was thrown into a public well. Apparently the Madonna got the point, for her *contrada* won the next *palio*, whereupon the image was retrieved from the well and reinstated in glory in her chapel.

Since the odds favored the Turtles, I deserted the Panthers for the consecration of the Turtle horse. The Turtle clubhouse was new; it had clean marble floors and fresh pastel walls. Its rooms were filled with the usual *palio* memorabilia of trophies, spears, armor, vestments, and livery. On one wall hung the fourteen *palio* banners won by the Turtles. The oldest was dated 1633. There were six from the first half of the nineteenth century; the most recent was 1933.

In the adjoining chapel, thirty six-foot candles flickered in a baroque setting. There were veined green marble columns, gold altar vessels, red draperies. A red rug was laid on the floor to keep the horse from sliding on the marble. Above the altar was a statue of the Virgin with the *bambino* in her lap and St. Anthony praying at her feet. The peaceful group was in dramatic contrast to the hysteria below. People were pressed together beyond the capacity of the church. Outside, others shouted to get in. Children slid under the red tasseled ropes which blocked off a free place before the altar for the horse. The hot day was heated still more by candles and people; the sweet, sickening aroma of incense blended with the smell of unwashed Sienese. A bearded Englishman focused a movie camera. Old ladies in black mumbled litanies. Behind me a plump little woman, wearing a white lace collar, fingered her rosary and said to her friend, "*Ave Maria*, I wore a sleeveless dress, *Ave Maria*, so if I meet one of those prostitutes of the Panthers I will kill her, *Ave Maria*. . . . " One thing concerned everybody. Would *il bello cavallo* (the beautiful horse), perform his excretory functions on the altar? For him to do so would be an omen from the saints in heaven. Were he to urinate, ah, that was a very hopeful sign. Should he empty his bowels on the altar, *gloria in excelsis*, that would be a positive portent, a sign of certain victory from the Mother of Heaven herself.

There was a rustle of excitement; someone was coming in. The crowd pushed to see. It was the priest, followed by page boys with yellow curls who were panting with open mouths like tired dogs. They carried spears. The Turtles' captain, a blustering V.I.P., pushed the crowd back with his hairy arms. Men became angry and women hysterical. My stomach became unsteady, but there was no way out. One could not move except to sway with the crowd. The priest tried to bring order by crossing his hands in a blessing, but no one paid him any attention. "*Silenzio*," he shouted angrily, "*Questa e la casa di Dio* [this is the house of God]." A child sobbed and a woman screamed, "*Mamma mia*. Oh, holy Mother. . . ." In the frescoed cupola above, fat cherubs billowed on clouds. St. Anthony, marble tears on his marble face, beseeched the Virgin.

The Swaggerer, resplendent in silks, stalked in and kneeled with a flourish at the altar. The priest waved the golden sunburst over him and grumbled a prayer. The Swaggerer went for the horse, but the horse, too frightened to enter, danced nervously on the steps. Someone suggested that the blessing be taken to the horse. The woman in the white collar protested, "The blessing is no good if not done properly. *Povero cavallino*." she wailed. "The poor sweet dear is frightened."

Finally they put blinders on the beast and led him in. The priest changed into lavish golden vestments. Women purred over the horse. "See his strong legs, his grace! How beautiful he is!" "Sainted Virgin," the woman with the rosary prayed, "please break the leg of the horse of the Panthers. . . ." Those near the blinded beast reached out to touch his quivering flesh. Many kneeled to the floor and gazed under him, watching hopefully for the promising twitchings of his organs. The priest droned in Latin, and the people responded:

"Let this animal receive Thy blessing, O Lord . . ."

"*Ave Maria*."

"whereby it may be preserved in body . . ."

"*Ave Maria*."

"and freed from harm . . ."

"*Ave Maria*."

"by the intercession of the blessed Anthony . . ."

"*Ave Maria*."

"through Christ our Lord . . ."

"*Ave Maria.*"

Someone in the front shouted excitedly, "*Il cavallo* is extending his *membro*. He is going to . . ."

The horse did. An amber spray covered the altar and the hem of the priest's gown. "It is the sign," they all said at once. "The sign from the Blessed Virgin." A stream of urine flowed from the altar down through the sanctuary. The priest raised the golden Eucharist over the horse and silence covered the chapel, for this was the holy moment of consecration. The priest was silent. All were silent but the horse. He raised his tail and with full percussive accompaniment completed the portent.

"Christ," the Englishman with the camera said reverently, "the bloody bastard's got the shit scared out of him."

A steaming mound of manure dropped to the red velvet carpet. The joy of the people was marvelous. "*Grazie, Madonna,*" the cry went up. Now, at last, it was an absolute certainty that the Turtles would win the *palio*. Women danced up and down in each other's embrace; men kissed each other on the cheek. The stench in the chapel was monumental. The priest smiled broadly, waved the sunburst, and blessed us all.

Full of confidence, the Turtles marched to the cathedral square to join the *palio* parade. I met some brother Panthers; they were disconsolate because their horse had offered no signs. One after another, the *contrade* arrived on the square, each a medieval procession led by *alfieri*, flag throwers who embroidered the sky with their banners. Pages led the race horses. Armored knights rode sorry nags wearing helmets and weighted with clanking steel. They looked like Don Quixote's steed.

Every street was a stream flowing to the campo; there was no swimming against the tide. The field was already filled. It took a half hour to push through to my reserved seat. People hung from the roofs and windows of the palaces; it was a miracle they didn't tumble off. Mary Louise Grottanelli, the sister of Giovanni, had her seat beside mine. She reported the latest gossip: the enemies of the Turtles and Geese had combined forces to prevent a Turtle victory and to throw the race to Mezzetto and Salome. "It will be the best *palio* since the peace *palio* of 1945," she said.

Our seats were near the starting line. Tourists filled the bleachers and Sienese stood inside the campo. Mary Louise estimated there were a hundred thousand of them. Facing us on the other side of the field were acres of white faces; on our side, the half turned away was a sea of black heads.

The crowd was watching a fight which had started somewhere in the center. A squad of *carabinieri* in white uniforms pressed in to stop the rioting. As the fight moved through the crowd, the design of faces and heads changed like a wheat field shifted by the wind.

A flair of drums ended the fight. A lady fell headfirst out of the bleachers onto the tracks and her relatives became hysterical. This terrible human trap gave me a feeling of claustrophobia. In the tower the great bell pealed the signal for the parade. Thirteen *carabinieri* rode into the track on matched black horses escorting the commune banner, on which were three black eggs representing the hills of Siena. The officers were a noble sight in their black and red uniforms, their fur epaulets and tricolored plumed hats. The workmen's guilds followed with trumpeteers and drummers, and then, one at a time, the *contrade*, each with its drum corps, its flag boys, its horse, and its jockey. The jockeys were the most wildly received. True to his name, Giancione swaggered; the Raspberry waved to the women and blushed at their cries. In his blond wig, tiny Mezzetto looked like a girl. A band of ten adolescent pages, bound together by a great garland of laurel, walked ahead of Siena's golden *carroccio*; it was drawn by four garlanded white oxen, and from its standards floated the prize of the race, the banner, from which the Mother of Heaven smiled aloofly on the tumult. The parade moved slowly, for each *contrada* stopped for a performance by its *alfieri*. At the end seventeen teams of flag boys performed simultaneously, their flags blazing into the sky like brilliant birds, careening back to the ground where the boys caught them in the crooks of their knees, danced with them, and then sent them looping back into heaven. Trumpets and drums conversed across the campo. With the brilliant phantasmagoria of a thousand knights in tights and tunics, the campo was a tumultuous assault on the senses.

The evening shadows mounted high on the tower. The gnomes with the black brooms swept the tracks and trundled away with the parade's horse droppings in their wheelbarrows. Suddenly children released hundreds of multicolored balloons. It was part of the *palio* ritual, Mary Louise explained, a last effort to foretell the outcome of the race. It was believed the Virgin guided prevailing winds to carry the balloons over the *quartieri* of the *contrada* which she had selected to win. But this time the Virgin was capricious; the balloons sailed gently over the horses of the Rams, which were not running in the race at all. The white *carabinieri* carried the *palio* banner to the judges' stand on a bridge over the starting line. The sight of it caused a woman to faint; the *carabinieri* carried her off, rigid as a corpse. Suddenly there was a rash of fainting women.

The sun was behind the face of the tower clock at last, and the white flag was hoisted on the city hall. Twenty policemen escorted the starter, a wizened little man with a torch. "If he were not guarded, the mobs would kill him," Mary Louise said. "Often it is necessary to guard his life for three or four days after a race." Mary Louise was close to fainting herself. She sat tensely beside me, the perspiration beading on her brow. The horses emerged from the city hall, each prancing nobly to the starting point behind a police escort. The horse of the Worms, absent since Monday from the rehearsals, was limping. *"Ah, poverino!"* the women cried sympathetically. "What brutes those Worms, to run the poor beast!" The jockeys had shed their silks and velvets for coarse canvas doublets; in their hands were the fearful *nerbi*. The horses leaped and reared at the starting rope. It took several minutes to corral them into a line. Only the gray Salome was tranquil. While the others leaped about, she slipped quietly into the preferred place inside the track and waited. The jockeys who were united to prevent a Turtle victory tried dismounting the Swaggerer by beating him with their *nerbi*. The Snail and Eagle jockeys leaped from their horses to beat the Raspberry. The starter raised his torch to the powder charge and ducked under the wicker cage, holding his hands to his ears. The fuse spit and burned out. The crowd roared. The Swaggerer attacked Mezzetto in an attempt to crowd him from the inside and succeeded in doing so. Mezzetto's wig was askew; he could not see for the curls covering his eyes. Raspberry, free from his assailants, led a new attack on the Swaggerer. The crowd shrieked for blood, and the starter relit his torch.

Bang! The brawling jockeys were unprepared. Duchess Salome leaped to a long lead. On top of her Mezzetto fought with his curls, finally ripping them off and throwing the wig onto the tracks. For a moment, *contrade* loyalties were forgotten and everyone cheered for Mezzetto. A cluster of eight horses bolted after him, with one, the horse of the Worms, limping along in the rear. "It is a punishment," I heard a woman say. "The Holy Mother has lamed the horse to keep the sinful Worms from winning."

Mezzetto and Salome held their lead twice around. Behind in second place, the Swaggerer and the Raspberry, swinging their *nerbi*, tried to dismount each other. The distance shortened between them and Mezzetto. As predicted, the aged Salome was tiring; she would not hold her lead. Halfway around the last lap they caught up with her. To prevent their passing,

Mezzetto swung his *nerbi* to right and left, trying to hit both the Swaggerer and the Raspberry. The Raspberry and Mezzetto struck at each
other, while the Swaggerer, his dark face shining like polished wood, finished the race. Mezzetto came in second and Raspberry third. Six horses
finished in a cluster—one could not see how they ranked—and the hobbling Worm horse didn't finish at all. "It was the Turtles all the time," a
man bawled beside me. "They only let Mezetto take the lead twice around
to make it appear a contest. The old woman never had a chance."

The portents of the Mother of Heaven were fulfilled. The race was ended
and a new madness began. *Carabinieri* made circles around the jockeys to
protect them from the frenzied mobs. "It is good fortune that Mezzetto
didn't win," Mary Louise said. "If he had, they would have killed him."
On the steps of the *Costarella,* a band of Foresters waited for the Turtles,
who came bearing the Swaggerer aloft. After a volley of curses, the fight
began. Other *contrade* pitched in; the wide staircase of the barbers became
a battlefield. It didn't stop until the *carabinieri* came to beat them with
clubs. "Now the Turtles will insult the Panthers and Foresters by sending
them a bottle of castor oil," Mary Louise said. "The castor oil will help
their horses to perform in next year's consecration."

It was the Turtles' first victory in eighteen years, and they set out to
make the most of it. First they carried their banner to the chapel to present it to her who had won it for them. That done, they borrowed it right
back from the Virgin to lord it over rival *contrade* in a victory parade. The
Geese joined them; from *bambini* in arms to gnarled men leaning on
canes, Geese and Turtles marched across town and back, singing and jug-
gling the Swaggerer aloft. For the Swaggerer, there were temporal rewards.
Female Turtles threw themselves adoringly on him, offering kisses and
caresses. A young Turtle said, "Ah, to be a runt and ride a horse. Tonight
he will have his choice of the unmarried women and some married ones,
too." In home quarters, the streets were festooned with electric and oil
lamps swinging in the wind. The red and green flags of the Geese hung
side by side with the blue and gold of the Turtles. Children jigged on the
cobblestones to a blaring little band. Young boys, taking turns ringing the
bells, sat on the chapel floor pulling ropes with one hand and drinking *vino*
with the other. Women ate watermelons and spat the seeds under the
altar. Pious grandmothers knelt before the new banner; while they were
counting their rosaries, some drunken youths wearing steel helmets stalked
into the chapel, pushed them aside, and grabbed the banner for still an-

other victory parade. A reedy blonde English girl ran laughing into the chapel, pursued in dead earnest by a lusty young Turtle who cornered her behind the altar.

"Say," she shrieked as he fell on her, "you are a real crazy one, aren't you?"

"I will give you much fun," he replied in husky English. Over it all the marble Virgin smiled vaguely and St. Anthony prayed.

I followed the parade back into the town. It included the band, the flag throwers, a steel-helmeted guard to protect the banner from capture by marauding *contrade,* and some drunken youths who had stripped off their clothes and wore Turtle and Goose flags wrapped about them like shawls. The campo, three hours ago a sea of humanity, was deserted now, except for a solitary drunk sleeping on a bleacher. Pitch torches flamed from the towers of the town and a full moon rose over the city from the southwest, climbing directly over the ward of the Turtles, stage-managed, no doubt, by the Virgin. The *carroccio,* brought to the campo by the garlanded oxen, was being pulled away by a rubber-tired Farmall tractor. Except for the Turtles, no *contrada* had any further interest in its horse.

At the end of the Via Cavour on the Piazza Matteotti, thousands of people wandered about in weary despair. Something had happened to the transportation arrangements; the buses that had brought them were not on hand to take them home. They were peasants from the hills, laborers from Genoa and Milan, and a hundred sailors from Leghorn. Periodically, a bus loaded itself to bursting and groaned away, but it was not enough. People fell to the pavement and slept. Sailors teamed up with young women in the same predicament. Finally the police opened the gates of the *stadio* and hundreds of them crawled in there to sleep on the grass.

I sat on the steps of San Domenico. From one side of the town the wine fair bellowed forth "Deep in the Heart of Texas"; on the other side, a new battle raged between Turtles and Snails. Next door, a bald, white-robed Dominican monk was checking out motor scooters from an improvised parking lot in the convent. They roared into the night, one after the other, as fast as he could release them. Once he looked at me.

"A good *palio,*" I said.

"Yes, a good *palio,*" he said, patting his round belly. "Four hundred scooters at seventy-five lire each. Thirty thousand lire for the saints."

At ten o'clock the next morning there was yet another parade. The Turtles, joined by the Geese, had gilded their horses and were marching the wretched beast and the *palio* banner back over the town, penetrating into every side street. Rico at the Chiusarelli said it would continue all day and would not come to an end until Sunday night, still two days away. I met some brother Panthers on the street. "I don't have anything against the Swaggerer," one of them said, "but I wish he would have broken his head." Then he told me a story of Duke Leopold V, Austrian ruler of Tuscany in the early nineteenth century. The people of Siena petitioned Leopold for money to build an asylum for their insane. His answer was caustic and to the point. "You don't need an asylum," he said. "Just go home and lock up the gates."

In the afternoon I left for Florence. When I took my reserved seat on a bus from Rome, the stranded ones, still milling on the Piazza Matteotti, were calling on the Virgin for a bus to take them home. On our way out of the city, we came upon a curious spectacle. It was a funeral, of a distinguished corpse no doubt, for the horse-drawn hearse was followed by a band of black-robed *misericordie* and several carriages of flowers. Riding behind the flowers and at the head of the mourners, astride the golden horse and wearing his clown suit of gold and blue, was the Swaggerer. About him the *alfieri* wove their flags through the heavens. Drunken Turtles and Geese mingled with the mourners. From the *palio* banner the Virgin smiled down, a smile as cool and wise as the Mona Lisa's, a smile wondrously satisfied for having been so celebrated.

The bus passed out of the gate under the words *Sena Vetus Civitas Virginis.*

CHAPTER 12

THE CITY OF FLOWERS

I

MAY IS FLORENCE'S fashionable month. Coming between the wet winter and the hot summer, it is the most congenial season in the city of flowers. In the middle centuries, May was a time of bright Medician processions, of games and festivals in the country. Today it is the time of the Maggio Musicale, the first of Europe's great summer music festivals. The May I was there it rained almost every day. For this old natives blamed Americans, who, they said, were releasing atomic rays. In a town which rarely sees snow, it had snowed on Easter Sunday and that was evidence enough.

During two winter visits Florence had become my favorite Italian city. This time I found her frantic and unsympathetic. Tourists were everywhere. The migratory ones, familiar faces seen in Sicily, Capri, and Rome, winged in on gin fumes from the south. Like birds, they moved on schedule; between June tenth and twentieth they would go on to Paris, later Switzerland, Bayreuth and Salzburg, and finally back to Venice, completing the cycle with their autumnal flights to the south. A great many of the visitors seemed to be Americans, many of them students on G.I. allotments. The invasion brought out the worst in the Italians. Hotelkeepers became villains; tradespeople were sly and predatory. It was a time of tensions and short tempers.

If I was annoyed with Italians, I found the Italians even more irritated with Americans. An educated woman who had been an Italian tennis champion and now operated a tourist service bureau on the Via Tornabuoni said, "You are all such poseurs, you Americans. I've seen so many of you come in here and you're all the same. Tell me, why is that? Your country is a young country. It is not conceivable a young people should lose their vigor so quickly. We are an old people. We have inherited the illnesses of the ages and these things are understandable in us. But you are America. I can't understand you and I am shocked."

I replied that the Americans she saw in Florence were not representative of America. "The bulk of America's population are strong solid working people," I said. "They are busy with their jobs and families and not rich enough to travel abroad."

"This is a pity," she said. "Those are the Americans for whom the people of Italy would feel a kinship."

Tullio Vacini, who dealt with tourists from early morning until late night at his desk in the American Express Office, grumbled, "Americans is crazy peoples. Americans is completely crazy peoples." Once after an especially trying day he said, "There are times when I can only dream how hygienic would be an atomic bomb."

Like the people of Rome who have had Anglo-Saxon visitors for centuries, the Florentines withdraw. They are cynical and remote, not wishing to complicate a monetary relationship with sentiment. They know the importance of the annual influx of tourist money. But they feel resentment. This is understandable, for no man can love the intruder in his house who makes a servant of him even though he pays well for it.

Fashionable visitors made their headquarters in two bars. One was the Excelsior Hotel bar. The other, known as the American Bar, was in the same *palazzo* as the United States Information Service and the American Library. The American Bar was a place I could not persuade Tullio to enter. "For an Italian to go through that door," he said, "is to leave outdoors your reputation."

The door to the street was always open. English was the language spoken inside. The clientele was predominantly male, American and well tailored. I recognized Pittsburgh Tom and the bored Scotsman from Capri; also some music press agents from New York. As always in such a gathering there was a spate of "writers," writing being a safe mask for the idler, since no one ever asks to see a manuscript. I ordered a drink and tuned in on the chatter.

"Can she *really* be an archduchess? I hear she's just a broken-down old countess." The Oxonian accent came from a poetic-looking lad in a dark suit. I learned he was the son of a Paterson, New Jersey, butcher and that he kept a notebook catalogue of European titles. He was talking to a New York "count." "I never accept invitations from anyone less than a duchess, so I don't think I'll bother answering her," he said.

In a low voice the count replied, "You must promise not to breathe it to a soul, but this is big gossip. She's really only a cow-herder baroness from Calabria." The count was leaving shortly for Majorca where he had wired ahead for a villa for the summer. "Only six bedrooms and two baths," he said. "Naturally I'm in a panic that it's going to be just too primitive. I'm stopping in Paris to have some studies made by Man Ray. Man Ray is the only photographer *anyone* is done by these days." The butcher's son moved away and the Manhattan count turned to me. "Don't breathe a word of it, but I'm sure he's a Jew," he said.

A tall young-looking man wearing dark glasses and leading a carefully clipped black poodle entered. He wore a champagne-colored suit of raw silk, carefully tailored to accentuate his long willowy body. He greeted everyone loudly and was immediately surrounded.

"It's Ronny Stacey," the Manhattan count said. I had heard the name before. It was well known all over Italy, though I didn't know why. "He's an heir to a very large fortune and all his jewels are quite fabulous," said the Manhattan count. "Don't breathe it to anyone, but he's thirty-two years old and he hasn't been sober since he was seventeen."

At his end of the bar Ronny Stacey's voice rose to a nerve-jangling screech. "I'm waiting for my father to die," he was saying. "It'll be the first kind thing he's done for me."

My informant continued, "Well, I really shouldn't tell you, I really shouldn't, and you must promise not to tell a soul, but he's living with a marchesa. You see he's not getting as much money as he'd like from America and his liquor bill is enormous so he had to take up with her. They had a frightful scandal. He clonked her with a gin bottle, and when she came to in the hospital she called the police and ordered Ronny banished from Italy. The police took his travel documents and he went to Switzerland. But in Lugano he got new travel documents and he came back and now they're together again."

"My greatest pleasure is in reading the obituary columns and my greatest love affair is before the mirror," I heard Ronny Stacey say. And then, "It's the most beautiful, most profound, really most thrilling play of our time. I've traveled to every city in Europe where it was performed. Of course, to really *get* it you must see *The Cocktail Party* many times."

I had to remind myself these were Americans talking, not a bizarre species from a distant planet. In a back room I heard a familiar voice. It was not an American voice, but an English one, and it belonged to Cleves

Stotesburry, a large, flashily dressed man who traveled with a quiet little woman named Guiniver Loft. I had met them in Sicily and seen them in Rome. They were like a bird couple, he large and blustering and brightly hued in a light blue corduroy shirt; she small and demure in a sparrow-gray suit. Even his voice was like a raucous bird's. He told me he had come to write criticisms of the festival ballet performances for a London paper.

"Though, of course, I don't know how we'll stand it," he said. "My dear, Florence is just too Brompton Square. All these dreadful Anglo-Saxons. Guiniver and I have decided we're never coming back." I had not known he was a writer. "Oh, yes. My best book was *Third Passage*, all about vice in Berlin. I daresay I was somewhat of an authority. The book was a *succes d'estime*. The critics were lavish, but only the Bloomsbury set bought it. You know, those terrible people who borrow each other's books. Well, how much can you make on that? We shan't be going to any of the operas while we're here. I really don't care for opera. I'm a ballet fan, you know. I love the intellectual appeal of the juxtaposition of the human body in flight. The human voice appalls me. The only voices I can listen to are choirboys', which are pure and satin as a lily. Women's voices! Horrors! But I do have a great sensibility to the human body. I'd love to be invited to join that lovely boat club on the Arno, you know the one where all those young men sun their fashionable Medici bodies. I have some gold sandals from Capri and some shorts with gold thread pulled through them, just a suggestion you know, and they'd be perfect for the club. But like always, I have champagne tastes. It costs ten thousand lire to join."

"Darling," said Guiniver Loft, "it doesn't really matter. You know you can't row."

"Dear, you don't row," said Cleves. "You just sit and look at each other's bodies."

"Darling, don't mind," she said. "I've seen those boys in their doublets and they're singularly peasant. So swarthy and hirsute and adrenalin."

"I don't know what we'll do when the festival is over," said Cleves. "Europe is just filled with these terrible Americans and their vulgarities. One must go someplace. Perhaps Spain. They say there aren't many Americans in Spain, but of course that's only temporary. Americans get everywhere these days. And I must say, old Italy-lovers like Guiniver and me are very sick of them making everything over."

"Turning all this lovely medieval beauty into a lot of bathrooms," Guiniver said.

"That's it exactly, my dear." Cleves took back the conversational ball. "Americans are bathroom fetishers. They worship the *aqua calda*. Americans spend all their time looking for cleansing materials. They must have their baths. Then if there is time, they may go look at a church. As if taking baths really made you clean."

"It's more than bathrooms," Guiniver said. "It's the neon lights and the overstuffed furniture."

"Dreadful! All of Italy like an American hotel lobby. Just like this bar. Abominable taste. No taste at all really. It's in Coca-Cola style."

We looked around the heavily beamed, darkly paneled room. It seemed quite Renaissance.

"And, my dear, it's late Coca-Cola," Guiniver said. "If it were only early Coca-Cola. But it's *late*."

"To old Italy-lovers like us it's a bad outlook," Cleves said sadly. "Yes, a very bad outlook."

On my way out I stopped for a moment at the window of the American Library next door to look at a display of *"Le Associazioni 4H d'America,"* photographs of American farm children tending Holstein calves, Poland China pigs and Plymouth Rock chickens, of girls canning vegetables and sewing dresses. Hardly any Italian passers-by stopped to look at the photographs. They moved to the bar, standing in a cluster outside the open door, looking inside with the deep fascination of children before a cage in the zoo.

At least one of the American "writers" in Florence was legitimate. He was an expatriate who had adopted Florence as his home. One of his novels had been a best seller; his travel articles appeared frequently in American magazines. In Florence he was known as *"L'Autore"*—the Author—and his books were on display in the Via Tornabuoni bookstore windows. Every evening from about six o'clock, the Author presided over a sort of court in the Excelsior bar. The Excelsior is Florence's most fashionable hotel; the bar is an elegant marble and oak room in the style of New York's Plaza Hotel. It was dignified enough so that Tullio consented to go there. Being near the Teatro Comunale, it was always crowded during the festival. Scandinavians, Swiss, Germans, English, all gathered there, but Americans were in the majority. There were many beautiful women. I recognized a ballerina, a motion-picture actress, and a Metropolitan Opera star. Standing at his reserved place at the end of the bar, the Author surveyed its full length, drinking endless cognacs, his fluent Italian booming through the room. He was burly, virile, and handsome; an extraordinary specimen of a man. One felt his tremendous vitality. "He is, I think, two persons," Tullio said. "He is proud and happy only when he has had drinks and has an audience in the Excelsior bar. When he is alone on the street, he is sad. I think he must be very lonely. But," Tullio added wistfully, "he lives intensely. I should like to live intensely like that."

I told the Author I enjoyed his books and thought the critics somewhat too harsh on his last one.

"Those bastard critics!" he replied. "A writer can't write a line criticizing anything American. The critics won't stand for it. Italian critics adored the book. I think Italians are the greatest people on earth. They've got everything Americans haven't got. Italians are people of the heart; their country is the land of the soul. I love Italians. Italians love me. Italy is my home. You'll never see me leaving it."

He asked where I had been, and I said I had recently come from Rome. "I don't like Rome," the Author said. "I've never been able to get hold of Rome." He cupped a large hand to show what he meant. I was surprised that any place should be too large for him; yet I knew what he meant. It was necessary for him to be in control of his environment and Rome was too overwhelming. He would have had to be Pope to be happy there.

A young Italian girl entered the bar. She was pretty and simply dressed. One could tell she was ill at ease as she shyly looked over the people. Then, having made up her mind, she timidly approached the Author.

"You are Mr. ——, the famous American journalist," she said in painstaking English. The Author admitted he was. "Well, I am studying journalism at the university and I have taken you for a project."

The Author blossomed and spoke to her in Italian. She replied in her careful English. "You see, talking English with you is part of the project. I should like to know what you think of Italian journalism."

"Why, I think it is the freest in the world today," the Author replied.

"Do you think *Life* magazine is a good model for us to study?"

"I think it is a terrible model."

The girl's courage was ebbing; her English became more halting.

"Do you know about *Time?* About how it is written?"

"Naturally I do," the Author said. "I read it."

"Do you think *Time* is a good way to study English for us?"

"I would say it was the worst possible way. You see, my dear girl, it's not written in English."

The girl drew away as if she were frightened.

"Americans are a nation of illiterates," the Author continued. "They can neither write nor read English."

"Well, thank you for being so helpful," the poor girl said and fled. She may have seen that he was drunk; perhaps she thought he was mad. The young men at the bar laughed at her quick departure. One of them asked the author if he was currently writing. The Author said, "Right now I'm in a lazy period. I'm too god-damned happy. I can't write when I'm happy, only when I'm unhappy. It's the damnedest thing. It's beginning to make me unhappy as hell that I'm too happy to write, so I may start a new book soon." The youth asked what the new book would be about. The Author looked at him with the same scorn that had frightened the girl. "Love, of course," he said. "What would anyone ever write a book about except love?"

After this episode Tullio and I left the Excelsior and found a quiet *trattoria*. It was a modest place in which the owner waited on table and his fat wife officiated in the kitchen. The hour was early for dinner and there was only one other diner, a large, extraordinarily handsome girl. She had the full, symmetrical face of a classic Venus; her eyes were large and glistening. Over her monumental breasts, carried high and firm, she wore a soft white angora sweater. It was unabashed womanly perfection, and Tullio and I feasted our eyes. The *padrone* attended her like a courting cock. He had no interest in serving us. Her every wish, even if expressed only by the eyes, was a command. Her voice purred like velvet. She ate a huge plate of spaghetti with a neat and rare grace. The man brought her a large steak, one he had selected and prepared as she ordered it, still red with blood. He chose the longest loaf of bread and when he presented it to her they laughed heartily together over its size. He brought a platter of the pea pods that Italians eat green and selected for her a plate of the longest ones, dangling each pod lewdly. While she ate he stood by pouring her wine.

I could not take my eyes off them. "One can see what he considers the staff of life," Tullio said. "It is obvious she agrees with him. Theirs is a very Italian point of view."

I commented on how indifferent the wife seemed to the incident. "She does not care," Tullio said. "Many women prefer their husbands to be unfaithful. It makes life easier for them."

Finished with the steak, the girl tore a piece of bread from the loaf, used it to blot the blood from the down on her upper lip, and then popped it into her mouth. The man hand-picked a bowl of wild strawberries and brought them to her swimming in Marsala.

"They are two poor people pleasing themselves like a queen and her knight," Tullio said. "It is part of our pagan inheritance to make a sacrament of the satisfying of bodily appetites. No doubt you think we are crazy peoples. Well, it is only fair. In Florence we have the same thoughts about you."

We succeeded in tearing the restaurant owner away from his Venus to bring us some steaks and salad. When we finished eating we walked along the Arno. The river was silent and dark and exhaled a heavy warm breath. The pavements were crowded with people, Italians and Americans, moving as silently as the water below. Coming toward us in the darkness was a hulking figure, the face hidden in the upturned collar of a U.S. Navy trench coat. It passed quickly and did not speak. I turned back and recognized the frame of the Author.

"Crazy peoples," Tullio muttered. After a few steps he went on, "Every Italian he will meet tonight will be jealous of him because he is an American. We think to be an American must be the greatest happiness possible on earth. He does not think so. He is an American who wishes to be an Italian. We are both crazy peoples."

II

Simultaneously with the music festival, Florence was staging one of its most decisive political campaigns. Ever since Italy became a democracy Italian elections have been tempestuous affairs with Communism the major issue. In 1946 the Communist party gained control of two thousand towns and cities, largely in the industrial north, including Genoa, Leghorn, Venice, Turin, Pisa, Bologna, and Florence. In the parliamentary elections of 1948, an important test between the strength of Communism and friendship for the United States, Premier Alcide de Gasperi's Christian Democrat coalition won the parliamentary elections, but the Communists still clung to their northern cities. Now—the year was 1951—the forces of de Gasperi were making a desperate fight to win them away.

In his backfield the premier had two strong forces, good will toward the United States' Marshall Plan recovery aid and the Catholic Church. Religious leaders, including the Pope himself, made political speeches. In the archdiocese of Milan, churches held communion services for three days before the election, and in Tuscany archbishops proclaimed that a voter who supported Communism was committing a mortal sin. In Rome left-wing leaders demanded action against religious prelates for turning churches into channels of political propaganda.

The Florence campaign was the most interesting in Italy. One reason for this was the prestige connected with the control of the Italian city most loved by Anglo-Saxons, the city which is the greatest museum of art in the world. Another was the personalities of the candidates. The incumbent *sindaco*—mayor—was Mario Fabiani, who had held the job since 1946 when a Communist alliance polled 55.7 per cent of the total vote. Fabiani, a moderate man, was a public servant first and a Communist second, a conscientious official who believed in deeds rather than words and had a distaste for public demonstrations. He had guided Florence through the difficult postwar reconstruction. Under him the despairing town had emerged from the rubble and begun to build. Realizing the town's great-est recovery asset was its tourist appeal, he had carefully refrained from any political activities which might alienate visitors.

To run against such a man the Christian Democrats knew they needed a formidable candidate. Daringly they reached out for the one man they felt might defeat Fabiani. His name was Giorgio La Pira, a professor of law at Florence University and a member of parliament. Florentines called him their "Friend of the poor"; they believed him to be a saint.

But a saint is not easily controlled, and party leaders knew from past experience their selection would be a political compromise. For La Pira was a Christian Democrat in the spiritual, not in the political, sense. Not a Florentine at all, La Pira was born in Pozzallo, an impoverished town in Sicily. He studied at Messina University, where he distinguished himself intellectually and attracted the attention of a professor who took the twenty-two-year-old student to Florence with him. He lived with the Mis-sionaries of the Sacred Heart and on Good Friday night he prayed for eleven hours without rising from his knees. After a year of reading law in Munich and Vienna, he returned to lecture in Florence. He was moved by his study of St. Thomas Aquinas to take the vows of the Dominican Third Order for devout laymen, and he moved into San Marco Convent, the serene oasis of silence which is the repository of the lovely paintings of Fra Angelico. The convent is the one from which the militant prior, Savonarola, was taken to be burned in 1498. There, in a ten-by-twelve-foot cell furnished with an iron bed, a washstand, and a desk, La Pira lived in complete silence. During the daily half hour of conversation he discussed the writings of St. Thomas with the monks. Outside the convent he devoted his time to the poor. In an abandoned church in the heart of the city he started a poor people's Mass at which a blessed loaf of bread was given to each worshiper. Soon he had a congregation of more than fifteen hundred cripples, paupers, prostitutes, thieves, and beggars. He opened still another church and had separate services for men and for women. Instead of preaching to them of their sins he spoke to them as Jesus spoke to the thieves on the cross; he told them he hoped to enter paradise with them. With a staff of volunteer assistants he collected and distributed food, clothing, and medicine; to the troubled he gave free legal and professional advice. Of his own earnings he gave away every lira. He himself wore frayed, threadbare hand-me-downs. When an affluent friend sent him a new overcoat he gave that away too.

When Mussolini adopted Hitler's racial programs and began to hunt out Jews, La Pira founded a journal called *Principles* in which he denounced the Fascists. After eighteen months his magazine was suppressed. It was 1942, the midnight hour of Fascism, but La Pira lectured publicly on the brotherhood of men. Not until the Germans moved into Florence in 1943 did La Pira retire to a country hide-out. Three days after the Allied liberation of Florence he returned with a truckload of flour for the poor. In the terrible winter which followed a doctor found La Pira dying of malnutrition; he had been taking his meals out of the convent and giving them to the poor. He was moved from the unheated cell to a small hospital, where he has remained as a permanent resident.

In 1946 Christian Democrat leaders persuaded him to enter politics to assist with the political reconstruction of Italy. La Pira agreed and was elected to Italy's first postwar parliament. His humanity and learning won him the respect of political friend and foe; even the Communist boss, Palmiro Togliatti, confessed it was difficult to oppose him. Re-elected in 1948, he was appointed an undersecretary of labor. It was a time of Communist-inspired labor uprisings, and the new secretary's function was to arbitrate strikes. In this he was spectacularly successful. Frequently he suggested terms more favorable to unions than to management. He settled national strikes with gas workers, chemical workers, and agricultural workers. When the government failed to give him full co-operation he resigned. "I favor a policy of full employment," he told Ernest O. Hauser of the *Saturday Evening Post*. "Most party leaders don't. We must give people work. We must give them hope. After all, what is the purpose of government? To elevate human beings." In his dreams for a Christian Welfare State, the Dominican with the Franciscan spirit was finding himself closer to the Socialists in the Communist bloc than he was to the conservatives in his own party.

His party did not leave him idle long. In the political grapple for the important city of Florence, he accepted the candidacy for mayor. Florence was poor and the friend of the poor could not do otherwise. Half of its 380,000 citizens were not permanently employed. Across the Arno there were still gaping ruins of apartment houses run over with weeds. What he had failed to do for his country, La Pira believed he could do for Florence. He told the people so in the campaign.

It was a feverish struggle. The languid indolence of a pleasure-loving town was replaced with frenzied activity. The Piazzas Signoria and Repubblica, where visitors were accustomed to dine outdoors or idle in the late afternoon or evening over coffee or an *apéritif*, were taken over by political meetings. Nearly a dozen parties had speakers. During May and up to the election on June tenth, the city was papered with posters; except for the late hours of the night, the cacophony of sound trucks never stopped. For visitors, so used to having their way with the town, the campaign was an affront and an inconvenience. They became displaced persons; there was hardly a place for a bird of passage to roost. One noisy afternoon I met the English writer Cleves Stotesburry and his friend, Guiniver Loft. "It's just too dreadful," he said. "It's making us terribly nervous and I don't know how much longer we shall be able to bear it." Tullio Vacini thought that the large number of tourists in Florence during an election would help the Communist cause. "It's bad that so many Americans should be here," he said. "The Communists are very clever. They point to the Americans and say, 'Look at them! They are dollar capitalists, parasites who live from the labors of poor men. These are the people who are friends with the Christian Democrats.'"

Despite the heat of the campaign, it was amazingly free of rancor. The two candidates respected each other. Knowing that any attack on the sainted friend of the poor would boomerang, Mayor Fabiani concentrated on issues and his own record. A Communist senator who came from Rome tried to inject some humor into the campaign by referring to La Pira as the "little priest," but no one laughed. He spoke from among the Cellini and Giambologna statues on the *loggia* of the Piazza della Signoria where a few days before a committee had commemorated the anniversary of Savonarola's martyrdom by laying a wreath on the pavements where the flames had consumed him. The senator was accusing the Christian Democrats of pro-Americanism. *"Il partito Americano,"* he said fiercely. "It takes its orders from the White House, the American government of war. It promises America that the workers of Italy will fight our brothers, the workers of Russia, to save American capitalism." As he spoke I moved through the crowd looking at the eager, responsive faces. Workers listened from bicycle seats, supporting themselves with one foot on the pavement. They hung from the statue of Cosimo I and the Neptune fountain and filled the side streets leading on to the great piazza. Very young couples made love, yet paid attention. There must have been fifty thousand people. The night was dark, with a few stars showing through the mists. Above the city the tower of the *palazzo* glowed in white light that reflected on the statues below.

"Do we wish to go to war again for American capitalism?" the speaker shouted.

"No! No!" the crowd answered in unison.

"Then vote for the Communist party of the people."

The reply was a thunder of shouting and clapping. The workers spat their cigarettes to the pavements and shouted until hoarse. Several noted that I wasn't applauding.

"Un Americano?" one asked.

"Si," I replied. They smiled to one another and watched me with interest. Men started to sing militant workers' songs. I saw Ronnie Stacey and his poodle. Because the streets were roped off they were having to take a detour to the marchesa's hotel. "I do wish they'd get this election over with," Ronnie fretted. "It's impossible to get anywhere. If they don't stop this everyone will leave Florence. Then where will they be?"

"Why not listen?" I said. "It's interesting."

"Don't be stuffy," he said airily. "It so happens the only Italians that are interesting are the ones who have culture and champagne and elegance and who speak English." Around us rivers of dark-faced men were emptying into the little streets. "You don't *really* like these people," Ronnie Stacey said. "They're quite impossible, really. They and I have absolutely nothing in common." The poodle led him into the stream of men dispersing into the night.

The same men that heard the senator came to hear La Pira. They listened carefully to both, weighing the arguments. Since they were working people their sympathies were with the unions, many of which were pro-Communist and which told them the Christian Democrats were responsible for their troubles. But the gentle little candidate held them. They knew he cared whether their *bambini* ate bread and drank milk, whether they had jobs and homes for their families. His speeches were unlike any they'd ever heard from a politician; indeed they were not about politics at all, but about the town's need for low-cost housing, for jobs, for schools, and for hostels for the poor. If he attacked Communism it was from within the depths of his own faith. "We fight," he said, "for the very soul of Florence." Small and bespectacled, he looked even smaller standing by the white statues of the *loggia*, facing the sea of people on the venerable piazza. "The Americans, the British, the foreigners who visit us come to look at those delights, those things of beauty created by faith for the glory of God," he said, indicating the majestic Palazzo Vecchio and the Michelangelo *David* guarding its door. "These are things incompatible with the Marxian system. How can we reconcile a system so strongly, so pointedly materialistic with this luminous transcendental culture, this almost heavenly architecture? This is the culture which can never be lost because it derives from Christianity. . . ."

They applauded, but not as robustly as they applauded the Communist senator. Perhaps they could not feel the urgency of preserving their city's spirituality for the pleasure of Americans and English. But they knew the man who spoke the words spoke them sincerely. I asked a worker for whom he would vote. "I cannot say," he said. "You mean you don't know?" I asked. "I cannot say," he repeated and then added thoughtfully, "It is difficult to know. I am a poor man and how can a poor man vote the same party as the rich. It is a dilemma most difficult."

Politics were also a part of the Maggio Musicale. Rather, it might be more accurate to say the festival participated in politics. This I learned the hard way. The festival, an Italian tourist attraction, was in part subsidized by the Ministero degli Spettacoli in Rome. I came to Florence with my ministry letter of introduction. My reception was considerably cooler than I expected. Requests for free tickets descend on every music festival like a locust plague, and I realized that the management couldn't possibly honor them all. I didn't mind buying tickets, but I did mind being a victim of political discrimination. This was partly due to the festival management's political hostility toward the government in Rome; partly due to the fact that I was American. American and English journalists were waiting at the gate while representatives of Europe's Communist press had tickets to burn; in some cases even the hotel bills of sympathetic journalists were paid by the festival management. A reporter from Paris who boasted he could get as many tickets as he wanted gave me some of his.

In spite of the administration's pro-Communist spirit, there was nothing proletarian about the festival. Tickets in the orchestra cost five thousand lire, and it was the world of society that sat there, film stars and nobility, elegant and overdressed. In New York, Mrs. W. R. Hearst, Lillian Gish, and others formed the "friends of the Florentine Musical May." Artistically the Maggio was less distinguished than Salzburg and Bayreuth and other festivals of the north. It opened with a lumbering production of Verdi's opera *Macbeth*, starring the American soprano Astrid Varnay as Lady Macbeth. There were productions of Schumann's lurid and rarely played *Genoveva*, Verdi's five-act *I Vespri Siciliani*, which continued until one-thirty A.M., and Haydn's beautiful *Orpheus and Eurydice*. There were also concerts, recitals, and ballet performances, the last starring Tamara Toumanova from America. Perhaps the program was too ambitious, for the Maggio bogged down at the halfway mark. The festival management was erratic and unpredictable; dates were changed, advertised performances were canceled, and unannounced programs were scheduled on short notice. For this reason few in Florence believed the rumor that swept the city. The Maggio was to be distinguished by ten of the greatest musical stars of the U.S.S.R., including the legendary dancer Galina Ulanova who never before had danced outside of Russia.

Nevertheless the ten arrived, with a dispatch that made it quite clear their mission was not purely cultural. In cities where municipal elections were already over, the news had not been pleasant for Moscow. The Communist citadels of Genoa, Venice, and Ravenna had been swept into the fold of the Christian Democrats. It was said that the Maggio directorate had extended an invitation to Russia and that Marshal Stalin himself had ordered the artists to appear. With Florence a strategic prize to be saved at any cost and hundreds of municipalities in the south still to vote, the Kremlin must have hoped that such an attractive pilgrimage of good will would reap a harvest of Communist votes. Perhaps they also wel-

comed the opportunity to show off the cream of Russia's talent before the
Western World journalists and tourists, especially those from America,
which the Maggio brought to Florence.

Whatever the Kremlin's motives, the artists arrived too late to serve
any political purpose in Florence. It was only a few days before the election when the Russian entourage swept into the luxurious Excelsior under
the watchful eye of a Russian minister of culture. The first performance
was scheduled for the evening of June 11, the day after the election. The
day before the election the city was surprisingly quiet. No sound trucks
blared in the streets; there were no meetings in the squares, and waiters,
carefully watching the weather, carried tables and chairs to the sidewalks.
Election day was like any other Sunday; people were on the streets making their Sunday *passeggiata*. So quiet and orderly were the polling places,
it might have been caucus day in a New England town. When the votes
were counted on Monday the Russians in the Excelsior learned that the
victory celebration they had arrived for would never be held. Bologna to
the north, Leghorn on the sea, and Florence's ancient Tuscan rival, Siena,
had remained Communist, but Florence, by a hairbreadth margin of six
thousand votes, had elected the little Christian friend of the poor.

The next Sunday in his church, the new *sindaco* greeted his unusual
congregation. "There's a lot of things I can do for you now," he told them.
"That's why I took the job."

III

The Russians' disappointment in the failure of their political mission
put them into an irritable state. They were not seen outside the Excelsior
except when they were chauffeured to the theater a few short blocks away.
Rumors spread that they were kept in their rooms under lock and key.
They seem to have made visits to the art galleries, for upon their return
to Russia, Ulanova, in an interview which was widely reprinted in Italy,
expressed her shocked disapproval at museums which charged admission,
thereby making their treasures inaccessible to the millions of Italy's poor.
What Ulanova failed to note was that the price of admission is usually fifty
lire—eight cents—and that each Sunday, when the working classes are at
leisure, most of the galleries are free.

Ulanova and her colleagues, however, had every reason to feel pleased
with the success of their artistic mission. Their audiences were large and
fashionable. The orchestra was filled with princesses and duchesses glim-

mering with hereditary jewelry, with austere counts and barons stiff as penguins, with English and American diplomats, government workers, and tourists. The enthusiasm was tremendous.

The first concert was by the pianist Emil Gilels. He was a chubby, boyish-faced blond man in his middle thirties whose tuxedo lapels were covered with gold medals. He entered fiercely, angrily pushed the piano seat to what seemed an absurd distance from the piano, and perched on the very edge of it. Hardly able to reach the piano, his body formed a triangle. All evening it looked as if he might fall off. He started with a Mozart sonata; it rang through the hall hard, staccato, and brilliant, but with little Mozartean lyricism. When it was finished the audience applauded wildly. Gilels bowed condescendingly. Without permitting the applause to spend itself, he began Beethoven's *Appassionata*. Beethoven was fine material for the musician's hard-hitting brilliance, but like the Mozart it was devoid of heart. When it was finished the audience lost all control. Unable to contain itself, it almost burst its blue-blooded arteries.

"Divine! Incredible! *Fantastique! Bellissimo!*" The English-speaking Italian manager of my hotel dashed up, embraced me, and chortled, "Too wonderful! Too utterly wonderful! I don't know what to do." So he kissed me.

Gilels ended the program with Rachmaninov and Prokofiev, to which his style was well suited. Obviously he exulted in the music of his compatriots; he was like a child showing how he could pound hell out of a piano. During a retarded rest, someone whispered in the theater, and Gilels beat more angrily than before. Occasionally he stopped in the middle of a piece to wipe his steaming face with a limp handkerchief, as if he were doing a difficult riveting job. When he finished, his listeners rose deliriously to their feet. "*Bis! Bis! Bis!*" they shouted, but the stern Gilels would not play an encore. "The way they shout one would think he had played with his feet," Tullio Vacini said. On the way out we met a young American conductor who lived in Florence. The conductor was starry-eyed. "It was genius," he said. Tullio looked the conductor over coolly and said, "It's five-year-plan music. Very efficient." The conductor replied haughtily, "Obviously you are permitting political considerations to affect your judgments." Then he walked arrogantly away. Tullio, slightly annoyed, explained to me that at his desk at the American Express he handled the conductor's money receipts. "I am happy to say his financial condition is very bad," Tullio said.

For two weeks the public excitement continued as eight winners of the Stalin Prize displayed their talents. There were two violinists. David Oistrakh faultlessly performed Mozart, Tchaikovsky, and Prokofiev and received nine curtain calls, and a blonde lady named Galina Barinova frowned at the audience while she raced formidably through Paganini and Moussorgsky. Tullio whispered, "She is like a lady demonstrating a new laundry machine." The climax came with the performances of Galina Ulanova and her partner, Juri Kondratov. Word of Ulanova's greatness had been coming from behind the iron curtain for several years. Balletomanes from everywhere had come to Florence to see her. The program listed some Chopin and Rubinstein waltzes and Glière's *The Red Poppy* ballet. Since there were only two dancers, no one knew quite what to expect and no one quite expected what happened.

The legends had not exaggerated Ulanova's beauty. She was said to be past forty but she had a breathtaking youthfulness and the slender, supple strength of a dancer in her twenties; she moved with liquid grace and she assumed endless statuesque poses with perfect muscular control. Juri Kondratov, her partner, looked like a graduate of a Times Square muscle school. His legs, arms, buttocks, and pectorals all bulged; his movements were arrogant displays of sinews and tendons. It was easy to see why he was Ulanova's partner, for what they did was tumbling as much as dancing. Most of it was neither classic nor modern, but a curious synthesis of the two, borrowing from Mary Wigman and Isadora Duncan, the revolt-from-tradition style that was popular before the First World War. Somehow it seemed like a parody. A scarf dance in which Kondratov pursued Ulanova at the end of a bolt of gauze recalled silent-film chases with Lillian Gish or Mary Pickford fleeing an ardent pursuer across a meadow.

Tullio began to laugh. The pious audience hushed him as sternly as if he'd desecrated a sacrament. In their most spectacular trick, Ulanova leaped into Kondratov's arms where she held herself rigid as a statue on a ship's prow and was carried off stage with ten meters or so of pink gauze fluttering behind her. This winged-victory specialty was so successful with the audience it was duplicated at the end of every dance, and each time the audience stood and shouted. A tall elderly Englishman beside us dropped his monocle and cried, "My word! This is bloody fine. Not too old-fashioned and not too modern. My word!"

To which Tullio said, "It is not ballet. It is a circus. It is plain to see the Russians have no souls."

The Englishman replied indignantly, "No souls! Young man, look at her!"

Tullio said, "It is bodies I see, not souls. No doubt that is how everybody dances on a collective farm."

Ulanova's great triumph was Pavlova's *Dying Swan*. Never wavering from her toes, she moved through the piece slowly and flawlessly, until she finally folded gracefully into a heap on the floor. When it was over Ulanova was presented with hundreds of red roses by Florence's defeated Communist mayor. The applauding audience had to be driven from the theater by darkening the lights. "It is very funny," Tullio observed, looking over the fashionable crowd. "The people who love these Russians so much would be the first to be liquidated should Russia ever conquer the world."

The snobbish cult of uncritically adoring the Russians spread over Italy. After Florence the artists performed in Milan's La Scala and in Rome. Finally, when they were in Venice, the government in Rome, its morale boosted by election victories, reminded the Russians that their month-long visas had expired. The Russians applied for extensions and Rome replied that extensions would be granted if Moscow agreed on a reciprocal arrangement for Italian artists to tour Russia. The next day the Russians departed for home. Moscow papers carried their descriptions of an "uneducated Italy" where "thousands of young people who are musically talented must give up their studies because of poverty." To which a right-wing Italian newspaper commented, "Posthumous vendetta."

The real climax to Florence's festival came after the Russians left. This was an outdoor production scheduled to coincide with June's full moon in the Boboli Gardens behind the Pitti Palace. Past outdoor shows had included Shakespeare's *A Midsummer Night's Dream* and *The Tempest* and Gluck's *Iphigenia in Aulis*. This time it was Carl Maria von Weber's aquatic opera *Oberon*. The Boboli Gardens are a vast Medici collection of manicured yews, swan lakes, and classic sculptures. For such a setting Weber's fantastic opera of elves and mermaids was an excellent choice. Theater on a lavish scale comes naturally to Italians, and *Oberon* is the sort of thing they do best. It is doubtful that anyone who saw the production will ever forget it. It was a show for swimming and physical-culture enthusiasts as well as opera fans.

The setting was a natural one on a circular, moatlike lake. Bleachers for the audience were floated on pontoons over the water. The "stage" included both an island in the center of the lake and the wide channel of water which divided it from the bleachers. Marble Venuses and Apollos glistened in the moonlight, both from the island and the water. In addition to the moonlight, thousands of fireflies flickered over the set, bringing to the performance the rich gaiety of a Versailles water carnival.

Casting for *Oberon* was something of a problem, for the principals not only had to sing loudly enough to be heard at a distance, some of them also had to be expert swimmers. Two of the leading sopranos were Americans. One of them, Jo Ann Sayers, sang the role of Titania. There were many technical problems. The ducks and swans who normally do their housekeeping on the lake had been caught and locked up for the week, but not so the bats who lived in the yew trees and who swooped about unnervingly, nor the frogs in the pond. The frogs were the greater menace. Thousands of them fell right into the spirit of the opera. With the first chords from the orchestra they began their fortissimo croakings. They sang in a sort of pattern and seemed to have their own conductor. A huge basso gave the signal, "Brrrrrrkookookoom" and they would all tune up; "Brrrroookookookoom," the bassos; "Brrrrakakakax," the tenors; and "Brrrrekekex," the sopranos. Finally they began to sing, responding especially to orchestral fortissimos, and to lights which were played on the water. Often the human singers could not be heard at all for the frogs. The artists naturally were unnerved. A fulsome Italian soprano stumbled on a rock on her first entrance; the stage director on one side of the lake shouted angrily in Italian to the conductor, who replied from the island in heated German.

After the first act, brown boys in G-strings paddled about the water with large nets trying to catch the frogs, a game which provided the audience with more merriment than the opera. The silly plot, which shuttled a pair of lovers across both hemispheres with sultans and pirates hot at their heels, continued with an aquatic procession of brightly illuminated gondolas carrying a singing chorus. The frogs, accepting the challenge, sang louder than ever, but the singers had primed themselves for the frogs so much of the time it was nip and tuck. Behind the gondolas came a score of mermaids who sang while they swam. Illuminated from beneath by green lights sunk into the lake, they seemed to be wearing nothing but long green wigs of seaweed. For a time even the frogs seemed awed into silence. Said Tullio, "The big frogs are telling their little ones to go to sleep and not look at those foolish naked peoples." The audience was awed too, for the night, unusually chilly for June, was hardly one for a moonlight dip. While the mermaids, sobbing plaintively, paddled about, a handsome and great-busted woman backstroked from behind the island. She swam into the center of the lake and climbed out on a rocky ledge, a Lorelei enticing amorous males to their death. In powerful voice she sang her aria, then dove into the lake, and, followed by her wailing entourage of mermaids, backstroked off the set. The feat left the audience breathless and stirred my chauvinism. The talented queen was a Tennessee-born American singer named Teresa Stich-Randall.

After this, the last act in which the lovers were blessed by Charlemagne, was naturally an anticlimax. As the night deepened a thick mist fell over the gardens. The bats and frogs became limbo creatures in the strange, erotic fantasy. On the island, knights and ladies rode horses whose rich medieval garb exposed only hooves and eyes; they were escorted by pages on little donkeys. On the water elegant barques lit by colored lanterns slid before us carrying singing choruses. Titania was drawn by swans propelled by boys swimming under water. Their breathing tubes sent bubbles to the surface like pearls, and the silver religious medals which dangled from their throats flickered like underwater stars.

The end came. The lights of the barques faded into the mist. There was only the moonlight and the yew hedges to guide us from the garden. The crowd melted quickly for the hour was late. The frogs still croaked. Tullio said, "It is the big old frogs telling the little baby frogs to go to sleep and not be afraid. The silly peoples does this every year."

CHAPTER 13

AN INTERNATIONAL FIGURE

In July while hustling my baggage through customs in Basel I reslipped the disk in my back. Two hours later I arrived in Zurich with a paralyzed left leg. After two weeks the Swiss doctor agreed to my returning to Italy providing I would spend my first week there in bed and arrange for frequent massaging of my leg. I wired ahead to Umberto Chioffi, manager of the Majestic Hotel in Florence. In a town where hotelkeepers are a ruthless breed, Signor Chioffi was a charming host with an unrestrained enthusiasm for Americans. When I arrived in Florence he had everything ready: one of his finest rooms overlooking the piazza of the Church of Santa Maria Novella and a physiotherapist to treat me twice a day.

When Signor Chioffi casually mentioned that the therapist was blind, I must have appeared a little startled. He assured me quickly, "But blind therapists are the best. Their hands are developed more strongly and sensitively." The therapist, he added, was a veteran who had learned his profession since the war.

My skepticism returned when the therapist arrived early and unannounced on my first morning in Florence. I heard a timid knock on the door. I called *"Avanti!"* The door opened slowly, an exploratory cane felt its way inside like an insect's antenna, and he entered carefully. He was small, frail, and pale and seemed terribly young. Large-lensed black glasses covered his eyes, but not so completely as to hide the horror of his upper face, with its deep blue scar tissue. His face was wide and his features were strong. His hair was brown and curly. He had probably been handsome. He was meticulously dressed in a fresh linen shirt, a solid blue tie, and a gray gabardine suit unmistakably American. I invited him to sit down, explaining the position of the chair. With almost imperceptible use of the cane he found it. I asked from where he had come. He replied, from the *diurno*, the public baths in the railroad station where he worked as a part-time therapist. As he talked his hands moved nervously. They were slender and soft as a woman's. Had he come from the *diurno* alone? I asked. The two piazzas between the hotel and the station were traffic hubs for trolleys, buses, and taxis, and the most hazardous in Florence.

"Of course," he said. "Is it true that in America all blind persons need dogs?" he asked.

I replied that many did. "It is better to learn without a dog," he said. "Is better to learn to see with the ear, the nose, the hands, and the feet."

He gave me a business card. "Nino Uccelli," I read *"Massaggiatore Diplomato. Massaggi estetici, sportivi, curativi. Casa Grandi Invalidi, Galluzzo."*

"You are American," he said. "America is a beautiful country. One day I hope to see it." His use of the verb *vedere*, to see, startled me. He asked me if I knew an American film star whom he named. I said I didn't, and Nino said, "He is my good friend." This I accepted as a young Italian's fantasy and let it pass.

He asked politely if he might remove his coat. When he hung it over a chair I noticed a Brooks Brothers label inside. I asked how he had come by the suit. It was a gift of the American film star. "It was too tight for him so he gave it to me," Nino said. "For me it was large, but the tailor made it fit." I asked how he knew the film star. "The manager of the Excelsior called me to relieve the film star's muscle cramp," Nino said. "He became my friend. Now he is in Venice but he will return to Florence in two days. He has promised to help me go to Hollywood. The climate in California is like Italy. California is a masseur's paradise. Old people go there to die. They like massaging and will pay dearly for it. In Hollywood there is also a great need for masseurs. Hollywood stars need massaging all the time. Imagine me, Nino Uccelli, massaging Lana Turner and Linda Darnell."

I agreed it was a pleasant prospect. Nino emptied a small package of talcum powder on my ailing limb. "For friction," he explained professionally. With a fierce spurt of energy he attacked my leg, beating and rubbing furiously. I cringed. "It is good to have pain," he said, and rubbed harder. I marveled at the power in the trained fingers, working over my flesh like shuttles.

The room was warm, and when he returned me to my back I saw he was deathly pale. His shirt was soaked to his skin and the sweat hung from him in drops. "Is very hot," he said apologetically and stopped to rest. He felt his way to the bathroom and returned with a towel with which he dried his face, carefully wiping around the black glasses so as to avoid removing them. When he had caught his breath he continued working more leisurely for another half hour. I prodded him to talk about himself. He told me he was twenty-six years old, the eldest of twelve children—eight of them living—of a factory worker near Grassina, about twelve kilometers from Florence. "At seventeen I was drafted into Mussolini's army," he said. "During the fighting for Cassino four of us were hiding in a cave. A bomb fell on us. When I awoke it was dark and I thought at first it must be night. Then I discovered that my eyes were gone. My three companions were all dead. Many weeks in the hospital I was sorry I was not dead with them. It took a long time before I learned that blind men also live. I was nineteen years old."

One eye had been replaced with a glass one; a crude surgical attempt had been made to repair the other. "In America there are doctors who are very great," he said. "The film star said if I have an operation in America it is possible I will see again. That is why I would go to America. Do you think American doctors can fix my eye?" he asked me anxiously.

"Perhaps it is possible," I said. In my heart I did not believe it. I had not seen under the glasses, but sometimes through the black lenses I glimpsed an outline of the terrible caverns beneath.

"The American doctors are the greatest in the world," Nino went on. "There is no doubt in America I would find help."

He told me that because of a technicality he had never been granted his government disability pension. "At the end of the war there were two Italian armies," he explained it. "One was Mussolini's nationalist army and the other an army that revolted and joined the Allies. I was a nationalist soldier and too young to understand politics. After the war the Italian government recognized only those who had ended the war as anti-Fascists." For four years, Nino said, he had pressed his case, going through the endless red tape of bureaucracy, pleading with public officials for the pension he believed was due him. "I went to Rome to see the Prime Minister," he said. "He received me and he talked with me, but he did not help me."

After the war Nino studied physiotherapy at a veterans' rehabilitation school. In three years he received a certificate to practice. For working four hours a day at the *diurno* he was paid ten thousand lire—about sixteen dollars—a month. The rest of the time he pursued his private practice, which was more lucrative. He lived at the Casa Grandi Invalidi de Guerra, a home for war invalids and orphans outside the city, but even here, being an unofficial veteran, he was given a bed only because of the director's pity. The home was at the end of a trolley line on which he commuted daily into Florence, making one transfer on the trip.

At the veterans' school Nino had also studied braille. "It has given me little pleasure because Italian braille is all *brutti romanzi* [lousy novels]," he said. "What I desire greatly is an Italian-English dictionary in braille, but it is too expensive. Perhaps you will be so kind as to speak English with me. It is, of course, necessary that I learn the language before I go to Hollywood."

How much English did he know? "Not much. I can say 'Good evening. What is the time please?' " He smiled mischievously. "It is very useful for meeting people along the Arno. You see I can never be expected to know the time." Whom did he meet in such fashion? I asked. His lips curled wisely and he did not answer for a moment. "Ladies," he said. "Ladies from America, England, Sweden, Switzerland. Ladies from everywhere. I like the Americans best. They have most money to be generous." He told stories of romantically inclined lady clients, including the nasty tale of one who falsely accused him of stealing her watch which was later found. "She was feeling guilty because of her husband in Chicago and she found it necessary to punish me," he said.

"I can also say in English, 'You like massage. I give good massage. I offer aesthetic, curative, and sports massages, and if you like, a *massaggio generale.*' "

What, I asked, was a general massage? He did not answer for several seconds. He laughed softly and a flush came to his face. "It is a favorite with ladies," he said. "For a general massage ten strong fingers are not enough. You need eleven."

When he finished I started to pay him. He refused the money. "When the leg is good you will pay me," he said. Such confidence in his therapy reassured me. I called a bellboy to guide him out of the hotel. Later when Signor Chioffi dropped in to see me I asked him what he knew about Nino's pension difficulties. I did not believe Nino had deliberately lied to me but I knew the Italian imagination to be a rich one and I also knew the great conviction Italians have about the naïveté of Americans. Signor Chioffi said he had investigated Nino's claims himself and had found that Nino was getting a small pension, but that his claim for the full disabled veteran's pension had never been recognized. The case was well known in Florence because Nino, not permitting it to rest, constantly pressed officials. As for the film star, Signor Chioffi said it was true, Nino had treated him. The actor had been moved by Nino's plight to exclaim, "Jesus Christ! Imagine being blind." He had given Nino the gabardine suit. Nino had attached great significance to the gift and imagined it indicated a deeper friendship than was intended.

Nino came to my room again just as the evening bells were ringing in Santa Maria Novella across the piazza.

"You see the Dominican pigeons?" he asked.

From the level of my bed I could look directly into the campanile where a half-dozen wiry boys pulled the bell ropes. Silhouetted against the evening sun shining through the Gothic arches, the boys, about twelve years of age, dangled from the ropes like sprightly black monkeys, making a game of the ringing. There was one boy to each bell except on the largest, which was pulled by two. They usually rang for a quarter hour, after which they loitered another ten minutes in the tower smoking cigarettes.

"It is a beautiful church, the Novella," Nino said. "When you are able to walk I will take you to see the paintings." I was no longer surprised at the suggestion, for I had become quite adjusted to his frequent use of the verb *to see*. He moved around my room with unfaltering confidence. Growing accustomed to his dark glasses with the blue scars underneath I came less and less to think of him as blind. On this, his second visit, the subject of his blindness was hardly mentioned. He spoke of paintings. His favorites, he told me, were Michelangelo's *The Holy Family* and Leonardo's *Annunciation* in the Uffizi, del Sarto's *Last Supper* in the San Salvi Church, Angelico's *Musical Angels* in San Marco, and Masaccio's Santa Maria del Carmine frescoes, all of which he remembered from the days when he had his eyes. "I was young and there are many paintings I did not see," he said. "It is a pity!"

I noticed his tie, a rather flamboyant one with a painting of the Arc de Triomphe. "*Le piace?*" he asked, as if he could see me looking at it. He showed me the label, "Fantasy Foulard styled by Curine." It was another gift from the film star.

When Nino was happy, he talked of America. "*Mi piace molto vedere America* [I wish very much to see America]," he said. He discussed New

York, Chicago, San Francisco, and New Orleans, and his knowledge of these places was astounding; he seemed to have grasped the personalities of each of the cities. I asked how he had done it. "I have treated patients from all these cities and when I rub they talk," he said. He remembered everything they had told him. He was an avid movie-goer, and at the veterans' home he listened for hours to the radio. His impressions of people were based on their voices. Dwight Eisenhower was a strong, courageous man, he said. Harry Truman was a "kind old man"; General MacArthur, an angry man; Spencer Tracy, a man with a warm heart.

Often while he worked he conjugated English verbs, opening his mouth wide for careful clear sounds. Almost always he conjugated "to see"—"I see, you see, he sees, we sees. . . ."

"No," I stopped him. *"We see."* He started over, rubbing my leg in rhythm, completing the verb correctly.

"Bene," I said.

"Pronunzio bene?" he asked.

Yes, I said, his pronunciation was excellent.

"Sempre progresso [always progressing]," he said. *"Attenzione,"* he called, like a military officer giving an order, and continued conjugating "to come," "to give," "to live." He attempted "I born, you born. . . ."

"No." I stopped him and explained the intricacies of the infinitive phrase. "I *am* born, you *are* born. . . ." In a second he had grasped it. "He *is* born, *we* are born. . . .

"Bene?" he asked.

"Benissimo!"

He beat his fists on the foot of the bed in his excitement. *"Sempre progressso!"* He started shouting through the forms of "to love," and out came an Anglo-Saxonism which was part of his basic English vocabulary and which to an Italian is synonomous with love.

I tried to explain that love and fornication were not the same, but the difference was difficult for him to comprehend. He conjugated perfectly and immediately began another. "I travel, you travel, he travel. . . ."

"No, no! He *travels*. . . ."

"I travels. . . ."

"No. I travel. . . ."

"Ah, that is what I like to do, travel." He was carried away. "I have been to Venice, which is exotic and beautiful. I have been to Milano, which is very like New York, and Rome, which is grand and very agitated." I asked whether he had "seen" these cities, before or after his blindness, and he replied after.

He learned with amazing speed. Still his efforts were heartbreaking to watch since there was no way for him to study. Pronunciation, especially, concerned him. Unable to watch a tutor's lips, he had to grasp it all by ear. He began making his own grammar. He brought to my room a small braille punch and some pages cut from heavy wrapping paper. Whenever he learned a new word he punched it on a page. He bound the pages together into a sort of book which he held against his chest and "read" with his fingers once or twice each visit. In this fashion he began to make sentences. One day he came with the words for the popular American ballad, "Give Me Five Minutes More." I translated their meaning into Italian for him and he learned the words. From then on while he rubbed my leg he sang the chorus of the ballad in Italian and in English. Both of us were in good spirits, Nino because of his progress in English and I because I was regaining control of my leg. When I was able to hobble about the room Nino made plans for a sight-seeing excursion.

On each visit more of his life unfolded. He told me he ate breakfast and dinner at the veterans' home; lunch he usually ate on the street, buying some bread and cheese or salami and some fruit. "It is cheaper than eating in a restaurant," he said. "I prefer to save my money to buy clothes. It is very important to be well dressed in my business." Like every young Italian he was keenly aware of his appearance and liked to be told he looked well. His wallet was filled with photographs of himself. "You have a camera?" he asked. "You will take photos of me. You will write my story for an American journal. A famous American doctor will read it and will send for me to operate on my eye." He laughed with delight. "I will be, you see, a sort of international figure," he said.

But his moods were never consistent. There were days when he could not hide from me the nightmare life of the blind. One morning—it was the last day of July—he arrived depressed and nervous. The veterans' home was closing for repairs, he said, and its inmates were being moved, for the month of August, to a seaside resort. Because his own status had never been official, Nino had been asked to leave. "After tomorrow I will have no place to go," he said mournfully, "and I have been thinking perhaps I will destroy myself."

I believed the threat an appeal to my sympathy and suggested that he go to his home to live.

"It is a small home and there is no room for me there," he said. "Living there I could not work. After I have traveled for an hour on the tram, I must walk for forty minutes into the country where the road is rough and it is very difficult. If I do not work, I cannot live, for there is no one to support me."

I suggested a room in town. "But how can I pay fifteen thousand lire for a room for a month when it is almost half what I earn?" His situation, indeed, seemed hopeless, and for the moment at least he was apathetic about solving it. I had to remind myself he was blind to keep from being annoyed. The next morning he was optimistic and excited again. From August tenth he would be able to live with some friends in Florence. At the moment the friends were away on a holiday but they had an extra room and when they returned Nino was sure he would be invited to use it. In the meantime he would continue going to the veterans' home—he was sure no one would prevent him from occupying his bed a few more nights. The following morning—it was now August second—he arrived haggard and spent. The day was hot and he was sweating. He sat in the chair to rest. He told me when he arrived at the veterans' home the night before the door was locked. Two other veterans, one without a leg, the other without an arm, were in the same situation, and the three of them had taken the tram back to the city. The two amputees had gone with prostitutes. Nino spent the night by the Neptune fountain on the Piazza della Signoria studying his homemade English braille grammar. Working on my leg, he raced off his conjugations, repeating each one several times. If he sensed I wasn't listening, he yelled "*Attenzione!*" Each time he finished one he asked "*Bene?*"

"*Bene!*" I replied, and he repeated happily to himself, "*Bene! Bene!*"

When Nino finished I said I would speak to Signor Chioffi about a bed for him in the hotel. He asked me not to do it. He didn't want charity, he said, and a room in the Majestic would cost too much. He had plans to go to the office of the *sindaco*; he was sure that the kindly mayor who was "the friend of the poor" would know where he might find cheap asylum. When he returned in the evening he said the mayor had not been in his office but that he had made temporary arrangements to sleep on a cot in the *diurno*, the public baths in the railroad station where he was employed.

Before the week was out Nino had succeeded in activating my leg suffi-
ciently so that I was able to walk with a cane. We went on our first sight-
seeing tour, a short one across the piazza to Santa Maria Novella. "The
blind leading the halt," Nino joked wryly as we made our way across the
piazza, I watching the traffic and Nino offering support. He was in a gay
mood and insisted I take his photograph outside the church. He bought
corn from a vendor and covered himself with pigeons. They fluttered on
his shoulders, his arms, head, and shoes. "For ten lire worth of corn any
man can be St. Francis," Nino said. I remembered how in his last days
when he wrote his song to "Brother Sun, who gives the day and lightens us
therewith," the saint himself was blind.

Inside, the great church was illuminated with hundreds of flickering
candles. "Why are the candles lit?" Nino asked, feeling their warmth. We
asked a priest; it was some saint's day or other. With Nino leading we
moved through the architectural intricacies of the great old church to the
Ghirlandaio frescoes of St. John the Baptist and the Holy Virgin. I forgot completely about his blindness. Each painting was a theatrical tableau
of renaissance life, and in them Nino pointed out members and friends of
the Tornabuoni family, rich patrons of the frescoes. His greatest enthusiasm was for the elaborate Spanish Chapel, where the artist Bonaiuto
covered every inch of wall with a profusion of history and allegory, much
of it too stiff and rich for my taste. Nino seemed to have remembered all
the extravagant details of apostles, saints, and important personages. It
would have taken me hours to absorb it so thoroughly. Some fierce black-
and-white dogs guarding a flock of sheep from wolves Nino said were
"*Domini cani*," watchdogs of the Lord protecting the faithful from heretical wolves. "I think if you will look closely you will see some of the sheep
are looking as if they did not wish to be protected," he said. It was true.

When we left the church, I invited Nino to lunch with me. He said he
would take me to a good, inexpensive restaurant that was not known to
tourists. He led me through a crowded market district in an old section
of town, a casbah into which I could not have ventured alone without
getting lost. Motor scooters, bicycles, and tiny cars whirred through the
snarl of tiny streets, disregarding traffic rules. Nino wove through the
jungle never hesitating, arriving at last in a fetid hallway at the end of
which was a small dark room crowded with people. To get inside we had to
climb over a fat man sitting in the doorway. When my eyes became accustomed to the light I saw grotesques of all sorts sitting at the tables: crip-

ples, paraplegics, palsies, men lacking limbs, others pock-scarred. A hunch-back, having finished his meal, was taking a siesta, snoring loudly, his head on the table, his hump in the air. A busty young woman, brassily beautiful, shouted sardonic vulgarities in a husky baritone at a young fop dangling with bracelets. On the floor a cretin child with an oversized head and crossed blank eyes was playing with a cat. His father, the *padrone*, laughed hilariously. The restaurant was a repository for freaks; a place where Nino was at home.

We ordered steaks and wine. "*Bianco o rosso* [Red or white wine]?" the man asked. "Black," Nino answered. He laughed and the *padrone* joined in with gusto, his stomach shaking the blood-soaked apron which covered it. "*Vino nero*," he shouted out for all to hear. "He likes black wine." The whole room shook with mirth. I did not know what they were laughing at. Nino sensed my confusion. "For me all wine is black," he explained.

The steaks were generous. When they came, the owner carefully cut Nino's into small cubes. Nino's hand never touched the food. He guided his fork toward it with a piece of bread, doing it with such fastidious delicacy that I felt the bread must have nerves. Only once did his fork click on the plate; when it did he blushed with embarrassment. He told me his friend, the film star, was returning from Venice and he would see him, if not that evening, then the next day. They would discuss the plans for Nino's going to America and meeting the American doctors. "When I arrive in New York, I will walk down *la Quinta Strada* [Fifth Avenue] without a dog," he said.

The next morning Nino was in jubilant spirits. In the lobby he had met Signor Chioffi, who told him the film star had returned. He called the star's room from my telephone. The conversation was brief and left Nino crestfallen. "He is very busy today," Nino told me. "He has asked me to call him tomorrow. Perhaps he will invite me for lunch." He worked silently, without verbs or songs or stories. Toward the end he began to talk of America, cheering himself with fantasies of travel and restored sight. The next morning he phoned again; the film star said he was *troppo oc-cupato* shaving and Nino should call a little later. Nino hurried through the massage. When he phoned again there was no answer. Nor was there an answer in five minutes. I wondered why Nino, so uncannily intuitive about everything, had not sensed that the film star was giving him a brush-off. Obviously he did not want to realize it, but the fact was beginning to penetrate nevertheless. When he left he was sad. Later Signor Chioffi told me that the film star had left a message at the desk that he was out to the blind boy, and that every hour during the day Nino had arrived at the hotel to ask for him. The day was extremely hot and the thought of Nino's going back and forth through snarled piazza traffic on a fruitless errand angered me. I called the room of the film star. He answered himself; I recognized the voice. I said I was a fellow American who knew Nino Uccelli and I wondered if he were aware that the blind masseur was making hourly inquiries for him at the desk.

"So what?" he asked.

"I'm interested," I said.

"Well then tell him to stop coming," the film star said. "Jesus, a blind guy. It gives you the creeps. Tell him I'm not going to see him."

"Why don't you talk to him and tell him yourself?"

"Listen, fellow, I don't want to see him. I don't want to talk to him. Is that clear?" The film star hung up.

When Nino came for the evening massage I was still debating whether to tell him of the telephone conversation. There seemed no need. Nino was happy. He had waited for the film star in the lobby, and the film star had invited him to lunch the next day. The star was sorry he had been so busy. The next day he would be free. "No doubt I will spend all afternoon, perhaps even the evening with him," said Nino. "Your leg is strong enough so it will not matter if we miss a massage." That night Signor Chioffi told me that the film star was leaving early for Cannes.

It was not necessary to tell Nino in the morning. He had stopped at the hotel desk and knew. When he came to my room he spoke in English, "Mr. —— is gone. He is not good with me." Then he sat quietly in the chair while tears rolled from under the dark lenses, the first tears I'd seen flow from blind eyes. Soon he started talking, talking as I'd never heard him before, from the dark agony of his soul. *"Solo, sempre solo,"* he said. "Alone, always alone. In my dark world a man is always alone and the night of the heart is blacker than the night of the eyes. I shall never go to America. There are no doctors with miracles to give me light. I have no friends. I am a freak. People are ashamed for me. Men pity me, but no man will ever be my friend, no woman will ever marry me. Even in love I am a grotesque, *un nuovo succhiello,* a new thrill. Women kissing me make themselves blind as I, not knowing that I know they do not look on me. *Io sono brutto,* I am ugly, ugly, ugly...."

His narcissistic Italian soul was crying out a torment difficult for men of other races, to whom physical beauty is not the greatest virtue, to understand.

"You are not ugly," I said.

"Am I handsome?" he asked, his voice angry. He tore the dark glasses from his face. It was the first time he had removed them in my presence. I looked with horror on what were once his eyes. The glass eye was badly fitted; it rested in the center of a gory scar and there was no eyelid over it. The other eye, the one he hoped American surgeons would restore to sight, was worse. A fragment of it staring off at an angle from a mass of raw tissue almost seemed to have sight. Around it the twisted flesh was streaked with blue. "*Sono bello?*" he shouted, leaving me no time to reply. "Am I beautiful? Now you can see at last how beautiful I am. Where is your camera? Perhaps you will make a photograph." I said beauty of the spirit was more important than beauty of the body and realized how foolish I must sound. "But I am beautiful," he said. "I will show you." He opened his wallet and searched through a fat compartment of photographs, removing one of himself on the beach, wearing only the dark glasses and swimming trunks. It showed the body of a boy, delicately built, lean, white, and firm. On the breast there was a scar, a lesser one on a thigh. Otherwise it was a body of adolescent purity.

"Am I beautiful?" Nino asked, seeming to look at me from the sockets in his skull.

"*Si,*" I replied, "*sei bello.*"

Then came one of the quixotic changes of mood so characteristic of him. He put on his glasses and said, "*Sono contento* [I am content]. My life has been changed; I have new experiences, new sensations, and new thoughts. To be blind has its own sweetness. Now I know so many things I never knew before. I am content." Before he left he asked me the time. "You see I never know the hour," he said. "By the time I reach the Arno I shall have forgotten it again." He laughed wickedly.

My leg and back gained in strength. When I could walk without distress I discontinued the massages. The day I paid him Nino asked if I would like to go with him on the following Sunday to his home in the country. I was interested to meet his family and accepted the invitation. At first he was excited by the idea of my meeting his people, then he became depressed and began to apologize for their poverty and the *cattivo* (ugly) house in which they lived. I assured him I knew how country people lived and would not be disturbed. I suggested we make a picnic of the excursion and invited Tullio Vacini and a student called Randy from my American university who happened to be in Florence.

Sunday was a fine day with a cooling breeze. Carrying string sacks of cheese, salami, and bread the four of us took a tram across town to Via dei Saponai—the street of the soapmakers—where we mounted a second trolley and were off. Nino was irrepressible. He and Randy sang "Give Me Five Minutes More" at the top of their lungs. Tullio and I read the Sunday *La Nazione*. It was a typical Italian journal filled with the cheerless "black news" that Italians love. There was the long headline of a man "Found with his chest opened by a dagger on the banks of the Arno." The story told of the unfortunate fellow's unhappy life with his wife, and photographs showed them in "happier days" at the first communion of their daughter, a little veiled bride laden with arum lilies. There was another story of a *morte improvvisa* (sudden death), by a motor scooter on my own Piazza Santa Maria Novella and of the *ragazza* who, assisting at the scene, had fainted and had to be rushed to the hospital in danger of her own life. The most saddening story of all concerned a *pastorello*, aged nine years, who died playing with a snake; the snake bit him, and after suffering *terribilmente* all day he had finally been called by Jesus. "I think I am going to cry," said Tullio.

We rattled gaily through lovely Tuscan landscape with its terraced hills of olives and grapes and broad valleys of fruit and almonds. Underneath the trees grew small grains and vegetables. There was hardly a meter that wasn't producing double crops. It reminded me of Sicily, except that it was softer and the fields were separated with thickets of dark pointed cypress instead of cactus. The Tuscan sky cast a blue light over the silvery olives making them dazzle like a summer sea. When the tram passed out of Florence, Nino had to buy a ticket; up to that time he had ridden free, a community courtesy to the blind. We crossed an algal stream in which women were washing clothes and passed through one dusty workers' village after another, each a cluster of dusty hovels, surrounding an old and frequently beautiful church. Almost every village had an outdoor movie. Posters advertised third-rate American films luridly retitled for Italian tastes to *The Sin of Constance* or *The River of Blood*. The tram line ended at the village of Aquilla before a *birreria* next door to a little Franciscan church. We had a beer with our conductor and then, guided by Nino, who never faltered in his directions, we started up a long hill on a rocky country road. The day had grown warm. We climbed through olive groves of dazzling silver, quiet with Sunday peace. After a mile we came to a tiny village named Croce de S. Giovani, hardly more than a crossroads with four buildings. Laborers' work pants hung from windows for their weekly airing. We went into a cool cellar to buy some wine. The vintner drew it from a barrel, thick purple stuff. While it flowed slowly into a jug I watched a young boy pinching the bottoms of three little girls. The girls with pierced ears and Sunday ribbons squealed with joy. We paid the vintner four hundred lire, about sixty-five cents, for the gallon of wine and continued on our way. After another half mile Nino led us into a grove. There in the shade of olives and grapes we ate our bread and cheese, sausage, eggs, and fruit. The strong wine made it a jolly picnic. Nino talked English with reckless abandon. To entertain us he acted out one of his street encounters with an American lady.

"Excuse me, what time is it, please?"

Randy replied, acting the role of the lady. "Young man, I couldn't exactly say, but I'd guess it's almost nine o'clock."

"You are an American?" Nino asked.

"Suh, I'm Southern. There's a difference."

"At what hotel do you sleep?"

"Naturally, at the Excelsior."

"Excuse me, I am masseur."

"But you are such a young man."

"All the better for massaging, Madame. Maybe you would like massage?"

"Well, my ankle *has* been hurting, ever since Venice. It's very painful slipping in a gondola."

"I always give satisfaction, Madame."

"Well, you realize if it weren't for my ankle . . ."

"Perhaps a nice general massage, Madame. . . ."

"Welllll . . ."

Under the olives the charade seemed hilariously funny.

We continued our hike past a rambling villa of terra cotta. On its walls bundles of valuable alfalfa were drying upside down like old bridal bouquets. An old man slept by a shaded well. At the sound of our voices he nodded awake. "*È fresco,*" he said, pointing to the well. "The water is fresh." He drew an old copper kettle of it and we drank our fill; it was cool and tasted of the earth. We continued down a hill and came upon the house of Nino's family, one of several farmers' houses all alike. Approaching the house Nino apologized again for its poverty and ugliness. It was a square rectangle of stone with a few windows. Apparently several families lived in it. We climbed upstairs to the Uccelli quarters consisting of three rooms and an indoor privy. In the heat of midday, its stench was overwhelming. We were invited into the coolest room, a sort of combination living and sleeping room, where Nino's mother and two of her daughters greeted us. The mother was a small, delicately built brown woman with the sharp eyes and the nervous movements of a bird. She was dressed in black. The older daughter, Antonia, was a stolid, attractive girl in her late twenties. The younger, Justina, was more slender and prettier. She sewed silently on a dress, never stopping while we were there.

It was an old house with unplaned ceiling logs and whitewashed walls. The red tile floor was so uneven that furniture slid around on it. The room was scrubbed spotless and furnished with a dark table, three sewing machines, a day bed, several chairs, and two sideboards. One sideboard, plain and functional, held the dishes; the second, a heavy, ornately carved antique affair, was too elegant and imposing for the room. For decoration there were some dog statues, the kind of brightly colored pottery ones won at carnival games. Three oppressively framed photographs looked down from the white walls. One, a wizened, toothless face glaring fiercely from under a black cowl was Nino's paternal grandmother; another of a fulsome young woman was his oldest sister who died of an appendectomy when she was twenty-two. The most gloomy of all was a wedding picture of the parents. Married in 1913, it took them four years to save enough money to be photographed in 1917. Dressed in black, the bridal pair looked as stiff and formal as a pair of corpses.

The father, roused from his Sunday slumbers by our visit, greeted us and sank into silence. He was a beaten, silent man who gave the impression that he had had nothing to say for many years. He had none of the spirit of the old woman who had been his mother, the one who glowed like a witch on the wall. He commuted each day the long distance to his factory in Florence and he seemed to resent our intrusion into his Sunday calm. Ignoring us, he sliced himself some bread and cheese at the sideboard and poured himself some Chianti. The mother served us sweet cakes and Marsala. I would have preferred the Tuscan wine in the father's straw-covered bottle but I drank the thick sweet Sicilian wine reserved for guests.

A shining new bicycle stood in the corner between two of the sewing machines. It belonged to Antonia. She rode it over the rocky two-mile stretch to the station at six o'clock each morning to take the tram for Florence, where she worked in a sewing factory. Evenings she brought home work which she, her mother, and sister finished on the three sewing machines. With Nino, Antonia was tender and considerate; she had, more than anyone in the family, the compassion that comes of a warm heart and a deep imagination. Two younger brothers and a sister, it was explained, were off on their Sunday affairs, and an older brother and sister, both married, lived away from home.

The ice broke slowly. The mother, too nervous to sit down, kept flitting about the room, arranging furniture, refilling glasses. I had walked too much; I was tired and sore. Nino was no help. He set a phonograph on top of a sewing machine and played at full volume his favorite American records, "Bongo Bongo," "Boogie Woogie Blues," and "Give Me Five Minutes More." The music made conversation impossible but seemed to bring pleasure to all the Uccellis. Even the mother rocked happily to the jazzy rhythms.

When the records were finished the father broke his silence to address a question to me. "Is it true," he asked, "that when it is night in Italy it is day in America and when it is day in Italy it is night in America?" I said that generally it was true. He shook his head in wonderment over the strangeness of the world and sank back into silence. Later he spoke once more. It was when I asked if the handsome sideboard were a family heirloom. Nino explained that it was the gift of a gracious signora whose children Nino's mother had nursed simultaneously with her own. "She had no milk at all, this wife of a rich *padrone*, and my wife nourished her four children," the father said. It developed that the sparrowy little mother had, in order to help support her own twelve children, taken to nurse during her childbearing years a total of thirteen children—all from rich mothers who couldn't or didn't wish to nurse themselves. "She was a good cow," the father said proudly. "Lots of strong milk." Then he added that he and his two brothers had a total of forty-one grown children. "We were good bulls," he said.

When I refused a second helping of cakes, Nino told the mother that I wasn't feeling well. With a peasant's fascination for bodily ailments, she asked a detailed description of my difficulties. She insisted that I rest on the day bed, where she spread her motherliness over me like a blanket, bringing me trays of sweets and fruit, cups of wine and coffee.

Nino brought forth his greatest treasure, a box of photographs. There may have been a hundred of them, and he showed us each, taking it in his hands, touching it gently, and then explaining who was in it and the circumstances under which it was taken. Occasionally, when he was confused, Antonia helped in the identification. The adolescent pictures of Nino made before the war were shocking to see. He had been a plump, pleasant lad with a lively air and large eyes full of devilment.

"They were blue, his eyes," the mother said.

There were pictures of him after the war, pictures of him on the beach wearing the dark glasses even in the water, pictures with friends, many of them American, and a picture of which the mother was proudest, showing Nino in an audience with the Pope in Rome. While we looked at them, the mother with sorrow and anxiety spoke for the first time of her son's blindness. "Is it true that in America there are great doctors who can perform miracles?" she asked. There were many great doctors, I said, wondering how to deal with her peasant's faith in the omnipotence of all things American. "Is it true that they take eyes from the dead who no longer need them and give them to the living? Do you think American doctors could give Nino such eyes?"

Nino's head was lowered as if from embarrassment and across the room the father listened with contempt. Obviously he did not believe in the miracle. But the eyes of the woman and her older daughter were on me, full of hope, begging for affirmation. "Only a doctor himself could say," I replied. It was answer enough, for the women, wanting to believe, believed; the father looked silently from across the room on what he believed to be the foolishness of women. Beside me Nino did not indicate what he was thinking, but I knew that he sensed my doubts. "Nino wishes to go to America to see the doctors," Antonia said. "But the great doctors of America cost much money. Do you know how much?" I said that if it were possible to restore Nino's sight an American doctor would not hesitate for a fee. "Is it true," Antonia asked, "that the doctors would operate on a poor boy like Nino?"

"Yes, if they believed they could bring back his sight."

"America is a beautiful land," the mother said. "A good and beautiful land."

It was after five o'clock. Antonia made more coffee and pressed more cakes on us, apologizing because there was no cognac. Americans, she had heard, liked cognac. We started down the long hill to the tram, Antonia and Nino accompanying us part of the way. It was a quiet walk. The shadows were lengthening across the land, and we were all sad.

Nino thanked us for coming as if we had done him a favor, still apologizing for the humbleness of the home. Then he turned back with his sister to spend the night at home. We saw them climbing up the hill, his hand in hers. In the village, crowds were waiting for a bicycle race to pass. The people made a *festa* of the race, jamming the streets and piazzas. Vendors sold fruits and nuts and that shocking Tuscan delicacy, fried birds. They were pathetically small things shorn of feathers and crisp as fried shrimp. At the end of their spindly necks the eyes were open; so were the tiny beaks, as if there were still an unreleased song in the throat. "No doubt meadow larks," Tullio said. "They are the most delectable."

When the tram came it was filled with a noisy, frayed-tempered Sunday evening crowd returning from a holiday. We pushed into the crowded aisle and breathed garlic, salami, and stale sweat. Next to me a young father was holding his son, a fat, bland baby with watery blue eyes. The baby was eating a piece of cheese, "*Sempre mangiare* [Always eating]," the father bragged to me. The baby finished the cheese and began to yell. The father shook his head wonderingly. "*Sempre mangiare*," he repeated for all to note and drew from his pocket one of the fried meadow larks. The baby popped the bird's head into his mouth and I heard the sickening crunch of tiny teeth on the crisp little skull.

An hour later we arrived in Florence. A glowing sunset cast a soft rose twilight over the beautiful city. But it was too late to revive our sodden spirits; we separated and went to bed. Early the next morning I left Florence for Venice.

Two months later I was back in Florence, walking along the Arno. I saw Nino passing on the other side of the street. I crossed over to catch him. Before I could reach him he had stopped to speak to a fashionably-dressed middle-aged woman, probably American.

"Excuse me," I heard him say. "What time is it, please?" Not wishing to interrupt the conversation, I moved along and I never saw him again.

CHAPTER 14

THEY'LL NEVER FORGET US

I FIRST HEARD of the two women from St. Louis from a bellboy who told me they had hung their laundry on the chandelier. When the manager discovered it had washed off the decorations he tried to make them pay.

"Like hell," they told him. "If you can't make your decorations melt-proof you can pay for them yourself. We don't pay for any decorations in a lousy hotel like this."

"Lousy!" the manager echoed. "What means lousy?"

"My God, can't you understand English?" said one. "Lousy means lice."

The manager was very upset. "Oh, no," he assured them. "At the Excelsior we have no lice."

They had not been in Florence two days before they were a legend. Wrapping themselves in the stars and stripes, the two ladies were never shaken in their faith in the superiority of everything American.

I saw them for the first time under an umbrella at a sidewalk café and recognized them at once from the bellboy's descriptions. One was smallish and feminine, with graying hair and a billowy cotton dress. She gave the impression of quiet demureness that was in contrast to her friend, a tall bony woman with faded blond hair and a loud brassy voice. Both were in their early forties. They ordered a glass of water. The waiter stood and stared as if he hadn't understood.

"A glass of water," the tall one said. "What's the matter, can't you understand English?"

Doubtless the waiter could, but it was the first time in his experience anyone had ordered only a glass of water and he didn't seem to believe it. "Perhaps a *caffè*, after the water," he said.

"No," the small one said firmly. "I don't want any coffee. Italians don't know how to make coffee. It's lousy."

Since Italians are famous for their coffee, the waiter was naturally astounded.

"What are you waiting for? Can't you even understand sign language?" the tall woman said. The waiter opened his mouth to speak but she stopped him. "Now don't ask me what I'm going to do with the water. Just bring it and you'll see."

In a daze the waiter went for the water. The women saw me watching. "Hey there!" the smaller one called. "You American?"

I said I was.

"You are?" echoed the tall one. "How the hell did you ever get to this hick town?" They introduced themselves and seemed eager to talk. The smaller one was Sybil, a telephone operator. The taller was Laura; she had a job winding armatures for electric motors in an appliance factory. Their six-weeks' tour, arranged by a St. Louis travel agency, was taking them over most of western Europe. "All we got to eat in England was fish," Laura said. "I was talking to a bus driver in London, and hell, I make more in a week winding motors than he makes in a month."

"Paris was sort of pretty," said Sybil. "But no one could talk English. We had the lights on in our room all night because we couldn't find the switch and no one could understand us when we asked where it was. The second night I telephoned downstairs. It took me fifteen minutes to get the operator, so I said, 'How the hell do you operate this telephone? I've been a telephone operator for twenty years and I want to know.' They sent a man upstairs but he couldn't talk English."

"I told him, 'For Christ's sake if you're going to run a hotel the least you can do is learn English,' " Laura said. "What we liked best on the whole trip so far was all those catacombs in Rome. The Cappucini one and St. Sebastian. I'm crazy for catacombs and the Cappucini was handy, right near the hotel. I went every day. I love anything that has to do with dead people. In St. Louis I go to the morgue at least once a week."

The waiter brought two glasses of water. "What the hell, don't you have any ice in this whistle stop?" Laura said to him. This time he did not understand. "Ice, ice." Laura rapped on her glass.

"*Ghiaccia*," I translated, and ordered some coffee for myself. The waiter went off in a sort of stupor.

"These damned foreigners are all robbers," Sybil said. "In Rome a girl with us got her pocket picked. She'd been saving eighteen years for this trip and they stole it all. She called the police, but if you ask me it was the police that picked her pocket. You can't trust foreigners. I tell you it will be good to get back to God's country again where you can trust people."

"In the hotel here we have a private bath with lots of shining knobs and no hot water," Laura said. "I told the manager, 'How the hell do you expect us to take a bath with just knobs and no hot water? For the money we're paying there ought to be hot water. If you were in America you'd learn how to run a hotel,' I said."

The waiter returned, and in the glasses the slivered ice glistened. The women drank the water and got up to go. "Well, I guess we'll be seeing you around," Laura said. "Can't help running into each other in this hick town." I drank my coffee and left the waiter a hundred-lire tip.

That night there was a rumpus in the hotel. In the morning Laura and Sybil told me about it.

"When we wanted to press some clothes with our iron it was the wrong current," Sybil said.

"Yeah, direct current." Laura picked up the story. "The dumb manager tried to tell me it was regular current. 'Regular,' I said to him. 'I haven't been winding electric motors for eighteen years to have a jerk like you tell me about electricity. Direct current's behind the times and there ain't any of it in St. Louis except maybe in the black belt. This hotel is a real crumb joint,' I said to him."

They went sight-seeing during the day and returned unimpressed. "I knew the minute I got off the bus in this one-horse town we weren't going to like it," Laura said. "It's a dry hick town with nothing to do."

What had they seen, I asked. "Well, we went to one museum and some churches but our guide couldn't even *understand* English so there was no point to that. It was very dry."

"What's the point of a guide who can't speak English?" Sybil wanted to know.

I asked what churches they had seen. "Oh, it was that gold Baptist church right next to that synagogue," Laura said. "It was sort of pretty but the funniest Baptist church I ever was in. No benches at all."

I asked for more detail. "Oh, you know that Baptist church, the round one right in the middle of town, next door to that big synagogue," Laura said.

I no longer had any doubts. The synagogue they had seen was the Cathedral of Santa Maria dei Fiori with Brunelleschi's great dome. The Baptist church was the baptistery with Ghiberti's gold doors.

The day I got on the Venice bus there they were in bounding good spirits. "Hi, you," Laura said. "You leaving this hick town too? Boy are we glad to get away."

"We're looking forward to one of them gondola rides," Sybil said, and Laura, laughing loudly, said, "Sybil is all keyed up for a hot bath tonight in Venice, but I'll bet she don't get it."

"I'm going to get my bath one way or another, I can tell you," Sybil said firmly. "No foreigners are going to tell me I can't have a bath." Their boisterous spirits continued through the morning.

We stopped briefly in a small town to look at a cathedral and I remarked that the church had great beauty of design outside, but very little distinction inside. "Can you build one like it?" Sybil asked me, and she and Laura burst into gales of laughter. Laura said, "I've been in so doggone many churches this trip I don't ever have to go to church again." On the road they both slept with their heads thrown back on their seats, snoring in harmony. When they woke up we were passing through a mountain village in which all the women were dressed in black. "Why do they dress so old fashioned?" Laura asked the driver. "Nothing but black dresses with long sleeves. You wouldn't see that in the States, except maybe a hundred years ago."

At noon we arrived in Ravenna where the bus made a scheduled stop for lunch at a restaurant which served bus passengers. Such "official" restaurants on tourist bus lines are often diabolical traps in which as little as possible is given for as much as the traffic will bear. Bus operators who bring in the unsuspecting travelers are rewarded with a percentage of the take. Italians know better than to eat in them. The tourists who speak no Italian and want most of all to escape the embarrassment of a scene are easy victims for such petty extortions. Of such establishments, the restaurant in Ravenna was one of the worst. White-jacketed waiters with napkins folded over their arms smiled with servile, serene confidence as we unloaded. Standing in the door, beaming with happy assurance, was the manager, never suspecting what disaster we were delivering to him.

I studied the menu. As usual in such places, it was *"prezzo fisso,"* a fixed price for an entire meal as is the custom in American, but not in Italian, restaurants. The price in this case was twelve hundred lire and included spaghetti, scaloppine, salad, potatoes, fruit, and cheese. To this was to be added the *servizio* and *coperto*, the last being a sort of cover charge. Wine, of course, was also extra.

The moment we were seated, the waiters disappeared. Twenty minutes later, the spaghetti arrived. When it was served to Laura and Sybil, Laura told the waiter they hadn't ordered spaghetti and didn't want any. They wished for soup instead. The waiter explained it was on the lunch, and he could not take it back. When the two women insisted, the waiter, according to the strategy of the house, called the manager. The manager, a portly man, lumbered up to the table smiling with deceptive graciousness.

"We do not eat spaghetti," Laura said. "We don't want to be fat pigs." The manager thought she was calling him a fat pig. "I didn't say you were a pig," Laura corrected. "I said I didn't want to be one." The manager shouted angrily at Laura in Italian and she shouted at him in English. I stepped into the hopeless situation and explained in Italian what Laura had said. The man apologized profusely.

"What about the soup?" Laura asked.

"A thousand pardons," the manager said, bowing with elaborate politeness, "but there is no soup. It is better you eat the spaghetti which you pay for." To my amazement the two women began to eat. I suspected the manager understood more English than he pretended.

The time allotted by the bus schedule for the meal was one hour; twenty-five minutes of it were already gone. Service continued *adagio*. When the spaghetti was eaten, bottles of wine and bread began to appear. When twenty minutes remained of the hour, the salad was brought in. Fifteen minutes, then ten, and still no scaloppine. The diners impatiently called their waiters. They could not be found. One or two appeared to say the scaloppine was on the fire. In five minutes they said it would arrive *pronto*. The two bus drivers, apparently well nourished, emerged from a back room, climbed into the bus, and tooted their horns. The scaloppine had not arrived from the fire and it was time to leave.

Immediately the waiters appeared. Ah, it was too bad the bus could not wait longer, just when the scaloppine was prepared. All of them carried little silver platters with the checks for the meals which had been contracted for. With the wine and the *servizio* and the *coperto* they totaled two thousand lire for each guest. As bus horns tooted frantically and the battalion of waiters babbled excitedly, confused and hungry Americans,

Scandinavians, and English reached for their purses, wanting only to pay and get out.

But not Laura and Sybil. At their table the battle flags were at full mast.

"No god-damned foreigners are going to do this to me," Laura told her waiter.

"No understand," he said.

"I said I don't wind coils for two-twenty an hour to be robbed by lousy Dagos."

"No understand."

"You're damned right you understand." She spoke loud enough for everyone to understand and everyone held on to their money a moment longer to await the outcome of the argument. "I ate some spaghetti," Laura said. "How much do you charge for spaghetti?" Several waiters joined their unhappy comrade and discoursed wildly in Italian. Laura outshouted them. "You'd better tell me how much the spaghetti is or you won't get one lousy lire," she said. "No foreign crooks are going to beat me out of my money. I'm an American."

Outside the drivers blasted the horns; inside no one moved. The waiter called the manager, who waddled back to Laura's table and bowed. "Would the lady like to come into the back room with me?" he asked in good English.

"Like hell I will," Laura said. "We'll talk about it right here."

Keeping his voice as low as possible in an effort to maintain his dignity, the manager agreed to "adjust" Laura's and Sybil's checks. Spaghetti, he said, cost three hundred and ninety lire.

"Robbery," Laura said. He shrugged. *Servizio,* one hundred lire, he wrote.

"But we didn't have any *servizio* and we aren't paying for any *servizio* we didn't have." The manager crossed it off. *Coperto,* one hundred and sixty lire, he wrote.

"What the hell's this *coperto?*" Laura demanded. "We didn't have any *coperto*. All we had was spaghetti."

The manager explained it was cover charge and picked up a menu to show it was listed. Laura argued, but he refused to remove the *coperto.* "Okay," she said with sudden resignation, "I'll take that *coperto*." For the two checks she gave him fifteen hundred lire in two notes and waited for change. In the meantime everyone else demanded adjustments on their checks. The waiters refused and then realized they had no alternative. Outside the horns tooted. The manager brought Laura's change, a bowl of ten-lire notes. "Nothing doing," said Laura when he handed her the bowl. "You ain't pulling no such tricks on an American. I want you to count it." In scarlet humiliation he counted out the dirty brown little bills while she kept score. He was twelve short. "I'll be doggoned!" Laura said. "You're an even bigger crook than I thought you were." The manager sputtered that the amount was correct; it was she who had miscounted. "Okay," she said, "Count them again." The miserable man did and came out twelve short. "Is a mistake," he said. "Excuse me please."

"It's a mistake all right," Laura said. He gave her the twelve notes.

By this time the rest of the diners were paying adjusted checks to the band of unhappy waiters and the restaurant was emptying. Laura and Sybil picked up the tablecloth and the napkins from their table and started toward the door. The astonished manager followed, sputtering protests. They paid him no heed, but went into the street where they threw the linen cloths on the pavements and vigorously ground them into the dirt with their heels. "If we're paying for *coperto* we're going to have *coperto*," Laura said to the awed Italians.

The admiring tourists stepped aside and Laura and Sybil passed between them to the bus like royalty. On the steps Laura yelled back, "This is the lousiest place I've ever been. Boy, the Hawkins-James travel agency in St. Louis is going to hear about this."

The drivers, anxious to have an end to it, lost no time getting under way. Laura and Sybil leaned back in their seats and began to laugh. "Boy, we sure showed those foreign bastards," Laura said.

"They'll never forget us," Sybil said.

CHAPTER 15

BIANCA

I FOUND HER on my second day in Venice on the Lido beach. I was there for some sun and swimming. After a lunch of bread and cheese I lay on the sand and fell asleep. I was awakened by the pleasant sting of warm sand on my stomach and legs. There she was, lying near me, her delicate bones outlined like the ribbings of a ripened fig in her little body. Her skin was burned to the color of walnut, her eyes were large and black, her hair was spun of ebony. Beside her I looked pale and fat like a gross inhabitant of another world.

She pretended not to notice me at all, and when I spoke to her she ignored me like a well-bred young lady. But I was certain the sand which had pelted me had come from the pretty little hand now drawing finger pictures in the sand. *"Una lettera d'amore?"* I asked. "A love letter to a dolphin?" The question made her smile. Still she would not speak or look at me.

"I am called Niccoló," I said.

She paid no attention but continued to look away. Her femininity was irresistibly challenging. I lit a cigarette and offered her one. She took it.

"What are you called?" I asked, lighting it for her.

"Bianca." She lowered her eyes modestly.

Bianca! I was enchanted. If, like Shakespeare's Bianca, she couldn't be from Padua, Venice would do as well.

"Siete Americano?" Timorous as hummingbird's, her eyes darted about the beach, missing nothing.

"Yes," I said. "Do you like Americans?"

Bianca blushed shyly, as if I'd made an improper suggestion. She did not reply.

I stood up and stretched. " I am going into the water," I said. "Will you come along?"

243

"*Sarebbe uno scandalo* [It would be a scandal]," she said. She looked over the beach, lined with husky sun bathers playing at body-building.

"No one is looking at you but me," I said.

"I am not alone," Bianca said. "I have come with two friends. Two girls," she added virtuously.

"Are they here?"

She looked around. "No, they are not here. Perhaps in our cabin. Do you have a cabin?"

I said I hadn't and started for the water. I felt sure she would come. When she did it was in a spirit of combat. Without a word she swam by me, farther out than I had ventured. I followed her, beyond the bathers, beyond the point where the whitecaps burst. We played together like languid fish, inventing games, turning somersaults in the water. She played with the naturalness of a child, and like a bashful child she spoke no word. Then quite suddenly she started to swim in. Why? I asked.

"*Uno scandalo*," she said, though no one was paying us any attention. I swam in with her. On the beach she said, "Now I must go to my friends."

"You wish to say good-by now!"

"But you cannot come with me. *Uno scandalo!*"

She loved that word; it was a fortress with which she barricaded herself. I did not understand her. I was certain that I did not want to let her go, and suggested that we return to Venice together. She was shocked, and then, turning capricious, she said she might. A second later, indulging her feminine prerogative, she said she couldn't.

"I am a good girl," she said.

"If I didn't know you were a good girl, how could I suggest it?" I replied, playing her game.

"In America do good girls speak to men on the beach?"

"Of course they do."

"*Senza scandalo* [Without a scandal]?"

"One can see scandal has never touched you."

Her eyes fell innocently. "You are right, signore," she said, "but it is not easy. To be a good girl, one must pay much attention."

"It is true. Life must have many temptations for one so pretty," I said.

Bianca reflected a moment. "I can see, you are understanding," she said. "You would not betray the trust of a good girl."

"Then you will meet me?"

"In a quarter hour outside the gates."

"*Sicuro?*" I asked.

"For certain," she promised.

I wasn't sure whether she was sincere or merely getting rid of me. But I hurried to my stall, showered and dressed, and in ten minutes I was at the appointed place. It was late afternoon and people poured out of the gates. Five minutes passed and Bianca did not appear. I watched the crowds closely for fear I might not recognize her in her clothes. Ten minutes more passed. My heart sank; I knew she would not appear. I started to leave; then stopped and waited some more. I had given her up, yet I could not get myself to leave.

Then I saw her. She walked slowly, with a curious triumph, as if she knew I would be there. She was wearing a blue cotton skirt and a sweater under which her breasts pointed firmly; her waist seemed smaller than ever. She had her bathing things in a little string sack which I offered to carry. I wanted to take the bus.

"Oh, signore, it is too dear," Bianca said. "We will walk." Though the fare was the equivalent of about five cents for one we walked to the motor-boat, moving slowly through the warm afternoon like two idle children. Conversation was an effort. When I looked at her, she turned her face shyly away. Though I asked many questions, the facts she offered about herself were sparse. She lived with her mother, a widow, "who guards me very closely that I am a good girl," in the vicinity of the railroad station. A brother worked for a butcher; a married sister lived in a village near Padua. She was twenty years old; her twenty-first birthday was only a week away. I would have guessed her younger.

She stopped to remove a pebble from her shoe. "*Excusez-moi, eine minute, please,*" she said. I had the impression she believed she was speaking English. Obviously she had brushed against a number of languages in Venice. With startling abandon she latched her half-dozen or so English words onto bits of French, German, and even Swedish. Her favorite expression was "*molto* very much," *molto* being the Italian equivalent of *very*. As I looked at her, bent over her shoe, she seemed more wispy than ever, a toy girl I had drawn from the sea. When she had finished, I took her hand. She looked at me a moment from the corner of her eye. "Oh, signore," she said, "*uno scandalo!*" but she left her hand in mine.

She withdrew it when we joined the crowd on the motor launch. The Adriatic was blindingly bright; Venice glittered in the afternoon sun. On the deck we faced the dazzling golden city.

"Bianca, you are very pretty," I said.

She continued to look ahead.

"Oh, no, signore," she said. *"Io sono molta brutta* [I am very ugly]."

"You are pretty," I repeated, and as stubbornly, whether from demureness or perverseness, I knew not, she repeated, "I am very ugly." Making conversation with Bianca required effort; I was soon exhausted.

The dreamy air which she carried like a cloud about her and which had so ingratiated me was now annoying. When I spoke, she seemed not to be paying attention at all. She had the common Italian habit, when she did not understand what I said, of replying simply *"Si,"* and I had no idea whether she had heard me or not. This put me into a temper. It was too soon in our friendship to be taken for granted. I would have been relieved if at the end of the ferry ride she had said *"Buona sera"* and disappeared into the crowd.

But she didn't. She got off the ferry with me, though it continued along the Grand Canal to her home, and we walked across San Marco together. She sensed I was in a temper. From the sides of her eyes she watched me with a naughty roguishness and allowed me to hold her hand.

I invited Bianca to dinner and asked her if she knew a place that was not *"touristi,"* where Venetians ate. *"Si,"* she said. *"Andiamo."* She wove me through the crowded labyrinths of the city to a humble doorway over which I read *Trattoria Bolzano*. The inside was clean and bare and there were not many customers. Bianca led me to a small back room in which there were two girls, a very striking pair. One had extremely long waves of bright red hair which she wore flowing about her like a *quattrocento* Magdalene. The other, more severely handsome, was a Junoesque girl with a strong noble face and short black hair. With delicate fingers they ate tiny minnow-sized fish, complete with heads, viscera, and scales, fried in deep fat to a golden crispness.

The owner of the place was a good-natured old bawd named Pfeifer who was also cook and waitress. She wore a shapeless black dress and in a Venetian dialect which I did not understand she greeted Bianca like an old friend. When Signora Pfeifer discovered I could understand German, she spoke to me in that language, pointing out with considerable superiority that she wasn't Venetian at all, but a native of Bolzano, a mountain town near the Austrian border, after which she had named her restaurant. She was not even Italian, but Tyrolian with an Austrian father, which she explained was something quite different. She boasted of the American soldiers and sailors who had been her customers and brought out the post cards they had sent from their homes in Jersey City, Atlanta, and Minneapolis. We ate a thick black soup of mussels and squid, and followed it with steaks and salad. Bianca ate heartily for one so small, but she drank very little of the wine. The girls at the next table followed the fish with eggs and mushrooms, and the proprietress inquired if they wanted onions with their mushrooms. They said no.

"Of course not," the old woman said meaningfully in German. "They must work tonight. Naturally, no onions."

When she was finished eating the Magdalene voluptuously drew a pearl comb through her red hair. It billowed like a cloud, bathing her in an orange mist, until her face was covered, with only her eyes, like a cat's, peering out. During this breathtaking performance I forgot about Bianca.

"She is beautiful," Bianca said petulantly, "and I am very ugly."

"You are prettier," I said.

"*Sicuro?*" she asked.

"For certain," I said. I reached for her hand under the table and she blushed and lowered her eyes. The room was quiet. At the other table Juno watched the Magdalene's voluptuous toilet. Finally, without a word, the Magdalene put away her comb and got up, and the other followed her from the room.

"They are lovers," the proprietress enlightened us. "Both are whores, but they are lovers and the dark one is very jealous." For dessert she brought us a bowl of fruit. I selected a peach and cut it in half, exposing two fat worms cozily burrowed near the pit. I showed them to Signora Straeller. "Thank you for telling me," she said, laughing. "Tomorrow they will go in the soup." When we left she said, "You will come back tomorrow for the soup?" her laughter rang out behind us.

I wanted a gondola ride. It was to be my first, and Bianca was amused at my excitement. We examined all the gondolas on the quay, searching for a particularly grandiose one with a congenial gondolier. We found one decorated in red and gold, elegant enough for a queen, with Venuses carved at the stern and prow and a curtained sedan garlanded with fresh flowers. The gondolier was a swarthy rogue, proud of his handiwork. He bowed us into it and packed us in cushions. Then he lit candles in little lanterns hanging from bow and stern and pushed off into the night. A moment later he turned into a damp little canal, dark and hardly wider than a walk, where the only noise was the water lapping against the houses.

The boatman began to sing softly Alfredo's "When she is far" from *La Traviata*. For an hour we slid noiselessly through blackness, meeting at corners with gondoliers singing from *Rigoletto* and *Aïda*, unseen, husky voices blending in the dark tunnels. We joined a caravan of gondolas, illuminated with Japanese lanterns, in the first of which a lusty and passable soprano sang *Madame Butterfly*. This was Venice, better than the most lyric descriptions.

Bianca confided to me that she had a favorite American song, one which an American sailor had started to teach her. She sang "Don't know'why there's no sun up in the sky, stormy weather. . . ." It was the only line she knew and she sang it over and over. She asked what it meant, so I taught her the Italian words, "*Non so perchè non c'è il sole nel cielo, tempo tempestoso. . . .*" When she had learned that, I taught her another line, first in Italian and then in English.

"Since my man and I ain't together keeps raining all the time. . . ."

We were leaving the operatic caravan and slipping through darkness again. Our boatman was silent now.

"*Tempo tempestoso. . . .*"

Quite unexpectedly Bianca stopped singing and kissed me. Like soft roses she folded in my arms. As with everything about her, the embrace was fragile and lingering.

"I love you," she said. It was the only English phrase she knew and I wondered jealously where she had learned it. "I love you, Nicki," and then the strangely syntaxed question, "I love you me?"

We conjured them easily, the symbolic words and gestures that are the chips of the game played by lonely romantic hearts. We played bravely, believing in the game, trying to make it real in an unreal city, romantically deceiving ourselves among the props and backdrops of the world's most theatrical setting. I held my doll plaything drawn from the sea and trembled with the excitement of discovery, as if a youth fountain had washed a decade from my years. That the waters were dank and putrid didn't matter for the moment.

"I love you, Bianca."

"I love you me?" she asked again as if she didn't believe me.

"Yes, Bianca."

We met every day except one in the next two weeks, always at the same time, three o'clock after the siesta, and at the same place, *il nostro posto*, our spot, an archway in a corner of San Marco. Afternoons we went to the churches and museums, to the Lido for swimming, or simply strolled through the bewildering catacombs of the streets of Venice. One day Bianca led me past a shopwindow pointing out a dress she liked. It was a strapless party dress, as pink and airy as circus cotton candy.

"I have never had a dress without straps," she said coyly. "Perhaps I couldn't wear one. Perhaps I have not the body."

I assured her that she could wear the dress.

"Do you think so?" she asked coquettishly. "Perhaps you will come with me to try it one day."

Often we wandered for an hour or more without speaking, so at ease were we now with each other. Her vague, abstracted way of not listening no longer upset me. But I did not understand her, and the mystery of her fascinated me. I was curious about her home life about which she would tell no more than she had the first day. That her house was neat I had no doubts, for though the weather was hot she was always scrupulously clean and fresh. Evenings she never let me walk her home; for me to do so would be a scandal. I would walk part of the way with her, and then she would say "*È basta* [It's enough]," and continue by herself. I suggested that she invite me to her home and she seemed shocked by the idea. "You joke," she said.

"I am serious, Bianca," I said. "In America girls invite their friends to meet their families."

"In Italy it is different," she said. "It would be a scandal."

I was more mystified than ever and wondered if she had been telling me the truth. How, if her mother was so decorous, did Bianca explain the late hours she kept with me; how had her mother permitted her to go to the beach alone in the first place?

There were times when she lost her shyness and became ardently aggressive, when her whole personality seemed to change. When we entered a church and I forgot to genuflect at the holy fountain she was as deeply upset as if she had witnessed a mortal sin. One afternoon in the basilica of Santa Maria della Salute—Saint Mary's of Good Health—the great octagonal temple on the grand canal, Bianca took a step to prevent my heresy. She stepped inside the church ahead of me, dipped her hand into the holy font, and then, before crossing herself, touched my lips with her moist fingers to convey the blessing to me. The sweetness of the gesture brought tears to my eyes. A priest led us to the sacristy to see paintings by Titian and Tintoretto. When he disappeared for a moment, Bianca turned back to kiss me. Her thin body trembled. "I love you," she said and asked her curious question "I love you me?"

"Yes, yes," I said. "I love you."

But she was not to be comforted and as we walked from church to church, looking at Bellini Sebastians and monks' tombs, and squeezed through the Calle Querni Stamialia, a street hardly wide enough for one man, she said nothing and hummed softly to herself of stormy weather.

We usually ate at the Trattoria Bolzano, where Signora Straeller took a clinical interest in our friendship. Evenings we took a gondola or went to the cinema or both. Bianca loved movies, especially American ones, and I had passes to the Venice Film Festival. We saw *A Streetcar Named Desire*, through which Bianca wept profusely for Blanche DuBois who she felt did not deserve such a terrible punishment; and we saw *Born Yesterday*, which I tried unsuccessfully to translate to Bianca. Its idiom was too American. To Bianca it was the story of a girl who loved a handsome young hero but who, for reasons difficult to understand, was held to a fate worse than death by a cruel ugly bully. Bianca and Billie Dawn triumphed in this one.

What Bianca liked best of all were the Greta Garbo movies. There was a revival of them in Venice. Within a week we saw *Camille*, *Anna Christie*, and *Grand Hotel*, through all of which Bianca sighed and wept. It was a time of love and tears, tears and love, during which Bianca's life turned as tragic and noble as Greta Garbo's, and I became so immersed in the present, I had no memories of past nor thoughts of the future.

It was *Anna Karenina* which brought us face to face with reality. After this film, Bianca couldn't stop weeping. "So beautiful," she sighed. "She was so beautiful!"

"Remember, it is only a story," I said, wiping away her tears.

"It is real," Bianca said. "It is real to suffer for love."

We took a gondola. As we glided through a dark canal Bianca asked me, *"Nicki, quando parti?"*

The question startled me. When I was with Bianca I had no thought of leave-taking; departure was not a reality, only a date on the calendar. Now I remembered I had an appointment in Padua on Saturday, just three days away.

"Why do you ask?"

"Because you will leave," Bianca said. "No one ever stays in Venice."

"I will come back," I said.

"You will not come back." She said it over and over again. "You will not come back. I shall never see you again."

"I promise to return, Bianca."

"You say so to please me, but you will not."

"No, Bianca, it is true." I believed what I was saying. "I will be back."

"When?"

"A year, two years. As soon as I can."

"Nicki, I love you. I love you *eternamente*. I love you me *eternamente?*"

"Forever, Bianca."

Her mood was quixotic now, changing as a cloud in flight, believing in our love and then not believing, solemn and tragic one minute, capricious and gay the next.

"It is not true that you will love me forever," she said.

"Bianca, I believe that we never lose the people we love, that in some way they remain with us forever. I know I shall never forget you."

"All of them you love?" she asked.

"Yes, all," I said. "One does not forget."

"It is a great many to carry inside you," Bianca said coquettishly, "all that you have loved."

"A great many for you?"

"For you, I think," she said. "Will you write me from America? I will await your letters."

"I will write."

"*Promesso?*"

"I promise."

Bianca tapped her fingers on my chest as one taps a typewriter.

"I am writing a letter," she said, dictating to herself in English. "Nicki, I love you. I love you, Nicki. I love you me, Nicki?"

The gondola was approaching music, hot American jazz which ricocheted through the dark somnambulant streets like gunfire. We followed it to a strange scene, a red and gilded ballroom in a sixteenth-century palace, a room with a voluptuously frescoed ceiling lit with hundreds of glowing candles. Through great arched windows opened to the night we could see elegantly dressed men and women dancing and drinking champagne poured by Negroes in the costumes of blackamoors. Outside the palace, the moonlit square was alive with kibitzing poor. Neighbors who could not sleep had gathered to listen to the music and others hung out of their windows to watch the candlelit revelries. On the cobblestones the young were dancing to the music of the band. A luminously white American sailor jittered with a dark Venetian girl. I asked the gondolier to stop and invited Bianca to dance. She shrugged decorously, as if dancing in the streets were a common thing to be doing. "See the candles burning," I said, "and the splendor of the room. We have drunk champagne, magic champagne which has turned you into Garbo and me into Count Vronsky. See how handsome we are, you in a silver dress without straps and me in my uniform." Bianca smiled. I could see she liked the game. She stepped from the gondola and the orchestra accommodated us with a waltz. We danced with the others in the moonlight. But my heart was heavy. I had yet to tell her that I was leaving her and Venice within the week.

Next day we met at our arch earlier than usual. It was the day Bianca had told me was her birthday and as a celebration we planned a boat trip to the island of Torcello, where I might see the Byzantine mosaics in the cathedral. For Bianca's birthday I had brought some gifts: a bottle of scent and a silk scarf. "For me?" she exclaimed when I gave them to her. On a card I had written *Buon Natale*, which provided much merriment because in mistaking *Natale* for *Nato* I had written "Merry Christmas" instead of "Happy Birthday." She thanked me for the gifts, but I could see she was disappointed at their modesty. Obviously from an American she had expected something more lavish. When, on our way to the boat she walked by the shopwindow to see if the pink dress was still there, I realized it was the dress she had expected me to buy as a birthday gift. It was a troublesome thought. I was sorry to have disappointed her. I had never bought a dress for a woman in my life.

On the boat Bianca was even more abstracted than usual. We passed Venice's island cemetery of San Michele, and I said I should like once to go to the cemetery to watch the arrival of a funeral by gondola. "Why?" Bianca asked. "They're *all* dead." Our boat was made of steel and the sun burned hot. The crowd was largely tourists and a band of young stonemasons returning to their island homes, each with his own tool kit. Sitting beside us was a British honeymoon couple. The groom was an academic type, about thirty-five years old; his bride was younger and pathetically plain. Her fat face was without make-up, her hair was straight, and her eyes did not focus. The Italian men stared at the couple with fascination, feeling pity and contempt for a man cursed with a woman so lacking in charm, making obscene jokes among themselves.

"It is a terrible sorrow to be so ugly," Bianca said. "How can he love her?"

The couple, completely oblivious of the interest they were arousing, discussed art and architecture with an impressive intellectuality. I told Bianca that they seemed very much in love.

"It is not possible," she said. "He will leave her. No man can love a girl so ugly."

The boat stopped at Murano, where the young masons disembarked, Burano, and finally Torcello. The little island, the historic mother of Venice, once a bustling capital of commerce and military operations, is now a sleepy meadow of vineyards and salt-water rushes. It has a few peasant houses and two antique churches. Of these, we had come to see the cathedral of Santa Maria Assunta. This fine church is so close to the level of the sea that part of its mosaiced floor was lying under salt water. We had to step carefully to keep our feet dry. The great twelfth-century mosaics on the entrance wall were perfectly preserved. They are more beautiful than the mosaics of Ravenna and Venice, more imaginative than the inferno paintings of Siena and Florence. They showed sea monsters with dogs' heads devouring sinners, snakes crawling in and out of the eye sockets of unrepentants, the damned squirming in flames of blood stoked by devils. I looked at the fantastic details until my neck ached. Bianca began to sulk impatiently. I pointed out to her the *paradiso*, which was as usual filled with ecstatic angels singing hallelujahs to the Lord. "A boring thing to be doing all through eternity," I said. Bianca crossed herself hurriedly for having heard such a blasphemy. "*Mamma mia*," she said.

I pressed the point. "But would you want to sing *Ave Maria* and *Alleluia* forever and ever without stopping?" I asked.

"I wouldn't like it now," she admitted. "But in *paradiso* it will be different. No doubt I will like it there."

She did not sound very enthusiastic. "Even if there are no men to kiss and no handsome American sailors to sing 'Stormy Weather'? Will you like it then?" I teased.

"It is very wicked to have such thoughts," she scolded. We drank Coca-Colas at a tourist inn and walked along the canals through the tall grass and vineyards with only the water insects and some long-legged birds to break the silence. I wanted to visit the fishing village of Burano, which I mistakenly believed was on the same island as Torcello. Our walk was so pleasant I asked Bianca if we might continue it to Burano. "*Si*," she

answered in her familiar abstracted manner. Soon we arrived at the
water's edge, where I discovered that Burano was separated from us by
a broad expanse of Adriatic. As usual, Bianca had not understood my
question and as usual she had answered. "Yes" just to be agreeable. It
sent me into a temper.

"*Stupida!*" I said.

"*Stupido!*" she fired back. "It is you who are stupid thinking one can
walk on water." Her dark eyes flared with sudden hatred.

"Only someone who is stupid would answer a question she does not
understand," I said.

"How can one understand when you are too stupid to speak Italian
properly?" she flashed back.

"It is stupid to answer 'yes' to everything," I said.

"You are rude and ugly," Bianca snapped. "Just like all Americans you
are a beast."

I spoke to a fisherman who said the departed ferry was the last boat
from Torcello, where we were indeed stranded. If I wanted to leave the
island I must hire a gondola to Burano, from which there would be a later
boat to Venice. I found a gondolier willing to take us for three hundred
lire, a sturdy, bare-chested youngster who steered his craft skillfully in
and out of the bayous. A gondola was no place to quarrel so I folded
Bianca in my arms and said I was sorry.

"You said I was *stupida*," she wailed.

"We were both stupid," I said. "You must forgive me for being angry."

"You were very cruel." She sulked, determined to punish me further.
She permitted my arm on her shoulder, but would not let me hold her
hand. We glided silently through a series of Japanese landscapes dotted
with graceful herons and storks and high-arched bridges.

The *Guide bleu* says of Burano: "A very animated fishing center famous
for its lace." It does not do justice to this captivating place. A miniature
Venice embroidered with canals, it is only five miles from Venice yet separated as completely as if it were another land. As we slid into the harbor
at sunset the terra-cotta village glowed with a coral light. At first sight
it hardly seemed real, but more like a stage setting of a toy village. The
people were lean and handsome; even the old ones had the rugged and
noble beauty of people who live with the sea. Spare barefoot fishermen returned with their fleets of fishing boats, sailing in from the open sea like
swans in the evening. Farmers returned in flat-bottomed dinghies from

which they tilled the muddy fertile silt of Burano and its neighboring isles. Lined up on benches along the canals to catch the last light of the day, black-robed wives spun lace around hard cushions the size of melons which they held in their laps.

I was enchanted; the salt air was so exhilarating I wanted to race around to see it all before dark. Bianca could not understand my enthusiasm. To her the village was *primitivo* and common. She could not see why it should interest an American, and she hated it as she hated everything which distracted me from her. She followed me petulantly, deliberately lagging a few steps behind, holding herself aloof like a lady of quality among the peasantry.

To please her, I went to the cathedral, where for the first time in a week she failed to touch the blessing to my lips. It was a spooky place, hung with black curtains, and except for a few red altar lights, completely dark. Bianca knelt to pray before a nude Christ of shining black marble. When she pressed her face against the black feet and kissed them an eerie chill passed over me. Outside I took her picture against a tower which leaned precariously toward the sea. Unlike Pisa, which is famous for one leaning tower, most of the towers around Venice seem to lean; occasionally one topples over, as did the San Marco tower in 1902. We walked along the canals following a woman driving a flock of geese. In the lagoon a band of boys were training a puppy for bird hunting, conditioning him to gunfire by shooting at the same time they skated a piece of wood across the water for the puppy to retrieve. I saw a Coca-Cola sign nailed ludicrously to a house, and a barber's den with the Communist hammer and sickle painted on the door, symbols which also appear on the sails of fishermen's boats. A priest was making his weekly door-to-door collections and children were everywhere. Little boys played with cards and dice and little girls cuddled lacy dolls or skipped rope to their own singsong. Infants held court on grandmothers' laps. All girl babies, even those pink and shriveled with newness, wore tiny gold earrings as if they had been born with them. An old woman emptied a chamber pot into the canal while Bianca daintily looked the other way.

There was no privacy anywhere; life was as public as church. We looked into open doors at walls from which rows of shining copper kettles gleamed in candlelight like burnished armor and portraits of grandmothers and grandfathers scowled stiffly. There was no electricity, running water only in the canals, but everything was spotlessly scrubbed. Wondrous odors

rose from cooking fires. Those women who were not cooking remained outside, piercing the darkness with their needles, harvesting a few more
stitches from the last light of the dying day. Raised high in a window so
she might watch life outside was a sick child, seven or eight years old, pale
and listless as a corpse, dressed all in white as if awaiting death, and hanging over her like a black angel itself was an old black grandmother feeding
her broth with a spoon. In another sick house an ancient parched husk of a
woman was strapped like a crucifixion to a board. Tilted slightly to face a
candlelit Christ-on-the-cross over the door, she too awaited the dark angel.
By the door sat a lovely girl of fifteen, fair of skin and dark of eyes, alone
and pensive in the evening light. Her haunting Madonna expression was
incredibly beautiful, as if she were awaiting an annunciation. I looked
again at the woman on the board, and I felt as if the hand of death had
been laid on me. Shuddering, I reached for Bianca's hand to hold to life,
but she was reluctant to give it. I was acting strangely and spoiling her
holiday. She seemed so suddenly alone, I felt sorry for her. I wanted to
enfold her in what for me was a wondrous richness of life, but it was not
easy. "Come," I said, "let us have some wine and food, a feast for your
coming of age. . . ."

She looked at me with dark suspicion, suddenly seeming to be more
Spanish than Italian, but allowed me to lead her into a place called Romano's, the only restaurant on the island.

It was a huge noisy place, more like a lodge hall than a restaurant. At a
dozen tables some forty banging and shouting young men from the ages of
fifteen to thirty were playing an animated card game called *scoppa*, and
another fifty noisy young kibitzers stood at their shoulders. Romano himself was a man of fifty with a distinguished manner and a household knowledge of English. When he learned I was American he took personal charge
of our table. In a great square autograph book he pointed out greetings
from Ernest Hemingway and the late Sinclair Lewis. Bianca paid no attention but kept writing on a piece of note paper. I asked what she was
writing.

She did not answer but continued to write. "Is it a letter?" I asked.
Still she did not answer. I became angry. "A letter to a sailor perhaps?"

The thought made me very jealous. I demanded to see what she had
written. Without a word she handed me the paper. *"Oggi Nic e io siamo
andati a Torcello e Burano. . . ."* I read. It was the beginning of an entry
in her diary.

Because we had little time before the last boat, Romano rushed our food. We had a thick and mysterious soup, superb enough to have been cooked for angels, a fish with wine sauce served with marinated artichoke hearts, and for dessert a cornucopia of nuts and fruit. We had no time for coffee, for outside someone shouted the boat was about to leave. Romano wrapped us a parcel of grapes and nuts and we ran to the dock.

We arrived just as the boat was pulling out. I helped Bianca onto the deck and nearly fell into the Adriatic leaping after her. The ferry was almost empty. We joined two young swains and their maids in the stern. When the steward refused to let the youths extinguish a ceiling light, one of them discreetly dimmed it by removing his shirt and wrapping it around the bulb. Like high-school spooners the six of us sat in friendly semidarkness, singing Italian and American songs, eating grapes and spitting the seeds into the Adriatic. Bianca nestled in my arms, forgiving me the errors of the day. My senses swam as her delicate body warmed under my touch. She was softly singing: "Stormy weather, stormy weather, since my Nicki and I ain't together. . . ."

And then, "I love you, Nicki. I love you me?"

"Yes, Bianca."

"Per sempre?"

So we repeated the cant of love. "Forever, Bianca, as long as I live. . . ."

"Promesso?"

"I promise." For you I promise even to pretend there is no death.

The boat was passing the cemetery of San Michele, inky black in the night. Bianca asked, "Do you wish to visit the dead now?"

"No, Bianca, not now." The death we were embracing so feverishly was enough.

"When you are in America I will write you every day."

"Thank you, Bianca."

"And you will write me every day?"

I'll write a letter every day the rest of my life, and after, two a day from heaven or hell, whichever the case may be. "Bianca, will you come to the train with me on Saturday?"

She straightened herself up like the lady she was.

"Alla stazione? To the station? Oh, no! Someone would see us and it would be *scandalo!"*

Of course. For a day I had forgotten about scandals. Love was eternal but scandal must be avoided at any cost. I lay back and watched the sea,

listening to one of our fellow spooners sing a saucy song about an ardent
gondolier and his lady fair. In a moment we were docking at the Fonda-
menta Nuova. The two girls pertly walked off ahead, looping their arms
and chattering like jays. Their young men followed with their arms about
each other. With her animal certainty, Bianca led me through the snarled
maze of dark alleys straight to the piazza of a little church where I had
photographed a gondola wedding several days before. It was our good-
night place. Here she let me bring her each night and no farther.

"Nicki, I say good night for two days."

"Not two days, Bianca. Until tomorrow."

"Tomorrow I must accompany my mother on a visit to my sister. There
is a new *bambino*."

It was a shock. A day in Venice without Bianca seemed inconceivable.
There were only two left.

"I am very sorry," she said. "But I cannot change it."

It was logical, of course, this demand by the mother who hovered in the
background, for whom we had always to consider the effects of a *scandalo*.

"*Ti dispiace?*" she asked. "Does it make you unhappy?"

"Of course, Bianca. Couldn't you postpone the trip to your sister, say
until Saturday when I have gone?"

"How could I explain it to my mother?"

I did not know.

"You see, it is necessary that I go," she said.

"Then we must wait until Friday. Meet me early, at eleven o'clock, and
if the weather is fair we will go to the Lido."

"I love you, Nicki. I love you me?"

"Yes, Bianca. Please believe me, I do."

"*Si, lo credo* [I believe]," she said. Then she kissed me, more ardently
than ever before. "This is good night for tonight," she said. Then she
kissed me again. "This is for tomorrow." Her body was quivering and I
could taste the salt of tears. "And this is for Friday."

"But I shall see you on Friday, Bianca."

She caught my lips with her little teeth.

"And this is for Saturday and for Sunday and for Monday, for all the
Saturdays and Sundays and Mondays until you come back."

"I shall count the hours until Friday, Bianca."

She loosed herself and with a sob ran away. I followed, but she was
quickly lost in the labyrinths.

The next day she was never from my mind. In the morning I paid a deposit on the pink dress so the storekeeper would not sell it before I could bring Bianca to buy it the following day. I passed the hours looking at pictures in the Accademia and the masterpieces of Tintoretto at San Rocco. But my wanderings were lonely and restless. I ate with some American friends and in the evening I went to a concert in the Teatro la Fenice. In everything I was killing time; my heart was in the next day. I kept reassuring myself that only in this unreal city of fantasy was Bianca indispensable. Left behind for other cities and other friends, both city and girl would be quickly forgotten. By remaining in Venice I must play the little drama to its final pathetic curtain. By leaving at once I could have it over and done with. Late that night, with the canal cats as companions, I was still trying to make up my mind to go in the morning. I could not. I wanted the happiness of another day with Bianca, even with the sorrow of saying good-by.

Next day I was waiting at our arch fifteen minutes early, watching the gold clock on the piazza, wiping anxious moisture from my palms. At eleven she was not there. I scanned the morning crowds for her arrival. Time moved agonizingly. It was five minutes after eleven, then ten, and finally fifteen. She had never been late before, but I reassured myself that I had told her eleven-thirty, that in my anxiety I had imagined it eleven. I bought a newspaper and sat on the steps to read it. But the words danced in front of me and I could get nothing from the columns. Eleven-thirty, and no Bianca. She would come, I promised myself. It was something with the mother that had delayed her. We had not made a practice of meeting so early and it would be difficult for her to get away. The piazza pigeons fluttered around me, sharing my misery, for by this time I was without hope.

At a quarter to twelve I knew she would not come. I remained under the arch another miserable fifteen minutes. Then I crossed the piazza to the canal, walking along the lagoon past the Bridge of Sighs and three American warships in the harbor for a week-end holiday, past a covey of gondolas where the gondoliers tried their animated persuasions on me. I tried to laugh at myself for having taken a light-o'-love so seriously when the rules of the game were so clearly posted from the beginning. I argued that I should be grateful to Bianca for having spared me the agony of a farewell. I even reminded myself that I had saved the price of the pink dress.

Thinking of the dress, I remembered the times Bianca had led me past the shopwindow. Perhaps if I went there and waited she would pass. It was my only hope. I passed the familiar landmarks, the American Express, the café where we stopped often for a good-night coffee. Then I saw her, the back of the dark head, with the hair tumbling to the shoulders, the familiar delicate little body. She was standing with an American sailor, spotlessly white, with his cap hooked jauntily to the back of his head. Beside her he seemed enormous. They were at the window looking at the pink dress. As they talked, the sailor reached out to take her hand, which she drew delicately back. I could hear her saying, *"No, signore, uno scandalo."* They entered the shop, and I left the little square, my heart heavy and sick. I was not jealous of the sailor, nor even angry with Bianca. But I was hurt, terribly hurt that she hadn't put him off another day, that she hadn't waited until Saturday.

Five months later when I returned to the States I found a card awaiting me from Venice. It was a Christmas greeting with a wintry snow scene and the words *Buon Natale.* On the back I read in English, "I love you. I hope I love you me. Please write to me. Bianca."

I wondered with the pain still in my heart who had taught her the new English words. There was no return address. I had already forgotten her last name.

CHAPTER 16

THE GOLDEN LILY

ORVIETO IS THE NAME of a wonderful golden wine. I drank it in Sicily when others drank Marsala and in Tuscany where Chianti is the *vino di campagna*. It was only after I had been in Italy for a time that I began to hear of Orvieto as a town with a cathedral known as "the golden lily."

Orvieto is north of Rome on an isolated plateau of tuffa stone a thousand feet high. From the station I rode a funicular up to the medieval town. I found it jammed with soldiers. An army camp near by was having a holiday and fifteen thousand Italian servicemen crowded the little community (population eight thousand) seeking *divertimento*. Italian soldiers are notoriously poor. There was a pathetic desperation about their endless search for women, cheap American cowboy films, or even a traffic accident or street fight to distract them. On the main Via Cavour and all the narrow side streets, it was the everlasting *passeggiata*, like brown currents of sand flowing in different directions. The weather was cold, and to escape the eternal rains the soldiers clustered under every portico, into every urinal station, any nook that was free. They were brooding and silent.

I registered at a hotel and ate lunch, after which I walked toward the cathedral spires rising above the roofs of the town. The cathedral is not in the center of town, but on a ledge looking down the precipice. It was the grape season; street gutters were purple as if wine were flowing in the streets. I met donkeys carrying baskets of grapes and others carrying wine barrels. The Via del Duomo was a tourist street of restaurants and souvenir and post-card shops. One window featured a life-sized photograph of a smug little boy with a dwarfish precocity and a feathered Alpine hat. It was captioned in English: "Roberto, the little polyglot guide."

To come on the cathedral as one does, entering suddenly the expansive piazza, is a staggering experience, comparable to approaching the cathedral of Chartres across the plain of Beauce. The cathedrals of Siena and Orvieto are sisters, the two great Gothic monuments in Italy. Only a moment is necessary to feel the greater beauty, harmony, and spirit of Orvieto. It has been called a miracle cathedral, and indeed, as one sees it rising with lofty and divine elegance, a heavenly apparition above the huddle of tightly packed slate roofs in the humble town, it is almost impossible to believe that it was put there by man. Its façade is a lacy filigree of saints, apostles, and graceful angels grouped around golden mosaics and a marble rosette known as the Wheel of St. Catherine. In the heart of the wheel is a head of Christ, a bearded young Apollo carved from marble luminous in its purity. The most astounding parts of the façade are the four pilasters carved by a genius named Lorenzo Maitani. In some eighty sculptured bas-reliefs of Bible history, of the last judgment and of heaven and hell, this great artist has chiseled the physical and spiritual universe of man. Maitani's art, so fiercely dramatic and mystic, is the essence of medievality. Yet the world has all but overlooked this Giotto of stone.

Unlike its sister cathedral in Siena, a museum cluttered with good and bad art, the inside of the golden lily seems empty. Its art is spare, and almost all good. It has spaciousness, majesty, and a feeling of holiness. It was empty when I entered, but soon a busload of English-speaking tourists unloaded on the piazza and clattered in. I recognized the Alpine hat of the little polyglot Roberto hustling among them. "Now if you will come with me I will show you . . . ," he was saying in precise English. But the tourists had their own guide. Outside, the rain beat with swift suddenness on the roof. To get out of it a hundred or more soldiers entered the cathedral. An excited priest herded them together. "Come to the Chapel of the Holy Corporeal," he commanded. "See the miracle of Bolsena." With the unenthusiastic reflex action of military men responding to an order, the soldiers followed the priest into a side chapel. Beside me the little polyglot said, "Naturally, you will want to see the miracle." He was an eerie little monster with his chubby body and round pink face. I guessed him to be about seven years old and small for his age. He wore German-style *Lederhosen*. I tried to discourage him by paying no attention, but he attached himself firmly and followed. He recited his spiel smugly in a precise machinelike staccato. I wondered if he knew what he was saying.

"In the fourteenth century in France, the heretical priests denied the presence of Jesus Christ in the Eucharist," he intoned. "A Bohemian priest on his way to Rome stopped at Bolsena to say a Mass. He strongly doubted the presence of the body and blood of Christ in the bread. As he held it in his hand it turned into flesh from which warm blood poured out. It stained the communion cloth and ran down the stones of the altar."

The Chapel of the Corporeal contained a gold tabernacle mounted on an altar. In the tabernacle the bloodstained cloth was accessible only by climbing a flight of steps. Soldiers waited at the steps as if they led to chow or a prophylactic station. The priest opened the golden doors of the tabernacle and prayed; the soldiers knelt mechanically. Then they started a long slow procession up one side of the ladder and down the other. "They are looking at the inside of a corporeal," an English lady said to her husband. "I don't think we need bother."

Neither did I bother. Beside me the polyglot whispered hoarsely, "Now if you will come with me, I will show you something very important." I asked him why he wasn't at school. "I do not go to school," he said like a talking toy. "I study with my father. My father is also a guide and speaks perfectly four languages. I also speak perfectly four languages. You are American, of course. I can always tell." I told him I would pay him the guide's fee if he would leave me alone. He took the money. Apparently he believed I had arrived with the bus, for a quarter-hour later he came to tell me with ill-restrained glee, "The bus has left."

"I didn't come on the bus," I said with equal pleasure. The news made him disconsolate. I knew I had made an enemy.

I was now free to see the most important paintings in Orvieto, the frescoes of Luca Signorelli which the young Michelangelo traveled from Florence to study. They are in a chapel locked by an iron gate; to see them I had first to find the sacristan who had the key.

Signorelli's large frescoes of judgment day, of the inferno, and of paradise are crowded with vigorously realistic male and female nudes. Hell is tumultuously crowded with virile sinners, and heaven is an idyllic nudist camp in which even the tonsured monks are built like wrestlers. The most startling of the walls portrays the resurrection of the dead. Skeletons pop out of graves and then, the moment they are above ground, miraculously assume handsome molds of flesh. None of the resurrected dead are children or old people; all are in the prime of youth and beauty. By taking judgment day to Olympus, the artist created a holy peep show, cloudy in its theology but remarkable to look upon.

When it was far too dark to see anything, I left to wander through the wet streets choked with soldiers. Tired and frustrated, they still walked their never-ending back-and-forth like caged leopards. For the most part they were orderly; only a few were drunk. A block-long line waited in the rain to see a film entitled *The Return of the Apaches*. A shuttered house of tolerance enjoyed a boom. From behind the doors of wineshops I heard boisterous singing. On a lonely piazza a soldier played a harmonica and a score of his comrades waltzed together on the wet pavements. A *carabiniere* was standing under a portico watching them.

In the morning the soldiers were gone. Except for vintners' donkeys carrying grapes the early streets were empty. I'd hoped for sun to light up the cathedral but in that wet season there was no sun in Italy. I trudged through the rain to historic churches, first the San Domenico where St. Thomas Aquinas taught and composed his office of the Sacrament. The crumbling old church was locked. Persistent ringing of the sacristy bell finally brought out a wizened little crone, a woman all in black like a folded bat. She giggled foolishly when I told her I wanted to see the church. As she led me inside she babbled that few persons came to see the church now, no more than one or two a month. I asked her to show me the sepulcher chapel of the Petrucci family, praised by Vasari in his art chronicles. The little grandmother shrieked delightedly and with a holy candle from the altar lit my way down dank steps. Her whooping mirth echoed through the dark bowels of the church. The Petrucci tomb, a small octagonal chapel decorated with minute Doric columns, had fallen on evil times. Neglect and dampness were rotting it, but its worst enemy was the Italian tourist's pencil. The walls and columns were covered with signatures and epithets, mostly dating from the Fascist years of the twenties and thirties. The grandmother pointed with a bony index finger to a pornographic drawing and convulsed herself with shrieks. "Is that art for a tomb?" she chortled. "I ask you, is it, and in a church too?" She returned me to the upper level with a candle and when I gave her some money she asked if I was American. "One can always tell an American by his generosity," she said, still laughing as I went out into the rain.

The most beautiful church I found was San Lorenzo, a lovely little jewel cast in Lombardian style. In its dark interior a woman was teaching two tiny girls to pray and kneel at the altar. Outside, the gutters flowed with wine dregs, and a brawny white-haired Hercules rolled a gurgling barrel back and forth on the street to stir the wine inside. My course along the edge of the town, over a broad valley of olives and grapes, led me back to the cathedral. It was empty and dark as the day before. In Signorelli's chapel, the sacristan brought me a chair so I might study the paintings in comfort. For four hundred lire I bought one of those guidebooks so common in Italy, written with the help of a dictionary by someone who doesn't know English. I turned to the pages about Signorelli's frescoes. About hell, I read: "In the middle of the picture a devil carries pickaback on his shoulders a beautiful handsome woman and drags her to hell, that opens below awfully imposing. Here new tortures and new tortured; dreadful-muzzled devils, tearing-faced damned among that fearful and wonderful confusion."

I turned to the page on heaven, and read: "Choruses of angels play sweet harmonies on mandores and zithers, while others scatter flowers and garlands of roses on the blissful. These, all charmed by the heavenly beauties, raise looks full of sweetness, anxious of being able to accept the invitation of the angels pointing out the gemmed doors of paradise."

As I read, the door squeaked behind me and the sacristan admitted a young man in baggy ski pants. My guess was that he was German; he was blond and stalwart enough to have delighted the heart of Hitler. He admired the long-haired big-bosomed Magdalenes with which Signorelli had populated heaven. "In paradise it looks very happy," he said, speaking faulty English with an obviously bad cold. I replied in German that Signorelli had made heaven a considerably more lively place than I was accustomed to picturing it. He told me his name was Reinhold Fauermann, that he was twenty-five years old and a medical student on his autumn holiday from Heidelberg. For six weeks he had hitchhiked through Italy, going as far as Sicily, sleeping in student hostels or in a tent which he carried on his shoulders, cooking all his own meals. The journey had cost him sixteen thousand lire, or approximately twenty-five dollars. At the moment he had only eighty lire—about twelve cents—left, but he was on his way to Florence where he hoped to find some money from his family awaiting him. He had hitched from Rome to Orvieto that morning, planned to go to Siena in the afternoon and on to Florence that evening. I said that was quite a schedule, especially since he had caught such a bad cold.

"*Es geht leicht,*" he said. "It goes as a matter of course if you have had military experience."

I asked him what his military experience had been.

"I am a veteran, having been called into Hitler's army when I was seventeen." He said it proudly with painstaking solemnity. He was humorless and heavy; even his good looks were heavy. He asked me if I knew the way to the Etruscan tombs. I didn't but I was going there myself so I suggested we hunt them together. He accepted, eager for companionship. He loaded a rucksack on his back; it weighed more than thirty pounds and contained the tent, some clothes, food, cooking pans, and a benzine stove. We walked down the hill and out of town, asking people along the way the path to the *tombe Etruschi*. No one knew. A few pointed in the direction we were going, but they gave the usual vague information of Italians who seem to prefer sending strangers out of their way rather than admit ignorance. We were misdirected by several shepherds, who it turned out later were grazing their sheep in a field adjacent to the tombs. It began to rain hard and our clothes were soaking. My companion maintained a Spartan spirit while I grew short-tempered. Finally we came to a little hut with its door open; inside it was piled high with chestnuts. In an orchard behind the hut a bent old man was harvesting more nuts. We asked him.

Yes, he knew. He was the caretaker. He shuffled inside for a key and led us up a muddy path to an iron gate secured with chain and lock. Before us was a sunken quadrangle of square little cellars. Grass grew on them and from each rose a round stone, like a cylindrical chimney. The quadrangle covered perhaps two acres. Each unit had a square entrance so low one had to stoop to get in. The tombs were empty. Their art, of course, was in the museums and nothing remained but dank dark holes in which the rain collected in pools. The old man, accustomed to disappointed visitors, tried to stir up our interest.

"See the inscriptions," he said, pointing to one of the phallic stones. "It is a language most mysterious. No one has ever been able to read it." Yes, we said, we knew. "But I am working on it. For eight years I have been studying and working. I shall one day have it. Yes, sir, I shall have it."

We wished him well on the project, gave him his tip, and began the steep climb back to the town. It was now pouring. The pack on Reinhold's back was heavy on his shoulders and on his face sweat mingled with rain. I suggested that he lunch with me at my hotel before setting out for Siena. He accepted gratefully. Then, at the door of the hotel, he hesitated. His eyes were cold and hostile.

"Sir, I have killed Americans," he said.

It took me a moment to catch my breath.

"I cannot accept your friendship falsely," he said, showing his self-conscious sense of Teutonic honor. "I hate Americans."

"Do you hate me?"

"No. You are the first American I have known that I have not hated."

"Then let's go eat," I said.

He followed me, sullen and foreboding. I ordered steaks—he asked for his *blutig*—and some wine. Then I asked Reinhold why he hated Americans.

"I have two reasons," he said. "The first is the destruction of our cities by American bombers."

What about the bombing by Germans of London and Leningrad? I asked.

"It was nothing like Germany," he replied. "Have you seen Frankfort? Have you seen Berlin and Munich?"

I hadn't. I asked what the second reason was.

"The inhuman treatment of German prisoners by Americans," Reinhold said. His first reason was the familiar one I had heard from many Germans. The second surprised and startled me. "The Americans starved Germans and buried them alive," he said. Was I hearing correctly? "In an American camp in France Germans were given only one hundred grams of bread a day. Many starved to death."

It made me angry. "Please don't say such things," I said. "You have told me you hated Americans and that I can try to comprehend. But don't repeat to me lies which insult the intelligence of both of us."

"I was there," he said, his voice unfeelingly cold, cruel. "In April, 1945. In four weeks my weight dropped from one hundred and fifty pounds to one hundred pounds. The day the war ended we were given a little more bread to eat, but only for one day. After five months the Americans turned us over to the French. The French fed us better and I gained weight. French guards are not very attentive, so I escaped."

The wine came. I filled his glass and then my own. We drank in silence.

"I do not believe you," I said.

He continued, not heeding my remark. "We slept without shelter *unter dem Himmel*. When the weather turned cold the Americans ordered us to dig pits in which to sleep. One night when it rained the pits collapsed and hundreds of Germans smothered to death."

The steaks came. He cut his carefully and began to eat. There was blood on his knife, and a drop in the corner of his mouth.

"The sadistic American officers were pleased when this happened," he said.

"You are making a mistake," I said. "You are speaking of Dachau and Buchenwald."

"The Dachau and Buchenwald you mean did not exist," he said. "It was all greatly exaggerated by the Americans."

"You cannot have seen the films," I said, "or you would not say they never existed."

"The films were clever propaganda made in Hollywood," he said.

He continued to talk and eat, not noticing that I was doing neither. "Things are going well enough in Germany now," he said. "Though of course it was better under the Führer." It was two o'clock when he finished his meal. It was raining harder than ever. I could not conceive of a human being setting out on foot in such a deluge and offered to buy him a bus ticket. He accepted stiffly, but the hotel manager told us there would be no bus until six o'clock. Reinhold would not wait.

"I must be in Florence tonight," he said. "I have an agreement with friends. A German does not fail in his word."

"It is raining too hard," I said.

"A soldier is accustomed to rain," he said. He loaded his rucksack. I noted that his raincoat was tied in it.

"Aren't you going to put it on?"

"When I have found a ride I will put it on," he said. "It is very ragged. It is not easy to get a ride in a ragged coat. And it is not good for Italians to see that a German must wear a ragged coat."

Should I give him my own? I thought of it, but instead I put it on myself. I was no saint; my charity couldn't go that far. I walked through the rain with him to the edge of town. The long hill down was shining wetly. As far as I could see there was only a cart and donkey on the road. "Now it is better that I go alone," he said. He reached out his hand and I took it.

"It may be necessary for you to hate Americans," I said. "But tell me, tell me in the name of God that you do not believe what you have told me."

Again he ignored me.

"Among all peoples there are good men and there are bad men," he said. "You are the first American I have spoken to as a friend."

He started down the road. I watched until I could no longer see. My spectacles were wet, outside and in. I turned back and faced the golden lily.

CHAPTER 17

THE CONSECRATION OF THE GRAPE

"There is a devil in every berry of the grape."
—THE KORAN

DURING THE OCTOBER GRAPE HARVEST wine towns celebrate a religious festival known as *La Sagra dell'uva*. A Roman actor named Gino Gini offered to take me to such a "consecration of the grape" in Marino, one of the *Castelli Romani* in the Alban hills about an hour's ride from Rome. Gino described the ancient rites as a sort of wedding of the Virgin Mary with the grape god, Bacchus, followed by a bacchanalia at which the municipal fountains flowed with wine instead of water. It was, he said, an affair more popular with men than with women.

Gino and I took a bus in which we were packed as tightly as stalks in a bound sheaf of wheat. A vicious little dwarf, apparently enraged because I was tall, bit me in the leg. Except for a woman sullenly nursing an overgrown baby in a corner, the passengers were all men. Having already jammed his vehicle to three times its capacity, the driver was considering whether to start the trip or to squeeze in some more. While he argued with himself there was a crisp little rap on the door of the bus, like the tapping of a woodpecker. Looking through the glass was a plump blonde with masses of reddish hair cascading to her shoulders. There was a chivalrous stir among the men. *"Una signorina!* Open the door!"* they called to the driver.

The men squeezed and pushed to give her foot space. A swarthy Don Juan appraised her with a purposeful Latin eye and offered his hand to help her up. I guessed her to be in her mid-twenties. She was somewhat lavishly gotten up for the occasion in a flower print dress and a string of pearls.

"Mercy, this is a crush, isn't it?" she said crisply. I was not surprised to learn she was called Hortense, nor even that her last name was Peartree. Obviously she was new in Italy, for she didn't seem to know that conversing with strange men was to invite their ardent attention. Speaking a halting Italian she told the men she was from Brighton and an ex-*soldato*, a fact which excited them very much. "Ah, a lady *soldato*. Such a one would know what there is to know," they murmured to each other. The dark-eyed Don Juan supported her in the crook of his arm and the men crowded each other for the pleasure of jolting against her body. In the back of the bus the nursing *bambino* began to squall. "Pietro!" the mother called sharply, and the Don Juan took a sticky rubber nipple from his pocket and handed it to the woman. She thrust it into the yowling face and buttoned up her dress. She was the man's wife, but he paid no attention to her. She, in turn, was completely indifferent to his preoccupation with the Englishwoman. On the other hand, Hortense Peartree was becoming worried. "Do be Boy Scouts and pretend you're old chums," she begged Gino and me. Some of the men were discouraged by our English-speaking familiarity with her but not the Don Juan. When the bus emptied out at the edge of Marino he left his wife and child behind to follow us into the village. "I am very sorry for him," Gino said. "To have to bring one's wife to a grape festival is a great mortification."

Hortense apprehensively surveyed the streets filled with men. "Please be darlings and don't ever leave me alone," she begged. We promised we wouldn't.

For a bacchanalia it was an odd setting. Cruelly mined and shelled in the war, Marino's scars were still brutally unhealed. Buildings not destroyed were riddled with bullet holes. Empty walls and rubble piles were covered with moss and weeds, like a green mold of death. For their *festa* the people covered the decay with a camouflage of life as gay as the Dionysian revelries of antiquity. Clusters of grapes as large and golden as hives of swarming bees arched the streets and covered terraces and doorways. At the entrance to the town stood a forty-foot Bacchus. He was not a conventional Bacchus, but a grotesque with beaming nose and cheeks and crazily rolling eyes. In his hand was a wine bottle turned upside down. The heart of the festival was in the Cathedral Square. The corso, a wide thoroughfare leading to it, was lined with the stalls of vendors of wine, olives, mussels and clams, endless sweets, nuts and fruits, dolls, paper hats, noisemakers, and phallic-shaped balloons. Musicians and beggars wandered through the crowds. Rows of roasted boars with loaves of bread in their open jaws instead of apples grinned at the spectacle like gargoyles.

The most popular stall belonged to a swaggering satanic-looking young fortuneteller in a striped shirt. As a come-on, the fellow had squeezed a monkey and a cat into a small bird cage. The monkey, a revoltingly libidinous beast which the man kept prodding into a frantic state, had mounted the cat. The cat put up a fight, and the cage bounced wildly on its steel spring as the two beasts scratched and screamed in bloody combat. This sent the crowd into guffaws. Soldiers and sailors rolled in the streets choking with uncontrolled laughter. "Oh, dear me, this is rather thick," said Hortense. "I'm afraid I'm much too Anglo-Saxon for this sort of game."

As Gino bustled her away, I could hear the voices of children piping a hymn at the head of the street. The Virgin was approaching, a silent plaster figure with folded hands, riding the shoulders of priests. She was attended by acolytes carrying a banner showing Christ changing water into wine, by little girls flapping tinseled wings wired to their backs, by little boys in the robes of priests and cardinals, and a procession of women dressed in the inevitable black, chanting the litanies. *"Evviva la Vergine* [Long live the Virgin]!" the crowds on the street cried out. Old women watched in safety from the balconies and terraces above the street. As the Virgin approached the stall of the fortuneteller, the soldiers and civilians turned from the monkey and the cat and genuflected to the Virgin. The little girl angels fell out of step as they turned their heads to watch the monkey and the cat bouncing in the cage. The priests, pushing them along, drowned the screechings of the metal spring with a loud *Evviva Maria.* When the Virgin was passed, the crowds returned to the fortuneteller's stall.

We followed the procession to the cathedral for the dedication of the grapes to the Virgin. The crowd, mostly women, was noisy and so large there was hardly room for us to enter. Inside, the lovely renaissance building was illuminated by the rich golden light of hundreds of candles. A choir sang, and a priest could be heard in the distance. Three of the child angels, their wings wilting like tired butterflies, rested at the foot of the holy fountain, and a band of twenty mothers, waiting for a communal christening, proudly wrapped and unwrapped their whimpering infants.

Outside, men awaited the end of the Mass. We joined them as they started back up the hill to the village gate. This time when we passed the monkey's cage Hortense looked daintily the other way. At the gate a band bellowed brassily while lines of buses and trams poured out men from

Rome and the surrounding hill towns. Many were in uniform, including the bright gear of Roman firemen, the endless variety of military uniforms, and the flashy *bersaglieri* with their cartwheel hats covered with clusters of rakish feathers. All of them crowded under the red-nosed Bacchus with empty bottles and canteens, waiting for the wine to flow.

Finally it came, first a feeble trickle and then, after a faltering moment and a loud flourish from the band, a steady stream. The men pushed forward with their containers and scores of hands reached up to the amber stream, hard knotty hands of peasants, soft white hands of boys, scarred hands of fire fighters, strong brown hands of soldiers, and the twisted hands of a cripple. For some it wasn't enough to fill the bottle or the pitcher; they stood under the spout, letting it flow into their mouths and spatter their faces and clothes until they were pushed aside.

It was the official opening of the festival. Wine flowed everywhere. Since Italians are not accustomed to immoderate drinking, many were soon drunk, their boisterousness filling the streets, squares, and rows of caves where wine barrels as wide as a man is tall were piled. Gangs challenged each other to drinking jousts which developed into fights. Among them were bands of boys, adolescent satyrs with wine bottles dangling from their belts. When they drank they arched their bodies in classic poses, like bacchants in the Naples museum, heads backs, legs apart, groins projected.

"Mercy, it's getting quite out of hand," said Hortense and clung tightly to Gino. "Whatever would have happened to me without you?"

I wondered. There were other women on the streets, but they, according to Gino, were not from Marino. The men hooted and jeered them.

"It seems to me the men are behaving shockingly," Hortense said.

"For a young woman to appear at a *sagra* is to cast away her good name," Gino said.

"Mercy!" said Hortense. "Whatever do they think of me?"

"That you are without morals," Gino said. "They know that you are a tourist and it is what they believe of all Anglo-Saxon women, so they are not surprised to see you. The Italian girls are from Rome and they are not surprised to see them either, for the girls of Rome are known to have taken up tourists' ways."

A number of the women were American or Scandinavian. A few native grandmothers guarded children and on the fringe of the gaiety some country wives silently nursed their *bambini*. Otherwise the women who had been to church in the morning had taken refuge indoors and watched from the balconies and windows above the streets. Not even the prostitutes ventured forth. Instead they hung over the iron railing of the bordello balcony to watch the male rites below. In their bright chenille robes they looked like pink flamingos.

Now I understood why the Roman Don Juan on the bus was ashamed to have his wife follow him. The *sagra* was a breaking forth of the Italian male's smoldering sexual war with women, his struggle for domination by possession. It was a man's act of rebellion against woman's tyranny, his pagan answer to the virgin cult of female chastity with which the church tried to subdue his passions. Church belonged to women; the *sagra* belonged to men to pay tribute to licentiousness. Roaming from fountain to fountain, from cave to cave, they fired the fever of their blood with wine and still more wine; the altar they sought was the fortuneteller's where with blasphemous ribaldry they flaunted their brute passions for women, their coveting lust, and their hatred. From the safety of the balconies, laughing girls threw confetti at the men and pelted them with grapes, as children tease animals in a zoo.

I raised my camera to take a picture of two English-speaking priests filling their bottles at a fountain. One of them, a gay bird around fifty years old, wagged his finger at me. "Naughty, naughty," he scolded. "I know you! You're from *L'Unità*," he said, referring to Rome's Communist anticleric newspaper. A blithe American with a camera shouted, "I want bacchanalian faces, lots of bacchanalian faces," and a score of leering youths accommodated him. Like silent judges dressed in black the town's aristocrats watched austerely from the terraces of their bullet-riddled palaces. Old peasants who had no balconies sat aloft on rubble piles to see.

The smell of roasted pigs made us hungry. We bought slices off a leering carcass, and from a row of vendors we bought bread and clams, a kilo of olives, two kilos each of nuts and grapes, and a sweet confection in which grapes and nuts were baked together. We carried our food to a cool wine cellar where for a hundred lire—sixteen cents—we bought a liter of excellent wine. There among the barrels, sitting on a split-log bench at a rough plank table, we had our feast. It cost us less than a dollar for three. The dark bread was fresh from the oven, the pig was sweet and tender and its skin crisp. While we ate, an alarm came over the public-address system in the piazza. "*Un piccolo bambino di tre anni si è perduto,*" said the voice. "A little boy of three years has disappeared. He wears a sailor suit, his eyes are blue. This little sailor's name is Ambrogio. If anyone sees him, pray return him at once so his weeping mother will be comforted. . . ."

A temple of the grape, a Greek columned affair overflowing with grapes like a huge cornucopia, had been set up in front of the cathedral and beside it a platform for dancing. At one end of the platform, twenty young musicians, their white uniforms tasseled in red, were playing a tango. The gay jerseys they wore said they were the *Orchestra Mandolini della Rocca di Papa*—the mandolin orchestra from the town known as Fortress of the Pope. The platform was filled with drunken men dancing together.

"Mercy," said Hortense, "the police would never allow *this* in Brighton."

I had seen men dancing together several times in Sicily, but there it had been ebullient and playful. This was something else. A few dancers were pink-faced puffing men, but most were youths. Some wore rough worker's clothes, with their wine bottles swinging from their waists. When I raised my camera, a row of dark-eyed, curly-headed adolescents crowded the front of the stage and posed like a band of Caravaggio satyrs. The orchestra played *raspe* and *tarantelle,* through which they whirled like dervishes, and waltzes, in which the dancers swooped and dipped romantically in each other's arms. When the orchestra played a rumba, the hips of the dancers rolled as if on swivels while their feet hardly moved at all. In the large audience that the dancers attracted, I saw the two priests and two young Americans, one pushing the other, a legless one-armed paraplegic, in a wheelchair. Both were drunk and the cripple waved a bottle of wine with his remaining arm. A Scandinavian couple with two boys around eight and ten years old arrived on the piazza. The mother, catching sight of the platform, immediately turned her sons back. As she drove them away, the two little boys kept turning to look back like Lot's wife.

What had begun as innocent exhibitionism was becoming menacingly serious. Rivalries developed and in the choosing of partners jealousies were stirred. The most precocious dancer was a youth so thin he seemed little more than limbs and a head connected with a gelatinous spine. One could not look at him without shuddering. His face was a lean and brutal mask; long hair, slicked down in a black bob, cascaded over his face like a sheep dog's when he danced. He weighed hardly more than a hundred pounds, but he was a fountain of energy. With his partners, he played the woman, winding his body over them like a snake, biting their ears, rubbing the backs of their necks. His favorite partner was a manly lad who danced with stiff solemnity.

This handsome one was the favorite of others too. When an intruder cut in on the dance, the snaky one snarled like a challenged beast and struck at the intruder. Others leaped into the fight. The simpering dancers turned into a mob of swashbuckling pugs who fell on each other in a brawl which threatened to collapse the platform.

The musicians knew what to do. Loudly and furiously they played "Alexander's Ragtime Band." The men paired off and fell into a mass epilepsy that was partly Charleston, partly jitterbug. Obviously it was their favorite piece, its power to distract them was a sort of sorcery. The pattern was repeated. During a slow waltz, the men lay dreamily on each other's shoulders, and the snaky one nuzzled his hero. An interloper cut in; the snaky one struck at him. Each time the orchestra played "Alexander's Ragtime Band" the brawlers fell kicking and whirling into each other's arms.

"It's aboriginal," Hortense said.

"Pagan!" someone answered her. "It's pagan, that's what it is."

It was the priest from the fountain, the one who had accused my camera of Communism. A brightly scrubbed young man in a tweed jacket and knit tie was with him. The priest, a large blond man, was in very high spirits. He asked me for copies of the photographs I had just made of the dancers.

"Without photographs they'll never believe it in Dublin," he said. "Never!"

"Having fun, father?" I asked.

"Haven't had a drink all day," the priest said. "Not a drop!"

My eyes dropped to a bulge in the folds of his robe. He brought out a bottle. It was two-thirds empty.

"Just warming it for a friend," he explained, laughing slyly. He looked at two sailors dancing together on the cobblestones. "I've never seen anything so shocking," he said and went off to a fountain to replenish the bottle he was warming for a friend.

The young man in the knit tie introduced himself as an attaché of the Irish Embassy. "Father Donnelly is from St. Patrick's," he said, naming the Irish church in Rome. "He is a great fellow. Now don't you go teasing him," he scolded sternly. A vendor interrupted to sell him a phallic-shaped red balloon attached to two blue ones. These grotesque objects were worn by men, and when they tired of them, they were released to rise languidly over the cathedral where the great stone angels on the cornices watched them float by.

Dark clouds blanketed the afternoon, and the town grew dark. Lights came on, lights of every color strung over the streets and squares. Over the microphones came the news that another child was lost; *"Cecilia, una bambina di undici anni,"* a little girl of eleven years. "Pray," the anguished announcer pled, "help us find this little angel." Gino took a cynical view of Cecilia's fate. "No doubt she is in a cave with a sailor," he said. "She will be found, but no longer an angel." I had the feeling that a monster, like the Berne *Kindli-Fresser* must be lurking in one of the dark caves feasting on children.

Back on the piazza, a woman was dancing, a droll Chaucerian bawd, who had taken it upon herself to entertain the crowd with a hula, or at least an Italian's version of a hula. Her partner was a stocky blond soldier who looked exactly like her, obviously her son.

"Heavens," cried Hortense. "It's incest."

It wasn't really. The game they played was not sex, but a parody of sex, like a pair of *commedia dell'arte* characters. Mother and son were proud of each other. *Mamma* lifted her skirts high enough so the men could point at her quivering fat thighs, while the *bambino* rotated his groin. Both were drunk and an audience of drunken men gave them vigorous applause. Even the pink flamingos looked down and laughed from their ledges upstairs.

Their comedy was interrupted by the long-awaited parade. It came down the corso, a score of tooting musicians leading a procession of gaily decorated donkey carriages of wine barrels and grapes and finally a *carro di vino*—a float most *magnifico*—on the top of which rode the virgin queen of the grape. It was the second time the virgin symbol was borne through the streets that day. This time she was alive, a girl fair and blonde, perhaps eighteen years old. Nobly ensconced amid a sea of grapes she sat on a pedestal high above the crowds as stiffly as a statue, one hand supported by a long shepherd's crook. Her long dress was of flowing blue stuff and a crown of grapes was on her head. Below her on the *carro* stood her ladies in waiting, a half-dozen girls who tossed grapes at the drunken mobs in the piazza. Men caught the flying bunches in their hands.

Hardly had the chariot come to a stop in front of the cathedral when the cry went up, *"Andiamo* [let's go]." The men stormed the chariot, bombarding it with grapes. It was a development the girls hadn't anticipated; as the grapes pelted their bodies they screamed. Their cries excited the men to attack; like crazed warriors they leaped into the temple of grapes to gather up ammunition. Grapes struck the girls on their faces and arms and spattered over their crisp skirts. The ladies in waiting tumbled from the chariot and ran into the cathedral for protection. On top, unable to descend without a ladder, was the pathetic queen.

"*Aiuto! Aiuto!*"

The queen was crying for help. Her hair disarrayed, her dress stained, she tried to beat off the attack with her shepherd's crook and, failing, threw it down at the men. The men, making a sex symbol of the stick, held it aloft like a battle standard and sent a new volley of grapes into the air.

It was the unpremeditated summit of the consecration. With their drunken desecration of chastity, the men were repaying at last the hilarious good joke of the church. On her pedestal the queen crouched to protect her face and burst into tears. The men only threw their grapes harder. The queen raised her skirts to cover her head from the assault. As she did so she revealed her rayoned thighs and buttocks.

"*Evviva la Vergine!*" the men shouted, pointing and laughing. "Long live the virgin!" Roaring like bulls they aimed their grapes at the pink exposures. The pelted queen screamed out in terror. *Carabinieri* threw her a tarpaulin and she covered herself. The orchestra played to distract the men, but music only excited them and the thud of grapes on canvas was louder than the beating of the drums.

"*Evviva la Vergine!*"

Those who knelt and genuflected to the Virgin as she rode through the streets in the morning now rolled on the piazza cobblestones in each other's arms shrieking their mirth. Hortense, ready at last to return to Rome, led us briskly toward the station. On the way we heard the announcer report the progress of the *Kindli-Fresser*. Little Carlo, "a good boy of four years" had wandered off somewhere in the vicinity of the St. Benedict fountain, and his mother was weeping; Ambrogio, the three-year-old sailor, was returned by a gentleman who found him drunk under a fountain. Of Cecilia, the angel of eleven years, there was still no sign.

I had hoped for a peaceful ride back. The train, though still in the station, was filled twice over and still they crowded on. Men climbed into the luggage racks above the seats and lay there like suitcases. We stood on the platform. In the town the fireworks were beginning. Thousands of heads turned up as they burst over the cathedral. Charges of silver, pink, blue, and orchid cascaded over the ruins, lighting the ghost town like neon and then evaporating into darkness.

As the train started, six pugnacious young drunks leaped on the platform. I remembered seeing them on the dance platform in the afternoon. One pinned another youth against a glass wall on the platform and an argument began.

"I fear something nasty may develop," Hortense said. We pushed inside the jammed car. We barely made it before the brawling began. From the platform came a crash and the sound of splintering glass. A crazed youth pushed through the train, smashing every window with a bloody fist. A woman was cut by the glass. She shrieked out in pain, but no one could get to her. Women joined a chorus of screams and men fought the length of the car. The punching youth had finished with the windows; glass and blood lay everywhere.

In the dark country night they stopped the train, turned out the lights, and locked the doors. Gino, Hortense, and I were caught in the middle of a car with a brawling inferno on both sides. The injured woman wailed so that I feared she was dying. Someone was sick and the smell of vomit was added to the smell of blood. One of the men curled asleep on the luggage rack awoke and shouted, *"Calmi! Calmi! Troppo confusione! Io voglio dormire!* [Quiet! Quiet! All this confusion! I'm trying to sleep!]" Then he turned over and went back to sleep.

The conductor's psychology proved sound. In the dark, the fighting subsided. With the lights still out, we started to move again. At the first village, three *carabinieri* got on board. In their custody the train continued. The night wind blew cold through the shattered windows. When the train arrived in Rome an hour late, the passengers were quiet and subdued.

In Rome's Piazza dell' Esedra we said good night. "Thanks awfully for being so decent and letting me trail along," Hortense Peartree said. "It's been a most merry day, hasn't it?" she added brightly. "Such a terrible lot of tickle stuff." She left me trying to explain in Italian to Gino what "tickle stuff" meant.

CHAPTER 18

THE ROY ROGERS POSTMAN

I

IN THE VILLAGE OF TAORMINA, telegrams and special-delivery letters are delivered by a messenger dressed like an American cowboy. The story of how this came about is a rambling one, beginning with the Feast of St. Martin. On this boisterous holiday on the eleventh of November, wine-growers in the hills hold open house for village lowlanders who climb to the cool mountain caves and cellars to taste the new wine of the year.

For ten days, since the Feast of All Souls, the young men of the town talked of San Martino. They promised me on that merry day roasted chest-nuts, hot country sausages, cool country girls, and all the wine I could drink. It would be the true *vita Siciliana*, something an *Americano* would never forget.

The day fell on a Sunday. It was cloudy, with the sun occasionally breaking through the mists. I made the ascent in the morning with two English-speaking Sicilians, Carlo, a shopkeeper, and Nino, a university graduate in law. Carlo wore a red shirt and green velvet trousers, a gift from Truman Capote; Nino a pink shirt and a scarf fashioned into a cum-merbund. But we were a drab party compared to the festively dressed natives we met on the way. On donkey paths we snaked across the face of Mt. Ziretto. Carlo led the way, leaping over the hazardous path like a satyr.

"Carlo is very happy," Nino explained. "You see he is fallen in love last night with a beautiful Danish girl. He has had a rendezvous with her in the hotel in the middle-night. The Danish girl is here on her honey-moon," he said casually. "Taormina is very popular with northern peoples for honeymoons."

Wasn't this unusual behavior for a girl on her honeymoon? I asked.

Nino shrugged indulgently at my Anglo-Saxon stuffiness. "It is a quite common thing to happen in Taormina," he said. "After being all the time with her new husband, a girl welcomes greatly a little Sicilian *divertimento.*"

I was intrigued. How was it arranged? I asked. Didn't honeymooning husbands usually keep a close eye on their new brides?

"Of course," Nino said. "Sometimes Danish and Swedish men get quite angry with jealousy. But you know women are very clever and it is easy for a bride to say she is going to take a manicure or a bath, and then go to another room in the hotel and *dedicate* herself for a half hour to someone else. Things happen very strange in Taormina," he added loftily.

Nino shared the conviction of Sicilian men that they are the most ardent lovers in the world. "It is well known that we are the most hot. That is why the Swedish women have such a preference for us," he said, using "Swedish" in the Sicilian sense of including all Scandinavians. "Northern peoples have sex complexes of inferiority, and the women need us Sicilian men to make them feel in sex a complex of superiority. There are no prostitutes in Taormina," Nino said, speaking on a subject about which he was probably well informed, for his father was the chief of police. "The reason there are none is there is no need for them. There are always enough Swedish girls for all of us, and we are quite content to help them out."

Our first sampling of St. Martin came on the hoof. A young woman, tall, commanding, and pregnant met us on the path. On her head she balanced a small keg of wine. She carried her burdens with sure-footed grace. Her wine was called *nettare di Venere,* and she was carrying it from her home on Mt. Venus to relatives in Castelmola. We drank of her Venus' nectar from a cup she carried in her skirts. The wine was well named.

We climbed through a grove of olive trees. A mother and her adolescent daughter were gathering the last fruit of the season. The soft brown olives appeared to be rotten.

"It is the way olives are best for eating," Nino said. He scooped up a handful from the girl's basket and gave them to me. Their wet smoky flavor was unlike anything I had ever tasted. The girl, a perfect Saracen beauty, spoke not a word. While they ate her olives, the Sicilian boys appraised her in English.

"When she is completely ripe," Nino said, digging his hand deep into her basket, "she will taste very good also."

We passed primitive peasant dwellings which were built into the cliffs like dugouts. On the ground floors pigs lazed in smelly sties and chickens scratched in the manure. From paneless second-story windows families invited us to stop and drink their wine.

But we continued on to the Casa Intelisano, where we were expected. Intelisano is a common name in the hills. The house we were going to was that of Nunzio Intelisano, whose son-in-law was an acquaintance of Carlo's and Nino's. Nunzio and his wife Caterina were watching for us and ran out to greet us, like old people welcoming their children home for Christmas. Nunzio was a quiet, kindly man in his sixties with an apostolic white head and a face that crinkled with pleasure. His multi-patched clothes were neat and fresh; where the buttons were gone, they were tied with strings. Catherina wore her traditional somber black, but holiday earrings dangled to her shoulders. Her graying hair still had shadows of red in it. She was in a festive mood, as gay and articulate as Nunzio was quiet and dignified. They led us through a pungent stable past two horses and a cow whose rough tongue licked our hands, on into a low dark cave heaped with manure. Under the steaming piles Nunzio fermented his wine. It was named *pista e mutta*—Sicilian for "crush and carry"—because Nunzio's method was to fill his bottles with newly pressed juice instead of letting it ferment first in barrels. He dug out some bottles and poured the wine into glasses. In the dank cave the rose wine glowed radiant and clear. On the tongue it was dry and wonderfully fragrant.

We toasted San Martino and, with our second glass, Santa Maria, the mother of Jesus. Then Nunzio carried an armful of bottles up to the house. Its one large room was furnished with two beds, a table, and chairs. A ladder led to a loft above the beds. On the walls were lithographs of saints, kings and queens from the defunct House of Savoia, and photographs of the three Intelisano daughters with their husbands and of Giorgio, the son. To the front a large window looked down on white clouds rolling up from the valley below. In the back was the kitchen, a dark chimneyless cave into which Caterina went to prepare food.

I asked Nunzio to tell me of his life on the mountain. He said: "To this mountain men can come only by donkey or on foot. From its starved soil I have brought wine and olives, exchanging the oil for flour to make bread, and I gathered the herbs and wild fruit that grew among the rocks.

"Since God made man, men have lived on this mountain. With each generation the work grows harder and the fruits less; each year the soil is thinner, and the flour is dearer in the town. Someday the time of man on this mountain will be ended."

Caterina came from the kitchen to scold her husband for darkening the *festa* with his thoughts of doom. Nunzio filled our glasses with *pista e mutta* and we toasted another saint. Each time we toasted a saint, Caterina scurried in to join us. The pink was rising in her cheeks; she was drunk, less with wine than with the excitement which the presence of *un Americano* had brought to her house. To allay our hunger until the cooking was finished she brought us thick chunks of dark goat's cheese. Its saltiness increased our thirst, and we continued to celebrate the saints.

Caterina spread the rough table with her bridal treasures, old heavy silver, linens golden with age and soft as cashmere. Before each plate she set a full bottle of wine. She served several kilos of spaghetti on a steaming platter. After that, we ate hot sausages, rich with chunks of fat and peppercorns, and coarse rich bread baked over hot coals. For dessert there were bowls of almonds and apples. While we ate, the room filled with people, for the word had spread on Mt. Ziretto that an *Americano* had come to take San Martino at the Intelisanos. Neighbors and relatives came to invite us to their wine cellars. Outside, the clouds crept over the mountain until we could no longer see the olive trees. But in their branches we could hear birds singing so that it seemed we were suspended not far from the gates of paradise and that the saints we were toasting were feasting with us on laughter, good food and *pista e mutta*.

I offered Caterina a cigarette. She accepted the first cigarette of her life and with reckless abandon shocked the roomful of men. Between self-conscious puffs she held the cigarette delicately between her thumb and forefinger. Smoke was floating about her head like a halo when the kitchen door opened.

A sturdy young man, carrying a rifle and wearing ragged G.I. trousers, stood on the threshold. It was the son, Giorgio Intelisano, returned from hunting. The sight of his mother smoking so startled him that he remained staring in the doorway. He refused both wine and a cigarette. Later when we set out to visit wine cellars farther up the mountain, he walked behind me, politely offering his support when my foot faltered on the path. The mountainside was alive with bands of boisterous Sicilians weaving up and down the trails. Giorgio kept proudly aloof from the chattering and laughing.

In response to my questions he told me he was eighteen, that he went to school until he was twelve, at which time he stopped to help his father with the wine and the oil and to hunt rabbits for food.

"I have never before talked with an American," he said.

"There are many Americans in the village to speak to."

"I do not have clothes to wear in the town, so I do not often go," he said.

I could see that his ragged trousers were not the clothes for one so proud as he to wear in the village.

The interest of everyone in the *Americano* created a formidable problem for me. Each wine maker insisted that I sample his product. Underneath this hospitality there was also a curiosity to see how much an *Americano* could handle. The strength of the U.S.A. was being gauged by my capacity for Sicilian wine. I tried to beg off at the cellar of a peasant named Alfio Galiano, but the uproar was so great and Alfio was so insulted that I accepted my beaker full. It was called *Vino Monte Ziretto* and was thick and sweet. After one swallow I knew I could not risk it; I was already too heady from *pista e mutta*. While the men joked loudly about the effeteness of Americans, I emptied my glass between some rocks. Only Giorgio saw me do it, and he smiled his promise to keep the secret. The rest of the afternoon, Giorgio, who drank no wine himself and who knew the mischief the men had in mind, watched over me like a guardian. Whenever it was possible I made my libations to Mother Earth. At one farm we were herded into the house so the farmer's grandmother might see an American. The old lady examined me quizzically for a minute and then dozed back to sleep in her chair in the corner. Her grandson poured the wine. When it came to the toast, our supply of Italian saints was exhausted and we were at a loss as to whom to honor.

Carlo solved the dilemma. With a sweeping flourish, he raised his glass. *"San Truman!"* he shouted. The toast was like an explosion. The sound of clinking glasses rang throughout the room. Even the children cried *"San Truman!"* I wondered which of the two Trumans was intended—Capote or Harry. I knew Carlo's original toast was for Truman Capote. While I was speculating, the old grandmother jerked to sudden life, took a glass from the hand of her grandson, and raised it shakingly. *"A San Truman,"* she echoed in a husky voice. "To Saint Truman, who brought me DDT so for the first time in the eighty years of my life I now sleep without *pulci* [fleas] in my bed."

I asked the grandson if *Il Signor* Truman Capote had brought the grandmother a present of DDT from America. He said no, the DDT had been distributed by the UNRRA agents of the American government. The old lady had always looked upon it as a personal gift from *Il Presidente* Truman.

Caterina awaited us on the top of the mountain, in the home of one of her married daughters. The entire Intelisano clan seemed to be gathered there. There were hordes of children; a solemn and beribboned little girl named Elvira was guarding the family pig, which grunted amiably over a holiday dish of acorns. Carlo swung Elvira up in his arms. "In ten years you and I will make our San Martino together," he told her, and the relations rocked with laughter.

In addition to the usual wine, we were served a supper of roasted chestnuts, bread, cheese, and apples. Of the new Intelisanos I met, one made a particularly strong impression. His name was Carmelo; he was a town Intelisano who had climbed the mountain to spend San Martino with his country cousins. I remembered his face from Taormina, where he delivered letters and telegrams from the post office. Once you had seen him, you were not likely to forget him. He looked about fourteen and was elfishly small, even for a Sicilian. His ragged clothes flapped loosely about his slight frame. His handsome head was out of proportion to the rest of his body and covered by a thatch of black curls. His ears stood at right angles and he had the curiously chameleon green eyes so common in Sicily. His most characteristic feature was a thoroughly happy face. He was quick to show his country cousins he was quite at ease with an American.

"*Conosce il Signor* Truman?" he asked me. By this time I knew that when a Sicilian spoke of Truman he meant Capote and not the President.

I said I had never met him.

"*È un mio buon amico* [He is my good friend]," Carmelo said, growing an inch or two as he spoke. "*Conosce il dottore dell' intestini* Gaylord Auser?"

I confessed I had never met the intestine doctor, Gayelord Hauser.

"My good friend also," Carmelo said, and explained to his awed relatives, "Doctor Hauser is a very important specialist who has flown to Hollywood to treat the intestines of film actors. On television he is paid five thousand dollars a week."

Everyone, myself included, was properly awed. What, after all, was more fascinating than the ailing intestines of Hollywood's stars and the fabulous fees of television? This was the America Sicilians loved to hear about. Carmelo made the most of it. He told of the *grande feste* with which

Dottore Hauser entertained guests in his Villa Turca down by the grottoes of the sea. "There are always twenty kinds of wine and cognac," Carmelo said, "and the tables bend with turkeys and hams, roast beef and lobsters. Of course, he always invites me. Signori Truman and Hauser are the two most distinguished men of American letters."

The spellbound House of Intelisano turned to me for verification. Was it true that these two part-time citizens of Taormina were the most important writers in America? Carmelo looked at me, his chameleon eyes twinkling confidently. I could not betray him. "Yes," I said, "*Dottore* Hauser and Signor Truman are certainly distinguished American writers."

"They are my dear friends," Carmelo added casually.

St. Martin's Day was ending. In the valley below, it was already dark. A Castelmola bus which covered the last half of the descent was due to leave in half an hour. Since I had lost Carlo and Nino, Giorgio Intelisano offered to take me to the bus, but Cousin Carmelo assured Giorgio it was not necessary. He would see that I was safely escorted. It was a nightmarish pell-mell rush down the mountain. Everywhere men were running for the bus, stumbling over loose stones, and cursing each other when they fell into a thorny cactus.

Carmelo kept a firm hold on me, guiding and offering support when I needed it. He was as solicitous as if I were a fragile invalid, but he accomplished the miracle of getting me to the bus with no greater mishap than a bruise on my left knee. The bus was too jammed with drunken Sicilians to close the doors. As we swayed around the hairpin curves, many got sick, and the driver had to stop so they could unload their stomachs. My own stomach threatened to rebel but didn't. My head was another matter.

Meanwhile, Carmelo's air of proprietorship was beginning to annoy me. I had seen too much of predatory young Italians' attaching themselves to Americans, especially when the Americans have been drinking. In order to avoid an unpleasant situation, I decided to ditch him. But when the bus emptied, I did not know where I was. Carmelo walked beside me. "*Dove vai*, Niccolò?" he asked, using the name with which my Sicilian friends had addressed me. I gave the name of a hotel, not mine, but one near by. He pointed in the direction opposite from the one we were walking. "This way," he said.

We lumbered along together. On the corso we met gangs of festive young men. Carmelo spoke to each of them by name, thereby calling their attention to his *amico Americano*. My irritation increased. Below us, the sea was dark. There were no boats out; the fishermen also had been celebrating San Martino. We passed the ruins of a bombing which workmen had lately been clearing away. In the midst of the rubble stood an incandescent white-marble Madonna. Six young men solemnly surrounded her. Illuminated by the moon, the classic stone face glowed tragically. The Madonna, ascended after eight years in a rocky tomb, had reason to be sad. The bomb had damaged her *bambino*; the child nestling in her arms was without a head. Bearing in her arms a terrible token of war, she was able to halt, for a moment, the drunken prowlings of men.

Ahead of us was the ancient Porta Messina. Suddenly Carmelo stopped dead. "Signore, it is not true that I was invited to the *feste* at the villa of *Dottore* Hauser," he said. "I ate turkey and ham, but it was in the kitchen, and the wine I drank was red, and not white as they were drinking outside."

I pondered what I might say. Since I had never believed the story in the first place, I had not expected a retraction.

"I am sorry to have told you an untruth," he said. Somewhere from the heights I heard a wail, a solitary flute keening a private sorrow; Daphnis, perhaps, weeping for Chloë in a moonlit grotto on Mount Venus. There was a plaintive answer. Two pipes conversed with each other like echoes lost in the hills.

"The shepherds," Carmelo said. "Each evening for six weeks before Christmas they tell us on their pipes that Jesus will be born."

I said good night.

"What is your name, Niccolò?" Carmelo asked.

"Niccolò is enough," I said guardedly.

"My friends call me Melo," he said. "You are my friend."

"*Buona sera*, Melo."

With his hands in his sagging trousers, he trudged away. In my hotel, I opened the terrace doors and filled the room with silver night. The pipes of Pan, heralding the birth of Jesus, lulled me to sleep.

II

I awoke with a guilty conscience about the little messenger boy. In my caution, I had been too brusque with him. He had, after all, guided me safely home. I would, I thought, give him some packs of American cigarettes. I would be cautious as one must be with young Italians who seek American friendships. Their objectives are usually immigration visas (which are not procurable) or expensive gifts to be sent from America. The post boy need not know my name. I would leave the cigarettes at the post office and say they were from Niccolò.

I didn't have to bother. I was at breakfast on my terrace when the waiter came to say the post boy wished to see me. "He has some letters which he says he must give you in person," the waiter said.

The post boy came to my room. He looked even more ragged than I remembered him.

"*Buon giorno,* Signor Erberto." In his hands were several letters rifled from the morning's mailbags. I wondered if he'd had his clothes off since I'd seen him, or if he'd slept in them. The roguish look of his face put me on guard.

"Is it your duty to deliver mail to this hotel?" I asked.

"No, Signor Erberto. Only the specials and the *telegrammi.*"

"Is there not a regular carrier to this hotel?"

"He does not come for two hours. I bring them to you immediately."

"Why?"

"Because you are my friend. For a friend one does favors."

"How did you find out my name and where I live?"

He shrugged impudently and smiled. "Only an *uomo importante* could receive so many letters," he said. "I do not think it can be anyone but yourself, Signor Erberto."

I thumbed over the letters.

"You are disappointed," Melo said. "Why?"

"A letter I have been awaiting is not here."

"From a *signorina?*" he asked. To a Sicilian it was inconceivable that a letter from anyone but a *signorina* would be important.

"Yes," I said.

"What is her name?"

"Rosemary," I said.

"Rosamaria?"

"Yes, Rosamaria."

His face filled with compassion as he shared with me my sorrow over the betrayal of a *signorina.* "Have you waited long for it?"

"Almost a week," I said.

His concern was so exaggerated one might have thought the post office was at fault. "There is a mail from Messina this afternoon. If it arrives, I will bring it at once."

"That will not be necessary," I said. "The regular delivery will be time enough."

"Of course it will come," he said, with the lack of conviction of one who knows the ways of the world. I asked him how old he was.

"Eighteen," he said. "In the spring I will have nineteen years."

I laughed. He was immediately crestfallen.

"You do not believe me, signore?"

It was possible, of course, I thought, looking at his face, intelligent and full of expression. But his slight and undeveloped body betrayed him. He kept thrusting his head forward, a habit which curved his back. No, I decided, sixteen at the very most. Even then he was abnormally small.

"I will have my mother tell you how many years I have," he said.

"Why?" I asked. "It is of no importance to me how old you are."

A cloud passed over his face. I had hurt him.

"Not important at all?" he asked.

"I mean, you're a good fellow, no matter how old you are," I said, feeling sorry.

"But you do not believe me?" he asked again.

"I believe you and I don't," I said. "When I was fifteen I lied about my age."

"Was it because you liked girls that were older?" he asked.

"Precisely," I said. "So I gave myself years."

"Women are the sorrow of my life," he said. "They never think I am old enough."

I dug several packs of American cigarettes from my bag.

"*Mille grazie*, signore."

"You are welcome. From now on let the regular carrier bring my letters."

"*Si*, signore." On his way out of the door, Melo turned back. "How many years do you have, Signor Erberto?"

"How many years do you think?" I replied.

He appraised me as thoughtfully as a carnival weight-guesser.

"You are not *very* old," he said. "Perhaps twenty-seven years. . . ."

I could find no clue in his smile as to whether he was serious or flattering me. In our curious little battle of egos, I realized that Melo had won the first round.

Of course, he chose to forget my instructions about mail. The next morning I was again at breakfast when he came running down the road.

"*La Signorina Rosamaria!*" he shouted a hundred meters away. He was waving an envelope. "*La lettera da Rosamaria!*" He was so excited that I hadn't the heart to tell him the American *signorina* was a *signora,* that her husband also was an old friend. Melo anxiously watched me read. The letter told about snow and ice in a raw New York winter.

"*Buona notizia?*" he asked.

"Yes," I said, "things are very well."

"*Mi piace,*" he said. "I am happy things are well."

"*Grazie,*" I said, "for bringing the letter."

He shrugged it off. "For a friend it's nothing at all," he said.

I had no more American cigarettes, so I offered him a hundred-lire note. He refused it. "You are my friend," he said. "One does not take money from a friend."

I wished he had taken it. I was wondering if he was building up for a big kill.

"Perhaps you might like to know that there is an American film at the Cinema Coco tonight," he said. "It is said to be a film *molto comico.*"

"Does one go to the cinema with a friend?" I asked.

His face lit up. "Yes, signore, one does," he said.

That evening we met outside the cinema. The audience was entirely male, for Sicilian men seldom appear in public with their women, and a woman does not venture out after dark. The men were convulsed by the film, a twenty-year-old Harold Lloyd comedy. When it was over Melo and I walked along the Via Roma, a cliff road which hangs over the sea almost a thousand feet below. As he trudged along, Melo told me his story with complete candor and without self-pity. He basked in the luxury of an interested listener.

It began with the war. Up to 1940 his life was like any of the other village *bambini,* a little more fortunate than some, a little less fortunate than others. He had a baby sister named Giuseppina. His father had a job working on the land and there was usually enough to eat. Melo went to school.

The father became a soldier. In 1943, when he was barely thirty years old, he was killed. The circumstances of his death were never made quite clear to me. "He was split down through the middle, even the head. There were two halves of him!" Melo told the story with a true *Italiante* fascination for gore. Six months later an American bomb struck the house of Melo's grandmother. "The two sisters of my mother were torn into fragments. They found the head of one aunt by the church of the San Carmine and a leg on the Piazza del Tocco."

Melo, a ten-year-old schoolboy, became head of a family which now included an infant brother, Carlo, born after the father's death. The Germans had occupied Sicily. Melo quickly learned to ingratiate himself with the German soldiers, who gave him food for his family. When the Germans left and the Americans came, Melo attached himself to Americans. He ran errands for K rations and searched the mountains for wild fruit for which the Americans traded him chocolate. When fighting to survive, one had no loyalties. "The Germans were very generous," Melo said, "more generous than the Americans."

It is easy to understand this impression, so common with Sicilians. When the Germans occupied Sicily, they were fresh from Germany, full of their dreams of conquest, and rich with supplies from the homeland. The Americans who followed were battle-weary sick veterans of Africa who could not afford to be generous with their limited supplies. "Of course, Americans are the best people in the world," Melo said, quick to make amends.

When he was fourteen, Melo became a post-office delivery boy. Since then he had worked without holidays, eleven hours a day, six days a week; and five hours on Sundays. For this, he said, he was paid twenty-four hundred lire a month, or approximately four dollars. His gay disposition, however, paid off. Many letters and telegrams went to visiting Americans who were generous with their tips. In a peak month, Melo boasted, he made as much as ten thousand lire on tips, or slightly over sixteen dollars.

Of his earnings, he kept for himself only an occasional fifty lire for the cinema. Cigarettes were not in the family budget. In their home, Melo's mother operated a tiny food shop. Her income from it was less than his. The family ate mostly the macaroni, dried bread, and overripe fruit from the shelves of the shop. Often there was not enough of that. Melo had even tried to raise money by the usual method of the *giovani* of the town: the selling of himself in *amore*, but his ragged clothes and childlike appearance were handicaps, and not much came of it.

"My mother has been eight years a widow," Melo said. "Now she has taken off her black dress and wears again a bright red dress as she did when she was a girl. It is because she has an *amico*—a widower—who comes from Messina two times a month. He and I are not sympathetic. I do not care for his three daughters who are too forward and use lipstick as freely as American and Swedish women. But in another year, perhaps, my mother will marry him. Then I will be free."

"What will you do then?" I asked.

"I have never told anyone what I desire to do. It would make people laugh. You will not laugh?"

I promised I wouldn't.

"I should like to study in a university to be a journalist."

The revelation was a surprise, but only until I started thinking about it. If Melo took a vocational test, it would doubtless indicate a strong aptitude for journalism. He was intelligent and likable, and made friends easily. He had an insatiable curiosity and a deceptively disarming aggressiveness. These were valuable attributes for a journalist.

"It is because you are a journalist that I wanted to be your friend," Melo said. "When you arrived in Taormina it was quickly known in the post office that an American journalist is in the town. I knew you were the one when we met on the mountain."

I told Melo how I had come to know the Italian people when I was a police reporter, and used to wander around in the Italian section near police headquarters, especially during the Feast of San Gennaro on Mulberry Street. My covering of *la cronaca nera* (the black news) interested Melo far more than San Gennaro and Mulberry Street.

"How many pistols did you carry?" he asked me.

I said I had never carried a pistol in my life. This Melo refused to believe. "But there is a great danger," he said. "There are many robbers and murderers in New York. The police are very sympathetic with criminals and it it not safe for a man to leave his house without a gun. I have seen it all in *La giungla d'asfalto* and *La città nuda*," he said.

It was the old story. How could I explain that *Asphalt Jungle* and *Naked City* do not present the same true picture of America that realistic Italian films present of Italy?

Melo asked if I knew the Sicilian *sindaco* of New York. I said I had never met Mr. Impellitteri.

"He is very rich, this Sicilian, who lives in a *grande palazzo*."

I said I didn't think Signor Impellitteri was very rich, and that the "grand palace" he lived in was the property of the City of New York.

"He is not a loyal Sicilian, this *capitano?*"

"He is an American, not a Sicilian. I believe he loves deeply the Sicilian people."

"No, it cannot be. He is *il capitano* of New York where all the ships go, is he not? If he is loyal to his people, then why doesn't he help them to come to America?"

It was a difficult question to answer. What can quotas and population balances possibly mean to one whose small island country has a population of ten million people?

"I should like to be a journalist in America," Melo said.

"Italy also needs good journalists," I said. "In the years to come, the whole world will need courageous journalists."

I thought of what would happen to a boy with such an ambition in America, even if he were poor. Scholarships and part-time waiter's jobs would put him through a university; he would graduate high in his class and begin at once what might be a distinguished career. In Italy there was no opportunity and no hope for Melo. At eighteen—if he really *was* eighteen—his six years of elementary schooling was all the formal education he could expect. To be poor in Italy and have ambition must be a terrible torment. I wondered how long it would be before Melo's high spirits were broken.

"Do you think I might go to America?" Melo asked.

"There are ways," I said, "but they take much time. You are young and you must have patience." The idle words I spoke did not deceive Melo.

"The poor become old quickly," he said. "I think that I am already old."

We were walking by The Club where I once paid a thousand lire—almost two weeks' salary for Melo—for a bottle of German beer. The band was playing "These Foolish Things." A cloud passed over the moon. Below us fishermen's lamps were lighting the sea. The smell of lemon was in the air.

"Why do you want to leave here?" I asked. "Why does anyone want to leave here?"

Melo rubbed his thumb and forefinger together significantly. "It is easy to see beauty when there is money in the pocket," he said. "But the eyes are not the stomach."

Melo invited me to visit his family, suggesting that I come the following evening. I told him I was going to Catania for a performance of *Norma*.

"Ah, *Norma*," Melo said. "My favorite of all operas. You will hear

Maria Callas, who is the greatest Norma in Italy." He sang several bars of *"La Casta Diva."* "I have never heard *Norma,"* he said. "I have heard *La Traviata, La Bohème* and *Aïda* in the films, but I have never been to an opera. I have thought many times to go to Catania, but the ticket and the trip cost too dear."

If he had never heard *Norma,* how did he know it so well? I asked.

He looked at me as if I'd asked a foolish question. "Everyone knows Bellini," he said.

On Sundays Melo usually accompanied his friend Nino, also a letter carrier, into the mountains to take a week's supply of bread to Nino's grandmother. He asked if I would like to go along. I said I would, so we made a date for Sunday.

The next day I took a bus to Catania with a young Taorminesi named Umberto who was also going to the opera and spending the night with relatives in the city. Like the director of La Scala in Milan, the management of the Teatro Massimo Bellini invited me to sit in the royal box. An official impressed upon me the importance of the occasion. Only a handful of distinguished persons had been so honored since Italy had disposed of her king after the war. He requested that I not enter the box until the house lights were dimmed and leave it before they were turned up. This caution was necessary because the monarchical Sicilians would be incensed at the sight of the gold throne of the House of Savoia occupied by a foreign commoner. I invited Umberto to share the box with me. He brought a relative named Peppino. At first the two Sicilians were too awed to enter. Once inside, they made the most of it. Umberto, assuming that all Americans were ignorant in operatic matters, briefed me with whispered footnotes. "Now will immediately come out Norma," he said. "At this moment she learns he has loved another woman. . . . Now she will walk into the fire." The performance, commemorating the 150th anniversary of the death of Bellini, Catania's most noted son, was a splendid one.

Umberto and I had been back in Taormina hardly an hour before the tale of the royal box swept the village. On the corso Umberto's aged grandmother corralled villagers into her little notions shop to hear Umberto tell the amazing tale over and over. "So, *il professore,* he is the king of Italy," Umberto said. "And I myself am sitting in the chair beside him and I am the queen of Italy, and Peppino is the captain of the guards. . . ."

The people of the town shook their heads in wonder; some were indignant. War was still too fresh in their minds to have forgotten that Allied bombs destroyed a third of their town and killed three hundred relatives and friends. There were all kinds of rumors. Some said I was a distinguished American traveling incognito, perhaps even a relative of *Il Presidente*. Others, pointing to my khaki pants and frayed jacket, said I was not distinguished at all, but doubtless an impostor; that my presence in the royal box was a mistake. Melo, who gleefully carried the rumors back, needled me for details. Had the throne been real gold or was it merely painted? Had people bowed to me? Had I met the diva, Maria Callas?

On Sunday Melo picked me up at my hotel. On the way we stopped at his house so I could meet his mother. Wearing her bright red dress, she waited with her two younger children in the door of the little shop. She was a little woman with attractively lustrous black hair and skin the color of oak. It was easy to see where Melo got his elfish frame and his happy disposition. By contrast, his sister, Giuseppina, a graceful and slim child, seemed infinitely sad. She wore the wooden clog sandals worn by the poor children of Italy. The little brother Carlo was bright-eyed, lean, and long-limbed. The store was a tiny place with a stock consisting of some bread, onions, and a few prickly pears. Draped in black crepe were photographs of the father, and some women who, Melo explained, were the two aunts killed in the war. The father, looking stiffly from the wall, was easily recognizable, for his face was the face of Melo but without the smile.

I asked the signora if the father had been small. "Small, yes," she said, "but not so small as Melo. After he died there was seldom enough to eat, and Melo didn't grow. Now he is only one and a half meters tall (five feet) and he is only forty-nine kilos (a hundred and nine pounds)."

The family slept and cooked in a small room behind the shop. I sat in the only chair while the signora poured a fiery orange liqueur. It glowed like sulphur in the tiny glasses and was phosphorescent at night, Melo told me. *Mamma* made it herself from an old and secret family recipe; it was named *dolce incanto*. We toasted each other's health with "sweet enchantment."

"*Mamma*," Melo said, "when was I born?"

The signora was puzzled by the question. "*Il ventuno Aprile, del trentatre*," she answered.

"Understand?" Melo said to me. "I was born on April twenty-first, 1933."

III

The door opened and a boy carrying a string bag filled with loaves of bread stepped in. He blushed and bowed. This was Antonio, to whose grandmother on Mount Venus we were taking the bread.

We set out like a procession. Nino walked ahead, carrying the bread as if it were the Eucharist, and Melo and I followed.

"Buon divertimento," the signora called after us, adding warnings to take care on the mountain trails. Children playing in the caves of the hills waved to us.

The path was narrow and perilous, often nothing more than a rocky ledge. After climbing for a half hour, we descended into a ravine, crossed a gorge on a foot plank with no railing while the mists rose about us from the waterfall below, and started to climb again. We walked through orchards and vineyards, past whitewashed stone cottages. Nino was too shy to talk, and I was too short-winded, but Melo, in his most allegro mood, chattered like a magpie. He identified trees and plants for me and gossiped about the people in the houses we passed.

One of the houses was the home of Giorgio Sterrantino, a letter-carrier colleague of Melo's and Nino's. We stopped to rest. Giorgio was a modest and gentle Philadelphia-born American who spoke no English. He was twenty-seven years old. When he was six, his father had returned to the homeland to buy the tiny farm with his American savings. A heifer lived in one room of the house; a fence enclosed a peaceable ménage of chickens, turkeys, and rabbits. Their feed and water dishes were an assortment of German, American, and Italian soldiers' steel helmets, which Giorgio had collected in the hills after the battle of Sicily.

Our host piled dried figs on the table and set a bottle of wine beside them. Flies from the manure pile outside the house swarmed on the figs and crawled over the edges of our glasses. The Sicilians paid no attention. While Giorgio recalled his Philadelphia childhood, I watched drunken flies stagger into my glass and drown. The wine was rich and potent, and I reflected how pleasant it would be to die in it.

We started to climb again. Melo invented a game which he called *Tarzan*. I was Tarzan and he was an ape leading us through the jungle. Melo loped forward, grunting and swinging his arms, and I whooped like Johnny Weismuller in the movies. Nino forgot his shyness and collapsed on the path from laughing.

The house of Nino's grandmother was on the side of Venus facing Etna. It was whitewashed and without windows; beside it was a great shed with a wine and oil press that had a screw the breadth of a tree trunk. When we arrived, the grandmother was in the hills gathering firewood and the men of the house were off on some mysterious Sunday business. There were only women about. A young aunt with two wide-eyed girls clinging to her skirts took the bread and carried it into the house. A neighbor wife helped another aunt, a widow crippled with dropsy, draw fluid from her swollen legs with a hypodermic syringe. The women spoke only Sicilian, and it was difficult for me to talk to them. But my camera made friends. The large-legged aunt was carried into the sunlight. Children were herded in front of the camera along with a donkey, a cow, and a pig. A bottle-fed lamb presented a problem. The lamb had adopted a chicken without which it refused to be photographed. The chicken ran away, the lamb ran after the chicken, and the women ran after the lamb.

Into this melee walked the grandmother, a wiry, cackling little woman with a bundle of faggots balanced on her head. She embraced Nino heartily, the sticks still on her head. In this women-ridden family, the only grandson was obviously a favorite. While she was unloading the sticks, her son-in-law, the father of the two *bambini,* came home. A gentle young farmer in his dark Sunday suit, he covered his shyness by pouring us beakers of wine and filling our pockets with chestnuts. I asked him to demonstrate the wine press, in turn for which he asked me to make a photograph of him astride the donkey. The sun was setting behind Etna, and Melo worriedly pressed us to start back. Nino and I were in no hurry. But as I read my light meter I suddenly realized Melo was indeed right, and that it would soon be dark.

We started at once. Because we were descending Mount Venus on the side away from the sunset, we were soon in darkness. Since it was too early for the moon, we could not see a yard ahead of us. When we heard someone approaching on the path, we called out to determine how close they were. To make way for a woman leading a cow and a man riding a donkey, we had to press our backs close to the mountain. Near us we heard a woman singing. It was a sweet, soft song, the sort of tragic dirge which Sicilians are always pouring from the ancient sadness of their hearts. Melo said it was a young mother singing to her child.

When the voice was still, the two boys told of mysterious soft voices which led men to death in the mountains. Had I ever fallen off a mountain?

they asked. Not off a mountain, I said, but I had twice fallen over embankments. Once, as a boy, I had stumbled from a cliff on my father's farm, and another time just ten years ago, I had rolled over a hill in a car. I told how a psychologist had said these two incidents were caused by a strong wish to die. Melo thought this very foolish. For instance, he asked, if a donkey fell off a path, did it mean that the donkey wanted to die?

Nino said that donkeys never fell off paths. Melo distinctly remembered a donkey falling from Mount Venus and breaking so many bones it had to be shot. Nino said it was impossible, donkeys were absolutely surefooted, and when faced by danger, they would refuse to go any farther.

We flipped cigarettes over the cliff. They cut a flare like rockets and disappeared in the canyon below. We walked in silence until Melo started the game again. This time he beat his chest like Tarzan and I grunted and swayed like the ape. We continued this way until I heard again the sad song of the mother, farther away this time, more will-o'-the-wisp than ever, fleeting as a dream. I stopped so I might hear better and turned to the edge of the path. My foot slipped. I faltered on the precipice for a moment. Melo and I cried out, and I plunged into darkness.

It seemed that I fell forever. Several times I scraped against a jut of rock or a cactus. Each time I reached out to grasp something, there was nothing there and I continued to catapult down the wall of the mountain. I felt the imminence of death. The sins of my life flashed like speeded film across the screen of my mind.

When I finally came to rest in a cactus bush, I realized I had not fallen as far as it had seemed. I was a mass of pain, and breathing was difficult. My clothes were in shreds; my glasses were gone. I was cold with sweat and sticky with blood. In the distance above I heard my name, "Erberto" It was the voice of Melo crying, *"Dove sei, Erberto!* Where are you?"

I thought I answered. Fearing broken bones and afraid of plunging even deeper into the abyss, I did not move. Slipping away as in a dream was the terrified voice above me. "Erberto! *Responde! Prego*, Erberto! Please answer!"

Then Melo and Nino did a wonderful thing. They set fire to the clumps of coarse dry mountain grass that dotted the slopes. The grass popped and sizzled, making fiery torches up and down the mountain wall. Venus burned like Etna in eruption, her leaping flames causing shadows to dance on the side of the canyons. It was as if hell were preparing a *festa grande* to welcome a distinguished sinner. Mountain people were attracted by the flames. Soon the slopes were alive with searchers, all directed by Melo, who shouted commands like one possessed. Though none could see me, I could see them all. It seemed a long time before they reached me, but everything was distorted, time most of all.

Melo was there first. *"Mi dispiace, Erberto,"* he cried like a man crazed. "I'm sorry, it's all my fault, forgive me!" He bent over me, trying to lift me. I tried to stand and was violently dizzy. Melo kept blaming himself for the accident. Of course he had not the slightest responsibility, but I couldn't convince him.

Others came to help, and slowly over a zigzag route I was returned to the path from which I had fallen. I lay down to rest, for I was sick to my stomach and trembling with shock. Melo ordered the men to return to the pit to search for my glasses. I protested. To hunt glasses certain to have been broken on the side of a dark mountain seemed like madness. The men agreed, but Melo, prompted by his peasant frugality, could not be dissuaded. He went into the canyon himself to look for them. Within a half hour he returned with the glasses. They were unbroken.

I was loaded onto a donkey for the painstaking jog down the mountain. Melo walked beside the beast to support me. Though a taller man might have served me better, he refused to leave my side. An argument developed between the men as to how far I had fallen. One said it wasn't more than ten meters. Melo argued as if my honor were at stake. He assured me that I had fallen at least thirty meters. So relieved was he that I was not seriously injured that he became positively gay. My cut and scratched hands, he said, had been blessed with *stimmate,* and he called me San Tommaso. As we descended Venus clumps of grass still glowed red behind us.

Under a twenty-five-watt light on the counter of their little shop, Melo and his mother picked the cactus spines from my flesh. Melo soaked each wound with *spirito* of alcohol and poured me tiny glasses of *dolce incanto*. Anesthetized with "sweet enchantment," I endured for an hour hundreds of little stinging operations. When they were finished, my legs seemed solid enough to undertake the walk to my hotel. On the corso we met Umberto, who looked at me and said, *"Mamma mia!* You must be just returned from Korea." Afterward Melo went to the cathedral to light a candle to St. Anthony.

Next day I was nervous and lightheaded and ached all over. A Dutch doctor found a sprained rib, attributed my dizziness to shock, and ordered me to stay in bed. Word of my mishap swept through the village. Among the Sicilians there was great concern for my welfare. They came, a caravan of them, to the hotel, shuffling past hostile attendants to visit me. Don Carlo Siligato, the old artist of Via Teatro Greco, nervously rolled his hat in his hands while he waited out a thunderstorm for an hour, entertaining me with tales of his youth in Taormina, and how he had been taken to Leeds by a rich Englishman but had quickly fled its foggy darkness to return to the sunlight. "A bird cannot live in a cave like a bat," he said. Melo came four or five times a day, managing always to have a letter or telegram to deliver in the neighborhood.

By Wednesday I was well enough to make a bus trip to Catania. The purpose of the trip was to discuss with the director of the opera a plan I made while convalescing.

The director was anything but sympathetic. "*Un contadino*—a peasant —in the royal box?" He reacted as if I'd suggested treason. "It is impossible!"

The "peasant," I said, would come as my guest.

"If you wish to bring a guest," the director said, "he will be welcome. But in the royal box he cannot sit. We will find another post for him."

"It would please me if he would sit not only in the royal box, but in the royal chair."

The director grew pale. "*Dio mio.*" He shuddered. "You want to make a ragged country boy the King of Italy?"

"No," I said. "That's not what I have in mind. I want to show that in a democracy, a poor country boy can sit in the throne of a king."

"Impossible," he said. "There has never been a peasant in the royal box."

"But you had one in the royal box last week," I said. "I am a peasant."

"You are a *professore*," he said.

"My mother and my father are peasants who milk cows. I myself have milked cows."

"In America things are possible that are not possible in Sicily," the director said.

I changed my strategy. "Think of the story it will make for the newspapers: 'A poor war orphan hears his first opera from the seat of kings.' "

"It would be a *tempesta*," he said, thinking of the aristocratic subscribers who still bemoaned the loss of their monarchical privileges. I showed my letter from the ministry in Rome that was helping to subsidize the Bellini commemoration. It requested I be shown every courtesy during my visit to the opera house.

"Does the ministry know what crazy thing you ask?"

"Not crazy," I said. "It happens all the time in America."

"I suppose ragged children sit in the *palco reale* at *Il Metropolitano*?" he said.

"Certainly," I said, forgetting along with the director that there was no royal box in the Metropolitan Opera House in New York. "In a democracy, poor children are often the guests of the management at operatic performances."

"This is not democracy," the director said, coming to a grudging agreement. "It is extortion." He returned the letter. "This is what comes of de Gasperi's visiting with the President in the White House. We have peasants in the *palco reale*!"

Before I left Catania I bought a shirt and a necktie for Melo. The shirt was for a fourteen-year-old boy. As it turned out it was too large and Melo's mother had to take it in.

The next day was Thanksgiving and the American-English colony bustled with cocktails and turkey. I invited Melo to have dinner with me on the American holiday. I knew it would not be wise to take him to my hotel, where the traditional feast was being prepared under the supervision of an American guest who did not like rubbing elbows with Sicilians. We went to one of the restaurants in the town. It was a dingy place, as they all are, with perhaps a half-dozen people scattered at tables. Melo apologized for his manners because, he explained, "I am not accustomed to eating in this manner. I have never eaten in a restaurant before." He ordered a *bistecca,* potatoes, vegetables, and salad, everything but *pasta,* of which he doubtless had enough at home. He ate with a delicate neatness, cleaning up the last crumb and drinking the last drop of wine. After some sweets and fruit, we moved on to a *caffe*. While we were having our coffee, I told him we were going to the opera on Sunday to hear Bellini's *La Sonnambula.*

He laid down his cup. "*Sicuro*?" he asked.

"For certain," I said.

"Do you have tickets?"

"You will sit in the royal box as a guest of the management."

"I do not think it possible they would permit me in the royal box."

"It is already arranged. All you must do is ask for Sunday off. If necessary, I will speak to the postmaster."

"It will not be necessary when I tell him I'm to sit in the royal box," Melo said. "But, of course, he will not believe it. Who will believe it? Me, Carmelo Intelisano in the box of a king. I do not believe it myself!" He started to laugh in the anticipation of it.

He said he had a dark suit, one of his father's which his mother had altered for him. We went to the hotel to get the shirt and tie. On the table in my room was a loaded tray, left by the waiter who had missed me at the Thanksgiving feast. I was not interested in any more food, but Melo tackled it with relish. It was one of the most spectacular eating performances I've ever seen. I marveled that a person so small could contain so much food. Everything disappeared, the turkey, dressing, potatoes, and vegetables. Not a crumb was left. Having been hungry much of his life, Melo could not stop eating as long as food remained. He stored it up inside himself, like an animal who eats for three or four days. When everything was gone, Melo sighed and smiled. *"Ho mangieto bene,"* he said, "I have eaten well. I like very much the American holiday, Thanksgiving." Then, the shirt and tie under his arm, we walked together to the cathedral, where, in honor of the American *festa*, the monsignor was screening an American film called *Hellzapoppin'*.

I asked Melo to keep the opera plans secret because I feared a public reaction before the performance might change the mood of the director. He did his best, but the story was too exciting to keep to himself. By Sunday morning word had gotten around that the little letter carrier was to occupy the throne of the king. I had asked Melo to meet me on the piazza at eight-thirty, fifteen minutes before the bus departed. At seven-thirty he was at my hotel, worried lest I wouldn't awaken. I could hardly believe what I saw. He was as scrubbed and brushed as a Sunday-school boy. His neat dark suit was pressed and clean, his shoes had laces and they were polished.

The townfolk gathered on the piazza to see for themselves whether it was true that *il piccolo* Melo was going to Catania with an American friend to sit on the king's throne. They brought their donkeys and their goats; one man carried two tethered roosters in a basket, as if he didn't want *them* to miss the sight. Melo's fat aunt clutched him tearfully to her opulent bosom. For the benefit of his audience Melo played the role of a casual cosmopolite. Opera in the royal box! It was nothing. A stranger would never have guessed it was his first trip to Catania, only twenty-eight miles away. The bus, delayed by the excitement, finally got off. New snow covered Etna and the sea was as blue as the sky. Red and white poinsettia blossomed along the highway. The morning was clean and pure.

In Catania the director, having decided to make the best of a bewildering situation, had instructed his staff to treat the country boy like a distinguished visitor. The performance was in the late afternoon; in the morning arrangements were made to conduct *il piccolo re* (the little king) through the Bellini Museum and the opera's backstage areas. We were delayed in the executive offices when Melo caught sight of a blonde and buxom secretary named Maria Spitale. Signorina Spitale was Melo's senior by eight years and fifty pounds, but he refused to begin the expedition without her. A hurried consultation decided the king should have his wench, and Signorina Spitale accompanied us to the museum. We looked at original manuscripts, models of stage designs, and old pianos. What most interested the king was a death mask made some forty years after Bellini's death, when the composer's corpse was returned to Catania from a cemetery in Paris. It was a gruesome affair with taut lips and half-opened eyes. "Incredibly preserved," Melo said to Signorina Spitale, "a beautiful thing."

In the opera house, he was shown the dressing rooms, sets, drops, and switchboards. He critically examined ballerina's tutus, and when the curtain was raised so he might see the century-old theater from the stage, he exclaimed, "A masterpiece! How much did it cost?" At the end of the sight-seeing Melo invited Signorina Spitale to lunch with us. She had news for him. She could not lunch because her *fidanzate* would understandably not approve.

So we lunched alone, Melo and I, in an open sidewalk restaurant on *scaloppine al marsala* and fresh Sicilian peas. Even though the food was excellent, lunch was a depressing affair. A parade of beggars, men, women, and children, stared hungrily at our food. The waiter gave them one or two *panini*, little rolls of bread, which was kinder than most *restaurateurs*, who scold beggars and send them away. Everyone seemed sad, the waiters, the customers, the people passing by. The inevitable funeral came darkly down the street, followed by a swarm of curious children. Even babies followed the dead in Catania. Melo ate slowly and thoughtfully. "There are more unfortunates in the city than in the country," he said. "Life in the country is better for poor people."

Back on the street we shook off our gloom. The Sunday was full of girls in twos and fours taking their *passeggiata*. Like a true country yokel, Melo ogled them all. Before the opera Melo got a flower for his lapel; then, as the crowds gathered around the opera house, a shine for his shoes. The mayor of Taormina, a pompous, rotund little man in an afternoon cutaway and top hat, passed before the elevated chair of the shoeshine. Melo greeted him with the familar *"Ciao,"* and the mayor bowed stiffly.

The house was jammed. The soprano, Margherita Carosio, sang a great Amina that afternoon. One gorgeous melody after another flowed as easily and naturally from her throat as from a bird's. Under the great gold crown which hung over the royal box, Melo looked smaller than ever, less like a king than an impish dauphin. His behavior was instinctively noble. With journalists he discussed the performance like an old opera patron. Carosio was *"magnifica"*; but *"il tenore!"* Melo shrugged. *"È meglio che ritorni a pescare* [It would be better if he returned to his fishing]." To a pair of befuddled old monarchists who came to see the blasphemy that was being committed, he offered cigarettes and then led them on an intermission promenade to see the Bellini portraits hanging among the crystal and tapestry. People asked each other who *il ragazzino importante* might be. Melo gave them no clue. To everyone with whom he came in contact, he demonstrated that poise and good manners are not the exclusive attributes of those born in luxury.

The only bus returning to Taormina left immediately after the performance. It was a lively ride, for the bus was crowded with high-spirited students who had been at the opera. They sang all the way, Italian student songs, Sicilian dialect songs, and a repertoire of American songs. Sicilians owe their cultural heritage to a variety of invasions beginning with ancient times. Their cultural legacy from the American invasion included "Deep in the Heart of Texas," "Yippee-I-Ay," "Dixie," and some thirty ribald stanzas of "Roll Me Over."

In Taormina, the piazza was deserted. Passengers quickly disbanded. The fantasy was over. Even Melo, back among the realities of daily life, was tired. He walked with me to my hotel. I told him I would be leaving Taormina in three days.

"It's a long journey to America," Melo said.

"Yes, it's very long."

"Do you wish to leave Sicily?"

"No," I said. "I do not want to leave."

"Then, why do you?"

"There are many reasons why one must return to one's home. Job, family, friends. . . ."

"Perhaps an American girl. . . ."

"No, no American girl in particular."

Melo shrugged. If there was no girl, obviously there was no necessity to return.

"Why do you not remain here? You should take a villa, perhaps the Fontana Vecchia. I will cook for you and keep your house clean."

"I must go back."

"When will you return?"

"As soon as I can. Two, perhaps three, years."

"It is a long time," Melo said. Hunched up and alone, he trudged up the hill. It was after midnight and everything had turned to pumpkin again. In the morning he would be the ragged letter boy.

v

It was an electric Monday in Taormina. Women shouted to each other from windows; men clustered in the streets. So it was true, then, the small boy had sat in the throne of the Bourbons and Savoys. Those that had disapproved were proud at least that it had been one of their own townsfolk in the royal box. After all, who was better qualified to be so honored than one of their public servants. Melo told the story with every letter and telegram, and with each telling the account became more wondrous until the golden throne, the crimson velvet hangings, the voice of Carosio, the crystal salons, and the elegant ladies might as well have been in *paradiso* as in the Bellini Theater of Catania. The people shook their heads and marveled. "It is an American idea," they said, "this *democrazia* in which a poor orphan from the country may sit on the throne of a king."

On my last day I went down to the beach to say good-by to the fishermen. Though it was December I swam and baked in the sun for an hour and visited with an old man who was spinning a rope, holding the hemp between his gnarled brown toes. In the middle of a sentence he indicated with his head for me to look up the beach. A girl was striding across the sand, her blond hair, bright blue slacks, and crimson sweater making a bright eyeful against the autumn sea. I decided to catch up with her, and the old fisherman bowed me off with understanding graciousness.

Her name was Gwendolyn, and she was a painter; an Australian by way of London who had only arrived in Sicily that morning. We climbed through the orange and olive groves, talking a flood of words to find out as much about each other as possible. To make the meager travel funds permitted by England last as long as possible, she had taken a room in which she could cook her own meals. It was obvious that Gwendolyn's stay in Taormina was not going to be a friendless one. As we walked up the corso together, the young men of the town watched with fire in their eyes, ready to go into action. Gwendolyn told me how, when she stepped from the bus and asked about a place to stay, one of them had suggested she come to meet his family. If everything was agreeable, he would marry her and her housing problem would be solved.

I took her around to meet my friends. We went to the notions shop of Umberto's grandmother where a dozen old widows and wives were gathered to say good-by to me. Amid ribbons, buttons, and spools we drank kümmel and ate cookies.

After dinner I introduced Gwendolyn to Melo. He was obviously enchanted. The three of us set out to pass the evening. The town glistened with moonlight and smelled heavily of mimosa and lemon. Shepherds' pipes sighed in the hills. We drank coffee and walked, drank more coffee and walked again. Our moods changed from allegro to *triste* and back again, as capriciously as a Sicilian song. Melo was full of flowery Sicilian phrases. *"Saremo amici per sempre* [We are friends forever]," he said to me. As a token of his esteem, he promised to learn English during my absence. But I knew his sadness at my leave-taking was greatly diminished by the advent of Gwendolyn. He had already invited her for *il cinema* the next evening. The town was quiet and it was necessary to say *buona notte.* It was my last night in Taormina and Gwendolyn's first. Above us the white cross of Jesus glowed in the night, and higher still, Etna burned red. Where in the world could man live so closely to heaven and to hell?

In the morning they were at the bus to see me off—Melo, Gwendolyn, Don Carlo Siligato, the fishermen, barefoot as usual, and some people of the village whose names I did not know. Melo gave me a small package wrapped in tissue paper. It contained an antique silver cross, a beautiful thing on a silver chain, the gift of all the friends who now crowded about me. I promised to wear it as protection on the voyage and as a promise for a quick return. Sicilians, like all Italians, love tears, and there was a rich flow of them in the gathering by the bus. Melo had a request which he was too embarrassed to make aloud. *"Prego,"* he whispered in my ear, "please send me a Roy Rogers *co-boi* suit."

When I embarked from Naples two weeks later, there were two letters waiting in the cabin of my ship. Melo wrote: "I am thinking how sad it must be for you to go away from this land which you love. I remember with a sad heart of when we were in the *palco reale* to hear *La Sonnambula*. The fishermen speak always of you, as do Nino and Don Carlo and Umberto, also Lady Gwendolyn. . . ."

And "Lady Gwendolyn" wrote: "Melo always carries my mail separately and produces it like a rabbit from a conjurer's hat. Yesterday he took me to see his grandmother. It was four hours' climbing, and four hours back, and very rough going. The old brown grandmother was weaving cloth at a loom. We lunched on bread, cheese, hard-boiled eggs, figs, sweet apples, wine, and a black country pudding made with wood ashes.

"Melo has such an air of proprietorship with me that I've had to invent a London fiancé who comes in very handy in an emergency. I am looked upon with scant approval by my fellow English, because I have chosen the Sicilians for friends. It is slightly more *pericoloso*, [dangerous], but infinitely more entertaining. Melo and his friends make me feel practically Etruscan, but in this country, I grow younger and younger. I do indeed, and can do nothing about it."

Another month and I was at my university in the heart of wintry America. One day the department secretary telephoned me at home to say that a letter marked *urgente* had just arrived from Sicily. Fearing that something might have happened to one of my friends, I went after the letter at once. It was from Melo. He was worried. "The Roy Rogers *co-boi* suit has not yet arrived in Taormina," he wrote.

I went immediately to Sears, Roebuck and bought some pegged trousers, a red-checked flannel shirt, and a belt. I was pleased with the belt. It was studded with nickel and brass and colored glass. I sent the parcel at once.

That is how one month later, the people of Taormina had their letters and telegrams delivered by a five-foot *co-boi Americano*.

CHAPTER 19

LA CASA DELLO SCUGNIZZO

No AMERICAN WHO ARRIVES in Naples can escape the terrifying onslaught. The moment one steps off a train or a ship, he is the unwitting Pied Piper of a horde of nipping, clawing demons, chanting their evil litanies like choirboys of *l'inferno*.

"Hey, Joe, wanna change money; wanna taxi, Joe; wanna woman; carry bags, Joe; wanna buy cigarette *Americano*; lika dirty pitchers, Joe; wanna nice clean hotel, Joe; hey, Joe, *sono affamato*, I am starving; I take you to girl, Joe, nice blonde clean girl. . . ."

These are the *scugnizzi*, the homeless children of the streets. Naples has more than any other city in the Western World. *Scugnizzo* is a Neapolitan word meaning "top"; the verb *scugnare* means "to whirl like a top." It is an appropriate name for these grubby, tireless delinquents.

They can be found wherever Americans congregate in Naples. The public gardens around the bay, the Piazza Municipio adjoining the port, the door of the American Express, and especially the Via Roma and the well-known Galleria Umberto are some of their important bases of operations. Their professional language is a G.I.-Italian patois. With it they pimp, sell black-market cigarettes and contraceptives, act as come-ons for hotels and taxis, pick pockets, rob drunks, and, with a studied pathos, beg. The nub of their activities is sex; none of them ever doubts that the first thing an American male wants after a long hot train ride or ten days on a boat is a woman, *pronto, presto, subito*. One Sunday afternoon when I was hurrying to a performance at the San Carlo opera house, one of them, about eight years old, followed me down the Via Roma: "Hey, Joe, wanna buy my sister, a thousand lire, Joe, eighteen years old. . . ." Singing the eternal refrain, he followed me into the opera house, where he was turned back by a doorman. Three hours later, the opera over, I crossed the Corso Umberto for a *Cinzano* at a Galleria café. There he was waiting for me. "Hey, Joe, wanna buy my sister now, I make you special price. . . ."

Why so many *scugnizzi* in Naples? The reasons are obvious. In a country of impressive fertility, the temperamental and amorous Neapolitans are the most fertile of all. Lower-class Neapolitan women have one occupation—childbearing. Because of the terrible poverty of the people there have been *scugnizzi* in Naples for three hundred years. Naturally the war increased their numbers. Bombings destroyed houses, making thousands homeless. Then the German occupation and later the Allied occupation destroyed morals more thoroughly than bombs destroyed houses. Children were bred like insects with no thought for their welfare. In every corner of the world there are always children who do not know their father. In Naples many *scugnizzi* do not know their mother.

During the war they prospered, these *bambini terribili* of the streets, providing a variety of services for G.I.'s, of which the most respectable and least lucrative, performed largely as a come-on, was the shining of boots. They do not go to school. Street education sharpens their wits and their inherent Neapolitan shrewdness; their dark eyes are glistening pools of diabolical mystery. Many of Naples' adult criminals are *scugnizzi* alumni. To the police a *scugnizzo* is a "pro" if he sleeps in the streets. When I was in Naples there were at least four hundred pros between the ages of five and twenty. Thousands of amateurs lived in the streets and crawled in with friends or relatives at night. When the United Nations' Mediterranean Fleet established its headquarters in Naples, it became a sailor town and the *scugnizzi* prospered again.

In 1949 an idealistic young Franciscan priest named Mario Borelli performed a most unclerical act. He abandoned his ecclesiastical robes, dressed himself in old clothes, and took to the streets disguised as a *scugnizzo*. The role was not a difficult one, for Father Borelli is only five feet, five inches tall, and he appeared even younger than his twenty-five years. With *scugnizzi* he cooked his food over rubbish fires in alleys; on cold nights he huddled with them for warmth over the window of a basement bakery, and he slept with them in bombed grottoes. From them he learned a lot of things priests don't ordinarily know, such as how drunk an American sailor must be before he can be rolled, and how to pick pockets on crowded trams.

When he had familiarized himself with their life and gained their confidence to the point of becoming their leader, he invited his gang to join him in organizing *una casa dello scugnizzo,* a house for *scugnizzi.* He had no money and no building. Religious prelates, suspecting the opportunism of a young upstart, offered neither help nor encouragement. But for journalists, Father Borelli's activities made good copy. He begged enough money from private citizens for a start and moved his twenty buddies into the bombed and abandoned Church of the Materdei. The *scugnizzi* took to the project with enthusiasm, restoring as much as possible the crumbling church, doing their own housekeeping, and going to school for the first time under a volunteer teacher. For the older ones Father Borelli sought apprenticeships with photographers, furniture builders, and shoemakers. To all the boys he became parent, teacher, priest, disciplinarian, friend, and beggar; beggar of funds, beggar of clothes, and beggar of food from produce merchants.

One April day Dr. Guido Botta, an Italian staff member of the United States Information Service in Naples, asked if I'd like to meet Father Borelli and his *scugnizzi.*

I would indeed! Dr. Botta told me to be ready in an hour. When he called for me with his beautiful Swiss-Italian wife in their little Topolino, Dr. Botta said we were going to Naples' race track, the Agnano Ippodromo.

Mrs. Botta told me that not only would I meet *scugnizzi,* I would also encounter a well-known ex-fellow patriot, the gambler "Lucky" Luciano, Since he had been deported from the United States for peddling narcotics, the Ippodromo was Lucky's base of operations.

It seemed a curious place to meet reformed *scugnizzi.* The story the doctor subsequently told me could happen, I believe, only in Italy. Among Italy's most popular pastimes are national lotteries. There is always one under way. In a lottery which the Ippodromo had just concluded, the winning ticket had been held by one of Lucky's colleagues. This aroused public indignation to such a pitch that the lottery sponsors were forced to recall the ticket and give the winning forty-four million lire to charity. In a public poll conducted by a newspaper to select a beneficiary, two institutions were tied, a home for unmarried mothers and Father Borelli's *casa dello scugnizzo.* The checks were to be presented that day at the races. The unmarried mothers were not present at the track, but the *scugnizzi* turned out in full force to accept their check.

Every Italian is a gambler; in a country where life itself is a gamble against overwhelming odds, the betting of a few lire on the horses is the salt in the soup. The Ippodromo, developed by Mussolini inside the crater of an ancient volcano as a lush playground for the gambling rich, had grown somewhat shabby since the war. Now it was crowded with poor Neapolitans come to gamble a hundred lire or two on the dazzling chance of winning a few thousand. Immediately upon our arrival the doctor and his wife queued up in a long line before one of several dozen betting windows. It was a turbulent scene. Long lines of bettors, frantically waving fifty- and hundred-lire notes, mobbed the windows before each race. Running between the betting windows and the grandstands, they put in more leg work than the horses. Milling through the confusion was a variety of stock characters: whores, touts in pin stripes, pimps, effeminate millionaires in capes, con-men, and pickpockets, the latter holding close to the betting and paying windows.

At the last window in the row there was no line. This was a special one for the exclusive use of Lucky Luciano. There I saw the gambler, surrounded by a battery of flashy cronies in bowler hats. Luciano himself was dressed like a groom in a dark suit, a Chesterfield coat, and a soft black hat. His cynical face was as expressionless as a corpse's. It had a curious familiarity. It was not a Sicilian face, for Sicilian faces, subtle and evasive though they may be, are a constantly changing screen of emotion. Nor was it an American face. It was the face of a movie gangster; the Hollywood concept of evil.

He didn't speak. At the window he simply waved a pink hundred-lire note to the clerk inside. Unlike other bettors he did not deposit the note, but walked away with it in his pocket. The triviality of the bet astonished me until Dr. Botta explained that the pink note was part of a code with which Lucky communicated with his own bookie. The gambler never bothered to pay or collect individual debts; everything went into accounts kept by a bookkeeper inside. By flashing a hundred-lire note Lucky signaled a bet of a hundred thousand lire; a brown five-hundred-lire note meant the bet was for a half-million lire, and the flash of a thousand-lire note placed a bet of a million lire. Lucky was known as a quiet fellow. No one had ever heard a word cross his lips at the races.

Up in the grandstand Father Borelli's *scugnizzi* were more articulate. Leaning over the railing to cheer the horses, they were probably the only ones at the Ippodromo enjoying the races solely for the pleasure of seeing the horses run. They were an astounding contrast to the mangy rogues on the Via Roma and in the Galleria. The younger ones were identically dressed in new blue levis, zipper jackets, and solid brown shoes, bought for the occasion. One extremely handsome lad with only one leg had a shoe as new and shiny as the others. The older boys, in suits and ties, were like any gang of dressed-up adolescents at a sports event. Every boy was scrubbed and brushed. Each of the little ones was the ward of an older *scugnizzo*, who looked after him with the protective tenderness of a parent. It was the easiest thing in the world to make friends of them. Well experienced in the art of persuasion, they were all extroverts. Some of the smaller ones spoke a Neapolitan dialect which I could not understand; others spoke their own peculiar jargon of G. I. English.

"Hey Joe!" A small skinny lad with bright eyes and sores on his leg was speaking. He winked at me and pointed to the cigarette I was smoking.

I asked him his age.

"*Quattordici anni, signore,*" he said.

I did not believe he was fourteen years old. Later I found out he was; almost all the *scugnizzi* were older than they looked, having been stunted by malnutrition.

"Does Father Borelli permit you to smoke?" I asked.

"Certainly," he replied in Italian, as if the question were a foolish one. I gave him the pack. He passed it among his buddies. It was emptied in a flash. The one-legged lad saw another pack in my pocket and nudged me for it. His name, he told me, was Gregorio; he was thirteen years old and a trolley wheel had cut off his leg. He asked if I was a chronic smoker who couldn't stop smoking. I boasted that I was sure I could stop if I wished. He bet me that I couldn't.

"To prove it you must give me the pack and not keep any for yourself," he said. I gave it to him.

The time had come for the whitewashing of the scandalous lottery. The ceremonies arranged for the presentation of the money were as absurdly pompous as if they had been staged by René Clair. To a platform in the grandstand crowded officials, politicians, and gamblers. Around microphones and newsreel cameras they bowed formally and kissed each other like a meeting of the Japanese diet. The mayor of Naples made a flowery speech congratulating the donors for their charitable act of mercy to "the little unfortunate soldiers of Christianity," after which an officer from the national treasury handed the check to Father Borelli.

It was the first time I saw the father, and it was hard for me to believe that the pink-faced young man in the black robe and inverted soup tureen, was a priest. Some of the bigger *scugnizzi* appeared older than he. To great applause he announced that the twenty-two million lire would begin a building fund for a new *casa dello scugnizzo*. *Scugnizzi* were photographed with public officials and sang Neapolitan ballads for the grandstand audiences. One little unfortunate soldier of Christianity blew smoke rings into the microphone from one of my cigarettes.

"Hey, Joe, wanna buy a tip on next race?" a *scugnizzo* asked me.

I said I wasn't betting, but he did not believe me.

"Ma lei è un Americano! No?"

Did being an American make it necessary that I bet on horses?

"Si, signore, Americans have money for gambling. There is an American here . . ."

He pointed to the dark shadow of Lucky Luciano.

". . . who is a very distinguished bettor. You must be a *poor* American."

I admitted I was. When I went to find Dr. Botta and his wife, I saw boys filthy as chimney sweeps crawling like animals among the feet of the crowd under the bleachers, scrounging for cigarette butts. They were the little soldiers of Christianity not fortunate enough to know Father Borelli.

II

In December I returned to Naples to visit the *casa dello scugnizzo*. I had the address—Largo San Gennaro a Materdei 3—but Dr. Botta was then in America and no one at the USIS knew where it was. A taxi driver promised to find it. His machine was old and lofty, like a Model-T Ford. He scrambled to the front and cranked vigorously. Finally the motor fired and the machine shimmied like a reducing vibrator. The driver had the idea I was someone of importance so, as we chugged up the Via Roma, he counterpointed the motor's coughs with beeps which he milked from a red rubber bulb. It was a joyful ride until I noticed the outrageous arithmetic of the antiquated meter. It seemed to be connected with the red rubber bulb, for it spurted astronomically with each beep.

We drove by the National Museum and turned left, into one of those crowded quarters of Naples where every intimate secret of the inhabitants is clinically bared. We encircled fruit and fish counters, brushed under laundry hung in the street to dry, and collected a caravan of children who ran shrieking at our side. At every corner my driver asked directions and, as is usual in Italy, each time they were different. Finally, I paid him off and offered a boy fifty lire to walk me to my destination. It was hardly more than a block away. The piazza was a jungle of bombed rubble. It was late in the afternoon and the winter sun had sunk behind buildings, leaving the square cold, dark, and depressing. Most of the children who followed me were barefoot. The largest building on the square was the scarred Chiesa Matterdei, the Church of the Mother of God. Its front entrance was boarded up, as buildings are after a fire. I rang the bell on a small door to the left.

A gray little man answered. When I said I was an American, he fell to his knees and kissed my hand, as if I were a king or a bishop. Then he bustled me into a tiny cold office where Father Borelli was talking to two visitors. With his long black robe, the priest seemed smaller and more boyish than ever.

His visitors were Swiss. The woman, a Frau Weller, was director of an organization known as Lucerne Charities. She wore a fur coat; her face was coarse and humorless and she spoke with businesslike intensity. The quiet young man with her seemed to be a sort of secretary. Obviously Father Borelli considered them important. He did not seem pleased with my interruption. While he talked with them, I looked at a large album which bore the label *Prete Scugnizzo*. It was filled with photographs of *scugnizzi* cooking in tin cans in the streets or huddled together like dogs under newspapers in the night. These were followed by photographs of the same boys, scrubbed and neat in the dining room of the *casa*, at work clearing away rubble, on a swimming expedition to the sea, and kneeling in prayer beside their beds. There were also photos of Father Borelli as a *scugnizzo*. In beret, ascot scarf, and sailor trousers he looked more like a Parisian apache than a Neapolitan street boy.

The Swiss and I were introduced to three members of Father Borelli's staff. Father Francesco Spada, a twenty-seven-year-old Franciscan, was in charge of housekeeping. Another young priest, twenty-three-year-old Father Luciana, had joined the staff three weeks before to assist Father Spada. Guido di Vincenzo, a thirty-two-year-old layman, was the schoolteacher. They were all kindly modest men with soft voices, a striking contrast to Father Borelli's forceful personality. The schoolteacher was the only one who spoke English.

"Today I have good news," he said. "Before two years ago, none of our boys attended school. Now nineteen of them go to public school. This week they have made the best examinations in their classes."

"I am more impressed with another examination we have passed,"

Father Spada said in Italian. "I speak of the Wassermann health examination. It is always a happy event to make a hundred per cent in the Wassermann."

Father Borelli escorted the Swiss on a tour of the *casa* and I followed in the custody of Father Spada, Signor di Vincenzo and a half-dozen boys. *Scugnizzi* life in the old church was centered about the nave, which at the moment was serving as a football field for thirty boys playing vigorous *calcio* with the marble altar as a goal post. Their shouts were amplified into a frightful din by the hollow dome. No doubt they were playing to keep warm as much as for pleasure, for the bomb-shattered windows had never been replaced and the room, open to the night, was cold as a tomb. The floor was cement and mercilessly dank. I drew my overcoat tighter. Di Vincenzo told me it was impossible to heat the ruin and the greatest concern of the *casa* was to try to keep the boys warm. The smaller ones wore heavy sweaters and flannel knee pants. Not all had socks. "Now we are badly in need of overcoats," the schoolmaster said.

I was looking at the dust which lay thick everywhere. The schoolmaster read my thoughts. "You must think we are terribly dirty," he said. "We have tried to fight it, but there is no way. Since the bombing the old stones just crumble away into dust. It is everywhere; there is no end to it. The boys wear clean clothes, but at the end of each day we all look like cement workers. There is only one way to fight it—to keep the boys as clean as possible. Our one extravagance is the hot showers with which the boys must wash every night."

"It is a great problem," Father Spada added. "Visitors are often discouraged because they think we are so dirty."

I asked how the dust and the cold affect the health of the boys.

"We have not much sickness," Di Vincenzo said. "Our boys are well immunized to dirt and cold before they come to us. There is now one boy in the hospital with tuberculosis, but we think that he brought it with him."

Space behind the altar was converted into two dining rooms, one for older and one for small boys. On the floor above, a space was partitioned into dormitories. Each had from five to twenty steel cots with plenty of blankets. A towel was folded over the foot of each bed. The bed tables of the older boys were cluttered with combs, razors, endless bottles of lotions, and bits of broken mirror. Two boys were in bed with the flu, one of them the one-legged Gregorio. He asked for a cigarette.

It was, I learned, against the rules to cadge cigarettes from visitors, but the boys did it all the same with a subtle wink and a flick of a finger to simulate the dropping of an ash. I distributed my pack as far as it would go. One small boy didn't get a cigarette and began to cry. Father Spada took him into his arms.

"He is very sensitive and his feelings are easily hurt," the father said. "He cries often and is therefore a problem, but he is really very lovable."

Those with cigarettes carefully broke them into two, storing half behind their ear for later. I noticed that even the little ones had an impressively experienced manner with a cigarette.

"They are not as young as they must seem to you," Father Spada said. "Giovanni," he called to a serious dark boy who looked about seven or eight, "how many years are yours?"

"Thirteen," the boy said, drawing a long puff from his cigarette.

"He is telling the truth," the father said. "Giovanni is half Greek. His mother is dead and his stepmother sent him into the street. He has a very sad heart and it is necessary for him to be loved."

He called to another, "Ciro, what years do you have?" He addressed a wizened dwarf with crumbling teeth and the wrinkled face of an old man.

"Sixteen years," Ciro replied in Neapolitan dialect.

"Ciro is one of our brightest boys," Father Spada said. "He came to us voluntarily, with his brother, Vittorio, who is fourteen, to ask if they might live here. They are from a family of ten children and their parents sent them into the streets seven years ago. They do not understand Italian, only Neapolitan. They now have jobs. Ciro works in a bakery; Vittorio is apprentice to a stonemason."

"You see it is not tobacco that has stunted their growth," the father said. "It is hunger."

As a final fillip for the Swiss, Father Borelli halted the football game and lined up the *scugnizzi* for a concert of Neapolitan songs. The singing had barely begun when a whoop of laughter echoed from the back where the kitchen was located. It infected the boys and they began to giggle foolishly as children do. Father Borelli started them over.

Again came the laughter and again it spread like a contagion through the choristers until, overcome by giggles, they were unable to sing. The Swiss Frau Weller was plainly mortified.

Failing to gain control of his choir, Father Borelli ushered the Swiss apologetically into his office. Father Spada's face was covered with despair and he also left the room. Di Vincenzo and I were left with the yowling *scugnizzi*. A sad sort of smile was on the schoolmaster's face. Not even he could entirely resist the hellish merriment.

"We have now a very great problem," he said. "It is the custom of the police to bring us stray boys from the streets. Two nights ago they brought us a laughing boy. He is feeble-minded and he knows nothing, not even his name. He cannot speak, but he laughs. He never stops laughing. He makes all the other boys laugh and for two days and nights we have had a nightmare of laughing. There is nothing to be done. We cannot hold school because of the laughter. At night there is laughing in the beds. We removed the boy away from the others and set him by the kitchen fire where it is warm, and the cook laughed so hard he was unable to prepare the food. It is a terrible thing to have a laughing boy."

Father Spada returned with him. He was shocking to look at, like a hairless stratospheric monster in an Al Capp comic. His bullet-round head was shaved smooth for vermin. He was small and stocky and unbelievably dirty. His clothes were in tatters. He clicked his heels and raised his arm in a salute. Then he took my hand, pumped it enthusiastically, and laughed more than ever. His empty eyes rolled idiotically. The military click and salute were his two tricks, the priest said, and, like a dog eager to show off, the boy never ceased performing them. Since he had arrived at the *casa*, he had stopped laughing only when he slept.

Father Spada had named him Carmelino; it had taken two days for him to learn to answer to the name. The priest estimated he was about thirteen years old. Looking at the grotesque boy, I wondered to what extent he was able to share in human experience. He saluted me, and the *scugnizzi* shook the church with their mirth. Father Spada put his arms about Carmelino and drew him to his breast. Watching him, I felt the cold sweat inside my clothes.

"He has been often lonely and hungry," the priest said softly. "Perhaps he is expressing to us his simple joy for the bread and companionship we give him."

A bell clanged supper. The *scugnizzi* pushed into the dining room for a meal of noodle soup and cheese served out of tin dishes on bare tables. To avoid pandemonium in the dining room, Carmelino was kept in the kitchen where he ate by himself. He did not know how to eat from dishes, even tin ones, but he laughed happily over a piece of bread which he had already soiled on the kitchen floor.

The Swiss were gone. Apparently they had left favorably impressed, for Father Borelli was in high spirits. He invited me into his office to see the architect's drawings for the modern *casa dello scugnizzo* to be built on the rubble-covered lot next door to the church. Four hundred square meters of land had been purchased with the *casa's* twenty-two million lire lottery windfall. The design showed an airy modernistic structure of glass, steel, and cement with private sleeping rooms and study and recreation facilities. Construction was to begin in a year. Father Borelli discussed plans for a modern *scugnizzi* schoolhouse, a factory and crafts center for the boys to earn their own living, and a *scugnizzi* summer camp at Posilippo on the sea. Obviously he was thinking in terms of billions of lire. The Naples *casa* would be a parent house to other scugnizzi homes in Rome, Milan, and especially the impoverished cities of the south. In his grandiose dream of a *scugnizzi* empire, Father Borelli had been influenced by the American motion picture of Father Flanagan's Nebraska Boys Town.

"It is a terribly cruel thing to have to turn away, because there is no room, boys who come to our door and beg for a home," he said. "The time will come when no boy will be turned away from the *casa dello scugnizzo.*"

Supper was finished and Father Spada and the schoolmaster brought several *scugnizzi* into the office for me to meet. The smallest of them tugged shyly at my hand. He told me his name was Franco and added something in Neapolitan which I did not understand. He was asking me, the schoolmaster translated, whether I had an airplane.

I said I hadn't and he frowned with disappointment. "Every American has an airplane," he said. "My father said so. When my father finds work he will buy an airplane."

It was an unlikely prospect, the schoolmaster said. Franco, five years old, was the youngest of the *scugnizzi*. His mother had run off with another man, leaving the father with three small sons, of whom Franco was the oldest. The father had brought him to Father Borelli six months ago and since then had shown no interest in the child whatsoever. To me it was astounding that a parent could have no feeling for such an appealing and affectionate child. His body was sturdy, his legs solid and strong. He had a beautiful head with large dark eyes set far apart. The most ingratiating thing about him was his expansive, trusting smile. It seldom left his face. He seemed to have one small defect, an exceptionally short neck with a slight curvature of the spine, which gave him an irresistible elfin quality, as if he were trying to dodge the blame for some mischief.

Father Spada asked him to sing for me two Neapolitan dialect songs, called "The Silken Handkerchief" and "The Market Girl." The priest boasted that the child knew fifty such songs, which he had memorized from hearing them on the radio. When he finished singing he climbed on my lap and sat there quietly, beaming with pride to be close to an *Americano*.

"Franco has the happiest disposition in the *casa*," the schoolmaster said. "Of all the *scugnizzi* he is the smallest trouble."

"*Il Nostro bambino*," Father Spada called him. "Our baby."

One by one, the other boys introduced themselves. The first was a tall, quiet fellow of twenty-one with twinkling eyes. I noticed that he was limping.

"I am the Zoppo," he said. The schoolmaster explained that his name was Bernardo, but that he was known as *lo zoppo*, which means "the jumper," because of the way he walked.

"When I was a baby, my mother threw a chair at me and broke my foot," the Zoppo said. "The doctor cut away the foot." Zoppo was now a tailor's apprentice and returned to the *casa* each evening to help care for the younger *scugnizzi*. "He is one of our best boys," Father Spada said.

A young man with his right hand missing presented himself. "I am the Mozzo," he said, speaking the Neapolitan word for "cut." His real name was Antonio M. He was short and dark, with black curly hair, a hearty, extroverted type, twenty years old, not as polite as the others. An old mine which he found in a rubble heap after the war had exploded and ripped away his hand. He was interested that I, with two hands, should write left-handed, a feat he was trying to master. I asked him if he had a job.

"No one will employ a *mozzo*," he said. "It is easier to work with only one foot than with one hand." Mozzo, said the schoolmaster in English, was a psychological problem. His feeling of inferiority made him extremely aggressive and he was not popular with the other boys.

Next came three serious, round-eyed brothers, graduated in size, but otherwise as like as peas. They were Vincenzo, nine, Carmino, seven, and Giovanni, five. Father Spada told their story: "They lived with their father and a woman who was not their mother. Because the rent was not paid on their two rooms, the family was evicted one rainy night by the police. Later in the night the father broke into the rooms so that his three boys might have a dry place to sleep. In the morning he brought them to us. Then he disappeared so the police could not arrest him for house-breaking."

Antonio B., a thin, delicate lad of thirteen told me he came to the *casa* voluntarily to escape his father, who sent him to beg and beat him when he did not return with money.

The next, a droll, beady-eyed boy of nine, had his shaved head wrapped in medicated bandages for the treatment of an impetigo infection. His name was Giacomo; for as long as he could remember he had been a professional beggar.

"When he was a baby, his mother, who had other children she used herself, rented him out to women for begging purposes at fifty lire (eight cents) a day," Father Spada said. From begging, Giacomo had graduated into robbery, working with a gang of pickpockets and shoplifters who wore metal plates on their shoes with which they tapped signals to each other on a job. Most of the members of the gang were now in the *casa*. One of them, Antonio L., seventeen, used to rob Giacomo's pockets when they slept together in the streets. Later, when Antonio came voluntarily to the *casa*, he brought Giacomo with him and continued to take a protective interest in him.

"To boys without family ties, friendship loyalties are strong," Father Spada said. "Friends on the streets usually remain strong friends in the *casa*."

Such a bond existed between Ambrogio, sixteen, and Davido, fifteen, a handsome, gentle pair of boys who, Father Spada said, were the students of the *casa* and spent all their time reading books. A more curiously matched pair were Mario and Antonio T., both sixteen. Antonio T. was the archtype Neapolitan, if one exists, a garrulous cock of the walk, precociously intelligent, full of fantasy and grand talk. He was small and dark, with flashing eyes and black hair slicked down to his scalp. He gave off an odor of strong cologne and wore an untidy silk ascot. He spoke an amazing English, picked up on the streets during the war years. More than anything it struck me as the English of an Italo-American burlesque comedian. Immediately he established himself on familiar terms by placing his arm on my shoulder.

"Dese blokes, dey no talka da English," he said. "I lika be your friend in Naples. Okay?" His story, which he told me himself, was the most bizarre of all the *scugnizzi* stories.

"I am begin a-worka da streets when I have six years old. I starta with da pickpocket and maka big success. The besta way picka pocket is in da movie or tram. From da jewelry store I taka da rings and cigarette lighters. Comes de war, I maka big prosperity. In da Galleria I polish da shoes of da Americans, see, not to maka da money, but to maka da acquaintance of da soldiers and sailors. I maka da big money working for da whores. When I have eight years, I have twenty-two whores are my clients. I bringa dem da soldiers and sailors. My price is thirty per cent. If da whore maka three thousand lire, she gava me nine hundred. From da soldiers and sailors I get more money for taking dem to da whores. Da English is stingy bastids but da Americans pay me thousand lire. I got another racket, see, I sella da drunk soldiers and sailors to older guys dat roll dem. I say to da soldier, 'You like nice woman, you lika drink, dance and fuckee?' He say 'Okay.' and I taka him into da alley, and dere is older guys who got us little bastids working for dem. We're too little, see, to roll da soldiers, so we sell dem to de big guys who knocka da shit outa dem and taka everything, even da clothes. Da big guys pay me eight hundred lire for an English bastid and a thousand lire for an American. If he is a Nigger bastid I get fifteen hundred lire. When business is good I catcha maybe five, six a night.

"I was richa like hell. I eata da *bistecca* two times a day. But wid all da dough, I am too little a bastid to renta da room in da hotel. So here I gotta my pants full of dough, maybe a hundred thousand lire, and I gotta sleep in da god-damn street wid da other fuckin' bastids."

I mistrusted Antonio; his easy confidence made me ill at ease. The priests understood none of his amazing recital, but the schoolmaster, who did, said Antonio was telling the truth. "He is one of the most trustworthy and co-operative of our boys," the schoolmaster said. I found it hard to believe in the reformation of one with such a lurid past. It seemed incredible that he should be satisfied with the life at the *casa*, his piano-polisher's job, and its pay of a thousand lire a week, not enough to keep him in hair oil and cigarettes. "I lika da work, see," he said. "I lika be a good man."

"Respectability is very dear to their hearts," Father Spada said. "A Neapolitan will fight enormous social and economic odds for the right to a job and a home and children. These are the things Antonio wants."

Antonio's close friend was his opposite in every way. Mario was tall and blond, more like a Teutonic young Siegfried than a Neapolitan street boy. He had blue eyes and hair like barley straw. Whereas Antonio had an extroverted, allegro disposition, Mario was a proud and sensitive boy in sullen rebellion to life. His intelligence was not as keen as Antonio's; he was shy and usually followed the leadership of his friend. Mario was one of the *scugnizzi* who had never learned Italian, who spoke only the Neapolitan street dialect. The schoolmaster translated his story for me.

Mario's mother, a north woman from Lombardy, had married beneath her when she became the wife of a Neapolitan fisherman. Mario, her twelfth child, was born after the father's death; there were more children later by another father. During the war, the family's three rooms were badly bombed, Mario, aged seven, left the family to make his own way in the streets.

On Piazza Garibaldi, he joined the railroad station gang, learning to pick pockets and steal women's purses. Like Antonio, he was soon working for prostitutes and a gang which rolled drunken English and American servicemen. Once an English sailor, less drunk than he seemed, fought off his assailants and with Mario in hand went in search of a policeman. Mario bit so hard into the sailor's arm that the sailor let go, and Mario escaped.

Father Borelli found him sleeping in the *stufarella*, which means "warm place," in this case an alley heated by steam escaping from a basement bakery. The *stufarella* was the most popular *scugnizzi* sleeping place in Naples. During his first month at the *casa*, Mario left it several times for what Father Spada refers to as "the call of the street." Each time he returned voluntarily. When Father Borelli found him, he was a small boy, but in two years he shot up into the tallest and handsomest of the *scugnizzi*. With his growth in stature there was also a change in personality. From a good boy, Father Spada said, he changed into a recalcitrant and moody problem. Mario loved his mother passionately and each Sunday he went to see her, taking for her half of his weekly salary of a thousand lire he earned as a photographer's apprentice. While we talked about him, Mario looked at me with the mute anguish of a trapped animal.

III

Inside the church, some *scugnizzi* had started another football game. Father Spada herded the boys out of the office. Little Franco remained on my lap. He was shivering with cold, so I wrapped my overcoat about him and covered his blue legs with my hands.

I was thinking of Italy's irresponsible, compulsive spawning of children;

the uncontrolled race between birth and death. I did not have to speak my thoughts. Father Borelli sensed them.

"It is not our fault we have so many children in Italy," he shouted, as if he were angry. "God has made us prolific. What is the sin in creating children when there are places in the world that are without men?"

Father Borelli paced his little office energetically and addressed me with rhetoric as passionate as if he were preaching a sermon. I began to get the feeling that he resented me because I was an American.

"I can offer no future to my boys in Italy," he said. "What good do I do a *scugnizzo* if I take him from the streets when he is ten, give him a home and make of him a good man, and then when he is twenty, I say, 'Now it is finished. *Arrivederci,*' and send him back into the streets to a life of crime? If the boys must live their lives in the streets, it is better that they be educated for life in the streets. The street gives them an education, a primitive education which prepares them for the only kind of life that is open to them, which helps them to work out their own solutions for survival. If I give them a hunger for a better life and then cannot make such a life possible for them, what is the point of my work? *Io farei una cattiveria* [I do them a cruel injustice]. I serve no one, rather I do a great harm by promising something which, when the time is finished, I cannot give. Unless I find a solution to this problem, my work is useless. I cannot take them from the streets without giving them a life to live. I cannot do one without the other."

Father Borelli's solution was to enlist the co-operation of philanthropic agencies in other countries which each year would welcome his come-of-age boys, find them homes and jobs, help them to lead honorable lives and become good citizens of a new land. Because young Italians love horses and machinery, he had in mind such great agricultural countries as the United States, Canada, South America, and Australia. He asked if I could arrange for immigration of his boys to America.

I explained the difficulty of what he asked. I pointed out that the Italian immigration quota for the United States would be filled for years to come with applicants holding affidavits from American relatives, that to bring an Italian into the United States any other way would require an act of Congress.

The little priest whirled on me. "Then have your Congress make an act," he said. "Don't your Congressmen know that in these sad times there are thousands of hungry and homeless children in Italy? Do they not understand that a country which is very rich has not the right to close its doors to the very poor? Do they not know that if a rich man has a house with ten rooms and he lives in it alone while there are nine people with no rooms, he is not a Christian and not fit to live in the brotherhood of man?"

The unalterable, impregnable problem of Italy's poverty and overpopulation had existed for a thousand years, I said. It would doubtlessly continue until eternity.

"It is not my problem, nor is it the problem of Italy," Father Borelli continued angrily. "It is the problem of the entire human family. The world is a body. No one man is disaffected by what happens to any other man. An infection in any part of the body spreads through the entire organism; one fever makes ill the entire body of man. No nation can live in health when there is infection in one corner of the world. The boundaries of nations are not natural to men; they are injustices that make peace impossible in the world. God has given the earth for all men, not for a few. The time has come when politicians must be humanists or there will never be peace in the world. How can there be peace when one nation has all the riches of life and another has not its necessities? Uneven distribution is not a natural phenomenon. The masses of hungry people want to eat. As long as there is hunger in the world, Russia will spread her myth that she is the mother of all downtrodden people. Communism, if it conquers the world, will do so because there are empty stomachs."

I could not argue with the priest. As a man of God he was right, unalterably right. If I thought him unrealistic I had only to remember that Jesus himself was considered a rabble-rousing anarchist by the realists of His time.

It was after nine o'clock and neither Father Borelli nor I had had any dinner. On my lap Franco was asleep; Father Spada came to carry him to bed. I invited Father Borelli and the schoolmaster to be my guests at dinner in a restaurant. Father Borelli declined. He had an appointment, he said, with the architects who were planning the new *casa*. He walked part of the way with the schoolmaster and myself, talking of his ideas for expansion. I doubt that he ate any supper that night; he seemed driven by a mysterious dynamo that did not need physical nourishment.

The schoolmaster took me to an excellent and inexpensive little restaurant near the Porta San Gennaro. He was carrying a curious package wrapped in newspaper which he laid beside him on a chair. We ate veal with new peas, salad, and wine. The schoolmaster ate and drank sparingly, as if he were unaccustomed to such extravagances. He was a good man and an exasperating one. Life had defeated him; he seemed to have no fight left. Laughter was no friend of his; tears were more ready companions. Like a martyr he was bearing the cross of Italy on his shoulders, but in a way more Slav than Latin, for he had none of the *scherzo* which has sustained Italy throughout a stormy history.

In appearance he was an aristocrat. His almost bald head was finely shaped, his features were strongly classic like those of the Pompeian portraits in the National Museum. His poor clothes were neatly pressed; the shirt cuffs were fastened with bits of string instead of cuff links. When he saw me looking at them, he quickly drew them into his sleeves and blushed with embarrassment. He told me he was a graduate in engineering from the University of Naples. When there were no engineering jobs, he worked for a time as a journalist. In one week during the war, he lost his entire family—father, mother, and a younger brother. The loss stunned him, left him a wanderer without roots through the rubble of Naples. When he met Father Borelli, he offered his services as a schoolteacher. "The boys call me *il professore*," he said. "With them I have found a family again. It is because I loved my brother so much that I can now love the *scugnizzi*. More than anything they need what they have never had, someone to give them love. I know what they have suffered and I have love to give them."

He taught them mathematics, geography, history, and Italian.

"They all wish to learn English," he said, "even those who cannot speak proper Italian. I have promised them English when they have all learned Italian."

Classes were held in a rough frame shelter which the *scugnizzi* built beside the church. During the day the schoolmaster worked with the small boys; evenings he instructed those who attended public school during the day, or those who held jobs.

In the early mornings, he often accompanied Father Spada, the housekeeper, into the streets to search for food bargains. Like frugal housewives they found the most for the least. The schoolmaster said, "Our boys eat macaroni twice a day. It costs less than spaghetti, which is served once a week as a special treat. Our most frequent dish is macaroni and cheese. It is cheap and most filling for hungry young stomachs. Cheap cuts of meat are served twice a week, on Wednesdays and Sundays, and eggs on Tuesdays and Thursdays. On Friday we have fish. Occasionally there is a treat of potatoes, and once a week there is fruit. A dairy donates milk, five gallons a day for seventy persons. We have bread and milk for breakfast. The entire food budget for seventy persons is ten thousand lire." It was sixteen dollars a day, or slightly less than twenty-five cents per boy. I asked about the disciplinary problems with such a group of seasoned delinquents.

"There are none," the schoolmaster said. "During the week they are all very busy. On Sundays they are free to do what they like. Those with relatives or friends in Naples go to visit them; otherwise it is the *passeggiata*, or the movies. Linda Darnell, Esther Williams, and Gary Cooper are their favorite stars.

"They are free to come and go as they wish. Often a new boy will disappear for a day or two to answer to 'the call of the street,' but almost always he returns. Food and a bed mean so much to a boy who has been without both. Also the presence of his companions. We have several gangs here. The boys have the same friends in the *casa* as they had on the street. This makes them feel immediately at home and removes their fear and insecurity. It is the first step in making them law-respecting citizens.

"All of them want to go to America. It is their leading subject of conversation. They know America through the motion pictures, and they are eager for the bright, shiny pleasures which Hollywood shows. They have not yet accepted the fact that America does not want them, that they must remain in Italy where there is nothing for them but frustration and hunger. We have no bad boys. They become bad only to the degree of badness in the world around them. Their tragedy is that the only world that awaits them is a bad one. It is sad to know these things when one is trying to make them good. You see, I have learned that for the young, Italy is a hopeless trap, a nightmare from which one can never awaken.

"One day they will know that we have lied to them and they will become bitter. Some of them will become Communists, for Italy is rich only in the conditions that make Communists. It is because I know what our boys must suffer in the future that I love them. But when that time comes, they will not even remember that we loved them."

I wondered about the homeless little girls of the streets, the persistent little beggars that lurked at all hours of the day and night in and about the Galleria? What was being done for them? I asked.

"We have hopes," the schoolmaster said sadly. "It is one of the things I cannot forget when I am on the streets. But now it is impossible because of our troubles with the church. The fathers of the Neapolitan church fought strongly against the *casa* when Fathers Borelli and Spada started it. When the stories appeared in the newspapers they tried to close the *casa*. Now Father Borelli would like to open a *casa* for girls, but the church, wishing not to recognize the fact that little girls also live in the streets, has refused permission."

The schoolmaster was deeply troubled by the attitudes of Naples' Catholic prelates. "They do very little to help the poor of Naples," he said. "What they do is make the poor even poorer by building new churches to extend their power and influence. The Protestants of America and Switzerland do more to help the poor of our city than do our own people. This is why I have decided to make a study of Protestantism and perhaps become a Protestant."

We were the last ones in the restaurant. The waiter hovered about trying to remind us of the lateness of the hour. As we left I noticed the schoolteacher forgot his newspaper-wrapped package. I called it to his attention and asked what it contained. He tried to avoid answering. Finally he told me the package contained cold fried potatoes. "They are cheap," the schoolmaster said. "I buy them in the afternoons and eat them late at night in my room before I go to sleep. It has become impossible for me to eat the macaroni of the *casa*."

Sleep was settling on the raw night. In the dark little canyons of the city, vagrants warmed their hands over the red coals of chestnut vendors. A wild eerie wail pierced the calm. It sounded like the skirl of a bagpipe. It *was* a bagpipe, the schoolmaster said, an Italian bagpipe called a *zampogna*. There was also a whining pipe called a *cornamusa*. They were played by shepherds at street shrines of the Virgin. Each Christmas, the schoolmaster told me, shepherd boys come down from the hills outside Naples to pay musical tribute to Naples' hundreds of street images of the Virgin. The serenades continue for a month until Christmas Eve, with the pairs of shepherds making nightly rounds of their assigned Madonnas. For this the shepherds are given a gift of money by Neapolitans.

We followed the wails to their source and came upon two small shepherds in coarse herdsmen's clothing, one with an untanned hairy leather bag strapped to his shoulder, the other with a thick pipe of wood. They stood before a blue plaster Madonna, illuminated by a candle in a glass. The wind-fanned flame sent wild shadows leaping through the dark streets, and the curious music sounded like the sobbing of ghosts. When the little shepherds finished the serenade, they went to seek another Virgin, and we started into the town. Via Roma was dark and deserted except for drunken

American sailors whose white caps glowed like crescent moons in the night. We passed three supporting each other as they walked. Close on their heels two ragged little *scugnizzi* were closing in.

"Wanna girls, Joe, nice clean girls?" The little ones yapped as tenaciously as terriers. "Hey, Joe wanna good . . . ?"

The sailors reeled into consultation. The *scugnizzi* waited knowingly, ready to open negotiations. In the hills behind us the shepherd boys had found another shrine. Their serenade to the Virgin filled the night like a cold chill.

IV

The next day was Sunday. I dropped in on the *casa dello scugnizzo* before taking the noon train for Rome to wind up my affairs, for I had only two weeks more in Italy. It was wet and misty on the little square of the Mother of God. Chickens were scratching in the rubble; a couple of tethered cocks crowed lustily. A herdsman, delivering the morning milk, drove his black goats to the open doors and milked them into housewives' pans. A butcher boy on a bicycle delivered the *casa*'s dinner meat; *scugnizzi* crowded around his wicker basket to admire the red fibrous flesh which an American housewife would hesitate to use for a Thursday stew. To them they were the Sunday *bisteccas,* a cause for celebration.

I had my camera. Each boy wanted to be photographed; by himself and with his buddy. The camera drew people out of tenements until the piazza was filled with mothers holding their babies, black-hooded grandmothers, and rakes in pin-stripe suits all clamoring to be photographed. Into this orgy of picture-taking stepped a *carabiniere.* He ordered me to stop "making pictures of our slums to be published in America." Father Borelli rescued me by explaining to the policeman that I was a friend of the *casa.* I squared myself with the law by taking a photograph of the policeman.

Inside the *casa* a whistle shrilled the signal for the Sunday Mass to begin. Older boys arranged the chairs, some without backs, some hobbling on three legs. To avoid a disturbance, Carmelino, the laughing boy, was not brought to the Mass. Huddling by the fire munching a piece of bread, he chortled happily when Father Spada came to the kitchen to bless him. Antonio and Mario, scrubbed, perfumed, and wearing blue serge suits, flanked me on each side and little Franco crawled on my lap. There was no organ; the *scugnizzi* sang their hymns in most unmusical *a cappella.* Since I was a *protestante,* Antonio took it upon himself to guide me through the Mass, telling me when to fold my hands and when to kneel. Franco watched slyly, his chubby hands in a this-is-the-church, this-is-the-steeple clench.

Father Spada presided over the poor shrapnel-scarred altar and sang the Mass. Taller than Father Borelli, Father Spada was dark and good looking. In order to focus through the thick lenses which corrected his extreme nearsightedness, he had to hold his head high, thus giving himself an air of remoteness. Nothing could be further from his true nature. In his heart was a love and compassion rich enough to embrace all the boys in the *casa*. From their six o'clock rising until the last ones were in bed at night, he watched over them. He personally bathed the little ones and put them to bed in an effort to bring them the security which a normal child gets from his mother. Without becoming angry or excited, he maintained constant harmony in his large and curious family. While it was easy to love the bright and responsive *scugnizzi,* there were others less lovable, the wizened, pinched little ones, twisted in body and spirit. It seemed to me that to love such a creature as the laughing boy took the stuff of saints. Like St. Francis, Father Spada was a gay man, responsible for much of the merriment in the *casa*. Father Borelli, with his promoting, planning, and fund-raising, was the physical body of the *casa*, but Father Spada was its soul.

The Latin phrases rang through the bleak church; I felt the miraculous presence of God and raised my face to the tortured image on the crucifix above the altar. Here, at last, was something He would approve of.

The boys voices shouted the *Ave Maria*. Outside it began to rain and the drops beat through the broken windows on our faces.

When it was finished, the schoolmaster, Antonio, and Mario accompanied me to the station. Antonio carried my bag and my camera; Mario my typewriter and my coat. We arrived early, in time for coffee and pastries. The boys ate four fruit tarts apiece. Antonio brought out his wallet, fat with photographs of himself. There were some of himself as the shrewd kid of the streets, as the boon companion of American soldiers, as the athlete in swimming trunks, as the natty man-about-town in flashy suits. There was also one picture of a plump, plain little girl of perhaps fifteen whom he described as "my woman." "Natch I ain't yet old enough to getta married but in two years I'm gonna marry my woman," he said, adding as an afterthought, "Of course, if I go to America, I ain't gonna marry dis one. I like better da American women."

He removed one snapshot from the collection to give to me; he signed it with a crude childish scrawl. "When I was little bastid," he said, "dere's dis American soldier, he likes me, thinks I'm cute kid. Wants to taka me to America wid 'im. But I'm making too mucha money in Naples and I don' wanna go. I'm dumb bastid, see. Now I kicka myself in da ass every day."

Through all this Mario quietly sat eating his sweets. I asked him if he had a *fidanzata*. He said he hadn't, but that he hoped in another year to have enough money to afford one. "But I will not marry an Italian *fidanzata*," he said. "I will wait until I am in America and marry an American one. They are much more beautiful." It was a fantasy obviously based on motion pictures. On our way to the track he linked his arm in mine. "Will you take me to America?" he asked. "Take me to America and I will be your brother the rest of my life."

The train rumbled into the station. I promised to return once more before I sailed for America. As the train pulled out, Mario's eyes followed me, mute and beseeching. They followed me to Rome.

While I was there I could not get the *scugnizzi* out of my mind. When I saw that I would have some lire left over, I had the idea of giving them a Christmas party the night before I sailed from Naples. I wrote to the schoolmaster, who responded with enthusiasm. I directed him to arrange for a dinner with authentic *bisteccas*, wine, fruit, sweets, and anything else that would make for a memorable feast. The schoolmaster wrote that a gift which would be most appreciated by all but the smallest boys would be American cigarettes. On the open market, American cigarettes cost about four hundred lire—sixty-five cents—a pack, but I knew that the United States Embassy sold them to diplomatic personnel tax free for approximately ten cents a pack. I went to an Embassy official and asked if he would arrange for me to purchase five cartons of cigarettes, which would provide one pack for each *scugnizzo*. I explained carefully why I wanted them, and I promised not to smoke a single cigarette myself.

The diplomat said it was against *the rules*. Italians, he said, were not allowed to consume tax-free cigarettes. His secretary said primly she didn't think boys in an orphanage should be smoking cigarettes anyhow. Next morning in the society column of the *Rome Daily American*, I read details of a formal reception for the American blues singer, "Bricktop," in the Ambassador Hotel across the Via Veneto from the American Embassy. The listings of Embassy and American military personnel, along with the usual assortment of princes and marchesas at such affairs, filled a column. Based on the assumption that each of the two hundred official Americans had smoked ten tax-free cigarettes during the course of Bricktop's party and had given another ten to their noble Italian friends, I made a little computation, arriving at three thousand cigarettes, or exactly three times as many cigarettes as I had wished to buy for the *scugnizzi* Christmas party. I sent the computation to the diplomat, who responded that I was "impulsive." At their Christmas party the *scugnizzi* smoked Italian cigarettes.

More or less in secret, I was working in Rome on another project, one very close to my heart. While I knew it was virtually impossible to arrange for mature Italians to go to America, there was no reason why the same restrictions should apply to children. What could stop me from adopting a small child and taking him back as my own? I had in mind Franco, the *scugnizzo bambino*. I had talked it over with the schoolmaster and the priests and had their enthusiastic approval. Franco seemed to me a perfect age. It gave me pleasure to think of this Neapolitan boy growing up in a midwestern community, of watching the impact of America on him, and his impact on America.

Again I went to the Embassy. I was told that the legalities and expense involved in adopting an Italian child made it almost impossible, that Italy, though it had several million children it could not feed, did not want to part with a single one of them. The fact that I was a Protestant would increase the difficulties. (Father Borelli had not considered this an issue.) The first step in the long process, I was told, would be to obtain permission of the child's next of kin, and the next of kin, even though they had not the slightest interest in a child, when they learned that an *Americano ricco* (the adjective *rich* was used to describe most Americans) wanted the child, could be counted upon to discover that they loved the dear little one more passionately than life itself and couldn't bear the thought of parting with him, that is for less than several hundred thousand lire to soothe their broken hearts.

Then, if by a combination of miracles and good fortune one might get a child *out* of Italy, I was warned that the problem of getting him into the United States was an even greater one, requiring nothing less than an act of Congress.

With a gambler's heart I said I would try for an act of Congress. Since there was obviously no chance of Franco's accompanying me to America in ten days, I would have plenty of time to consult a member of Congress.

The idea of that austere body's taking time from its solemn responsibilities on behalf of little Franco appealed to my imagination. Once everything was in order, I would return to Italy for Franco.

I wrote to the schoolmaster asking him to locate Franco's parents and get their permission. He replied in two days. The mother was not to be found. The father, however, was in Naples. Indeed, he had said, he would be very happy for his little pigeon to go to America, providing, of course, that he was also adopted so that he could accompany his favorite child, from whom he could not bear to be parted. The father, who was nine years my junior, was adamant. No papa, no Franco. His sudden paternal attachment for Franco apparently did not include his two younger children, whom he quite willingly would have left alone in Naples. The situation was hopeless. Because the Italian law was on his side, I was forced to abandon plans to bring Franco to America.

V

On Friday, two days before my sailing, I said good-by to Rome and went to Naples. It was my last train ride through the Italian landscape and I watched it with a broken heart. The day was warm and the hills were alive with country people harvesting olives and oranges and watching their cattle and sheep. Along the tracks brown men lunching on *panini* stuffed with cheese and greens and, if they were lucky, a bit of meat, waved purple bottles of wine at the train. Women were everywhere, carrying baskets of fruits and vegetables and bottles of oil and wine on their heads. They also waved, as countryfolk do who live by the railroad but seldom ride on it.

A psychologist in Zurich once told me I had the soul of a peasant. He must have been right, for the people I loved most in Italy were the farmers and shepherds, the fishermen, and the growers of olives and wine. Married to the sun, the soil, and sea, they are people who have not alienated themselves from the earth mother or from God. Now as I passed them, I felt as if they were waving a farewell to me whom the train was hurrying to the end of an odyssey among them. Although I had never met them, I felt I knew them, and I loved them as friends.

All too soon we were in Naples. In the station I was attacked by the usual ragged *scugnizzi* who offered me the usual commodities and grabbed at my bags. I had to beat them off with my cane until I was rescued by the schoolmaster, who had come to meet me. We took a final walk through the National Museum and saw a small crucifixion by the Florentine Masaccio, a *Slaughter of the Innocents* by a Sienese, of course, and a Sodoma *Resurrection* in which the fleshly Christ rested his weight on a cloud instead of soaring spiritually toward heaven. We saw the dark-eyed somber Madonna of Pacecco de Rosa, which so strongly resembled my mother as I remember her when she was young and I was a child. Finally we saw Brueghel's ironic faces of human sheep called *The Blind Leading the Blind*, in which two blind men catapult over an embankment and four others follow in good faith to self-destruction.

We ended our tour in the Pompeian and Herculaneum galleries. Walking backward through time, we seemed to be going forward in human hope, for here the mosaics and paintings are a liberation from mysticism and agony, from martyrdom and death. Here it is all life. Every face is a noble one with the eyes looking honestly at you. Each body is beautifully formed and gracefully at ease. Plato converses with his students; Sappho, quill in mouth, reflects on a poem. These healthy and sensual sun worshipers were Mediterraneans caught in the greatness of their youth, the ancestors of her citizens of today. Indeed, as the schoolmaster stood before the paintings, his own strong head and steady eyes were mirrored on the walls.

The lesson of art is a brutal one, and nowhere so brutal as in Naples. On the street outside we met the same faces, but scarred with avarice, hunger, and hate, their bodies frail and twisted. These are also the descendants of the noble race within. Generations of man, each hoping for a rebirth and moving further and further into the abyss. The blind leading the blind indeed!

Over dinner the schoolmaster told me of a crisis at the *casa*. Four of the older boys, Mario among them, had taken to pooling their meager lire to raise the two hundred (thirty-two cents) necessary for a cheap prostitute with whom they crawled into an alley where she served each in rotation. This little enterprise had come to light when one of the boys became infected with gonorrhea. Father Spada's first move was to take the sick boy to a doctor for a penicillin cure; then he had a serious talk with the offenders. The talk had apparently not made a strong impression, the schoolmaster said, for Mario and the other two were still secretly playing their street games.

"I think it would be good if you were to talk to Mario," the schoolmaster said.

The suggestion startled me. If Father Spada had been unsuccessful, how could I do anything?

"Mario is becoming rather a bad boy," the schoolmaster said. "He pays no more attention to us. I think it is possible that he would listen seriously to you. He admires you very much."

The idea of my giving a Dutch-uncle talk to someone who had pimped for a battery of prostitutes at the age of eight was a sobering prospect. The next morning the schoolmaster brought Mario to my hotel. I gave each of them a wool muffler which I had brought from Rome. In a curious little gesture Mario kissed his twice and then wrapped it jauntily about his throat. The schoolmaster began to weep. "We are very poor in Naples," he said. "You see we do not often get gifts for Christmas."

Mario invited me to come with him to visit his mother. Being the widow of a fisherman, the mother lived close to the sea. We wound our way through bombed tenements along the harbor. It was a chilly morning, but thinly clad children wandered around barefoot and an old lady sat in the morning sun, peeling tobacco from a harvest of cigarette butts as if she were shelling peas. We entered a smoky black tenement gaping with bomb pits and climbed several flights of crumbling stairs. Mario led us into a cavernous dark flat with old paper cartons serving as walls. Gaping holes five stories above the street were patched with cardboard and rags. There was no glass. The kitchen, charred by the smoke of chimneyless cooking, had no water or sanitation. Unwashed cooking pots were piled about a stone hearth.

It was colder and damper in this dark cave than outdoors. Living there were Mario's mother, a younger brother, a sister with three girl babies, and the sister's husband, a merchant seaman, home only three or four times a year. The ragged children, sticky with running noses, had the sick and listless look of the children in the black Capodimonte grottoes. It was what Mario, aged seven, had fled from to live in the streets.

Obviously *la mamma* had once been handsome. Except for the absence of teeth she did not look like the fifty-two-year-old mother of fourteen children. Unlike her children, who spoke only a raucous Neapolitan, she talked cultured Italian with a soft Lombardian voice. She had the gentility of the north, a quality which set her apart from her sordid environment. Mother and son embraced each other. One could see that Mario, so much like her, was the mother's favorite child.

The most presentable corner of the flat was partitioned for the daughter's bedroom. There the mother served us "*caffè*," chicory that was strong and black and very pleasant. Brass cupids entwined about the bed and a shrine of St. Anthony, patron saint of children, burned over it. There were photos on the walls, wedding pictures of other daughters, snapshots of sons in seamen's uniforms, and a large fading one of the moustachioed father.

After the *caffè*, the mother brought us tiny glasses of a strawberry liqueur of her own making. It was rose colored and sweet. She talked of Mario and the sorrow he had been for her. "He was never a happy child, even though I did everything for him I could," she wailed. "When he left to live in the streets, I wept and I prayed for him, walking all night to look for him, but he would not come home. Who could blame him; it was ugly here, we were always poor. He went into the streets to search for better things. What he found was only evil things, bad people and wicked deeds."

Mario squirmed uncomfortably at her side, his face blushed scarlet. To distract *la mamma* I suggested she come into the street so I could take some photographs of herself and her son. The faces of the two older *bambini* were scrubbed and they were taken along.

La mamma posed straight and proud, her arm on her son's shoulder. After I had photographed the children, I said good-by. *La mamma* took my hand and burst into violent weeping. "Please, good sir," she begged, "take my boy to America. It is the only way he will become a good boy. In Naples life is ugly; there is no life for him here. If he must stay here, he will be a bad boy and live an evil life. There is nothing a mother can do to prevent it. For myself, it makes no difference. My life will soon be over. *Per favore, signore, per favore*, take my boy away from Naples. I would be happy never to see him again if I knew he will make himself into a good man."

I fumbled for words of reassurance, promised I would do what I could, but I had had enough of tears. With Neapolitans it was always laughter or tears. Naples had dehydrated me completely. I stopped in a bar to collect myself over a *Cinzano*. Mario calmly ate pastries. I told the schoolmaster I wished to buy some Christmas toys for Franco and the smaller *scugnizzi*, but the schoolmaster said it would not be wise, that private possessions at the *casa* only aroused jealousies and made trouble. Franco needed some warm gloves, the schoolmaster said, and I might buy him those. Not being able to buy a toy for Franco made me very sad. I was thinking of my last Christmas in the United States spent with three small nieces, of how the living room looked like a toy store and how, even before Christmas dinner, the grand destruction began.

The schoolmaster excused himself, saying he had to finish arrangements for the Christmas party that evening. Then I realized it was time for my talk with Mario. We wandered into the little streets above the Galleria, weaving in and out of the teeming Neapolitan humanity, past openhearthed tinkers' shops, counters of marvelously colored fruit and vegetables, the tables of macaroni hucksters. It was Saturday noon, the weekend was under way. The streets were filled with sailors, mostly American, some quietly pursuing their solitary hunt, others, in pairs and trios, already drunk, followed by the inevitable escort of yapping *scugnizzi*. "*Come durante la guerra* [Just like it was in the war]," Mario said.

We found a *trattoria* where Mario ate the usual *bistecca*; I had liver cooked in the Venetian manner with onions. Conversation between Mario and me was not easy. But he understood my Italian better than I understood his Neapolitan, and the subject of women came up easily enough, for Mario was distracted from his *bistecca* by every woman under thirty that passed the restaurant. I prodded the Don Juan in him and soon he was telling me about his sordid alley tomcatting.

"Did it please you?" I asked.

He shrugged. "Of course not. Such women are dirty dogs. It is over in a minute, like a rooster covering a hen!"

"Then why bother?" I asked him. Any Italian would think my question absurd, and Mario was no exception.

"A man's got to have a woman," he said.

I might as well have ordered the Tiber to flow north as to suggest chastity to a Neapolitan.

"How would love please you?" I asked.

"If I had a job with enough money to have a *fidanzata* who would love me, that would please me." It was the Italian male's concept of love; always "who would love me," not "whom I might love."

"You say a man must have a woman," I said. "But you are not yet a man. First you must make yourself a man by learning a trade, so that you can make a life for someone who will love you, so you can support a wife and *bambini*."

"Perhaps if I were in America?" Mario asked.

He was right. I was speaking to him as I would to a boy at home where young men *can* learn trades and where jobs exist.

"In Italy too," I said. "One can make a man of himself in Italy as well as in America. America does not welcome men with bad characters. If one day you would like to be a good American, you must prove you can be a good Italian first. You don't do that by crawling into alleys with prostitutes."

"Are there no prostitutes in America?"

"Certainly there are. There are prostitutes in America as there are in every country. But in America, sixteen-year-old boys who want to live honest and good lives go to school and not to prostitutes."

"When they come to Naples, the American soldiers and sailors like very much the prostitutes," Mario said.

I felt I was muffing it badly. But I had promised the schoolmaster.

"There are different kinds of Americans, just as there are different kinds of Italians," I said. "One must take as an example the kind he would most like to be and work hard to make himself like that."

"If I do not go with prostitutes again, will you help me to go to America?"

Again the inevitable, heartbreaking question which I was asked at least once every day of my fourteen months in Italy. How could one make Mario see, how could one make them all see, that Americans cannot accomplish everything that is asked of them? How could I explain America's caution in not freely welcoming all the homeless people of the world?

"You must show you are worthy." I said. "You must study. Study everything that you can. If you want to go to America you should study English. If you do these things, I will do what I can."

There was still the afternoon ahead of us. I asked Mario what he would like to do.

"*Il cinema,*" he replied promptly.

A movie was not exactly what I had in mind for my last afternoon in Italy, but I was making it Mario's holiday. I asked if there was any film in particular?

"*La Figlia di Nettuno,*" he replied promptly.

Off we went to a dingy movie house showing the currently popular revelation of American life called *Neptune's Daughter*. In the dark theater I studied Mario's face while he watched technicolored bathing girls cavort like dolphins to Xavier Cugat's rumbas and a bronze young man make underwater love to Esther Williams, coming up only for an occasional glass of champagne. Mario's hands gripped the arms of his seat; his wide eyes never left the screen.

"*È bello*," he said, "*far l'amore sotto l'acqua* [Making love under water is beautiful]."

It was not, I said, the customary method in America.

"In a *democrazia* like America anything is possible," Mario said. "I will go to Hollywood and be a friend to Esther Williams. I will swim with her in her pool."

When we left the theater Mario was preoccupied and brooding, no doubt over the fact that tomorrow I was leaving for the wonderful land of aquatic love while he had to remain behind to eat macaroni in the *casa dello scugnizzo* and seek out diseased prostitutes in alleys. We stopped at a haberdasher's so I might buy a hat for shipboard. The shop was near the harbor and the prices were high; obviously it catered to foreign customers. The salesman, bringing out a fancy number, said in smooth English, "Now, this is a style especially designed for men of distinction." As I stood before a mirror the salesman spoke to Mario in Neapolitan and a loud argument developed. Mario, it seemed, was being ordered to leave the establishment as an undesirable person.

"He is here with me," I said. "He is my friend."

The salesman drew me aside. "Sir, you are a very kind man, I'm sure," he said. "But we must warn you. It is very dangerous to associate with street boys like him. One can see he is a bad boy, and it is the custom of his type to cultivate men of distinction like yourself and rob them or things even worse."

We left, with the salesman still babbling about the hat. Mario was wretched with shame and wounded pride. Tears filled his eyes. The implication was clear to both of us: there was little hope for a reformed delinquent in Italy. Nothing I said comforted Mario. We trudged silently to the Christmas party.

VI

The *casa dello scugnizzo* was in *festa* spirit. The *scugnizzi* were dressed in their best clothes, and Father Spada had cut his hair so that he looked as young as Father Borelli. Franco met me at the door; they said he had been waiting all afternoon for *l'Americano*. My party, I learned, was one of three events in a festive week end. First was the *casa*'s brand-new Madonna, which had just arrived. Franco led me to see her in Father Borelli's office. She was of pink and blue plaster; her robe was fringed in gold. Her glass eyes stared like a doll's, and her foot stomped on a green mottled serpent which wound around her leg and extended a long bright red fang at us. It was an artistic outrage of the kind so popular in Naples. The *scugnizzi* were filled with admiration.

"Ah, she is very beautiful!"

"Look at her eyes, so natural, like a real woman's."

"See how finely clothed she is, like a princess."

"Is she not a most beautiful Madonna, signore?"

"Yes," I said. "A beautiful Madonna."

The dining tables had been set up in a jungle of potted palmettos and flowers in the nave. I thought for a moment the floral tributes were in my honor, but the schoolmaster quickly informed me they were for the third event of the week-end: the presentation of a Lambretta motor scooter by the Swiss Frau Weller and her Lucerne charities. A most useful gift for hauling groceries and supplies, the schoolmaster said. It was scheduled for dedication at noon on Sunday. Would I come? Judging from the palmettos, Father Borelli was prepared to make quite a show of the occasion, and I didn't want to miss it.

The party was slow in getting started. The delay was in the kitchen, where the cook, inexperienced and ill-equipped, was struggling to turn out seventy steaks. He finally had them done, many overdone, at nine o'clock. In the meantime, Franco became very tired. Bravely he fought off sleepiness and hunger awaiting the party. The church was cold as usual, and he began to shiver. Finally he started to cry. It was the only time I had ever seen him unhappy and I was sure he must be sick. His little body shook with a chill. We put him to bed and Father Spada brought him some warm milk. He went to sleep almost immediately, missing the party he had looked forward to for a week with so much excitement.

For the rest, it was a roaring success. Some of the smaller boys served as waiters, performing like experienced *camerieri*. In addition to the steaks, there was an abundance of other things: spaghetti, salad, potatoes, fruit, cake, and a great deal of wine served from buckets with tin dippers. I sat at the table with the three priests. No one minded when the boys became mildly drunk and sang bawdy songs. The priests, enjoying the *vino* themselves, reveled in the exuberance.

"They are not normal, none of them are normal," Father Luciano repeated, and Father Spada said, "They are unique, unlike any other people in the world."

Father Borelli, not for a moment forgetting the future, leaned over to ask me if I would call on His Eminence Cardinal Spellman when I arrived in New York to discuss with him the possibilities of emigrating *scugnizzi* to America. I promised Father Borelli I would visit Cardinal Spellman.*

While Father Borelli laid plans, the old church rang with salutes to "Ollywood" and "Brook-lane," two American paradises, of one or the other of which each *scugnizzo* apparently hoped to become a citizen. To *scugnizzi* the map of the United States was nothing but a vast waste land dividing these two capitals, Hollywood and Brooklyn, where all claimed to have relatives.

Suddenly out on the piazza there were several explosions and a horn blared loudly. *Scugnizzi* and priests alike leaped up to tear away the boards that sealed the old portal of the church. With a great burst of noise, Frau Weller's motorcycle, jockeyed by a salesman, bounded up the church steps into the sanctuary. It came to a screeching stop in a cloud of smoke in front of the altar and was immediately surrounded by boys.

"*È bellissima.*" "A beautiful machine." "Look at the speedometer! It will go sixty kilometers." "*Una carina,* a dear thing."

Each *scugnizzo* had his turn on the seat, starting and stopping the motor. Even Father Spada raised his skirt, straddled the seat, and stood on the starter. The church was filled with blue clouds and monoxide fumes. I took my coat and left; in the excitement no one noticed. Behind me the explosions, amplified a dozen times over by the echoing dome, were like a fusillade of cannon fire.

Next day at noon, I returned for the dedication. The square was alive with inquisitive citizenry, gathered to witness it knew not what. The vegetable man's horse was tied to a post; little girls danced their singsong games around the beast. A platoon of uniformed *carabinieri* stiffly guarded the door of the *casa,* and a stream of red velvet carpeting flowed like blood from the heart of the church into the sunlight.

Shortly before noon a delegation of Neapolitan dignitaries and their ladies arrived and paraded through the police lines into the *casa.* A few minutes later, precisely as the bells of Naples pealed twelve o'clock, a caravan of black limousines ceremoniously encircled the piazza and came to a halt before the red carpet.

---

* When I arrived in New York Cardinal Spellman was in Korea. A call to his residence resulted in an interview with the Right Reverend Monsignor Swanstrom of the National Catholic Welfare Conference. Monsignor Swanstrom said he would have a representative from Rome visit the *casa.*

"*Gli Svizzeri,*" *scugnizzi* murmured. "The Swiss are here."

They were indeed. First came Frau Weller, flanked by a red-faced priest and a fat little diplomat in a Chesterfield coat. After them came a dozen gently superior ladies, more than half of whom wore hats with feathers softly curling down from the breasts of geese or stiffly quivering quills from the tails of pheasants. Father Borelli met Frau Weller at the door of the *casa* and escorted her over the crimson carpeting into the nave. Mounted on a red-velvet platform in front of the altar, shining like the ark of the covenant, was the motorcycle. It was surrounded by palmettos and burning candles and covered with a floral spray. On its side were painted the words "*Don de la Charité de Lucerne*" [the gift of Lucerne charity]. Around the vehicle was a circle of chairs. On one side sat the Italians, on the other side the Swiss. The two camps faced each other glumly. *Scugnizzi*, glowing with soap and virtue, lined up like a choir. Behind the altar Antonio and Mario administered a final application of perfumed oil to their hair.

Father Borelli mounted the platform. Like St. George covering the dragon's head, he rested one hand on the seat of the motorcycle. For twenty eloquent minutes the little priest extolled the virtues of the Swiss. He spoke of their nobility and their generosity. Indeed, they were a nation of saints; the world need only be populated with Swiss to make it a paradise on earth. On one side of the room the Neapolitans, believing not a word of it, nodded their enthusiastic approval. On the other side the Swiss, believing every word, pretended to believe none of it. Each time Father Borelli paused for breath, the *scugnizzi*, like well-drilled applauding machines, beat their hands together, the older ones somewhat cynically, the younger ones enjoying the noise they made. Each round of applause was a signal for the Neapolitans to nod and smile at the Swiss; for the Swiss to nod back and blush modestly. On the piazza outside a rooster crowed and across the room Fianco looked at me and started to giggle.

It was a *commedia dell' arte* farce. On one side the Swiss sat in tight-lipped righteousness, so certain that virtue and goodness are tangible things to be weighed like meal and counted like eggs, hating the disorder-liness of the Italians, their unbridled spontaneity, their guiltlessness. On the other side were the Italians, contemptuous of the cult of goodness, of discipline, of frugality and self-denial in the midst of abundance; a people to whom the materials of life, like its passions, are for expending, not hoarding.

So they faced each other, the haves and the have-nots, those who, loving the feast, are absented from the table and those who welcome the feast so they may abstain from it. They faced each other in fear, and because hatred is fear guised as a warrior, they hated each other. Divided by ten feet and a world of misunderstanding, they sardonically played at their comedy of brotherhood.

When Father Borelli stepped down from the platform, the Swiss diplomat stepped up. The motorcycle was nothing at all, he said solemnly, a humble gift to pass between brothers in Christianity. Father Borelli returned to the platform to make still another speech, this one in acceptance. When he had finished, a *scugnizzo* took the wreath of lilies from the motorcycle and handed it to Father Borelli; Father Borelli presented it to Frau Weller, who gallantly returned it to the *scugnizzo*, who returned it to the top of the motorcycle. The crucified Christ looked starkly down from the cross and the sun cast parallel rays through the broken windows, lighting the motorcycle like a holy thing. In a sense it was a miracle I was witnessing: I knew that never again would so many Swiss ride through the pearly gates of paradise on one motorcycle!

An orgy of hand-kissing and picture-taking followed. The Lucerne ladies photographed the *scugnizzi,* pinched the cheeks of the little ones and brushed the sideburns of the older ones. One of the photographers raised little Franco astride the driver's seat. His head ducked forward so he could reach the handlebars; he looked even happier than usual.

It was the last time I saw him, for I left without saying good-by. I had three last hours and I wanted them alone. My American ship was waiting, her red, white, and blue smokestacks rising splendidly above everything else in the harbor. It was warm as June and the Via Roma was alive with the *passeggiata.* Immediately I had an escort, chanting the Neapolitan litany.

"Hey, Joe, wanna change money, wanna buy woman, Joe, nice clean virgin. . . ."

Past the Galleria, past the Teatro San Carlo with its glorious memories of Renata Tebaldi's Violetta, through the colonnaded half-mooned Piazza dello Plebiscito, down the stairs to the bay where American sailors were racing horse cabs and barefoot fishermen were drawing their nets from the sea. The faces changed, but the scene was the same.

I would miss it.

CHAPTER 20

ARRIVEDERCI

> "Our future is temporary."
> —GIUSEPPE PELLA

I ATE MY LAST MEAL in Italy alone in the sun at the Ristorante Zi Teresa on the Santa Lucia wharf where the wine was good and the musicians noisy. A fisherman drew beside my table in his boat to sell me a ride in the bay. I refused, but a Neapolitan can't take no for an answer and this one stood up in his boat and argued.

"I'll give you a beautiful ride around Santa Lucia," he insisted. "An hour for five hundred lire, signore."

His sharp chin almost met his long nose in Neapolitan cunning, as he laughingly persisted in his persuasions.

"In an hour I will sail away on her," I said, pointing to the ship on the other side of the harbor.

"*Lei scherza* [you are joking], signore."

"*No scherzo. Sicuro,*" I said.

He bowed grandly. "*Mi saluti,* signore, on your good fortune. Happy is the man who sails for America. Would that I could go today to paradise and leave my toubles behind."

"You have troubles?"

"Too many, sir. Nine of them calling me *papa,* crying for bread."

"Nine children!"

"*Si,* signore, *e cinque morti,*" he said, proudly adding the five dead ones to the score of his virility. "Where's a poor man to get bread for nine mouths and his own? Where can they sleep when a house has but two rooms? Nine are too many, and still they come, signore."

"Why do you continue to make them?" I asked.

"Ah, signore!" A look of beseeching let's-be-reasonable sadness crossed his face. "What is there for me to do with my time? Does a man with nine little ones have lire for *il cinema*? Can a man without money spend his evenings drinking cognac with friends? Perhaps I could go to Rome to play cards with the Pope? I ask you, signore, what pleasures does a poor man have but the making of babies?"

The fisherman wished me Godspeed as warmly as if I were an old and treasured friend and rowed away to tackle a pair of American sailors at another table. The clamorous musicians approached me with a serenade, but my mind would not be diverted.

II

I was at the end of my sojourn. Now, facing west in the afternoon sun, I had to take stock. After living fourteen months with Italians I no longer thought wholly as an American. There were two of me, an American self and an Italian self. The latter, an articulate, troublesome self, rose frequently from my subconscious to bait me. I had long ago called him Esposito, the name given by Neapolitans to foundlings. Like all Italians, Esposito liked to talk and I often had to pacify him with conversation. He was there now at the table.

Esposito: Well, do I go with you? Do I stow away?

HK: If you did you'd only give me trouble.

Es: I don't need a passport; I'll ride on yours. I hide very well and if you're careful not to expose me no one will know I'm along.

HK: That's not the kind of trouble I mean.

Es: You mean that I'm a disturbing influence?

HK: Definitely.

Es: How would I disturb you?

HK: You'd never let me forget anything. That fertile fisherman, for instance.

Es: Ah! The Malthusian tragedy of Italy. There are forty-seven million of us on our overcrowded peninsula, two thirds of which is mountain and rock. We live in the sun and eat fish and we enjoy simple pleasures. Naturally we are a fertile people. We have four hundred thousand babies a year.

HK: You also have two million unemployed and the figure keeps growing larger. Two thirds of your industries operate at a loss and must be subsidized by your government, which operates in the red. And what do you do? You boast of making babies without giving a thought to what will become of them.

Es: Babies are a field in which we have been accustomed to a certain freedom. Manpower is our traditional export.

HK: But France's trade-unions don't want Italian workers in France and British miners no longer welcome them in England.

Es: And the United States, which used to be happy to absorb our over-flowing population, now has an immigration quota of only 5,645 Italians a year. Your Mr. McCarran pleases our Communist leaders very much. They do not like to have their voting members exported.

HK: The United States does not wish to import Communist voters.

Es: An Italian in the United States is not a Communist. Give him a job and he will become a Republican and dream of being a capitalist.

HK: Even if he votes Communist in Italy?

Es: Don't forget that Italians who work earn one half the salary of a Frenchman, one fourth as much as an Englishman, and one sixth as much as an American. The picture which is so bleak in the cities is even bleaker on the land. You have been in our "deep south" where one half of the land is owned by a handful of rich men and land reform moves at a snail's pace. Communist leaders do not let us forget these things.

HK: Who is at fault if your businessmen and landowners fail to meet their social obligations and give workers a fair reward for their work? Who is responsible for your selfish, untrustworthy, myopic rich with their political corruptions and tax inequities? It seems to me you're always passing the buck for evils that are of your own doing.

Es: No one will deny we have our share of human failings. Naturally it is the rich, not the poor, who can support the government with money, and Americans, by closing their eyes to these things, seem to us to be their conspirators.

HK: At the same time you take for granted everything that America does for you, as if it were an obligation. You seem to forget that we were not allies in the last war, but enemies.

Es: If you mean the money, the average Italian is vaguely aware that America is spending it in Italy, but his life is little touched by it. He sees everywhere the symbols of American life, for our land of Fra Angelico and Leonardo is invaded by Esso stations, billboards, Coca-Cola. Yes, even TV. But the symbols only increase our resentment, for they remind us of what we don't have.

HK: It isn't all Coca-Cola and TV. There are the new apartment houses and hydroelectric plants in Calabria, the Point-Four fertilizer, and the hybrid grains.

Es: The benefits of these things have not yet seeped down to most of us.

HK: Is that why you believe Communists when they tell you American dollars are buying allies for America and making the rich richer?

Es: Let us say we are easily persuaded. The Communists understand far more subtly how to appeal to us than the Americans. They let us talk.

HK: Perhaps they can't stop you.

Es: They listen, which is flattering to us.

HK: They parrot promises which they cannot keep and then they talk of the American betrayal.

Es: They do more than that. They use the United States as her accomplice. They understand changes are in the making in the world, that a new political generation is knocking on the door. Russia makes no loans or gifts. But while you are sending us your billions her agents work away, quietly as gravediggers in the dark, undermining American prestige and making converts of our youth.

HK: The Communists are making their biggest campaign outside the iron curtain in Italy. Naturally they would direct it at the youth who will determine your political future.

Es: What they understand so well is that our youth are *predetermined*. Each year more than a hundred and thirty thousand of them mature and join the unemployed. This includes almost all university graduates. Our spiritual sickness in Italy is a lack of faith. Young men need faith and a belief in political action. They must join something, and the Communists and neo-Fascists are their means of protest. Unless the democratic peoples of the world can give faith to youth, democracy will be lost to the new generation.

HK: I do not see how the Communists, even if they were successful, could make their philosophy work in Italy.

Es: You are right. We are a nation of individualists. We are not materialists, and Communism is materialism. For us Communism would be a terrible tragedy. I think it might even be tragic for the Russians. They would discover we are rather explosive.

HK: Then you admit democracy is preferable?

Es: Always. But it is a sad thing that the sacrifices of World War II should have led to such poor examples of democracy as those of Italy and France. To our youth the last fight has been for nothing.

HK: The next will be worth less unless you realize that what needs changing is not institutions but Man.

Es: That is a lesson for the entire world and not Italy alone. In the family of nations one sick member cannot set about to make herself healthy without the help of the others.

Across the harbor the ship's festive banners shone brightly in the sun. I was thinking of the ceremonies of the motor scooter and the polite words of brotherhood which had been spoken before the *scugnizzi*. A motor scooter from Switzerland; three and a half million dollars from America. What was the good of it when men did not understand each other?

Es: It is a beautiful ship. I'm sure I shall enjoy the voyage very much.

HK: I'm not sure you will.

Es: Why not? I'm a very affable fellow and I make friends easily.

HK: We haven't decided yet that you are going.

Es: You mean you don't want me with you?

HK: It's perfectly obvious you'd be bothering me all the time. I'm going back to take up a job teaching students in a university. It's much better for me to forget you.

Es: I've been with you a long time. You're going to be terribly lonely without me. We understand each other.

HK: Do we?

Es: Don't you think so?

HK: You are a citizen of a land that is Latin, pagan, Catholic, and poor. I come from a country whose culture is Anglo-Saxon, puritan, Protestant, and rich. I've heard you say it a hundred times.

Es: And I've heard you say we are allies united in fighting the dark clouds which threaten the world. I even heard you say it on the radio. Pretty fancy talk, I thought to myself.

HK: What I've seen of allies uniting has been more disheartening than encouraging.

Es: When there is failure the guilt lies on both sides.

HK: You Italians don't even understand each other. You're always talking of "hotheaded Tuscans," "lazy Neapolitans," "snobbish Romans." The poor are divided against the rich, southerners against northerners, nobility against industrialists, Republicans against Monarchists, laity against clergy. In the last elections there were ninety-nine parties on the ballot. With such a record of not understanding yourselves, it's not likely you would understand Americans.

Es: It takes two to tango, remember.

HK: It can't be done as long as Italians think of Americans as technical and financial wizards without culture.

Es: Nor while Americans think of Italy as a nation of spaghetti-eating fruit vendors and stone chiselers. It seems to me Americans fail even more dismally in understanding us than we do in understanding them.

HK: In a minute we'll be calling each other names. Wouldn't it be better to get down to specific points?

Es: Certainly. I'll begin with diplomacy. Your diplomatic colonies over here are miniature American resorts with English-speaking bars, restaurants, movies, and hotels where Americans drink and gossip, read American journals, and live more luxurious lives than they ever would at home. In them diplomats are safely protected from contact with the population of Italy, the little people of which we have such a great majority. Their native friends are the fashionable nobility who speak English and have palaces in which to serve American cocktails, Scotch whisky, and French wines. It does not matter to your diplomats that many of their fashionable friends were also friends of Mussolini's. It is because your representatives spend so much time with them that they seem to be against the people.

HK: There are diplomats who love Italy and have a genuine interest in the problems of your people. I have met them.

Es: Unfortunately they are not the ones that stand out to us. Italy gave the world Pagliacci, who laughs in the face of tragedy. Now we are laughing the same way at a United States Information Service director known to us as *il barone*. A baron is the lowest rung on our nobility ladder. When this American "baron" arrived at his post from America he and his wife made friends with the local nobility, most of them old Fascists. The baron kissed the hands of princesses, invited marcheses to lunch, and went to the opera with countesses. His Italian employees he treated like serfs. Naturally they spread the word, "Americans preach democracy but they don't practice it here." The staff members had to spend so much time making reports for Rome that they had no time to do the things they were making reports about. They gossiped that the baron did not know the difference between a cigar-store Indian and a Michelangelo, and when the USIS in Rome sent Aaron Copland to lecture in his city the baron asked one of his

Italian secretaries, "Who's this guy Copland?" The secretary explained that Mr. Copland was America's very famous composer of symphonic music.

HK: I know about the baron. He has since been removed from his post.

Es: And taken to Rome for an important job there. Diplomats are not the only ones who fail us. Your journalists, who report again and again in your newspapers that Italy is a safe and strong ally, do not see the forest for the trees. Your motion pictures, which are so popular in Italy, show you as a nation of rich and idle wastrels.

HK: That is a Hollywood myth which Americans themselves do not believe.

Es: Your tourists give support to the myth with their arrogance, as if they were superior persons visiting an inferior race.

HK: I've noticed that arrogance is not specifically an American vice. What about the Italian building contractor who was given an American architect's plans for some large-scale modern housing? "Imagine," he said, "they're telling us, the sons of Michelangelo, how to build houses!"

Es: He was being proud, not arrogant. The difference is obvious in our relationship. You give dollars; we take them.

HK: Are you suggesting that we have not given enough?

Es: Enough and not enough. You have done a great deal for us materially but you have failed to see that gifts without understanding can bring you only ill will, that suspicion cannot be halted by bread, that dollars and bullets do not win trust. You spend your billions selling yourselves, but very little making friends.

HK: Would it have been better to have given nothing at all?

Es: No, the gifts are necessary to both of us. For us your generosity is necessary for survival. You are, in comparison with us, unfathomably rich. So many of us must struggle from day to day just to keep alive.

HK: In this struggle we help with our agriculture, our food technology and our medicine.

Es: Because you think of the poor of any land as lower creatures to be given bread if it doesn't cost too much. The world's poor give you a feeling of discomfort and guilt. To you the gifts are necessary as a self-protection.

HK: Obviously you do not think we are humanitarians.

Es: Humanitarians, yes. I think you are the world's greatest humanitarians. But you are very poor humanists.

HK: What do you suggest we do about it?

Es: Share your riches without hoping to create the world in your own image. You must learn that you cannot superimpose the standards of a country as rich as the United States on a land as poor as Italy. Capitalist democracy, so successful in your vast land with its endless resources, cannot be made to work in our small and overpopulated land. The strong middle class which makes your democracy possible and which keeps democratic little Switzerland the most secure country in Europe does not exist in Italy, where a few are rich and many are poor. If we are to survive as a democracy we must look for our model to a more modest country, England perhaps, where many have learned to share little. Your failure to comprehend comes from thinking on too large a scale, from forgetting that behind budgets and programs there are men and women and homeless and hungry children.

HK: You admit that even with our failures Italy needs America.

Es: Yes. But America with all her vigor and technology and wealth also needs Italy. Technology is not a civilization but a tool of civilization. If civilization ever becomes a tool of technology, then civilization and men are doomed. Here on the Mediterranean we had a great civilization at least fifteen centuries before Christopher Columbus left Genoa. This is the meaning of Italy to America and to the world. If Western civilization would save its soul, it must save Italy.

HK: With such a severe opinion of America I do not understand why you want to go there at all.

Es: I am an Italian. I love America. I envy her. Of course I want to go.

HK: What will you do when you get there?

Es: Help you with the job we both have to do. Not to report the things we know, however disagreeable, would be to hide from the people the truth. Are you taking me with you?

HK: I don't see how I can help it.

Es: *Va bene.* Let's go. *Andiamo!*

III

The shadows were lengthening on the water, and across the bay my ship was waiting like a fate. I still had to go to my hotel for my bags. It was a short walk through the heart of the raucous, dirty, treacherous, beautiful city, teeming with vitality and the wondrous high spirit of a people bound together by laughter and lamentation and the eternal Neapol-

itan optimism. At the hotel the schoolmaster and eight *scugnizzi* were waiting to say good-by. Could they, they asked, come with me to the dock so
they might see the inside of the grand American ship? I agreed to try, and
we walked to the dock, a caravan of *scugnizzi*, each one carrying a bag or
two, and I following like an explorer on his way to the jungle.

Guards stopped us at the gate. The boys, they said, could go no farther;
visitors were not allowed on the ship. I knew this was not true. Perhaps
the guards feared the *scugnizzi* would stow away, or perhaps they thought
it necessary to protect the sensibilities of first-class passengers. Whatever
is was, the hour was too late to argue. Porters took my bags and there was
nothing to do but say good-by.

Each of the *scugnizzi* embraced me in his turn. Davido, the reader of
books, was weeping. "How beautiful it is to go to America on such a ship,"
he said. Mario was the last. His eyes too were filled with tears and mute
pleading.

"Send for me to come to America," he begged. He started to follow me
through the gate but the guards held him back.

CHAPTER 21

BY THE DAWN'S EARLY LIGHT

"Send these, the homeless, tempest-tost to me,
I lift my lamp beside the golden door!"
—EMMA LAZARUS

I

THERE WAS NO DENYING IT, I did not want to go home.

For weeks before sailing I had been in a turmoil of indecision. At least once each day I wanted to cancel my ship reservation and wire my university that I would not be back.

Compared to my Italian friends, my American friends seemed remote and cold. Their letters were filled with fears of an atomic war, with stories of air-raid drills in New York, of private bomb shelters in the suburbs, of fierce snow and ice storms lashing across the country. Why return to things such as these from a land where a June sun shone in December? Why leave a land where people poor in worldly things could still live richly together to return to a country where people, rich beyond their own comprehension, lived in a dark night of fear and anxiety?

Yet, here I was, going home. As the guest of my government, I had been on the most extravagant and enriching journey of my life. An inner compulsion, a sense of responsibility was drawing me back, in the hope that my experience might cast a ray of light on the problems of our time. The time had come when I could do more for Italy by going home than by remaining there. Standing now on a lonely spot on the upper deck, waiting for the ship to pull out of the harbor, I promised myself more fervently than I had promised the *scugnizzi* that I would return to Italy.

Darkness had fallen. On the crowded decks below, departing Italians sobbed; their relatives sobbed even louder on the pier. A conclave of twenty nuns waved white handkerchiefs to two departing sisters. The ship's orchestra played "The Sidewalks of New York" and "Deep in the Heart of Texas." The whistles blew and the orchestra played "Auld Lang Syne."

When I felt the ship slip gently away I could no longer bear it. Like the Neapolitans, I wept.

"*Ma lei non è Italiano!*"

I was being addressed by a pleasant frumpy woman of middle years.

"No, signora, I am an American," I said.

"You like Italy?" she asked in Italian.

"Very much, signora."

"You are not happy to return to your own country?"

"I am very sad to say good-by to Italy."

"Signore, you have a good character."

I thanked her for such a quick and favorable appraisal.

"I saw you arrive with your friends," she said. "Neapolitans are very shrewd judges of character. When they like *uno straniero,* he must be a good man."

We introduced ourselves. She was *Dottoressa* Esther Panetta, a professor of languages at the University of Rome.

"I am very happy," the *dottoressa* said. "You see, I am going to your great land for the first time. I am going to study at the University of Columbia as the guest of your government under a very noble plan of your Senator Fulbright."

So it was hail and farewell! The people on the pier became smaller and smaller until they looked like a colony of insects. The orchestra played "Jingle Bells" and from an American cruiser anchored in the bay, homesick sailors shouted, "A Merry Christmas and a Happy New Year!" Between us and Naples the night mists were descending like a scrim.

Already I seemed to be in America. The luxurious ship with its Otis elevators, its Brentano's bookshop, and its Helena Rubinstein beauty salon was as American as Fifth Avenue. My cabin was like a suite in a modern Manhattan apartment hotel. The heat stifled me, and I tried to open a porthole. It didn't open. The deck steward, an unfriendly Cuban-American named Diego, explained that the temperatures were automatically controlled and showed me the thermostat. I was, it seemed, hermetically sealed. The claustrophobic loneliness was too much to endure. I wandered through catacombs of gray and salmon-colored corridors, past gyms, ballrooms, a hospital, a Saks Fifth Avenue department store, until I found what I was seeking. The bartender was loudly vilifying Dean Acheson to some well-dressed customers who swore that what he said was the truth. I was, indeed, in America.

After a few Martinis I went down to ask the dining-room steward to put me at an Italian-speaking table. He served me well. My mess-mates were a Sicilian bride en route to join her New York husband; a first generation Italo-American college girl returning from a visit with Italian relatives, and an Italian businessman. The two girls, already at table, were a strange pair. The collegiate, whose name was Margaret, wore levis with one leg rolled to the knee and sandals without heels. She wore no make-up and her long dark hair was in a snarl. The bride, Maria, was frilled and flounced; she glistened with gold bracelets, brooches, pendants, and rings which she wore self-consciously like a child showing off. She was about twenty, blonde, pretty—if you like the type—and stupid. I had never known an Italian girl like her.

She talked freely about one thing—herself. She was the daughter of a Ragusa landowner, obviously rich, and she did not want to go to America. When she said this, she wrinkled her nose delicately as if America smelled bad. The course of Maria's sheltered life had changed decisively five months before when a young Brooklyn printer of Sicilian parentage decided to take a wife. Wanting a girl just like the one that married dear old dad, he set out for Ragusa, his mother's home town.

"For two weeks he searched everywhere in Ragusa," Maria said. "All the girls wanted to go to America and he could take whatever girl he desired. But he found no girl that pleased him.

"Then he saw me." Maria stopped and blushed. "It was at the feast of my saint, Maria Magdalene. I was praying in the church, and when I was finished, he followed me into the square. I did not like him and I would not let him speak to me. For a month he came to see my mother and father. He said he had made up his mind that no other girl in the world would please him. I did not permit him to see me, but after a month . . ." Maria fluttered her hands in a you-know-how-it-is manner. "He was very ardent and I said yes. All the other girls in the town were angry as cats. We married immediately and he returned to New York. I stayed as long as I could in Sicily. . . ." With more blushes her eyes lowered modestly to her ripening stomach. "Four months already," she said.

In Sicily, more so even than in Italy, a pregnant woman is the center of her universe. She is cajoled, spoiled, and humored. A whole set of superstitions surround her and each of her relatives becomes her slave. It was apparently what Maria expected of all her shipmates. "When I write my husband he is *estatico*," she continued her story. "Immediately I must come to him in an airplane. I write him that I will not go on an airplane. It would have a bad effect on the baby."

The businessman was of medium height with a suave, continental manner. His elegantly tailored clothes fit tightly over his muscular frame. He bowed formally to the girls, said his name was Fagioli and sat down. While he was ordering a French wine, suddenly, without any warning, Maria screamed.

She was pointing to the waiter. "*Il Negro!*" she gasped and screamed again. It was altogether too clear what was the matter. She was frightened by the Negro waiter. "*È brutto,*" she cried. "Ugly!" The waiter, who was as terrified as she, disappeared. Fagioli explained the situation to the headwaiter and soon another waiter appeared, an Italo-American who could talk to Maria in Italian.

"I cannot look on an ugly black Negro," Maria said. "If I do my baby will be black."

She was her simpering, primping self again, happy in the waiter's attentions, giggling with him over how she must "eat for two." The waiter translated the large menu for her. She wrinkled her nose over it. He brought her a delicately browned filet mignon; she sulked and pushed it aside. He carried it back and brought her some turkey. It also was not to her taste. He returned that and brought her some veal which suited her even less.

"American cooking is *brutto*," she said. "It is impossible for me to eat it."

Obviously Maria was geared to hate everything even remotely associated with America. My own thoughts went back to the wretched hunger I had seen in Sicily, of the lean poverty of my friends there. I was finding Maria a little hard to take. My resentment was mild, however, compared to Fagioli's. In his individual English he said, "She will make for her husband a great joy under his Christmas tree. I am very sorry for him. He will wish very much, I think, that he had stayed in America when he decided to have a wife."

After dinner Fagioli and I remained behind for a brandy. He was a delightful fellow who came of a wealthy Milan family. In his youth he had been an expert swimmer, but now "the breathe, it comes too short from too much cigarette." He showed me photographs of his low-slung racing car as other men show pictures of their children. Fagioli was forty-six years old, which he certainly didn't appear, and a bachelor. Marriage had never entered his mind, he said, because "it is to make yourself an old man to take a wife." Although marriage didn't interest him, women did. In addition to fast cars, his sporting life was divided between the stalking of two widely diverse species: women and sharks. He didn't fish the fish, he hunted them.

"I like especially to hunt of the family of sharks who is very aggressive," he said. "I walk on the floor of the sea. I go way downstairs very deep, into the underwater caves of Portofino where live the tiger sharks that are forty feet long. I am not scared of the shark and he is not scared of me. The shark is very stupid. Once I see big one but I have no bait, so I just put a towel on a hook and he eat and I catch.

"When I am downstairs in the sea, I am naked, with rubber fins on my feet and a glass helmet on my head. The shark is think I am another fish. He think I am a fish *simpatico* who will not eat him, so he does not eat me. I have a gun with which I shoot an arrow with a rope in it. When I have shot I go quickly to the upstairs with the rope, for the fish has great resistance to die and when he feels arrow in him, he is somewhat angry. Once I shoot one almost in two, but he get away. The next time I am walking downstairs in the ocean, I see him swimming about cut almost in two. He was a fish to look at very funny."

Although Fagioli had to forgo shark hunting on his frequent trans-atlantic trips, he managed to find other diversions. He had a subtle and diabolical fascination for adventuresome ladies. Women passing our table always hesitated; a few stopped dead in their tracks. He was no less stirred than they. Whenever an attractive woman moved into his magnetic field he bristled like a supercharged sexual Geiger Counter.

Fagioli invited me to join him for some shipboard sport. I accepted and he briefed me on a few essentials.

"Pretty women is stupid like sharks," he said. "They does not require much bait. It is the same as shark, upstairs in first class they are not very hungry. It is necessary to go downstairs to second and third class. Downstairs they are more appreciate and *simpatici* and more natural than first class. On a trip I usually catch two or three very pretty fish, but is better if they are not in same class as each other."

We made a speculative survey of the dining room and came to rest simultaneously on a dazzling sight. Sitting at a table in the center of the room was a cool young Sheba. Her skin was alternately pink and olive, depending on the lights. She had dazzling blue eyes and hair that was pulled by a ribbon to the back of her head, where it burst into a profusion of sunlight. She wore a dress of rainbow colors and a golden stole across her shoulders. I was entranced and so was Fagioli.

"The heart of a chrysanthemum," I said.

Fagioli surveyed her with a sporting eye. "A type very difficult," he said. "She makes of virginity a great treasure."

The Sheba caught our stares and coolly lowered the stole to show off her bronzed shoulders. With slow indolence she lit a cigarette and offered the gold lighter to her companion, a formidable-looking dark woman of middle years, dressed in black.

Fagioli seemed to be regaining his swimmer's breath. "Is I think her mother," he said. "A situation very difficult." We asked the dining steward for the women's names. They were indeed mother and daughter. The girl's name was Maira Kismet; the mother's, Fatima Kismet. They were from Istanbul. Fagioli shrugged. "Is better downstairs," he said. I wasn't fooled. Our partnership, so newly formed, was, in the case of the Kismets at least, already dissolved. It was going to be an open competition. Fagioli suggested that we go to a Jane Russell movie. "I have some interest in the contours of Miss Russell," he said. The film was a stupefying affair and after I made sure that Maira Kismet was not there, I excused myself and went to my cabin.

Sleep was not easy. I had still to accustom myself to American comforts. My cabin was excessively hot, so I turned down the thermostat. Several hours later I awoke sneezing; the cabin was frigid, and an icy blast of wind was blowing over me from the register directly over the bed. There was nothing to do but turn the thermostat up.

When I awoke again in a sweat, I knew I was catching cold. I rang for Diego. It was obvious he was prepared for my complaints, but he was in no mood to deal with them.

"Where I sleep is all cold," he said. "No heat at all. Maybe you like to sleep there."

"My concern at the moment is not your sleeping arrangements but mine," I said. "This cabin is a pneumonia trap."

"You are, I think, a little nervous," he said. He looked at my typewriter and the books on my desk, planted himself firmly in front of me and, flailing like a windmill, elaborated on his point.

"I got no school, not one day in my life do I go to school. Never once in my whole life am I sick. Never do I even spik to a doctor. I spit on doctors." He demonstrated this by spitting on the thick cabin rug.

"Why am I never sick?" he shouted. "Is because I am good Cattolick. I don't drink. I don't smoke. I don't do the other thing too much and I don't read books. I am in America for twenty-three year and I am not sick one whole day in my life. America is sick! America is crazy! The whole world is crazy. Everyone want to shoot gun all the time, and women is lousy. I got a son, he is nineteen year old, and he say to me, 'Dad, I cannot marry a woman.' Why, I ask my son, can't you marry a woman? He said, 'Dad, you don't know, but all American girls want to do all the time is make the sex. Just the sex all the time.' The world is crazy. I am fifty-two year old and never read a book and am good Cattolick and I am not once sick. I spit on books."

I was afraid he would spit again, on the Boswell's *Journals*, which I had borrowed from the ship's Brentano's. I was convinced that he was demented.

"All I want is to have this wind shut off," I said.

"Is no possible. When is shut there is no air and you die of sophistication."

Nevertheless he went into the shower and soaked a towel, which he pushed, dripping wet, into the air vent. It slowed down the gale considerably. As he worked, his anger turned from me to the shipping company.

"Is crazy thing, this air conditioning. On every trip is catch cold and last time three pneumonia. You are lucky is winter. In summer is much worse."

He stepped to the door. "I am good Cattolick," he said. Then he departed, leaving me to die of sophistication.

In the morning I went to see the purser. Diego, he said, was inclined toward temperament but was really very kindly. As for the air conditioning, I would accustom myself to it in a day or so. Everyone did. At breakfast the next morning, however, Fagioli said dryly, "This air conditioning is one of the lesser triumphs of your American science. For Europeans, who have not the habit of American heating, it is a foretaste of *l'inferno*."

II

Whatever disaster lay ahead, for the time being at least, things were as blithe and gay as the shipping line's advertisements in *Holiday* magazine. The Mediterranean was warm and serene. On deck, passengers swam in a pool surrounded by Christmas trees. On the second night out the captain had his cocktail party. Without telling Fagioli, I arranged with the purser to be introduced to Maira Kismet. Feeling adventuresome, I dressed for the encounter in white summer flannels. Following Oriental protocol, I was presented first to Madame Fatima Kismet, who was as forbidding as I expected. Maira, on the other hand, was even more enchanting. She was wearing the rainbow dress without the stole and a heavy bracelet. "Is very old," she said. "Like you say, to chain a slave." Her musical voice cascaded in a stream of unique and captivating English.

"We go to make visit to my aunt on West Seventy-third Street in New York," she said. "America to go is what I have always dreamed. I like so much zee American ladies, and I like also zee American men. I luf especially zee American language. It was such a sadness to get the visa. We wait a long time and then one day it is come and we go. Of course, I like Istanbul, but I think I will like so very much more zee New York and all zee America. I think I will like also quite much zee California. But more than anything in America I want to meet zee men," said Maira, blushing like a rose. "I luf all zee men have, I luf their manners and their eyes and their clothes and their voices. I hope zee men American will like me a small."

I swore fervently zee American men would. A waiter asked Maira what she would drink.

"I will take a coffee," she said.

There was no coffee, he explained; it was a cocktail party.

"Then you will bring me please a cocktail."

"What kind of cocktail?" the waiter asked. She flipped her wrist at him. "Any cocktail is good," she said.

The waiter returned with a tray of Martinis. Maira drank three in fifteen minutes. "Is my first time a cocktail," she said. "I think they are not very sweet. Perhaps much in America is not very sweet."

The orchestra was playing a Viennese waltz. I asked Maira to dance. She asked permission of her mother, who gave it grudgingly. As we whirled away, Maira said, "I am only child, zee papa is dead, and my mother, she love me too much, never she let me to go with myself. It is very difficult, zee life." Soon we were alone on the floor. The orchestra continued its medley, waltz after waltz.

"They are thinking we dance very beautiful," Maira said. "I luf very much zee waltz. I am not even a small tired."

Along a wall I saw Fagioli.

"Nor am I tired," I said.

"I have for me a new gown from Paris," Maira whispered. "Is much more beautiful than this one and I hope zee men in America will like me in it. Maybe even you will like me in it just a small."

In a rash gesture of sportsmanship, when the dance was ended I introduced Maira to Fagioli. He bowed, clicked his heels, and kissed her hand. "Countess," he said.

"But I am of course not a countess," Maira said.

"If nobility were beauty, you would be a queen," he said.

"You are man very polite," she told him.

The purser brought another man to the table, a tuxedoed Mr. Beach from Kansas City. Mr. Beach was in insurance; his territory, he said, went all the way to Oklahoma City.

"How very interest," Madame Kismet murmured, appraising him judiciously. By occupying the Madame Mr. Beach made it possible for Maira and me to have our next drink at the bar. Alcohol had loosened Maira's tongue. Candidly she confessed the purpose of the American trip.

"Is to find a husband, we make zee trip."

"For your mother?"

"You make of me zee joke. You think maybe I have very innocent?"

"But aren't . . . Haven't you?"

"Is my mother's fault. She make all zee men think I have very innocent. She think American man like Turkish man will to marry only innocent girl. In Turkey is not possible for girl to make marry two time if she have already one. So it is better to go to America."

Things were moving too fast for me. Maira continued her confession. "You see when I have but nineteen, I make marry with a Turk. He would seem very nice and has a villa and is professor of architecture. Mamma like him, and so we make marry. But he is very cold and for me make great *soffer*, very much I *soffer*. So I make divorce and we take visa for America."

"You are much too young for such an experience," I said.

"I am no more young," she said. "Is too old in Turkey to make marry, so must go to America for zee husband. Zee visa, it is only for three months, so must find quick zee husband. Then I will stay in America forever and make of me an American."

"Why is America so honored?" I asked.

"Is very romantic, zee American man. In Istanbul I have best friend, a girl who is older. She dream of zee American men. During war comes to Istanbul a rich handsome soldier of America and marry her and take her to New York. She is very much happy. Already she have made for him three babies."

Maira sighed with romantic rapture, and then showed that she could be objective, even about her best friend. "I do not understand what he see for to marry with her. She is not pretty at all. She have very funny nose. But of course, she is very good girl."

Faithful to her American dream, Maira had already turned down one proposal in Italy. "When we arrive in Rome there was young man in railroad station. He was much kind, he help us find water and show us how to go. Very soon he say he luf me very good and would I make marry with him. But I say, 'I don't know you and I will not make marry with you because I will to marry with an American.' He was very noble and said, 'I will wait for until death for you.'"

I was interested in the strategy with which Maira and her mother proposed to find the dream prince.

"He will be like a professor of medicine from a high aristocratic family with great riches," Maira said. "We will be acquainted by he come to take a tea with us at zee house of my aunt, and then we can go to his family to take a tea. This will be zee beginning for zee relations. I hope of course that we should go to zee theater and zee night club and do zee gay things like it is in America, but mamma does not like."

Tea drinking was hardly standard American procedure for snaring a husband in three months, but looking at the radiant Maira through a haze of Martinis, anything seemed possible. I even fancied myself in the role of a suitor. There was no doubt about it, Maira could liven up the pedantic life of a midwestern university professor. The idea seemed to have crossed mamma's plotting mind too. She asked me my profession.

"A professor!" I said, hitting it hard.

"Of medicine?" mamma asked.

"Of speech," I replied.

"Then is necessary in America professors for speaking?" mamma asked witheringly.

"Is why I think zee American men speak so beautiful," Maira said bravely. Mamma ignored her.

"Your family, they live in New York?" she asked.

"In Wisconsin," I answered.

"Is then a country place?"

It certainly was. I spared her the details of the Holsteins and Leghorns.

"Maybe," ventured mamma, "they will come to New York and take a tea."

It wasn't likely.

Mr. Beach, in the meantime, was extolling the beauties of Kansas City.

"Mother and I would sure like to have you drop in on us," he said. "Glad to show you the town. Even drive you down to Oklahoma City and show you an oil well."

"Is very interest, zee oil well," mamma said. "We will of course see all zee America." Then, moved no doubt by Mr. Beach's mature wisdom, she confided in him her fears for Maira's welfare in America. "She is so much innocent and in America zee girls is too much free."

Mr. Beach knew the answer. "You know, you're just gonna have to let her loose from the apron strings," he said.

"Zee apron strings?" Mamma was puzzled.

"Yeah. Teach her to be self-sufficient. Let her take care of herself. What"—Mr. Beach paused to make his point—"what if you should *drop dead* tomorrow? What would happen to her then?"

Madame drew herself up in horror. The conversation froze. I felt a twinge of real compassion for Madame. Mr. Beach, however, thawed quickly. "You know, you don't look like a Turk at all," he said to Maira.

"But I have only three-of-a-fourth Turk," Maira said. "I have had one grandmother from Vienna."

So that was it! In Maira Oriental beauty had been melted down and recast in gold by the blood of a blonde grandmother from Vienna. The orchestra played another waltz. "It is why perhaps I luf so great zee waltz," Maira said, "because I am one-of-a-fourth Viennese."

I bowed to mamma and led Maira on the floor. As we danced she told me of her plan to remain in America, should the three months not produce the rich and aristocratic prince.

"I will make of me a nurse in a hospital. They have much need of nurse, no? I am very fine for making zee sick. I will do many good works and then they will let me remain in America."

The orchestra played "White Christmas."

"Is song of zee Christmas feast, no? I am of course *Muslim*, but I like very much interest in your Jesus religion. It give me great joy to arrive in America for zee feast of zee Jesus birth."

Two lovely tears, like pearls on a Christmas tree, rolled down Maira's cheeks, one from each eye.

"It make me very much to cry to think of zee sweet little Jesus baby just born," she said.

III

Next day we passed Gibraltar into the open Atlantic. It was the end of the idyl. The weather turned wet and stormy; the winter sea was rougher than it had been in years. The ship's newspaper reported we were four hours ahead of schedule and gaining all the time. The ship was vibrating so violently passengers were calling her the S.S. *Bendix*. In the morning stewards distributed boxes of Kleenex to the cold sufferers; by noon passengers were beginning to be seasick. One of the first victims was Maria, the Sicilian bride. She went to the hospital and stayed there for the rest of the trip. At dinner time the dining room was two thirds empty. Among those absent were Maira and her mother, both sick in their cabin.

The next day things were even worse. "Is most terrible trip in my experience," Fagioli said. He also complained of no *divertimento* downstairs. "The ladies is all sick with the stomach," he reported. "Is no good love when stomach is bad." By a rigorous routine of light eating, no drinking, and much sleep, I was holding my own stomach together. The only first-class passenger who wasn't affected at all was a ruddy, vigorous priest of middle years named Father Gleason. This gray-haired man of God was on the side of the angels, no doubt about it. In the midst of so much despair his heartiness was disconcerting. At six each morning he arose to say Mass in the ship's chapel. After a breakfast of buckwheat cakes and sausages he worked out in the gym, played ping-pong, shuffleboard, and something called bullboard. At lunch, while others toyed with a bowl of broth, he ate three-inch sirloins with fried potatoes. After that, wearing a turtle-neck sweater, he loped about the deck like an Olympic runner, while everyone else huddled miserably in deck chairs. After dinner he sang Irish songs over a beer, or recruited hands for canasta or bridge. One night I joined him for bridge.

My partner's name was Bill Palmer; he was a tall, elegant man with a coldly arrogant face, a bloodless pallor, and deep-set blue eyes. His black suit and tartan vest, monogramed shirt, and knit tie were perfectly tailored to his emaciated frame. He wore a trifle too much monogramed jewelry and spoke with a slow, tired voice. I guessed his age to be about thirty-five. He played good bridge; after the game we went to the bar for a drink on our winnings. There he told me he was a dancer and had ended an engagement in a Rome night club to spend Christmas with his mother in America.

Was he an American? I asked.

"Oh, my, yes," he said. Under the fluorescent lighting of the bar he looked like a prize-winning display at an embalmer's convention. "*Very* American! We are Mayflower. Southern Mayflower."

I raised my highball. "Merry Christmas," I said.

"I'm not *really* up here, you know," he said. "I'm second class, but the purser is very nice and lets me use the lounges up here. Down *there*, there are such common people."

"Rough, isn't it?" I said. "The way there are common people all over."

"The dining steward is a bastard," Bill said. "He wouldn't let me eat up here, even though I told him I'd be traveling first class if I hadn't bought that terribly expensive Jacques Fath gown in Paris. . . ."

I gagged on my bourbon.

". . . for my mother for Christmas. It's amaryllis with a sequin train.

Boston's never seen a dress like it. I adore buying dresses for my mother. She measures like a doll. Mother and I always go dancing when we date."

"She must be a very extraordinary lady."

"She is! We're going dancing Christmas Eve at El Morocco."

"What a nice thing to do with one's mother on Christmas Eve!" I said.

"Oh, yes, isn't it? You can imagine how excited I am. I haven't seen her for two years! She's thirty-six and she doesn't look it at all. . . ."

For the second time I choked on my drink.

"I'm twenty. Mother was sixteen when I was born. She divorced immediately. I've never met my father, but everyone says I am the image of him. I've had three stepfathers named Peters, Plympton, and Phillips. Mother always marries men whose names begin with "P" so she doesn't have to change the initials on her luggage. We're from Memphis. When I was sixteen, mother took me to Hollywood to be in pictures. Then mother married in Boston—that was Phillips—and wired me to come to Harvard. But Harvard was stuffy about having me so mother sent me abroad to study dancing. It was terrible being away from her. I was so depressed."

"Now you'll get back just in time to be drafted," I said.

"Oh, horrors! Do I look like the military type to you?"

I admitted he didn't. "What are your plans?" I asked.

"Dance with mother," he said. "I suppose one day I shall marry a rich woman. Older, of course. You can only find those in America."

"Ever thought of going it on your own?"

"You mean work?" he asked incredulously. *"Never!"*

The bar was closing. "Well," Bill said when we parted, "it's down to the masses!"

IV

Next day I met another twenty-year-old in cabin class, an Italian named Giorgio Francesco. He was part of a group of seasick immigrants who were having a miserable time. They spoke no English and the crew, anticipating no tips, ignored them. The ship's doctor was too busy to give them much time.

I went down and found a row of sick young men huddled miserably in deck chairs, preferring the cold, wet outdoors to their foul cabins. All had affidavits from American relatives who had agreed to support them when they arrived and help them start life in the new land. Least ill of the group was the youngest, a solemn twelve-year-old named Teodoro. He and his brother Mario, aged fifteen, were on their way to "Artfore, Connatekut" to join their father, a shoemaker who had emigrated ten years before. Their mother and two sisters were still in Naples. The most wretched one was a small youth in a threadbare suit who lay knotted in a cramp with a blanket covering his face. *"O, mamma mia, perchè non ho viaggiato in aereoplano* [Mother of Heaven, why didn't I go by airplane]?" he groaned to himself.

Little Teodoro watched him soberly and said, "Giorgio thinks he is going to die before he arrives in America."

I tried to reassure Giorgio he wasn't going to die. He told me he had eaten nothing but a few oranges from his suitcase for three days. Though there was nothing on his stomach to rise, he was convulsed with vomiting spasms. I gave him some dramamine pills. In a few minutes he relaxed. Then I went to the dining steward and arranged for the Italians to be served some milk and soft-boiled eggs on the deck at lunchtime.

When I returned to see them in the afternoon they were feeling better. Giorgio's face was less pinched, his eyes were alive with interest. He asked where I lived, and if I'd ever been in "New Rokeyle." I asked him to write it, and it turned into New Rochelle, where I had been once or twice. "Was it *una grande città?*" he asked. "Were there many Italians there?"

New Rochelle was where he was going to live, with an aunt who had signed his papers and sent him his boat ticket. He had never seen the aunt, but she had sent her photograph. He showed me a snapshot of a good-natured round woman in a summer dress. Giorgio had sent her his picture. Did I think, he asked, that he and his aunt would recognize each other when she came to meet him? He was greatly worried they would not. He had come from Calabria, the most impoverished and backward part of Italy. He had gone to school only two years. Since his fifteenth birthday he had worked as a carpenter earning two hundred lire—thirty-two cents—a day. "Is it true that in America carpenters earn more than five dollars a day?" he asked. He spoke with the staccato excitement of south Italy, punctuating his words with his hands.

I said I thought they earned more.

"Ah, America is a land of good fortune," he said. "If I am paid five dollars a day I will save enough money in a year to send for my brother." He grimaced and put his hand on his stomach. "But I will not permit my brother to come by ship. He will come by airplane."

Giorgio showed me the contents of his wallet: the usual assortment of photographs and seventeen hundred lire in Italian currency. It was less than three dollars, all the money he had in the world. "I will not spend it, even for cigarettes," he said. "When I arrive in America I shall send it to my mother. She will use it well. In her house there is not enough to eat. *L'Italia va malissimo* [Italy is very sick]."

His face lit up. *"Io sarò un Americano! Che fortuna.* I cannot believe it. It is the greatest fortune in the world to be an American. Already I love America as if she were my own land. I will be a good American."

Next day, passing the Azores, the sea was calmer and the gloom of the ship lifted for a day. Giorgio was full of plans. "How long before I can be a citizen?" he asked. When I told him five years, he frowned. "A long time, five years," he said, and asked another question, "How long until I can make myself a soldier for America?"

I didn't know the answer to that one, but suggested it might be necessary to speak English first. "I have already thought of it," Giorgio said. "When I arrive in America I will do three things. First, I will find a girl; second, I will find a job; and third, I will go to night school to learn English. When I have learned English I will become a soldier to show America how grateful I am to be an American."

"All admirable ambitions," I said and suggested it might be good to modify the sequence, since knowing English would facilitate the business of finding jobs and girls.

"At first—for a month at least—I shall have an Italian girl," he said. "Do you think I will find a girl who speaks Italian?"

"I think perhaps you can count on your aunt to know one," I said.

"But if they speak Italian, they will not be blondes," he said. "In America I have decided on a *raggazza bionda.*"

"Perhaps it would be better if you had a girl that didn't speak Italian," I said. "Then you will need to learn English to speak with her."

Giorgio threw his head back and laughed. "That is true," he said. "I will have a blonde girl who does not speak Italian."

As the ship moved north the storm hit us again. The *mal di mare* was worse than ever. Decks, lounges, and dining rooms were deserted; doctors and nurses were haggard from lack of sleep. The ship's social staff dutifully tied Christmas trees to the walls with wires and draped the empty lounges with mistletoe and crepe paper. Recorded carols rang out from bow to stern. In the evening orchestras played in empty ballrooms. The few passengers who were strong enough to dance were prohibited from doing so by ship's officers, who feared accidents and law suits. To all complaints the crew had a comforting reply: "We are now seven hours ahead of schedule."

The last day at sea a miraculous recovery swept over the rolling ship. Dining rooms were filled. The afternoon was filled with Christmas spirit.

Free champagne before dinner brought out Maira in her Paris gown and a lot of other people not seen since Gibraltar. The captain's dinner which followed was a Tudor banquet served from oaken tables loaded with capons, turkeys, jellied hams, tongues, and roasted pigs. But the passengers played it safe and concentrated on simpler dishes. I asked the waiter what would happen to all the untouched food. "Into the barrel and overboard," he said. I was still close enough to Naples to be shocked by such obscene waste. Fagioli read my thoughts. "Is no wonder there is Communists in the world," he said. "For me, I like very much the simple things. I am very natural man." Then he ordered a filet mignon and some Château Haut Brion 1926.

I went downstairs to see the Italian boys. I found Giorgio pondering an ethical problem. Because the ship provided no facilities for the exchange of lire into dollars it was impossible for Italian passengers without dollars to purchase anything on board ship. Earlier in the day Giorgio had succumbed to the holiday mood by deciding to buy a package of cigarettes with money from his meager funds. A member of the ship's staff whose name Giorgio did not know offered to exchange a dollar for a thousand lire. After the transaction Giorgio began thinking it over. He asked me if the exchange had been a fair one. Since the official exchange was a dollar and sixty cents for a thousand lire, it was far from fair. Giorgio and I went in search of the culprit, but we did not find him. The episode troubled Giorgio deeply. Not only did it leave him with a thousand lire less to send to his mother in Calabria, but even more serious, it had shaken his faith in Americans. "I have believed Americans were the most honest people in the world," he said. I told him how, when I was new in Italy, I had been cheated by moneychangers in Naples and later in Germany, and how a friend had been swindled of a hundred dollars in Paris. "There are bad Americans," I said, "just as there are bad Germans and Frenchmen and Italians."

"But Americans are not poor," Giorgio said. "People who are poor do such things and Italians are poor."

"Rich or poor, there is no difference," I said. "Except perhaps that in a country which is rich dishonest men have more to cheat over," I said.

Giorgio began to see it philosophically. "Men are the same all over the world," he said.

I went with him to the ballroom. "Is very difficult, the American dancing," he said. "But I must learn it. No American girl will know how to dance Italian style." While we watched the dancing twelve-year-old Teodoro rushed breathlessly in from the outside deck. "I see a light," he sputtered, beside himself. "I think it is the Statue of Liberty."

We went out to see. Teodoro pointed to several lights, doubtless from a fleet of fishing boats. I explained to the Italian boys that the Statue of Liberty was still at least eight hours away. Two hours later Maira and I were walking about the deserted deck. At the prow of the ship, huddling under a canvas-covered lifeboat, I saw a small familiar figure with the shoulders hunched. "Giorgio," I called.

"I cannot sleep," he said. "I fear if I do, we shall pass *la libertà*. I must see her."

I said we would positively not arrive at the Statue of Liberty before dawn and it was safe for him to go to sleep.

"*Sicuro?*" he asked.

"For certain," I said. He continued to stare ahead of him into the black night. "Is the last night," he murmured to himself. "Tomorrow—America."

At five o'clock in the morning I was awakened by a knocking on my door. Everything was calm. The engines were hardly moving and the ship slid along as if carried by a current. I got up and opened the door. Outside were Giorgio, Mario, and Teodoro, bundled up in three shirts, two sweaters, and an overcoat apiece. "Is very cold in America," Mario said. "We are prepared."

"We think you will not want to miss *la libertà*," Giorgio said. "So we have come to awaken you."

I dressed and went out on deck with them. It was still very dark. Several lighthouses flickered through the mists. Each beam sent the three Italians into a fever of excitement. The weather was milder than it had been since we left the Mediterranean; I could not tell whether it would be clear or rainy. There was still nothing to be seen, so I took the boys into my cabin and arranged for some breakfast to be sent in. It was a struggle to make them eat. When they had bolted their food, we returned to the prow of the ship where we stood facing west. Behind us a faint beam of coral reached across the eastern sky. It was going to be bright and mild, one of New York's rare beautiful winter days.

We were moving so gently we seemed to be winged ashore by the gulls which swooped about the ship. Above us a crescent moon still hung pale white in the sky. It took a half hour for the world to light up. The familiar skyline emerged in a glow of pink and blue mists. It seemed the most beautiful thing I had ever seen. We stood with our arms interlocked, watching in silent wonder.

"America," Giorgio said softly. *"È finita la fame. Avanti la vita è bella. Avrò l'America per Natale."*

"America! Hunger is finished. A beautiful life begins. I have America for Christmas."

With these simple, moving words, Giorgio expressed what it meant to be an American; what the light of a bright morning of life and liberty can mean to the oppressed and hungry. I thought of all those who for three centuries have come as Giorgio, and how much in need of Giorgio's faith are their children and their children's children. I was full of humility and shame and could not speak. For Giorgio and Mario and Teodoro and me it was indeed a bright morning of Christmas.

Teodoro leaped to the railing. *"La libertà,"* he cried, pointing ahead. There she was, the familiar goddess, arising from the cloud, her torch aflame with the rose light of the morning. Teodoro was laughing and crying hysterically, *"La libertà, la libertà!"* His brother Mario looked at the statue intensely. "Is not to be believed," he said, "we are in America." People gathered about us. *Dottoressa* Panetta of Rome watched through a pair of fieldglasses. Teodoro asked if we were going to disembark at *la libertà* and the question set everyone laughing. I pointed out Brooklyn, the Empire State Building, and, looking at it myself for the first time, the United Nations Building. Giorgio's eyes could not be drawn from the statue. Slowly he spoke his first English words. "I love *la libertà*," he said.

Visitors were not permitted on the pier, so Giorgio's aunt and the father of Mario and Teodoro could not meet them until the confusion of customs was past. I accompanied the hopelessly bewildered boys and their sparse possessions through customs. All three swore they had nothing to be declared. But when the officers opened the pasteboard suitcases, Giorgio's contained olive oil and several Italian salamis, presents for the aunt sent by the home folks in Calabria. I persuaded the customs officer to pass on the olive oil, which was in tin containers. To Giorgio I explained the necessity of food regulations to protect the health of American people. He quickly understood and readily gave up the salamis. *"Una buona cosa,"* he said. "A good thing, these laws."

I delivered the boys to their relatives. The father of Mario and Teodoro was too overcome to speak. So he weepingly embraced us all. Giorgio did not have to find his aunt; she found him.

"Who is the stranger?" she asked.

"Mio primo amico Americano," Giorgio told her. "My first American friend."

Maria, the Sicilian bride, was gathered up by her frantic husband, and *Dottoressa* Panetta bustled away under an escort of nuns who had come to greet her. I hoped to see Maira for a second, perhaps to arrange to take a tea, but she was gone.

I said good-by to the three new Americans.

"Buon Natale," said Teodoro and Mario.

"Buon Natale," said Giorgio.

"Merry Christmas!"

I went to look for the friends I knew were waiting for me.

ABOUT THE AUTHOR

Herbert Kubly is a self-styled "Wisconsin farm boy who went beyond the horizon to the big city." All his ancestors came from Glarus, Switzerland to New Glarus, Wisconsin, making him a fifth generation American who is still of pure Swiss blood. After completing his formal education in the New Glarus schools and the University of Wisconsin, he moved on to Pittsburgh where he worked as reporter and then art critic on the Pittsburgh Sun-Telegraph. *Five years later he came to New York and to jobs as reporter on the* New York Herald Tribune *and music editor and critic of* Time *magazine. His first play,* Men to the Sea, *was produced in New York in 1944 under the direction of Eddie Dowling; his second,* Inherit the Wind, *at the Playhouse Theatre in London in 1948. It was as an Associate Professor of Speech at the University of Illinois that he was granted the Fulbright fellowship that resulted in this book.*

Mr. Kubly has written articles and short stories for Harper's Bazaar, Town and Country, Mademoiselle, Esquire *and other magazines but* American in Italy *is his first book.*